BRING OUT YOUR DEAD

Bring Out Your Dead

THE PAST AS REVELATION

Anthony Grafton

HARVARD UNIVERSITY PRESS

CAMBRIDGE, MASSACHUSETTS

LONDON, ENGLAND

2001

Library of Congress Cataloging-in-Publication Data
Grafton, Anthony.
    Bring out your dead : the past as revelation / Anthony Grafton.
        p. cm.
    Includes bibliographical references and index.
    ISBN 0-674-00468-X (hardcover : alk. paper)
    1. Europe—Intellectual life—16th century. 2. Renaissance. 3. Learned institutions and
societies—Europe—History—16th century. 4. Learning and scholarship—Europe—
History—16th century. 5. Italy—Intellectual life—1268–1559. I. Title.

CB367 .G73 2001
940.2'232—dc21

                                                                    2001039206

Contents

൭ᴥᴥᴥ൳

Acknowledgments

This book argues that some of the most remarkable intellectual achievements of Europeans in the early modern period sprang from and depended on the work of intellectual communities. They are no less vital now. It is my intellectual duty and personal pleasure, accordingly, to thank the members of my own communities: Lindsay Waters, whose encouragement and criticism brought this volume into being; Peter Miller and Ingrid Rowland, whose advice showed me how to shape it; Nancy Siraisi and Jake Soll, whose comments on a draft of the introduction materially improved it; and Greg Lyon, whose technical and editorial skills were essential to its completion. David Chambers, Joseph Epstein, Jill Kraye, Robert Silvers, John Sturrock, Jay Tolson, J. B. Trapp, and Leon Wieseltier originally edited many of the essays that reappear here, and Nancy Clemente extirpated errors and infelicities that had survived. To all of them, my heartfelt gratitude for their patience, their constructive criticism, and their generosity of spirit.

Introduction

⊙∞∞⊙

_A_ S WINTER turned to spring one day in 1522, the Ferrarese scholar
Celio Calcagnini sat in his study and remembered a freak show.
Calcagnini, known for his stylish Latin prose and verse, normally confined
himself to more dignified pursuits. He taught at the University of Ferrara,
served on diplomatic missions with members of the city's ruling house, the
Este, and earned the respect and praise of writers as diverse as Ariosto and
Erasmus. His interests ranged from Egyptian hieroglyphs to Greek astronomy, from Latin poetry to modern politics, and from the most esoteric
details of ancient history to the fashionable court and salon life of his own
time. Antonio Brasavola, the distinguished medical man who studied with
Calcagnini and edited his collected works, said that his teacher's motto had
been "nothing is sweeter than knowing everything."[1] Calcagnini suited his
action to his words. He knew and praised Raphael's efforts to study and
restore the ruins of Rome, catalogued the enormous Este collection of
coins and medals, and wrote a tract arguing, before Copernicus's book
appeared, that the earth could be rotating on its axis.[2] Readers savored the
brevity and wit of the epigrams in which he displayed a period taste for
paradox.[3] Calcagnini, in other words, occupied a central place in the
courtly high culture of elegance and erudition that had flourished in Ferrara for almost a century, and would eventually transform the city into a
theater of cultural memory, one that would fascinate and obsess later writers and artists like Giorgio De Chirico and Giorgio Bassani.

The day in question had apparently begun, like most of Calcagnini's days, in another key, as he read his way meticulously through a recent work of encyclopedic scholarship. In 1518, Marcello Virgilio Adriani, the chancellor of Florence and an established and influential humanist, had published a massive book: a new translation of and commentary on the treatise on the medical uses of herbs, minerals, and animal parts which the Greek writer Dioscorides compiled, largely from first-hand experience, in the first century C.E.[4] Calcagnini read this enormous work with pen in hand. Like most of his learned contemporaries, he saw reading as a discipline that had formal rules. True, he did not emulate Pandolfo Collenuccio, who used color-coded inks to identify the subjects of the passages he underlined, or adopt the widespread practice of using "little towers, pointing hands, and little columns" to serve as aids to memory.[5] But he did make a habit, as he remarked, both of copying passages into notebooks and of "making a separate summary, in the margin, of everything at all worthy of note."[6] In this case, he summarized both Dioscorides' text and Adriani's comments in the margins, taking a special interest in the niceties of Adriani's Latin style and the spurts of sarcasm that he had directed at another, more celebrated scholar, Ermolao Barbaro.[7] Occasionally he noted, with a devout "glory to God" in Greek, the date on which he had finished working through a particular section.[8] Like Adriani, Calcagnini was not a medical man by profession or training; yet he scrutinized the text almost as fiercely as the editor had.

At one point, Adriani, whose work had no illustrations, tried to depict a particular plant so vividly that its image would appear in readers' minds, even without an accompanying woodcut:

> Once I saw a human being of monstrous nature, which had been brought from France to Italy. Men took it from city to city to show it off for money. It was a boy that had not reached full puberty. From its front, between the bottom of the chest and the navel, hung another human figure, a little less than perfect, perhaps a third as large as the other, perfect being from which it hung. It lacked only the head and the top parts of the shoulders, which, as though by some process of grafting, were hidden in the complete body, and had grown together so neatly in the place I mentioned that two bodies, only a little less than whole, lived without difficulty or misery in one human being. It

appeared to have only stumps of arms; the rest of its body was perfect in every respect, and it moved in response to the other's senses and needs. The leaf of the Alexandrian laurel is just like this.[9]

"A monster from France," Calcagnini noted in the margin of his copy: "I saw it too."[10] In the midst of his studies—while carrying out a form of reading so intense and meticulous that it amounted to a precise, critical conversation with the ancient author and his modern commentator— Calcagnini took time off to meet Adriani, virtually, in the street, where carnies chanted to fascinated onlookers about the tormented being whom they would cart from piazza to piazza until he died. The high and the low proved hard to separate in the study—as hard as they did in the world of print, where erudite scholars and impoverished scribblers competed to publicize such monsters. Usually they took the existence of abnormal beings, human or animal, as signs of impending divine wrath and punishment—an interpretation soon to be borne out by the wars between the French king Francis I and the Holy Roman Emperor Charles V which raged across Italy in the mid-1520s, and climaxed in 1527 with the sack of Rome.[11] Adriani and Calcagnini were unusual not least in their ability to view a monster without alarm and to resist the temptation to make prophecies—an attitude perhaps befitting an official who had lived through the age of Savonarola, and a humanist who viewed with skepticism "the vanities of the magicians."[12]

The contact between Calcagnini and Adriani unfolded on many levels. At the most obvious one, it represented the continuation of a dialogue between Florentine and Ferrarese learning which had begun in the 1490s and showed no signs of abating almost thirty years later. In 1491, the Ferrarese scholar and medical man Nicolò Leoniceno directed criticism in a letter at errors in the elder Pliny's *Natural History*, a massive, magnificent, and sometimes weird compendium of the marvels to be found in the world of plants and animals.[13] The Florentine philologist Angelo Poliziano replied by challenging Leoniceno, in a letter, to something like a scholarly duel. Leoniceno, Poliziano argued, had misunderstood Pliny; one needed stronger grounds to shake the authority of so learned an ancient writer.[14] In December 1492 Leoniceno offered a retort courteous on the grand scale: an entire treatise "On Pliny's Mistakes in Medicine and Those of a Good Many Others," which he dedicated to Poliziano. This was in turn rebutted in 1493 by another scholar who admired Pliny, Pandolfo Collenuccio of Pesaro, and still others intervened in the discussion as time passed. The situation became even more fraught as two editions of the massive, long-awaited critical commentary on Pliny by the erudite Venetian patrician scholar Ermolao Barbaro appeared, in 1492 and 1493. For Leoniceno claimed that on many points he and Barbaro agreed. But the Venetian scholar had set out, in his own massive commentary, to restore Pliny's authority by cleansing the text of the *Natural History* printed at Venice in 1472 of its false readings, and Pliny's defenders considered him an ally.[15] The battle lines, in other words, tended to waver.

Leoniceno tried, at times, to portray the debate he had called into being in straightforward terms, as one about the errors of Pliny. The Roman writer had been a scholar, not a naturalist. He regularly went wrong because, as he copied what others had written, he applied passages on different plants to the same one, and vice versa.[16] Leoniceno carefully distanced himself from Pliny and his ilk, arguing that words should be secondary, in the eyes of the naturalist, to the plants, stones, and animals they referred to. He claimed that he would not even mind seeing Pliny's arguments defended and his own refuted, if the truth emerged intact, "since the question here has to do not with the weight of words, but with things, on which human health and life depend."[17] Here and elsewhere, Leoniceno suggested that the parties to the dispute used two radically different methods: the textual one of the Florentines (and Pliny before them), who assumed that ancient books offered authoritative information on all subjects, including the natural world, and the empirical one of the Ferrarese, who went out into the woods, fields, and apothecaries' shops to study the things that texts merely referred to, often in vague, puzzling, or unintelligible ways.

But as most scholars have recognized, the debaters usually formulated their positions in a far messier fashion than such formulas suggest. Leoniceno acknowledged that Poliziano's encyclopedic form of scholarship—which he pursued in collaboration with the dazzling young polymath and philosopher Giovanni Pico della Mirandola—gave him standing in the discussion.[18] He also argued that his chief concern was not with Pliny's mistakes, but with those of later Muslim medical writers like Avicenna, whose works, in Latin translations, played a major role in medical teaching and practice, even though the humanists had been denouncing them for some time. Like the Florentines, in other words, Leoniceno saw himself as waging a campaign to purify philosophy at the university level by extirpating the "barbarism" of medieval learning.[19] And he cited the evidence of books—ancient and later ones—at least as often as that of natural specimens and empirical investigations.[20] Collenuccio, who defended Pliny's authority ferociously, had fun satirizing what he described as Leoniceno's effort to make Dioscorides—Pliny's supposed source—into an absolute authority. He also took care to show that he too had watched druggists at work with mortar, pestle, and desk references—for example, the "not ignoble apothecary" at Venice, whose shop had an Ethiopian's head as its sign. There Collenuccio had seen "an herbal, illustrated with such skill and care that one would think the plants on its pages had been born there, rather than merely represented."[21] What counted as an authority in botany and pharmacology? Modern experience? Ancient texts? Particular ancient writers who had given special attention to and developed special expertise in the qualities of plants? Modern compilations based on empirical research? Material specimens? Vivid illustrations?[22] Scholars took all of these positions in the course of the debate, which ran on and on, attracting new interventions year after year. Calcagnini—a close friend of Leoniceno and his follower Giovanni Mainardi, but also a passionate admirer of Pliny—knew the different positions and attitudes of the debaters intimately.[23]

Adriani's edition of Dioscorides amounted to a complex and somewhat messy move in this protracted academic game. As he confessed more than once, the book did not meet his own standards for precision and completeness. A massively busy civil servant, Adriani took an active role in the violent and frightening politics of the early sixteenth century. Machiavelli worked in his department until 1512, when the Medici returned to Florence and dissolved the republican government that had replaced them. More adroit than the eponymous founder of modern politics, Adriani stayed in office, though he later fell from grace.[24] But that meant that his work on Dioscorides—parts of which were carried out under his direction by his secretaries, who also read the proofs and produced the detailed indices to his edition—had to be completed in the brief intervals left by many other demanding activities.[25]

Dioscorides himself, moreover, presented peculiar and intractable problems. Pliny's critics, noting many passages in the *Natural History* which corresponded closely to Dioscorides, argued that the Roman had taken most of his botanical information from the Greek. Where variations occurred, Pliny had misread or mistranslated the text before him. Others argued, however, that Dioscorides had actually lived and written after Pliny. Apparent agreements might show that the two men had drawn on common sources; variations, that they were actually discussing different plants. The subject mattered, in practical and urgent ways. Dioscorides' work, the most complete and accurate ancient source on *materia medica,* would become, in the course of the sixteenth century, one of the core texts of the reformed discipline of natural history.[26] The interpretation of its descriptions of leaves and flowers and prescriptions for their use had vital implications for the practice of medicine. But the more closely scholars inspected this long, intricate, and poorly transmitted text, the less clear it seemed how they should balance ancient authority with modern experience before deciding which herb or stone a practitioner should turn into pills and administer to patients.

Adriani's chief skill, as he knew very well, lay in the critical study of texts, especially the semantic analysis of the words of which they were made up. He had a schooled understanding of how the Greek language had developed over time. This enabled him to demonstrate, for example, that though the word *kardía* had once meant "heart," by the time of the Peloponnesian war both medical writers, like Hippocrates, and others who used medical terminology, like Thucydides, employed it to refer to the "stomach and its mouth"—the cardiac orifice of the stomach.[27] Accordingly, Adriani approached the text primarily as a scholar, bent on "cleansing and restoring everything that is or seems faulty or divergent in the printed Dioscorides, and clarifying the Greek and Latin words, and explaining the more unfamiliar and unusual points."[28] To that extent, his book must have seemed a characteristically Florentine product, a work of philology, to Ferrarese readers. No wonder, then, that Calcagnini showed special interest in recording what Adriani had to say about the details of both Greek and Latin usage.

Dioscorides, however, confronted Adriani with a whole range of obstacles, which slowed and sometimes halted his progress through the text. The Greek original, which swarmed with the names of plants and their parts, had been disfigured to the point of unintelligibility by scribes understandably unfamiliar with the technical terms of Greek botany. Worse still, the text had apparently been tampered with by later readers who used it pragmatically, without according it the respect usually shown to literary or philosophical works. Trying to clarify the difficult and complex text, medieval scholars reordered individual sections alphabetically and added material drawn from glossaries and other sources, some of which did not agree with the genuine text of Dioscorides.[29] These reasonable, if not always successful, efforts to make a rich but rebarbative text useful and accessible seemed, to humanists like Adriani, arbitrary and inexcusable: corruptions, not corrections. The "barbarous" later names for plants that medieval users had introduced, regularly but inconsistently, into the text as explanatory glosses posed a continual problem to the purist readers of the Renaissance.[30]

As a Florentine, Adriani knew the scholarly work of Poliziano intimately. The brilliant poet, critic, and philologist had insisted, sometimes ferociously, that the editing, translation, and interpretation of any ancient text must begin from a close study of the available manuscripts. Only manuscripts which did not derive from other existing ones, and which offered the text in a correct form, deserved a scholar's trust. And the scholar should resort to "divination"—efforts to correct the text by conjecture—only when the best sources still offered a clearly unsatisfactory wording. Poliziano's method—and his efforts to apply it in practice—occasioned widespread discussion in the 1490s.[31] But conditions had changed, for Adriani as for others: the age of crisis and desperation that followed the year of Poliziano's death and the French invasion of Italy, 1494, left few scholars in possession of the time and resources to pursue such austere and distant goals. Poliziano's methods, moreover, offered Adriani little help with this particular textual tradition. As it happens, he owned one very old manuscript, an illuminated one now in Munich, which contained the old Latin translation of Dioscorides, probably executed in the sixth century. Adriani described this as being written "in Lombardic characters," that is, an unfamiliar, early script, and like Poliziano he dated it backward to around six hundred years before his own time.[32] But this Latin manuscript did not provide anything like the basis for a critical edition, since it often deviated radically from the Greek text. And though Adriani also consulted Greek manuscripts and tried to establish that one of them was superior to the rest, he found that "something was lacking in each of them" as well. Accordingly, he could only do what "a talented painter once did when he painted a goddess for the citizens of Croton:

after collating five Greek manuscripts of Dioscorides, at each point where variation or corruption occurred, I chose the more certain and appropriate reading."[33] The story of the artist who had examined the five loveliest women in the city of Croton, naked, in order to choose each one's best parts and assemble them into an image of consummate beauty was very familiar in Florence, where Boccaccio, Alberti, Poliziano, and others had told and retold it. Adriani, accordingly, omitted the painter's name, which had become a byword—like the story itself—for eclecticism.

Calcagnini, determined to make his copy of the text as complete a reference work as he could, effortlessly supplied what Adriani had left out: "Zeuxis," he wrote, "was the painter of the citizens of Croton."[34] But if Calcagnini approved of Adriani's classical allusions, he did not find the Florentine chancellor's rough-and-ready, pragmatic method of editing to his taste. At one point, when Adriani explained that he had devised a very loose but plausible paraphrase of an unintelligible piece of Greek, because he thought it necessary to fill the space in question, Calcagnini noted that "I would simply have crossed it out."[35] Calcagnini's reading of Dioscorides and Adriani, then, reveals the high hopes that scholars still cherished about what ancient texts could reveal—as well as the practical and technical difficulties that arose when philological methods were put into actual practice.

Adriani, like Pliny, was chiefly a man of the word, as the botanical experts of the 1520s and 1530s noted more than once.[36] It did not take the gifts of Sherlock Holmes to make this inference about a scholar who investigated the effects of cooking on one popular vegetable by noting that, according to the Roman biographer Suetonius, Augustus had liked to remark: "that will take less time than it does to cook asparagus."[37] Yet Adriani did not confine himself to philological questions, or to the studies previously pursued in Florence. He echoed Leoniceno when he insisted that "this is a science of things, not of words and names."[38] And he emulated both the Ferrarese physician and his critics when he pointed out that he too "had sometimes consulted specialized herbalists who work in the fields, and had been an eyewitness of many plants"—and that he had also corresponded and conversed with experts and even ordered herbs sent from distant regions.[39] Adriani, in short, agreed with Leoniceno and Collenuccio that one could not understand, much less, correct, a text like Dioscorides' without some knowledge of contemporary practices in the same field. The high world of classical philology and the low one of herbal medicine must interact, if the interests of both were to be served. Adriani's reference to the Siamese twin, in other words, was only one of a number of passages in his commentary in which the present interfered with the past, personal experience with classical texts, and artisanal knowledge with learned medicine.

At some points Adriani went even further. He noted, for example, that even in antiquity, quacks had hawked love potions and other harmful "magical vanities." Even after pious Christians drove the ancient ones from the market, moreover, new ones had arisen to take their place.[40] At the same time, he remarked that his own project, which he defined as restoring "antiquity," had required him "to make diligent inquiries among the peoples and inhabitants of many places, if any unknown things of medical value lay hidden among them." Valuable herbs like lucerne had flourished through ancient Italy, where ancient farmers and herdsmen had used them extensively. But lucerne had vanished from Italy in later centuries. Careful inquiry, pursued to the limit—in this case, all the way to Spain—enabled Adriani to find lucerne. He set out, accordingly, "to bring it forth into the light and to restore it to cultivation."[41] Even the restoration of antiquity required knowledge of modern practices—since these, in some cases, preserved elements of ancient material culture. Ancient texts had value only insofar as they recorded genuine ancient knowledge and customs, and research into modern husbandry in one region of Europe might be needed to restore a feature of ancient agrarian life which had fallen into disuse in later times. Adriani the humanist had moved partway down the long road that Otto Brunfels, Leonhard Fuchs, and other sixteenth-century naturalists would traverse.[42] By mid-century, Fuchs and others would argue that ancient writers could claim authority in natural philosophy only to the extent that they themselves had carried out empirical investigations. In the realm of natural philosophy, the classics gained credence not from their confinement to the *hortus conclusus* of the library but precisely from the signs they had left of intimate acquaintance with men who worked in woods and fields.[43]

Learned men began to tear at the foundations of bookish culture, to unite the study of words with that of things, long before Francis Bacon and Tommaso Campanella began to denounce scholars' excess concern with verbal trivia. Adriani's commentary, that ocean of modern words dotted with an archipelago of small segments from the original text, was one of the many works of learning written about 1500 to show symptoms of this impending transformation. No wonder that Calcagnini manifested no suprise when he met the Siamese twins in Adriani's commentary. It was just the sort of place in which a scholar expected to encounter the most wonderful of nature's creations. Erudite commentators could not hope in this world—or any other—to separate their textual pursuits from their encounters with the harder, sharper worlds of nature and politics outside the library.

This modest case study has some large implications for the study of the world of learning in Renaissance Europe. In the mid-nineteenth century, students of the Renaissance and Reformation saw the scholarly world of the past as isolated, not only from real life in the sense of business and politics, but also from the arts and disciplines that made possible what Jacob Burckhardt called "the discovery of the world and of man." On the one side, Burckhardt and his followers arrayed the giants: the painters, sculptors, architects, and scientists, from Petrarch to Leonardo and Galileo, who created a new culture. On the other, they set the midgets: the scholars, men characterized by vanity, irreligion, and pedantry. The contest was clearly one-sided, and for a long time even the most erudite historians believed that the new forms of classical learning which took shape in Renaissance Europe were pursued in a haunted palace of erudition, inhabited only by cranky pedants and burning-eyed careerists.

In the decades just before and after 1900, the pioneering intellectual historian Friedrich von Bezold, the dazzlingly innovative art historian Aby Warburg, and other scholars began to draw new maps of Renaissance society and culture. They argued that classical texts had actually provided their Renaissance readers with essential, practical tools. And they showed that scholars had played vital roles, as the intermediaries who made ancient texts and ideas accessible to their contemporaries. The members of the Warburg Institute, as it took shape in the Hamburg of the 1920s, made clear that the fifteenth- and sixteenth-century scholars who examined classical texts with passionate intensity were looking for a moral language—one that could serve the needs not only of writers of learned Latin like themselves, but also of hard-pressed Florentine merchants like Francesco Sassetti, battered by what seemed the unchecked power of Fortune, which threatened their lives, their families, and their investments. In the 1920s and after, Hans Baron argued in pioneering articles that the humanists had found in the ancients and recovered for modern use a vision of civic life that proved essential to the Florentine elite of the fifteenth century. Evidently the recovery of classical texts and the mastery of modern politics were in some sense related—even closely related—enterprises.

Between the thirties and the seventies, finally, historians like Paul Hazard, Paul Oskar Kristeller, Eugenio Garin, Frances Yates, Erwin Panofsky and Arnaldo Momigliano drew new maps of what had been called, in the seventeenth and eighteenth centuries, the Republic of Letters. They showed, in a variety of ways, that the humanists were never the *Luftmenschen* that they seemed in the nineteenth century, but deeply rooted participants in the beliefs and institutions of the larger societies they lived in. My own work as a scholar, which began in the mid-1970s, was inspired by that of these great writers and teachers. The articles and reviews collected here record parts of a continuing historical effort to come to terms with the world of humanistic learning in early modern Europe and to trace the ties that bound it to other social and cultural spheres.

One central theme I have pursued for many years is the connection between the study of ancient books and that of material objects—both the physical remains of antiquity, such as buildings and inscriptions, and the physical world itself. Scholars and practitioners of the fine arts interacted, in varied ways, from the Renaissance onward. Both collected, studied, and tried to interpret ancient monuments and statues. And one result of their collaboration—and, sometimes, their conflicts—was the rise of a new scholarly discipline, usually called antiquarianism. Its practitioners collected ancient gems as eagerly as ancient books, traced the layout of ancient cities as well as the plots of ancient epics, and tried to recreate the forgotten institutions, beliefs, and rituals of ancient societies, often with striking success. In 1950, when Momigliano first traced the development of antiquarian scholarship in an essay of sovereign erudition and deep historical insight, even well-informed scholars were amazed to learn that the learned men of early modern Europe had created forms of history that adumbrated the work of the French Annales School of the twentieth century.[44] Historians, art historians, and others have retraced the grand lines of the antiquarian tradition, as well as many of its lesser branches, in the intervening decades.[45] Yet even now, the traditions of historical research and writing, with their emphasis on verbal as against visual sources, make it hard to do justice to the range and quality of this interdisciplinary and collaborative form of scholarship.

Much more has been written—chiefly, though not only, by historians of art—about the ways that scholars helped to reshape painting, sculpture, and architecture in the Renaissance and after. And a great many historians of science have examined the ways in which students of ancient texts resisted, contributed to, or stayed aloof from the transformation in the study of nature which took place in the fifteenth, sixteenth, and seventeenth centuries. Here too, however, far more remains to be done. The precise details of what practitioners of the fine arts actually learned from scholars—and the ways in which they interacted—remain controversial. So does the relation between the thought of writers like Bacon and Descartes, who called for the creation of new forms of learning, and the traditions in which they were educated. So, finally, does the role of creative misreading in the cultural survival and impact of ancient texts, motifs, and images—a subject to which historians of literature, art, and science have paid more attention in the past than intellectual historians, but a central one in the history of the classical tradition. Many of the essays that follow investigate these issues.

The relation between the discovery of the ancients and that of the wider non-European world, finally, has been a scholarly *casus belli* for centuries. The European landfall in the Americas could be seen as discrediting the authority of the Greeks and Romans, since they had believed that the world's land mass was much smaller than it is. But it could also be, and was, depicted as revealing the continued stimulus that ancient ideas about discovery and geography still afforded in the sixteenth century. The pervasive neo-classicism of early modern learned culture seems a perfect case in point of Europe's millennial tendency to see and represent itself as the center of the world. Yet classical texts and expert classical philologists also played a vital role in Europeans' sustained efforts to understand nonwestern cultures.[46]

Renaissance miniaturists often depicted scholars as isolated figures—immured in libraries, working alone at desks laden with classical codices, and accompanied, if at all, by a sleeping lion. A strong modern tradition of interpretation, one rooted in the Romantic moment of the early nineteenth century, takes such images literally. It treats the humanists the way contemporary satirists sometimes did, as so desiccated by their pitiless regime of classical studies that they could not sustain human relations with one another—to say nothing of less elevated mortals.

In fact, however, as Kristeller and many others have taught us, scholars rarely lived, and never worked, alone. They renewed the traditionally monastic customs and usages of academic life. And they created new forms of intellectual sociability and new academic institutions. Learned groups and societies, formal and informal, took shape, first in individual Italian and German cities and then across Europe. Eventually, scholars came to speak a republican language of their own. They represented themselves as citizens of a formal, international community, the Republic of Letters. Through the sixteenth and seventeenth centuries, even as religious polemic and warfare shook the world around them, they tried to set standards of intellectual interaction, to regulate one another's ways of pursuing learning, and to sustain an ideal of learned conversation that transcended the narrow loyalties of nation and church. Naturally, lived reality did not correspond perfectly to high ideals; but a number of the essays that follow show how real the imaginary Republic of Letters was.

Scholars also created, in collaboration with entrepreneurs and artisans, another sort of community: the brand new institutional world of the printing shop, where learned men found that they had to work with dirty, inky hands, and printers shaped the presentation—and sometimes the content—of works of high speculation or profound erudition. Even the most titanically learned antiquarians, the most heroic emenders of texts, could make a reputation and reach a public only after scribes and printers had transformed their drafts into items with a material form and a market value, books which could be presented to patrons or sold to readers. In some cases, hybrid styles of learned life came into being in the fertile locations where texts became books. Scholars tried to master the artists' skills of accurate and vivid drawing. Printers' correctors, often scholars who had not managed to climb the greasy pole of preferment in church or government, tried to stay abreast of both the physical technology of printing and the scholarly technology of artistic Latin prose and verse. These new forms of intellectual community are explored here in a number of complementary ways.

The scholars of early modern Europe, for all their commitment to the study of tradition, were by no means all traditionalists. Some of the most radical religious and political movements in early modern Europe—for example, the Protestant Reformation—began when scholars reinterpreted texts. And some texts that now seem almost absurdly harmless—like Livy's history of the early centuries of Rome—proved capable, in sixteenth- or eighteenth-century Europe, of provoking their readers to advance radically new theories about nature, society, and politics. The world of classical learning spawned not only an endless, and endlessly erudite, literature of commentaries and lexica, but also some of the most radical, iconoclastic theories of knowledge and interpretations of history to be created in premodern Europe. Giambattista Vico of Naples, rightly hailed as one of the creators of modern social science, was also a habitué of the humanistic tradition, from which he drew both many of the problems that preoccupied him and some of the methods that he applied to their solution. Seen in context, his career offers curious parallels to that of the now-forgotten Jesuit Father Jean Hardouin—another brilliant revisionist who lived in the decades around 1700, and tried, like Vico, to bring the disciplines of Renaissance humanism up to date in the age of Enlightenment. Bacon and Descartes—both proverbially innovative, even radical thinkers and writers—can profitably be examined from the same vantage point. The idea that reading itself has a long and complex history—and that the study of readers' practices can shed light on a wide range of questions in intellectual and cultural history—links many of the essays in this collection. So does the idea—not yet as familiar as this last—that reading, in early modern Europe, was a goal-oriented procedure, carried on with highly practical goals in mind.[47]

Many of the scholars who studied the early modern world of learning in the nineteenth and early twentieth centuries cut deeply impressive figures now. They knew the world of humanism at first hand. At the schools they attended, dark, heavily varnished portraits of bewigged sixteenth- and seventeenth-century scholars glowered on the paneled walls. In the libraries they frequented, seventeenth- and eighteenth-century editions and compendia were still standard fare. No wonder that their works call the forgotten worlds of early modern learning back to life more vividly—and more accurately—than many later books.

Yet these scholars had agendas of their own. They took positions in bitter controversies over the nature of classical scholarship, the best form of education, and the nature of literature and art. Their assumptions, and sometimes their prejudices, drove them to study the earlier history of scholarship, and continue to fix the ways in which we interpret the lives and works of early modern literati. Anyone who hopes to grapple with Renaissance humanism or seventeenth-century historical scholarship, accordingly, must engage with the lives and thoughts of its later interpreters as well. The complex, dialectical interplay of ancients and moderns—an essential feature of humanistic traditions, western and eastern—forms a central subject of the case studies of Jacob Bernays, Mark Pattison, and Erwin Panofsky that appear below.

All of these essays represent incursions into contested lands, voyages to the darkling plains where learned armies clashed by night. And many of the clashes they record are substantive and deeply felt debates about the nature of intellectual work and the definition of culture itself. Studies in learned, and sometimes arcane, pursuits, these essays also chronicle some of the early modern world's most passionately fought battles of books—and readers.

These, then, are the themes pursued in this collection, which itself still exemplifies, in a way, the new kind of scholarly miscellany that became fashionable in learned Italian circles in the 1470s and 1480s. Some essays began as articles, based on the interpretation of substantial masses of text. Others took shape as reviews of original works of scholarship. All of them—like the study of Calcagnini and Adriani from which this introduction began—rest on study of highly varied sources. All of them seek to show that the apparently arid ground of humanist learning brought forth not only multiple examples of lovable—and less lovable—pedantry, but also substantial efforts to connect the realm of nature with that of books, the realm of everyday experience in the street with that of passionate reading in massive tomes, and the realm of codes of etiquette and institutions with that of extravagant and joyous erudition. All of them, finally, represent efforts to understand how monsters could have been welcome in the midst of the life of reason and learning.

I

HISTORIES
AND
TRADITIONS

I

Panofsky, Alberti,
and the
Ancient World

ᏇᎢᏇᎢᏇ

𝓛EON BATTISTA ALBERTI could do many remarkable things. He leapt from a standing start over the head of a man standing next to him. He hurled lances and shot arrows with astonishing force, and threw a coin so high that it rang as it struck the vaulted roof of the church he stood in. A penetrating observer of society, he divined men's intentions toward him at a glance. He loved to look at dignified old men, but wept when he saw spring flowers or fall fruits, because they made him feel unproductive. He interrogated knowledgeable craftsmen about their skills, and eventually become a dazzling (if amateur) painter in his own right, one who could paint or sculpt the likeness of a friend while dictating an essay. The device for projecting images that he designed startled his contemporaries with its illusions of landscapes, the night sky, and the ocean. He trained himself to bear pain without flinching (he sang to distract himself) and even to tolerate the presence of garlic and honey, which had originally made him vomit.

All this we learn from the so-called anonymous life of Alberti, first published in the eighteenth century (sadly, most scholars now take the text as autobiographical and with at least half a grain of salt).[1] The Alberti of this anonymous account—the universal savant, the brilliant man of action, the cultivator of *sprezzatura* before Castiglione—enthralled Jacob Burckhardt, that passionate lover of the life of the Italian streets which Alberti prowled and the Italian landscapes which he found so beautiful. Alberti's character forms the core of the brilliant description of "the universal man" that lights up the second section of *The Civilization of the Renaissance in Italy*. In both the original account and Burckhardt's incomplete retelling, an encounter with the classical past plays only a supporting role—and a rather frightening one—in the lively cast of Alberti's tasks and hobbies. Both texts tell us that the very experience of textual study—at least when carried out on an empty stomach—proved unhealthy, almost lethal. Burckhardt treats the transition in Alberti's life, however, not as a crisis but as a natural progress from textual studies to science and the visual arts: "finding his memory for words weakened, but his sense of facts unimpaired, he set to work at physics and mathematics." This brilliant, iron-willed student of nature made the perfect prelude, in Burckhardt's eyes, to the true universal man of the High Renaissance, Leonardo. That self-proclaimed "man without letters," scientist, and artist was to Alberti "as the finisher to the beginner, the master to the dilettante." Burckhardt's Alberti—the universal man, the friend of artists who did not waste his time among the humanists—dominated the historiography for decades. He made a natural centerpiece for a vision of the Renaissance in which the discovery of nature and of man took center stage, and the rediscovery of classical texts had a strictly subordinate role.[2]

In the years just before the turn of the century, however, the nature and direction of cultural history and the history of art began to shift in momentous ways. The impact of the classical heritage on Renaissance art and artistic theory attracted attention from many quarters. Not only the brilliantly idiosyncratic refugee from a banking career in Hamburg, but Julius von Schlosser and Karl Giehlow in Vienna, Willi Flemming and a host of others now forgotten, broke the unpromising ground of dialogues on art, neo-Platonic treatises, and classical commentaries, searching for iconographical and biographical gold. Major Renaissance artists, like Albrecht Dürer, and influential theorists, like Alberti, were suddenly revealed playing an unexpected role: as serious readers as well as forceful writers. A century of subsequent work has proved that this approach is necessary (though not sufficient). Students of Alberti's works on the arts, for example, have shown in meticulous detail how closely he based each of his technical manuals for artists on classical prototypes, above all the rhetorical works of Cicero and Quintilian, and how densely he stuffed them with classical references. Unfortunately, the same century's work has not determined exactly how one should approach Alberti's classicism. Each new interpretation of *On Painting*—and every year brings forth a number of them—now routinely rests on an identification of Alberti's major structural source or sources. Unfortunately, some are no solider than Flemming's effort of a century ago, which Panofsky effortlessly refuted, to make Alberti a neo-Platonist on the strength of a supposed connection with Plotinus.[3] The great example of the Renaissance's discovery of the world and of man has become a central figure in the classical revival—and, even more paradoxically, the object of an unending paper chase.

Erwin Panofsky—whom, like Alberti, I know only from reading—could do almost as many remarkable things as the inventer of Renaissance perspective. His books, which I and my contemporaries encountered in undergraduate and graduate courses, won many of us to the study of the Renaissance—in cultural history as well as the history of art. They offered an attractive, if practically inimitable, model of interdisciplinary scholarship. Their author, after all, could jump as effortlessly as Alberti, and over higher obstacles. He leapt with a Nureyev's ease and mastery from visual material to texts, from literature to science, and from antiquity to the baroque. When Panofsky set out to define a Gothic form or the Renaissance view of the past, he retained the sweep and eloquence of a Burckhardt. He had learned, presumably in his early years of interaction with Aby Warburg and Ernst Cassirer, to see the central forms of cultures as coherent sets of symbols. He had also made discoveries about rhetoric—partly in the course of his collaboration with Fritz Saxl, that master of the capsule summary and the deftly chosen example; partly as a result of having to teach in America. In English, he realized, he could describe the basic western cultural forms to a new public and with a new clarity, partly because he was released from the toils of his Begriff-stricken mother tongue. But if his hypotheses towered into a speculative stratosphere, they were still firmly rooted in empirical soil. Thick, twisty footnotes made clear his mastery of a wealth of texts; numerous plates assembled an equal wealth of visual material.[4] Panofsky, in other words, supported his arguments with—and often built them around—precisely the sort of detailed interpretations of texts and images that Burckhardt had omitted. He seemed to have both the panoramic vision of the parachutist and the microscopic attention to detail of the truffle-hunter. Such at least was my experience of one Panofsky—the Panofsky of *Gothic Architecture and Scholasticism, Studies in Iconology,* and *Renaissance and Renascences in Western Art.*[5]

One of this Panofsky's formulations, in particular, won many hearts. In a series of brilliant essays, the fullest of which was written with Saxl, he set out to establish the difference between the several renascences of classical texts and forms which took place during the Middle Ages and the full-scale Renaissance, which he localized in fifteenth-century Italy.[6] Medieval artists and scholars, he explained, studied individual classical texts or imitated individual classical forms. But they did not see classical forms and their original content—or motifs and themes—as organically connected, as joint, though different, expressions of a single civilization. Only in the late fourteenth and early fifteenth centuries did humanists come to see the ancient world as a whole, a coherent culture that stood at a fixed chronological distance from their own. When they did so, the shock of recognition was immense, and the intellectual change involved revolutionary. It was, in fact, every bit as radical as the contemporary transformation of the visual arts by the formulation of a strict system of one-point perspective. Panofsky, characteristically, speculated over and over again on what he saw as these contemporary and analogous changes of cultural focus. The end of the medieval "principle of disjunction" and the creation of a modern system of perspective became, for him, the double expression of a single phenomenon: the rise of a naturalistic art, for whose practitioners the way to nature lay through the antique (eventually, of course, the classical form of realism would be overcome and supplanted, in its turn, by other forms). Panofsky's dramatic but flexible way of putting this point gave those interested in the history of the classical revival a vocabulary and a thesis. He enabled us to argue in detail about humanist scholarship without feeling that we were lost in the pursuit of details that had no larger sense. We owed him intellectual confidence—a hard emotion for intellectual historians to cultivate in the years when "real" political history gave way to quantification. No wonder that his elegant formulations inspired so much research and teaching.

Songs of innocence, however, turn into songs of experience. A richer experience of the texts and problems connected with the early and mid-fifteenth century has made me uneasy about the very claims that made me enter the field in the first place. If Panofsky was right, Alberti ought to be the nexus, the thinker in whom both forms of perspective, visual and temporal, come together. He formulated the rules of perspective, for the first time, in writing. He intimately knew, and celebrated in a phosphorescent prose poem, Filippo Brunelleschi and the other Florentines who devised them. He devoted much of his life to the study and use of ancient buildings. And in fact he reappears constantly in Panofsky's work, as a key witness to the existence of a real Renaissance. But the more closely one looks at the texture of Alberti's writing and creative work, the harder it becomes to make him fit Panofsky's splendid model.

Alberti certainly took a passionate and creative part in the fifteenth-century revival of antiquity. He studied the ruins of the city of Rome more systematically than any of his contemporaries, except his colleague Flavio Biondo. *De re aedificatoria* is, as Carlo Dionisotti pointed out long ago, not only a pioneering work on architecture but a *summa* of fifteenth-century antiquarian scholarship. Alberti also knew the crafts that his contemporaries used to elucidate ancient texts. He knew the techniques of humanist philology, for example, well enough to enjoy playing with them—always a sign, as Michael Baxandall has pointed out, that one has mastered a skill with difficulty and likes to display the acquisition in public.[7] Guarino of Verona translated Lucian's mock-encomium on the fly into Latin and sent it to Alberti, who was suffering from a fever. The text amused him so much that he immediately sat up and dictated a mock-encomium of his own. Alberti praised everything about the fly. The fly is heroic (he is willing to attack any opponent, without a leader or allies, at any time); he is pious (whenever the ancients sacrificed animals to the gods, the flies were the very first to attend); he and his female companions wear the same fine classical dress as their ancestors and show the same musical talent. Above all, however, Alberti praises the fly's erudition and antiquity. Flies are insatiably curious; in fact, they know the answers to questions that have tormented scholars for centuries. Flies know what Circe fed her suitors to turn them into pigs, what Andromache's breasts tasted like, what flaws appeared in Helen's *nates,* and what beauties adorned Ganymede's *occulta.* So much for exactly the sorts of historical and mythological questions most beloved of humanist commentators and schoolteachers. Even textual criticism, the humanist science of sciences, came in for its share of mockery at Alberti's hands. The flies, he explains, stood at the origins of ancient science: they had taught Pythagoras his new mathematics. A simple feat of textual criticism proved the point. The texts said that after Pythagoras proved his theorem, he sacrificed "musis," to the Muses. In reality, Pythagoras must have offered his hecatomb of oxen "muscis," to the flies.[8]

Most important of all, Alberti could synthesize his vast treasury of information. His probing, fluent inquiries into the history of western culture show how profound and flexible a historical imagination he had. Like Biondo—and in the teeth of the beliefs of many well-reputed scholars—Alberti argued that in the ancient world Latin had not been a special, learned language, as it was in his day. Rather, it was the ordinary language of the Romans, in which they had discussed everyday business with their wives, their children, and their slaves. Canonical writers like Cicero used it not because it had a special status but because they wanted readers to understand them. Alberti followed their example, he argued, when he wrote his dialogues On the Family in Italian, since he wrote to be understood, as they had.[9] More cogently than Biondo, Alberti turned the scattered hints of Vitruvius into a sharp, lucid, and imaginative history of how architecture was born in Asia, flowered in Greece, and reached maturity—thanks to the efforts of rival architects and the sound moral traditions of Italian patronage—in Rome. In each case, he clearly saw and treated classical culture as a whole, using developments in one area to explain those in another, and imagining Roman society in human and intimate terms—but also as very different from his own.[10]

But these examples of Alberti's historicism are as unusual as they are impressive. For as Eugenio Garin pointed out long ago in an article as short as it was brilliant (it is one page long), Alberti often cites or responds to ancient texts and ideas in ways that fundamentally alter, and sometimes radically subvert, the apparent meanings of the originals.[11] Garin supported his thesis with a number of examples of Alberti's inversions of Cicero. But the evidence is even more plentiful than he suggests. Each of Alberti's major works takes a radically eristic stance toward classical sources. On Architecture attacks Vitruvius on myriad details, explicitly and implicitly; the whole book challenges the very ancient source whose content Alberti made available, for the first time, to large numbers of modern readers.[12] On Painting describes itself, in a direct attack on the elder Pliny, as not a mere history of painting but a brand-new treatment of painting as an art—a subject on which no ancient *monumenta* had survived.[13] *On the Family* concludes with a book on friendship which, explicitly and implicitly, inverts the idealistic treatment given by Cicero in *De amicitia.*

Panofsky, of course, insisted that high Renaissance classicism always involved the creative reworking, not the passive repetition, of ancient forms and texts. He admitted that Renaissance artists and scholars frequently found themselves required to mix the classical with the modern, the Greco-Roman with the Gothic. Eventually they learned to appreciate the latter as historically correct, for its period. More than once he went further. In the beautiful essay on *Pandora's Box* that he wrote with Dora Panofsky, he argued that the most erudite and creative of Renaissance scholars, his beloved Erasmus, had conflated the archaic myth of Pandora with Apuleius's much later tale of Psyche, in order to create an effective but unclassical image of imprudence.[14] In the essay on Poussin in *Meaning and the Visual Arts,* he showed how radically new forms of sentiment were read into a classical adage, to the point of distorting its grammatical meaning— and how those who did this violence to Latinity expressed a new and powerful vision of the pastoral.[15]

When Panofsky moved from asserting the rigid purity of humanist scholarship to following its playful, arbitrary qualities, his approach changed—or so it seems to me. In these works—perhaps, one might say, in this second Panofsky, to whom I came later than I did to the first—the classical tradition looks very different than it did in the first. A carnival funhouse replaces the stately hall of symbolic forms that perfectly reflect each Zeitgeist. Historical accident and personal taste dictate the fates and functions of classical motifs. The fixing of the detail complicates—and even contradicts—the desire and pursuit of the whole. Above all, as in textual criticism, error, not accuracy, becomes the determinative element. Just as the occurrence of so-called separative errors proves the independence of one manuscript or family of manuscripts from another, so separative "errors" in interpretation enable one to see not only what early modern readers found most useful in their classical motifs, but also what they felt they needed to ignore or distort in the original texts or images. In later writers, the repeated presence of the error proves the persistent influence of the original re-former of the text. Only one difference—though a crucial one—calls for comment: the errors that merely disfigure a manuscript of a classical text may amount to room for creativity in a reworking of a classical artistic prototype.

This second Panofsky offers a much more effective model than the first for describing and understanding what Alberti did to ancient texts and forms.[16] Consider just one test case, drawn from *On Painting*. It is the famous story of Zeuxis and the women of Croton. Alberti tells it thus: "The idea of beauty, which the most expert have difficulty in discerning, eludes the ignorant. Zeuxis, the most eminent, learned and skilled painter of all, when about to paint a panel to be publicly dedicated in the temple of Lucina at Croton, did not set about his work trusting rashly in his own talent as all painters do now; but, because he believed that all the things he desired to achieve beauty not only could not be found by his own intuition, but were not to be discovered even in Nature in one body alone, he chose from all the youth of the city five outstandingly beautiful girls, so that he might represent in his painting whatever feature of feminine beauty was most praiseworthy in each of them. He acted wisely, for to painters with no model before them to follow, who strive by the light of their own talent alone to capture the qualities of beauty, it easily happens that they do not by their own efforts achieve the beauty they seek or ought to create; they simply fall into bad habits of painting."[17] This anecdote reached a vast public in the next two centuries. Writers on beauty, like Giangiorgio Trissino and Agnolo Firenzuola, used it to justify their endless catalogues of the ideal standard for each bit of the female anatomy (those texts that Burckhardt curiously took as witnessing to the enhanced status of women in Renaissance Italy). The story become one of the most popular of those classical and modern tags that floated from text to text in the sixteenth and seventeenth centuries, blurring as they moved. If we can trust the authenticity of Raphael's letter to Castiglione, it even became part of the normal language of the artist's studio.[18]

The story's meaning naturally varied with its use. Panofsky, in his early book *Idea,* points out that Alberti himself used it in diametrically opposed ways—in *De pictura,* as an incitement to the artist to form a conception of beauty based on meticulous study of the real world; in *De statua,* as an inducement to artists to base their work on a single coherent idea of beauty. Even Panofsky, however, did not examine the passage and its classical sources as closely as he did its later uses. This was reasonable; he saw Alberti's relation to the ancient past as relatively unproblematic, as belonging to a first phase of excited, whole-hearted rediscovery. But close, comparative study reveals that in this central, vitally influential text Alberti performed as radical an act of textual surgery as Erasmus did to Hesiod eighty years later. Alberti drew the story from two standard sources: Cicero's *De inventione* (2.1) and Pliny's *Natural History* (35.64). He craftily made clear, to the educated reader, that he used both. Alberti located the story in Croton, as Cicero did (Pliny put it in Agrigento); but he described the temple for which Zeuxis worked as that of Lucina, as he thought Pliny did (Cicero made it the temple of Juno). The passage thus amounts to an elegant pastiche, as Nicoletta Maraschio showed in a very attentive examination of it, almost thirty years ago.[19] As she also pointed out, Alberti's procedure responded in a very precise way to those of the authors that he exploited. Cicero told the story of Zeuxis as justification for his own eclectic use of several sources in *De inventione,* just as Zeuxis had used several models' bodies, Cicero would use several model texts. So Alberti, imitating Cicero, used another textual source as well.

Alberti, however, not only combined the two Latin models; he systematically abridged and altered them. Cicero told a far longer and quirkier tale than Pliny or Alberti. Zeuxis, he explained, asked the Crotoniates to show him their five most beautiful young women. They replied by taking him directly to the *palaestra,* the wrestlers' gymnasium, and showing him many handsome boys (as Cicero remarks, in those days the Crotoniates were great athletes). They then told him the good news: that the boys he saw wrestling had equally beautiful sisters. Unfortunately, bad news followed immediately: he had to infer their *dignitas* from that of the boys. Undaunted, Zeuxis begged the Crotoniates to let him see the five most beautiful virgins for just so long as he needed to transform the truth about them into a *mutum . . . simulacrum.* At last they agreed, and by a public decree gave him the power to choose his models. The point of the story is evidently double. A teacher's joke, inserted by Cicero to liven up the beginning of a textbook, it turns on a Roman's negative view of Greek naked athletics (and, perhaps, the adult Greek male's love of boys). It also shows the Roman's clear awareness that to paint a nude, the painter needed a naked model—and that respectable women and their parents could find this requirement of his art, with its erotic suggestiveness and social inversion, unacceptable. The story of Zeuxis had an erotic edge as well as a literary moral.

Alberti's version of the story, unlike its source, scrupulously avoids all erotic suggestion. The gymnasium and the Crotoniate boys have disappeared. Paradoxically—and, no doubt, deliberately—he has changed places with his source. Cicero, who used the painter and his models as an analogy for the rhetorician and his sources, described the episode in vivid physical terms. Alberti, who actually meant to tell painters how to paint and patrons what to buy, retold it abstractly. Not only did Alberti use Cicero's and Pliny's material, but he rewrote it to fit the ethical and aesthetic program for which he hoped to win support—one that emphasized the emotional, but denied the erotic, effects of painting in what ultimately became a very influential way (one might compare his account of sexual intercourse, one of the more displeasing male fantasies in the western canon, in *On the Family*). Because Alberti manipulated standard sources that his intended readers knew intimately, he could feel confident that they would understand and emulate his revision of the very authorities he used (as indeed, every one of them did, sharing the separative error with the intermediary source that shaped their vision of the ancient artist at work).

Alberti's attack on the passage seems no more classical and no less radical than that of his chief late-medieval predecessor—a man whom Panofsky would have tied rather to "i primi lumi" than to what he took as the pure classical revival of the fifteenth century. Giovanni Boccaccio told the story of Zeuxis in some detail in his commentary on Dante. Characteristically, he celebrated exactly the implications that Alberti chose to ignore, and cheerfully praised Zeuxis for having examined not only all the Crotoniate boys, but also all of their sisters, in his (admittedly hopeless) search for ideal beauty.[20] Alberti's version of the story, though better adapted to a Christian, moralizing readership, is no more scrupulous, no more inspired by a desire to reproduce ancient books or ancient life as they really were, than Boccaccio's.

It may seem curious that Alberti, who read the classics with such dedication, applied them with such arbitrariness. In fact, however, his rewritings of his sources fell within the norms of a certain kind of humanist practice. In his youth Alberti had studied with Gasparino Barzizza, who taught his pupils precisely to show their respect for and independence from classical sources at the same time. "Imitation," he explained to them, "is carried out in four ways, by addition, subtraction, transferral, and transformation"— never by straight copying. Simple verbal changes could make a single sentence new: "If Cicero says, 'Scite hoc inquit Brutus,' I will add, 'Scite enim ac eleganter hoc inquit ille vir noster Brutus.' See how it seems to have a different form now."[21] Mature humanists as well as schoolboys practiced the same form of aggressive imitation or emulation. Maffeo Vegio, the Roman cleric who wrote a thirteenth book for the *Aeneid*, spoiled the epic for generations of schoolboys, by grafting onto the real text a pastel-colored sequel in which Aeneas buried Turnus, married Lavinia, ruled his peoples, and finally ascended to heaven, to become a star. Yet Vegio knew what he was doing. He saw, under the august surface of Virgil's text, the same tensions that have bothered modern readers: the harm done by Aeneas in his travels, the innocent sufferers, the strange ending, so much less humane than that of the *Iliad,* in which Aeneas savagely kills Turnus, and the latter's death scream is the last sound heard. Vegio rewrote the poem, in short, because he understood it so well—just as Dante had inflicted Christian senses on Virgil because he understood the pagan ones so well. The boundaries between vernacular and classical culture, late medieval and Renaissance scholarship are simply not so sharp as Panofsky drew them. Ironically, the second Panofsky thus provides the best guidance in how to criticize the first.

To establish that Alberti's procedures fell within normal tolerances is not to explain why he chose them so consistently. But it seems possible to connect his commitment to emulative reading with a larger aesthetic project. Alberti loved the classics. He used classical rhetoric as his model of a well-organized intellectual discipline, took classical architecture as his prime source of principles and design elements, and pleaded for the unique intellectual and practical value of a classical education. But he also insisted, in his famous letter to Brunelleschi and elsewhere, on the legitimacy of the modern: on the power and uniqueness of the achievements of his fellow Florentines. His account of the family, with its systematic blurring of the distance between the ancient Romans and the ancient Alberti, used classical materials to find a voice for the ideology of later medieval merchant life. His architecture—like the Holy Sepulchre that he built for Giovanni Rucellai, with its classical inscription superimposed on a little gem of a Gothic building, or the Malatesta Temple at Rimini, with its triumphal

arch superimposed on a Christian church, or—if indeed it reflects Alberti's
ideas—Pienza, with its symphonic interweaving of pagan and Christian,
antique and modern forms—regularly combined classical and modern elements in radically novel ways.[22] Alberti, in short, committed himself
throughout his life to making classical texts, ideas, and forms live in what
he recognized, quite happily, as a nonclassical world. His appropriations of
specific texts amount to something more than a set of emulative readings
of passages. They made manifest a self-conscious, creative, and wholly consistent relationship between classicism and modernity. Applied to the
study of this relation, the first Panofsky's model fits only part of the evidence, and obscures almost as much as it reveals. By contrast the second
Panofsky's philological work, with its cheerful admission of the shaping
power of accident and the distorting pressure of personal taste, remains
exemplary.

Three morals remain to be drawn, and one question to be asked. First,
the tensions in Panofsky's thought were organic parts of it; for the philological seeds of the second Panofsky's brilliantly revisionist work were sown
at the very start of his career—for example, by the lovably pedantic Greek
teacher whose charming sermon on the importance of a comma in Plato
Panofsky evoked in his memoir.[23] The second Panofsky's work demonstrates the continued utility of a highly traditional philological method,
when applied with art and taste. Second, though the perceptions of the
second Panofsky were sometimes very narrowly defined, their implications
were very broad: more than once they undermined the wonderfully bold
and lucid symbolic forms that Panofsky pursued them to support. Third,
Panofsky's work on the vision of antiquity, like his work on perspective,
drew both energy and tension from his ability to tolerate internal contradictions and function, brilliantly. The question that remains is simple:
what factors—political, cultural, biographical—explain the prevalence of
the first Panofsky, the continual reappearances of the second, and the varied ways in which both segments of his individual talent interacted with
the classical tradition?

2

The Ancient City Restored:
Archaeology, Ecclesiastical
History, and Egyptology

ᏻᎷᎷᎾ

This essay first appeared in the catalogue of the 1993 Library of Congress exhibition *Rome Reborn: The Vatican Library and Renaissance Culture.* The original illustrations have been replaced with plates from a fifteenth-century collection of drawings and inscriptions by Giovanni Marcanova.

*B*ETWEEN 1400 and 1650 some of the splendors of ancient Rome emerged from beneath the shapeless pastures and deserted hills of the medieval city. Students of what we would now call archaeology plotted the regions and identified the buildings of what had once been the largest city in the Mediterranean world, *Roma nobilis.* In the later Middle Ages many classical sites lay in ruins; others had been incorporated into Christian churches or city walls. Thick layers of earth concealed locations and obscured identities. Roman masons constantly attacked the structures that remained above ground, stealing stones to insert them into new buildings or burning them for lime. And central portions of the classical city—the forum itself, the Capitoline and Palatine hills—were entirely deserted. Michel de Montaigne, who came to Rome after a century and a half of unremitting work had identified the primary ancient sites and uncovered hundreds of fascinating objects, thought the modern city so different from the ancient one he had read about that an ancient Roman, should he come back to life, "could not recognize the site of his city even if he saw it."[1]

Figure 1. Life among the Ruins. Princeton University Library, MS Garrett 158. Courtesy of the Department of Rare Books and Special Collections, Princeton University Library.

Worse still, a tightly woven fabric of popular errors and legends overlaid the whole city, confusing anyone who hoped to work out where exactly the great dramas of Roman history had been acted. The famed traditional guidebook, the *Mirabilia urbis Romae,* identified the Colosseum not as a place of gladiatorial combat but as a temple of the sun. It explained the great *thermae* (baths) of the emperors not as places where the Romans had gone to wash and sweat but as palaces with large underground chambers which were heated in the winter and filled with cooling water in the summer. And it divagated at far greater length about the golden palaces that had once crowned Rome's hills than about the stone ruins still to be found on them. It identified the equestrian statue of Marcus Aurelius, then at the Lateran but since moved to the Capitoline, as the image of a peasant who had saved Rome from the depredations of an invader. Pilgrims who used this text as their Baedeker would not leave Rome knowing where Caesar died or Nero fiddled.[2]

The Roman in the street, moreover, could prove as rich a source of misinformation as any book. As late as the middle of the sixteenth century, the German antiquary Georg Fabricius warned travelers that "one must not listen to the ordinary crowd when learning the antiquities of the city. They say that the brick structure before the Colosseum called the *Meta sudans* was Virgil's tower; that the temple of the four-faced Janus, a square structure in the forum Boarium, was the house of Boethius. They babble that the bronze columns in Saint John Lateran, which Augustus Caesar produced by melting the booty of the battle of Actium, after the defeat of Antony, were brought from the Temple in Jerusalem for the sake of religion."[3] He also complained that the Romans identified every large structure one asked about, whatever its real function had been, as a bath.[4]

Accordingly, even serious students of the Roman past found it hard to establish basic facts—especially in the early Renaissance, when little firsthand research had yet been done and brambles and legends still concealed most of the monuments. Petrarch, the greatest classical scholar of the fourteenth century, surveyed the city with his Roman friend Giovanni Colonna; they had delightful antiquarian colloquies in the Baths of Diocletian. He carefully compared what he saw and heard with what he had read in the Latin classics, which he knew intimately. Yet he still accepted and passed on, unscrutinized, many popular beliefs that a close look at the stones in question could have refuted. He went to his death thinking that

Figure 2. Monte Testaccio. Princeton University Library, MS Garrett 158. Courtesy of the Department of Rare Books and Special Collections, Princeton University Library.

Trajan, not Hadrian, built the Ponte Sant' Angelo and that the Pyra-mide—the large stone pyramid near what is now the Protestant Cemetery, built by one Cestius, whose name appears on it in large letters—was the tomb of Remus, one of the two legendary founders of the city. Petrarch vividly evoked the cityscape of republican Rome in his epic poem of the Punic Wars, the *Africa*. But his description contained jarring errors and anachronisms, and portrayed an urban fabric far too richly textured for the austere age of Scipio Africanus.

Archaeology and Antiquarianism: The Past Unearthed

In time, however, the physical city swam back into historical focus. The humanists gradually learned to take a serious interest in three-dimensional remains as well as literary texts. In the early fourteenth century several north Italian scholars inspected ancient sites and monuments. Their results were sometimes fantastic, but their methods could be surprisingly modern. Giovanni de Matociis, the *Mansionarius* of the cathedral in Verona, used Roman coins to illustrate the faces of the Roman emperors, and drew a diagram to shed light on his description of a Roman circus. Gradually new interests spread. Ancient inscriptions could provide evidence that complemented the classical texts. Direct inspection of tri-umphal arches, temples, and arenas could shed light on a great many aspects of Roman life, from political history to religious ritual, that the surviving histories did not fully clarify.

As the physical evidence attracted scrutiny, the society that had created it also came to be seen in a new way. Some ancient Roman scholars, above all Varro, had systematically studied their own ancient past. Unlike the ancient historians, who told stories of great men and dramatic battles, Varro and his ilk collected the fragmentary information that could show them what it had been like to live in Rome centuries before their time. These men rewove the textures of forgotten practices and beliefs, drawing their evidence from stone monuments as well as literary texts. Though Varro's own books survived only in fragments, a number of popular and authoritative works—above all Augustine's *City of God* and Macrobius's *Saturnalia*—exemplified his methods and preserved some of his discover-ies about early Roman rites and institutions.[5]

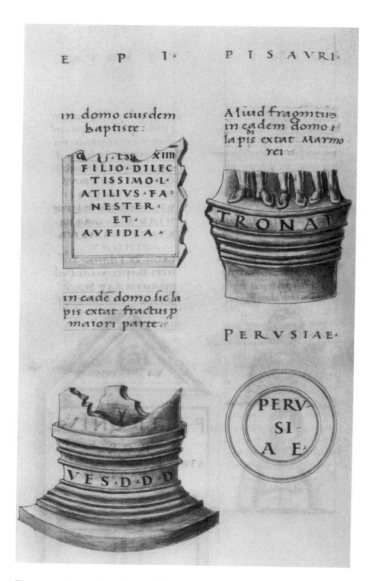

Figure 3. Inscriptions from Italian cities. Princeton University Library, MS Garrett 158. Courtesy of the Department of Rare Books and Special Collections, Princeton University Library.

Varro's branch of learning, usually called antiquarianism, began to revive in the fifteenth century. It gave the study of ruins a purpose and a context. Ruins and inscriptions could be studied not only for their intrinsic interest but for what they revealed about the lives and thought of past individuals. The antiquary Cyriac of Ancona, who traversed landscapes sown with ruins not only in Rome but in Constantinople and Egypt, and brought back wonderfully lively sketchbooks adorned with magnificent images of obelisks, pyramids, tombstones, and giraffes, defined his project as "conversation with the dead"—resuming direct contact with the ancients in a way that mere reading did not allow.[6]

As Roman social and cultural life reawoke, moreover, it became clear that individual relics still carried a powerful political and sentimental charge. The stones had always stimulated some excitement. In the eleventh century Roman scholars caused a sensation when they identified the tomb of a very large man as that of Pallas, son of Evander, who had fought on the side of Aeneas against the Latins (so, at least, Virgil said in the *Aeneid*). But in the Renaissance vivid, apparently unchallengeable evidence about an older, purer Rome could be revolutionary. In the mid-fourteenth century the republican rebel Cola di Rienzo found in the Lateran the so-called *Lex de imperio*—the bronze tablet bearing the decree by which the Roman people formally transferred its power to the emperors. He used this text effectively in support of his efforts—ultimately disastrous—to restore the city to independence from papal and imperial control. As he explained, he set out to make the Roman people "imitate . . . the will, benignity, and liberality of the ancient rulers of Rome."[7] Even so technical an area of the study of the past as the reading of inscriptions served clearly felt modern needs. Antiquarianism, in other words, could have a sharp political edge. But it did not need to aim at radical or subversive ends. Great Roman families, like the Orsini and the Colonna, actually traced their ancestry back to the aristocrats of the Republic. They regarded ancient Rome—like the modern city—as their legitimate possession. And their support made possible some of the earliest ambitious archaeological work. Cristoforo de' Buondelmonti, a Florentine priest, became the first western scholar to search the ruins of the Aegean world, examining both Christian churches and pagan temples. He braved terrible dangers—at least once he wrote his own epitaph in the expectation that he would soon die of hunger, only to be saved when a merchant ship turned up—and saw wonderful sights in the ruin-strewn landscapes of the Greek world. His lively first-hand account of the splendid antiquities and barbarous modern inhabitants of the Greek islands was dedicated to the great Roman book collector Cardinal Giordano Orsini. Its vivid reportage and evocative, sometimes fantastic illustrations reveal the double nature of early humanist archaeology, its characteristic mixture of serious method and romantic enthusiasm. The city of Rome naturally invited similar scrutiny.

The first intellectual to make a powerful literary case for the pleasures to be garnered from the ruins of Rome was one of the liveliest of the intellects that adorned the early fifteenth-century papal curia: Poggio Bracciolini. Toward 1430, Poggio explained, he and his friend Antonio Loschi had explored the deserted places of the city in free time made available by the pope's absence. They admired the greatness of Rome's past and mourned the devastation of its present. Climbing the Capitoline on horseback, they dismounted and sat down among the ruins of the Tarpeian rock, "near what I take to be the huge marble lintel of a temple gate, and a great many broken columns lying about; from here a view of much of the city opens out."[8] As they looked, they sighed. But after they sighed, they studied. And after they studied, Poggio gave their conversation a detailed and elaborate literary form. In what became the first book of a comprehensive text, *On the Mutability of Fortune* (*De varietate fortunae*), which he completed around 1450, Poggio described the Roman buildings he knew, site by site.

Poggio was no amateur archaeologist. When he criticized Petrarch's identification of the Pyramide as the tomb of Remus, for example, he knew that that "most learned man" had followed popular opinion instead of looking at the actual structure. He excused his great predecessor, who had failed to part the thick bushes that covered Cestius's name. But he also praised those who came later, himself included, who "combined more diligence with less learning" and actually read what the stones had to say. In fact, he had compiled a whole notebook of inscriptions, both public and private, from inside and outside the city, "copying them word for word, for general use, and digging up some that lay hidden amid the bushes and brambles, so that others might have access to them."[9] Poggio's collection— not quite the first, but one of them—marks the beginnings of systematic field archaeology in Rome. He compiled his notebook by direct inspection of the ancient sites as well as by reading and copying others' transcripts;

other scholars could test, correct, and add to his materials as copies of his work became available. Over the next seventy years, such collections, called *syllogae,* would multiply. They became the primary source of information about individual Romans below imperial rank: the thousands of Romans whose lives, careers, marriages, and beliefs can be inferred only from their tombstones and from their carved messages to their gods.

Poggio's literary survey of the city was brief and unsystematic, and it purveyed as well as corrected errors. He followed tradition, for example, in taking the small round temple on the bank of the Tiber near S. Maria in Cosmedin as the Temple of Vesta rather than that of Hercules Olivarius. And when he solemnly mourned the decrepit state of the aedes Castorum, "once the famous place where the Senate met," he was actually looking at the ruined temples of Venus and Roma near the Colosseum.[10] But he made clear how radically the city had changed from its classical state, when Augustus had rebuilt it from marble. Poggio's survey used literary texts to conjure up the myriad statues, temples, triumphal arches, public buildings, and private houses that had embellished the ancient city. He cited his own eyewitness inspections to prove that the city walls had been rebuilt and repaired many times over the centuries. And he drew on personal experience to lament the continual destruction to which even the fragments that remained were subject. In his own lifetime, Poggio reported, the Temple of Concord had been reduced from a state of nearly perfect preservation to a heap of lime. All that remained was an inscription (in fact not part of the temple), which ironically recorded that the Senate and people of Rome had restored the building after a fire. Antiquarianism and nostalgia—the desire to find what had been lost and the need to mourn what could not be saved—were linked, not for the last time.

In the Roman Academy of the later fifteenth century, the exploitation of ruins and inscriptions became more and more systematic. Pomponio Leto and his friends not only loved but revived the customs and culture of republican Rome. They identified and celebrated the Roman holidays—the Parilia of 21 April, the birthday of the ancient city, and the Robigalia of 25 April, on which they began what became the long-lived Roman custom of posting satirical verses on the statue of Pasquino.[11] They built their own classical theater, in which they could perform Plautus's comedies and Seneca's tragedies for the curia. And they traversed the city, penetrating into the catacombs below it and climbing the hills above it to look for new relics of ancient history and art. We even possess a record of Leto's standard antiquarian walk around the old city, apparently taken down as he spoke.[12]

Leto's circle studied inscriptions and ruins with a new care and made them available, in various ways, to a new public. Students' notes on Leto's lectures at the University of Rome survive. A detailed and elegant copy of his lectures on Varro's treatise on the Latin language reveals that he not only told his students about the origins of Latin words but showed them (perhaps in diagrammatic form) Roman places and things. The student, who at one point drew a nice quick caricature of his teacher, also inserted round temples modeled on the so-called Temple of Vesta and sketches of baths and temples into the margin of his notebook. Even Leto's students, in other words, learned to study texts and objects together.

Only fragments of Leto's notebook of inscriptions survive, one of them showing that he discovered a Roman rustic calendar, on stone. His copy of the calendar is unadorned and uninformative, but the Roman printer Iacopo Mazzocchi reproduced it in print, in a little pamphlet, now extremely rare. Thus an archaeological find was not only recorded but published (though, in fact, Pomponio had long since made the text available in handwritten copies to friends in other cities).

Eventually, in the 1520s, Iacopo Mazzocchi brought out a printed collection of the inscriptions of Rome, compiled by one or more scholars who remained anonymous. This collected dozens of texts, and dramatically portrayed the Pyramide, the Vatican obelisk, and other major sites with new illustrations. Though often inaccurate in detail, the book provided a basis for further study and a baseline for debate on the subject. The scholar could carry a copy of it into the field and correct it against what he saw. One could also record in it, as many owners did, oral and written reports of new digs and discoveries. Antiquarianism thus became a collective and cumulative enterprise.

The rise of a new art and architecture, finally, did much to quicken interest in Roman remains. As early as the beginning of the fifteenth century, the great Florentine architect Filippo Brunelleschi tried systematically "to rediscover" in Rome "the excellent and highly ingenious building methods of the ancients and their harmonious proportions." He took notes, examined ruins, made drawings, and even had excavations done. According to his biographer Antonio Manetti he and Donatello lived austerely, spending as little as possible on food and clothing in order to "satisfy [themselves] with these things to see and measure." They spent their money on porters and laborers. And though they gained, for their trouble, the reputation of being "treasuremen," they also learned—Manetti says— how to distinguish the styles of Greek architecture from one another and how the Romans had joined and finished the elements of their buildings.[13] On such foundations the new art and architecture of the fifteenth century were reared.

Soon humanists, clerics, and ordinary citizens began to see ancient structures and works of art as the artists saw them, as the unique and precious remains of a higher civilization. In the 1430s, when a laborer digging ditches to plant trees near S. Maria sopra Minerva found a colossal head, crowds came to see it; the owner of the land had to bury it again to keep them away.[14] And in 1485, when the perfectly preserved body of a young Roman woman was discovered in the Appian Way, all Rome came to see this classical equivalent of the mummified saints that inhabited so many Italian cathedrals.

Discoveries multiplied as the city revived. True, not all of them were systematically recorded or even preserved. As late as the time of Julius II, when a barber digging a latrine turned up the fragments of the great meridian instrument of Augustus and the broken obelisk that had been its enormous gnomon, no money could be found to perform a full-scale dig. Again the remains were covered over, not to be fully excavated until very recent times.[15] Other great objects—like the *Ara pacis*—were scattered across Italy as late as the sixteenth century.

Gradually, however, efforts at preservation became more systematic. Pope Sixtus IV set a vastly influential precedent when he established a museum on the Capitoline in 1474 and placed in it the famous bronze statues of the Spinario and of the lupa, or she-wolf, that nourished Romulus and Remus. Cardinals and popes competed to adorn their gardens in the Roman hills with sculptures. New discoveries, like the mosaics of Nero's Golden House and the Laocoön, attracted buzzing swarms of artists. Drawings, prints, and notebooks carried these newly canonical antiquities to a European public of artists and patrons. And some popes—like Leo X, who appointed Raphael to survey and preserve the ruins of Rome—made ambitious, though largely unsuccessful, efforts to slow the pace of the long-term cycle of demolition and construction that produced the fabric of Renaissance Rome. Sadly, other popes counteracted these wise measures.

Many ancient buildings and monuments were destroyed in the Renaissance and after. The notes of scholars and the drawings of artists have become the only firsthand record of them.

Still, archaeology had become more than a subject; it had become a craze. In the gardens on the Roman hills, cardinals, artists, and scholars met at dinner to discuss technical problems. What were the precise dimensions of the "foot" and "stade" that the Romans had used to measure the world on their expeditions? Where was the spring of the nymph Iuturna, the water of which could cure dermatitis? When was the city really founded? Scholars competed to find the decisive text or fragment—like the famous effigy of a foot that Angelo Colocci, the owner of one of the most famous sculpture gardens and the host at many an antiquarian banquet, used to answer the first question mentioned above.[16]

A whole antiquarian community grew up, and though some Roman experts died in the sack of 1527, others—many of them foreign—joined it. By the 1560s, when the brilliant young Flemish scholar Justus Lipsius found himself as dazzled and bewildered by the chaotic ruins of the Colosseum as he was by the Roman noonday sun, another Fleming, Nicolaus Florentius, calmed him with the assurance that he could explicate the entire structure, tier by tier, on the basis of the work already done by local experts. The antiquaries, like other scholars, were often as possessive and paranoid as they were learned. Their letters reveal them in action, and the scene is not always edifying. One sees them eagerly sniping at one another for everything from inaccuracy in copying out an epitaph to inability to order food in Venetian dialect.[17] But when major projects confronted them, they could pull together. In the 1540s, the fragments of the Roman consular *fasti*—the official lists of the consuls—turned up in the Forum. The greatest antiquaries of the day edited and commented on the texts, and advised Michelangelo—who reassembled the pieces of the *fasti,* so far as he could, on the Capitoline. The results were dramatic. Roman history—for two centuries a favorite subject of humanists teaching ethical principles and prudence in politics—suddenly became an object of microscopic scholarly attention. The precise chronology of the Roman past took on a clear shape for the first time since the fall of the ancient world.[18]

As the case of the Capitoline *fasti* suggests, the book-learned antiquaries were not specialists in a dry subject of no interest to others. By the end of the fifteenth century, the classical monuments in Rome had become an

Figure 4. The Equestrian Statue of Marcus Aurelius. Princeton University Library, MS Garrett 158. Courtesy of the Department of Rare Books and Special Collections, Princeton University Library.

essential stop on the itinerary of every promising artist and architect. Giuliano da Sangallo—Lorenzo de' Medici's favorite architect—was one of many who came, saw, sketched, and took away rich notebooks which students and others could copy in their turn. These collections of drawings, though more compelling in form than the work of the scholars, often drew as heavily on the rough sketches of the antiquaries as on direct observation—and the antiquaries in their turn relied on the artists to produce images in full perspective and proportion, as they themselves could not. The resulting vision of Rome, an idealized, almost Arcadian city of sweeping vistas and imaginatively restored buildings and friezes, had as powerful an impact as the real city on artistic and architectual practice.

The City Restored

As early as the middle of the fifteenth century, intellectuals at the curia began not only to prize and study individual sites and statutes but to recreate the city as a whole, region by region. Flavio Biondo, the papal secretary whom later antiquaries often saw as the founder of their discipline, wove a vast range of quotations and rich first-hand information into his elaborate *Roma instaurata,* which became the standard, and invaluable, reference work. Any reader of Biondo would know, for example, exactly where he could find Roman baths and exactly what purpose they had served: "They took the word *therma* from the Greek word for 'hot.' Hence we can see that the Latins properly called *thermae* the places which were set aside for washing and sweating, with heated water or in a vault heated without water. Everyone who has read about their history knows that the Romans, both in the austere days of their Republic and in the fastidious ones of their emperors, bathed often and almost daily. Hence although every modestly well-off citizen had his own private bath, many baths were set up at public expense, in which the people could bathe as they liked."[19] Arches, temples, hills, and obelisks received the same precise, rigorous, and comprehensive treatment. At last visitors had a full, informative, and generally reliable guide, if not to the city as it was, at least to what it had once been.

In other cases artistic and textual inquiries intertwined. Leon Battista Alberti, another member of the curia, was at once a brilliant student of classical texts and a pioneering writer on the visual arts. In the 1430s, amazed by the one-point perspective devised by Brunelleschi, he wrote the

Figure 5. The Baths of Diocletian. Princeton University Library, MS Garrett 158. Courtesy of the Department of Rare Books and Special Collections, Princeton University Library.

first elaborate account of it. His *De pictura* became a manifesto, in both Latin and Italian versions, of the new painting, which had a powerful impact on both patrons and artists in central and northern Italy. And he himself became Italy's greatest expert on the building forms and aesthetics of the Roman city. He probably served as Nicholas V's chief expert consultant as the pope worked out his detailed, quixotic plans for a holy utopia in the Borgo.

Alberti ranged the city's ruins with an informed and perceptive eye. Where the stones left off, the historians came in; and where both failed, surviving buildings could yield the evidence for a conjectural restoration of lost ones. "I discover," he remarks, "from the historians that the Circus Maximus in Rome was three stadia long and one wide. At present it is so dilapidated as not to offer the least impression of its original appearance. But by measuring other similar works, I have discovered that the ancients used to give the central area a width of no less than sixty cubits."[20]

One result of Alberti's research was his massive survey of the classical style in architecture, the *De re aedificatoria*. This text, which circulated widely in manuscript and was eventually published by another great scholar, Angelo Poliziano, commented in passing on a great many episodes in the creation of the ancient city. A second enterprise had even more remarkable results for archaeology. Fascinated by perspective and measurement, Alberti had laid down rules by which painters and sculptors could measure human bodies, in order to discover the ideal proportions that should govern the human figures in their work. In a little treatise written at Rome in the 1440s, Alberti explained how to measure Rome itself. The reader could stand on the Capitoline and use Alberti's device to plot ancient and medieval sites—the Pantheon, the Aurelian column, and the Lateran—on a circular grid, producing a scale map of the city: a coherent rather than a piecemeal vision.

No perfectly Albertian map of the city survives. But as early as 1457, the Roman illustrator of a copy of Euclid's *Elements* produced a perspective view of Rome. Drawn as if from the site of the present Vatican gardens, it shows the Pantheon and the Ara Coeli in the distance, and has in its foreground the Borgo that Nicholas V had meant to make the center of a reformed Church. The image represents not pagan but Christian Rome, the dramatic vision of the sacred city as a pilgrim would first see it, which

Alberti and Nicholas probably hoped to realize. But its technique could be readily applied by artists seeking to glorify the lost secular city of the Romans.[21]

As early as the 1440s, Antonio Averlino had made the Pantheon and other ancient buildings play dramatic roles in the richly worked bronze doors that he made for Saint Peter's. Scribes and illuminators of the 1450s often used the Colosseum, the Castel Sant' Angelo, Trajan's Column, and the Pantheon to adorn appropriate manuscripts—for example, luxurious copies of the *City of God*. After Biondo's and Alberti's work, however, images of the city became both more ambitious in coverage and more rigorous in form. Copies of Ptolemy's *Geography*, for example, were fitted out in the Florentine shop of Vespasiano da Bisticci with stunning views of the ancient sites, drawn by Pietro del Massaio. Less rigorous than Alberti's map, these too set the city's monuments—above all the ancient ones—in their rough locations. A schematic but vivid image and a written label identified each building. Biondo's *Roma instaurata* provided the detailed identifications and other information which Alberti's short work had not included. These views dramatized both the splendor of the city that had been and the devastation of the city that was. Classic and romantic at the same time, they became the prototypes for hundreds of perspective and bird's-eye views, plans, and guidebooks which recreated Roman history and topography for successive generations of students and tourists.

In the Renaissance as now, art, scholarship, and fantasy interacted in these efforts to call the past back to visible life. The first systematic map of the earliest settlement in Rome, for example, was created by Giovanni Nanni da Viterbo, a Dominican who served as *magister sacri palatii* (papal theologian) at the very end of the fifteenth century. Nanni, a man of immense learning and strong opinions who died by poisoning at the hands of Cesare Borgia, published in 1498 an enormous compendium of texts and commentaries on the history of the ancient world. A number of his texts discussed Roman history, and for one of them—Fabius Pictor's treatise on the Golden Age—he drew up the first, vivid image of Rome of the seven hills. Nanni's vision of the past was marred by anachronisms: the city walls were crenellated. In fact, however, not only did he make individual mistakes, but he actually invented most of the texts he published, forging them in order to discredit what he saw as the lying histories of the ancient world produced by Greeks and Romans. He wanted to show that the Etruscan culture that Rome had eventually conquered and replaced had been older and more vital than that of Rome.[22]

Nanni's histories seem obviously fantastic now. Yet in his time they exercised an enormous influence. The general of the Augustinian order, Giles of Viterbo, who gave the opening speech at the Lateran council, took much of his own idiosyncratic presentation of world history from Nanni; the margin of his annotated copy of the text, still in the Vatican, shows him poring over and summarizing Nanni's proofs that the Greeks and Romans had lied about the past. Pinturrichio's frescoes for the Borgia apartments in the Vatican took part of their iconography from Nanni's work. And even more sober efforts to represent the early history of Rome—like those executed by Fabio Calvo, Raphael's friend, who produced a kind of systematic classics comic book, using the conventions of late antique art to draw up diagrams illustrating the development of the early city—remained schematic and partly fanciful.[23]

Artists, of course, could be as imaginative as scholars. In the middle of the sixteenth century, the leading expert on Roman antiquities was not a humanist but an artist and architect: Pirro Ligorio. A man of gentle birth but no professional scholar, Ligorio spent his vast energies as lavishly on the study of the ancient world as on his practice as an architect (in which he often applied his own discoveries, as his papal patron Pius IV wished him to). He excavated many sites. He compiled enormous, systematic notebooks of visual materials and textual extracts illustrating ancient history, myth, and ritual. And though only a tiny specimen of his written work reached print, he became celebrated for his dedicated, lifelong effort "to revive and conserve the memory of ancient things and satisfy those who take pleasure in them," which had led him "to study, with enormous effort, every place and portion" of the ancient ruins, "not leaving a bit of wall, however small it was, without seeing it and examining it minutely: always accompanying this with the reading of . . . authors and . . . often having recourse to conjectures where the ruins were lacking."[24] His immense skill as archaeologist and his deftness as a draftsman made him indispensable to more erudite antiquaries like Antonio Agustín.

Unfortunately, Ligorio could be as irritating as he was necessary to the men of the book. He clung throughout his life to the archaeological tradition that had formed around 1500, with its combination of romantic fan-

Figure 6. A Triumphal Procession. Princeton University Library, MS Garrett 158. Courtesy of the Department of Rare Books and Special Collections, Princeton University Library.

tasy and serious scholarship. When statues lacked pieces, he added them. When a relic inspired him, he embedded it in a splendid classical frame. In the pages of his manuscripts, pagan Rome flickered back to a richly imagined life.[25]

Ligorio's most spectacular efforts to revive a dead world took the form of prints rather than drawings. He studied topographies as well as monuments, and published with Michele Tramezzino in 1553 an updated map of the ancient city, on which the major ancient sites were restored to wholeness and labeled—a more detailed version of what Pietro del Massaio had done a century before. For Ligorio, however, this was only a beginning. He went on measuring sites and reading texts. He systematically collected Roman coins, which often provided details and elevations of lost or decayed monuments. And he saw—as more learned antiquaries probably did not—that a full reconstruction of the ancient city must include more than the great buildings that still poked through the medieval fabric or that had left a paper trail in ancient sources. It must also show the ordinary two- and three-story houses and suburban villas in which the ordinary Roman family had lived. These, too, he found represented, evidently in a relief now lost.[26]

In 1561 Ligorio published, again with Tramezzino, what he called an *Anteiquae urbis imago*—an *Image of the Ancient City*. This colossal set of prints showed the city as an ancient relief would have—as seen from above, and flattened, rather than in the Albertian perspective of a normal Renaissance artist. Ligorio's work, with its respect for the magnificence of *aurea Roma* and its meticulous interest in the details of everyday life, summed up the antiquarianism of Renaissance Rome at its most imaginative. He did not make the dead speak, but he showed how they had lived—and with a combination of meticulous details, derived from the visual sources, that none of his book-learned critics could have rivaled.

In the later sixteenth century, to be sure, the directions of antiquarian research and archaeology both changed. Serious study of the ancient city continued to be carried out. A long series of guidebooks, topographical surveys, and texts had collected the main ancient works of art and classical sites. The French artists and publishers Jean Dupérac and Antoine Lafréry used the full panoply of High Renaissance techniques in their evocative, precisely detailed views of great Roman sites as they really were, ruined and overgrown. Their portfolios of printed images, based on close examination

Figure 7. A Sacrificial Ritual. Princeton University Library, MS Garrett 158. Courtesy of the Department of Rare Books and Special Collections, Princeton University Library.

of the sites, conveyed the nostalgic pleasures of Roman ruins to patrons, architects, and artists across Europe. Scholars and painters continued to brave the intensity of the Roman sun and the dust and rubble of the Roman ruins. But the Counter-Reformation gradually had its effects on archaeological as on historical scholarship, and reoriented this in ways that would sometimes have surprised—though sometimes they would have pleased—such pioneers as Alberti and Poggio.

The Christian City

From the start of the Renaissance, the scholars in the curia studied and tried to interpret the remains of early Christian as well as pagan Rome. They examined the relics and other treasures of Saint Peter's and others of the city's hundreds of churches. They translated Greek texts by fathers of the Church as well as pagan philosophers. And they argued about the nature of authority in the Christian as well as the scholarly tradition.

The ground these scholars covered was necessarily contested. The sources were complex and their analysis posed intricate problems—all the more so because both early Christian polemicists and medieval ecclesiastics had sometimes invented texts and tales to provide the authority for modern practices and beliefs. Revision could prove both hazardous and frustrating. Lorenzo Valla, for example, studied both the history of the Roman Empire and that of the Church in the fourth century C.E. in order to demonstrate the spuriousness of the Donation of Constantine. He quoted lavishly from texts of several kinds, and proved that the document represented the Romans as using words that had not yet been coined to describe institutions that they would not have recognized. A text that contained such anachronisms could not have been written in the time it claimed to come from. Unfortunately, Valla's demonstration threatened not only cherished beliefs but the political and economic powers of the popes. Since he could not be convinced of error, he was offered a good job at Rome. And since his thesis could not be refuted with solid evidence, though a fair number of scholars tried to do so, it was contradicted with powerful images. In the 1520s, when the Protestant challenge arose, Giulio Romano decorated the Sala di Costantino with magnificent frescoes of the battle of the Milvian bridge, the baptism of Constantine, and his Donation—the last two events set amid receding columns in crisply evoked classical settings. Archaeology reaffirmed mythology within the protective walls of the Vatican.

Even those who set out with the most honorable of intentions could easily take wrong turnings in this rebarbative intellectual country. The Camaldolensian Ambrogio Traversari did for the fathers of the Church what great collectors like Coluccio Salutati and Niccolò Niccoli did for the classics. On epic journeys he collected and copied the records of church councils, the texts of ecclesiastical histories, and the writings of the Greek church fathers, which he translated. As other humanists tried to revive the golden age of Roman culture, he tried to revive the golden age of Christianity: the religious thought and practice of the first centuries after the life of Christ, when belief was at its purest and ritual at its simplest.

One set of texts that Traversari prized consisted of the works of a particularly early Christian: Dionysius, the convert made by Saint Paul in Athens, on the hill of the Areopagus. Dionysius described the hierarchies of the angels in heaven and the clergy on earth, making both seem the logical expression of the divine order that ruled the universe as a whole. His ideas had much in common with the hierarchical picture of the world offered by some of Plato's followers. And though his work had long been available in a medieval Latin translation, this seemed "barbarous" and unintelligible to humanist readers, as did the commentaries that accompanied it. Traversari was delighted, then, when he gained access to the original Greek and could produce a new, elegant text-only version in a properly classical Latin. His translation in turn delighted his patron at the curia, Nicholas V, who said that "he understood it better in this simple text than in the others with the numberless comments and notes they contained."[27]

Unfortunately, the text was a seventh-century forgery which combined neo-Platonic philosophy with Christian theology. Some Byzantine Greeks had suggested as much, and Valla either revived their objections or arrived at them independently. But these criticisms were muffled, and Traversari's version of Dionysius, with its convenient implication that the whole complex hierarchy of the medieval church went back to apostolic times, enjoyed credit with most Renaissance readers. The best fifteenth-century scholarship on the Roman church, in other words, did not systematically purge the record of errors or even establish which sources deserved credence.

The sober Christian humanism of northern Europe and the Protestant Reformation, however, confronted the Church with serious and systematic challenges in the realms of history and philology. Erasmus printed Valla's notes on the Latin text of the New Testament and Dionysius the Areopagite. Protestant polemicists published Valla's criticisms of the Donation of Constantine. More seriously, they began to challenge some of the basic historical elements in the Church's ideology and practice. The bishop of Rome was pope because he was the direct successor of Peter, the first bishop of Rome, whom Christ had appointed the head of his Church, and whose body remained in Saint Peter's. But the New Testament did not mention Peter's coming to Rome, much less his bishopric. And Catholic preachers about the primacy of Peter's See began to be faced by pertinacious young men who pulled their Greek New Testaments from their rucksacks and insisted that "Saint Peter was never in Rome." More generally, Martin Luther and other Protestants insisted that the Roman church of their time had departed from the true faith and distorted the message of the Bible. To defend itself the Church had to fight on the ground of historical scholarship. Otherwise it could not prove its right to claim a direct descent from the Church of the apostles.

After the Council of Trent, Roman scholars dedicated themselves to the Christian past with the same sense of mission that had inspired their classicist predecessors a century before. They sought to reconstruct the experience and liturgical life, the saintly lives and terrible deaths of the early Christians. Time had destroyed not only classical colonnades and arches, after all, but also "basilicas, splendid [Christian] temples, the remains of martyrs and other saints, and the records of the translations of their [bodies]." Filippo Neri, the founder of the Roman Oratory, began to lead pilgrimages to ancient cemeteries and churches in search of any remaining tangible evidence of the fervor of the early Christians. Both his charismatic example and the lavish picnic lunches he provided had their effect. Scholars offered help and advice. Eventually specialized archaeologists of early Christianity like Alfonso Chacon investigated everything that remained with passion and exactitude. Chacon, for example, spent a whole year, accompanied by two scribes, diligently investigating the stones and the archives of "three hundred basilicas, temples, and other holy places," to make the sacred city as well known to foreigners and as safe for posterity as the ancient one.[28]

One particularly novel area of investigation lay literally beneath the city, in the catacombs where Christian communities had buried their dead. Members of Pomponio Leto's circle had penetrated these and left marks there. But it was only in the late sixteenth century that systematic investigation began, after the Catacomb of the Giordani was accidentally opened up in 1578, revealing Christian epitaphs, fragments of sarcophagi, and paintings that were suddenly charged with a powerful attraction. "The city was paralyzed," we are told, at the revelation of a subterranean holy city from the past. Chacon investigated, and hired painters and scribes to make detailed records of the works of art and artifacts underground. These records were certainly completed and colored, and some of them probably entirely executed, not in the catacombs themselves but in Chacon's house. Accordingly they are marred by errors: they placed some images in the wrong tombs and distorted others almost beyond recognition. But they still vividly evoke what Chacon called that "original age of Christianity," when Christ was depicted not as the ruler of the universe but as a gentle shepherd, and the Christians imagined themselves as his sheep.[29] The flavor of early Christian art and thought became more and more familiar in the seventeenth century. Antonio Bosio, the "Columbus of the Catacombs," who learned the mysteries of handling ropes and lamps underground and risked cave-ins and smothering to explore the underground city, supervised his artists more carefully than the pioneer Chacon had. He summarized their results in a magnificent printed survey of *Roma sotterranea (Underground Rome).*[30] The Vatican librarians brought to light new documents that confirmed and enriched the record of the catacombs—especially the remarkable text published by Lucas Holstenius, the *Passio* of Saints Perpetua and Felicitas, which showed what a prominent role women converts had taken in the heroic life of the persecuted early Church—and exactly how they had found consolation in the image of Christ as shepherd, about which Perpetua dreamed as she awaited death in a Roman prison. At its best the new scholarship on early Christianity was as wide-angled, as creative, and no more sentimental than the best of classical archaeology. Like classical archaeology, too, it inspired artists and architects: Chacon's meticulous work on ancient furniture and customs, for example, found creative use in Poussin's pictures of the life of Christ.[31]

The most ambitious and influential of all these scholars was a Vatican librarian: Cesare Baronio. Inspired by Neri and instructed in scholarly method by Cardinal Guglielmo Sirleto, Baronio joined in the expeditions into *Roma sotterranea* and read vastly in the published and unpublished sources. A man of almost superhuman energy, Baronio restored churches, carried out diplomatic missions, served as a cardinal, designed the liturgy of Saint Peter's, and fed twelve poor men at his own table every night. But he gave the best of his life to scholarship of a highly polemical kind. Protestant scholars at Magdeburg, in Germany, had published an enormous collective history of Christianity which challenged the Church's claim to direct descent from the Church of Peter. This Baronio made it his life's work to answer. He compiled an enormous Catholic counterhistory, the *Annales ecclesiastici,* which traced the history of the Church from its beginnings to the present in overwhelming detail. Baronio believed that the Church had never fundamentally changed, and he shaped his documents to prove that thesis. But he also believed that the truth was great and would prevail. He spent years comparing sources, critically and seriously. The Donation of Constantine fell to his criticism and made no appearance in his text. He even criticized the fathers of the Church where they went wrong. Baronio's book—which drew not only on his own research but on that of many distinguished Catholic scholars who helped him—became the indispensable guide to church history, even for Protestants. It went through more than twenty printed editions.

And yet Baronio's work had terrible flaws to match its shining virtues of erudition and criticism. In the end, Baronio was so certain that the Church had never changed or erred that he incorporated many traditional fables and mistakes in the fabric of his work. Baronio himself, moreover, lacked the expert command of classical history and of Greek that the best northern scholars possessed—and that his Italian predecessors had also attained when their interests were more classical. He therefore lent his authoritative support to many historical errors—for example, the belief, already present in the church father Lactantius, that an Egyptian sage, Hermes Trismegistus, had enjoyed a separate revelation of the truths of Christianity and the coming of Christ. In fact, the works of Hermes Trismegistus were Greek forgeries, made in Egypt in the second and third centuries C.E; their apparent anticipations of Christian doctrine were actually borrowings from the Septuagint, or standard Greek text of the Old Testament. And the language of the texts made all these points clear—as a number of scholars, some of them Catholic, had already argued. Protestant rebutters of Baronio enjoyed pointing out these mistakes in their critiques of the *Annales*.[32]

Baronio's work rested in part on a critical method of source criticism. But it also supported forgeries and suppressed countervailing evidence. Baronio dealt with the Donation of Constantine, for example, not by admitting that the Church had relied on a forged text but by omitting any reference to it. The sacred history of Counter-Reformation Rome unearthed new forms of Christian life and enriched the architecture and liturgy of the modern Church. But it was shaped as much by polemics and emotions as by facts and texts; and when it came into conflict with other forms of history, it did not argue with them freely but instead suppressed them.[33] No sector of Roman intellectual life in the sixteenth century was more creative than the new study of the Christian past; yet none more vividly reveals the perils of making scholarship the servant of extra-scholarly ends.

Egypt in Rome

The ruins of Rome were not entirely Roman in origin. One set of foreign artifacts in particular tempted the imaginations of humanists from the outset of the Renaissance: the enormous Egyptian obelisks that had once dotted the city, giving tangible proof of the power of the emperors who had been able to bring them across the Mediterranean from Egypt. The obelisks seemed a startling proof of the powers of ancient technology, and the hieroglyphic messages that adorned them—so the ancient Greeks and Romans suggested—might be more powerful yet. The hieroglyphs, the ancient Greeks and Romans had believed, were a powerful form of writing, one devised by the wise priests of ancient Egypt. The animals and other images used as characters expressed ideas naturally, not conventionally (a snake swallowing its own tail, for example, represented the ever-turning, ever-returning world). For the most part, to be sure, these ideas were late and erroneous, formulated by Greek-speaking neo-Platonists living in late antique Egypt who had only a tenuous knowledge of the real Egyptian language and culture; but until the time of Jean Champollion, they would dominate almost all efforts to decipher Egyptian writing.[34]

Roman humanists looked for the fragments of the obelisks described by ancient writers. Alberti found one by taking soundings in the area of the

Figure 8. A Discussion of the Vatican Obelisk. Princeton University Library, MS Garrett 158. Courtesy of the Department of Rare Books and Special Collections, Princeton University Library.

ancient Circus.[35] The discovery of another, which Augustus had used as the gnomon of his famous meridian instrument, caused widespread excitement in the time of Julius II. And the antiquaries loved to discuss the symbolic writing of the ancient Egyptian priests at elegant dinners in their gardens and on country picnics. Roman sources were probably drawn upon by the author and illustrator of the *Hypnerotomachia Poliphili,* a strange and wonderful romance published by Aldo Manuzio in 1499. The hero wanders in a dream through an Arcadian landscape richly strewn with inscriptions—including hieroglyphic ones—and obelisks, one borne by an elephant (an image that would be influential as late as the seventeenth century). One of the dominant scholars in Rome in the decades before the sack, Pierio Valeriano, compiled a spectacular encyclopedia, chiefly drawn from late antique sources, of every meaning-packed symbol he could illustrate and explain. His work became a favorite quarry for artists and writers for the next century and more. Egyptian mysteries could be dangerous as well as seductive. Giordano Bruno died on the Campo de' Fiori partly because he believed more strongly than a Christian should in the Egyptian revelation of Hermes Trismegistus. Egyptian relics had power.[36]

Sixtus V, the least nostalgic of prelates, transformed the relics of Egypt from objects of nostalgia to the pivots of Roman public life. He set out first of all to move the Vatican obelisk—the only one standing in the Renaissance—from its old position, at the rear of Saint Peter's, into its present, prominent place in the piazza before it. The engineering problems involved were staggering; even Michelangelo had refused to take them on. But Domenico Fontana solved all of them by a combination of meticulous planning and bravura improvisation. In elaborate ceremonies the obelisk was exorcised and rededicated to the service of the true God; a cross was set on its top, replacing the ball which had once been thought to contain the ashes of Caesar Augustus.

The keeper of the papal metallotheca, Michele Mercati, wrote a careful treatise to explain the obelisks, the hieroglyphs, and the meaning both took on as part of the papal rebuilding of Rome. They showed, vividly, that papal Rome had appropriated the splendor and power of both pagan Rome and Egypt itself, all in the service of a triumphant Christian God. More obelisks were raised; and soon five of them dotted the city, providing prominent focal points for processions and drawing down cultural, if not

·celestial, power from the skies. Like the chimneys of a magical Battersea power station, the mysterious Egyptian monuments dominated dramatic portions of the Roman skyline. The execution of Bruno, who took his Egyptian mysteries without theological salt, gives some sense of the energy with which they crackled.

Even in Counter-Reformation Rome, however, not everyone agreed with Sixtus that the obelisks were unclean or that the society that produced them had been as wicked as it was powerful. The brilliant Jesuit linguist Athanasius Kircher, who in the best seventeenth-century fashion traced the journeys of Noah's ark, did experiments to establish the laws of physics and optics, and revered the sages of ancient China, devoted himself to Egyptian studies. His knowledge of Coptic enabled him to make some progress toward understanding the nature of the Egyptian language. But his prejudices were far more important. Kircher believed, as Valeriano had, in the wisdom and piety of the Egyptian sages and the magical power of their symbols. He wrote vast volumes on the meaning of the hieroglyphs, which he decoded with startling ingenuity. And in the mid-seventeenth century, when Pope Innocent X decided to make an obelisk, once part of the temple of Isis but now some distance outside the city on the Via Appia, the center of a fountain in the Piazza Navona, Kircher provided the authoritative interpretation of its hieroglyphs and drafted the new Latin inscriptions for its base. He interpreted its message as a benevolent one about the life-giving forces of nature—exactly the sort of thing that the wise priests of the ancient Near East had known about. The fountain itself—a magnificently original piece of work by Giovanni Bernini, chosen over a more austere design by Francesco Borromini, his great rival—also represents the powers and harmony of nature. The base on which the obelisk stands uses dramatic figures to personify the four great rivers of the world, the Ganges, the Nile, the Danube, and the Plate, and by extension their continents. There seems to be a relationship between the program of the modern sculptor and the supposed meaning of the Egyptian enigmas on the obelisk's side. And it is certain that the completed work is not another effort to wrestle the horrors of Egyptian magic into the service of the Christian God—even if Kircher did credit the dove with defeating the "monsters of the Egyptians." The completed fountain forms not the focus of a pilgrimage route but a secular monument to Innocent's family, the Pamphili; their heraldic dove flies atop it. It is not aligned with any particular church. A monument to encyclopedic tolerance, it occupies the center of the most dramatic of all the public spaces of baroque Rome.[37]

Kircher's interpretations were "Wrong but Romantic." His program to renew the intellectual world of his own day by a return to the primeval wisdom of the Egyptians was weakened by his inability to distinguish between genuine Egyptian documents and late Greek forgeries. Yet his deep study of the hieroglyphs did provide the ideological underpinning for one of the greatest works of baroque architecture, Bernini's fountain. And to that extent, his Egyptian archaeology, however alien it may now seem, makes an appropriate conclusion to the larger story of Rome's rediscovery.[38] Scholarship and art, rigor and imagination interacted in the Piazza Navona as in Giuliano da Sangallo's sketchbook. The results irritated the Romans, who had to pay a special tax. "Pane, pane, non fontane," they shouted in the piazza. But the fountain survived their anger. It has stood ever since as an enigmatic but bewitching evocation of an antiquity too profound to be real and too splendid to be denied.

3

The Hand and the Soul

ᎧᏗᏗᏗᎧ

This essay was a review of *The Moment of Self-Portraiture in German Renaissance Art* by Joseph Leo Koerner (1993).

ALBRECHT DÜRER spent much of 1520 and 1521 in the Netherlands. His diary records in microscopic detail the trip he took, "at my own expense and outgoings, with my wife": travel expenses, rooms rented, engravings sold or given away to patrons, wine drunk and meals eaten, churches and townscapes. On Ascension Sunday in Antwerp he watched the great procession of the guilds, enjoying the spectacle presented by the three Magi on "big camel creatures," boys and girls in the costumes of many countries and "a big dragon, led by St. Margaret and her virgins on a leash: she was really pretty." In Brussels, the fountains, menagerie, and gardens of the royal palace resembled a paradise, and the things "that the King has received from the new Golden Land"—a golden sun, a silver moon, strange clothing and bedding from the New World—filled Dürer with amazement at the "subtle talents of men in foreign countries." The crowded town squares, the lacy spires, and the frenetic public life of the Low Countries rise before the reader, lively and vivid as a scene in one of the artist's engravings.

One scene Dürer did not record in writing—though he described it, later on, to friends. In 1520 Charles V, a Habsburg, became Holy Roman

Emperor. Dürer attended the coronation ceremony in Aachen; in September 1520 he accompanied Charles on his formal "Joyous Entry"—the customary euphemism for the mind-numbingly long and complex inaugural festivities of the time—into Antwerp. Beautiful young women served as living statues, wearing costumes so diaphanous that they were effectively naked. The emperor virtuously looked away. Dürer, by his own admission, went close up "to make a proper study of their perfection." "I looked them over," he later recalled, "a little shamelessly: but that's because I am a painter."

This episode does not figure in Joseph Leo Koerner's dazzling book, but it suggests many of the issues that engage his attention and something of the approach that makes his version of Dürer novel and seductive. The protagonist appears as an artist uncertain of his rights and prerogatives, a student of the human body curiously apologetic about his interest in naked women and curiously ambivalent about his own naked self. And no one could seem an odder candidate to fill these trembling shoes than Albrecht Dürer.

For Dürer has always played a starring role in one of the great dramas of European cultural history. Generations of art historians have dramatized his success at creating a modern artistic self and embodying it in the new high art of the self-portrait. Dürer represented himself over and over again, in every two-dimensional medium from the delicate silverpoint he employed in his first effort at fourteen to the vivid oil paint of which he was for a time Europe's unrivaled master. These lovingly precise images, closely observed, meticulously dated, and sometimes displayed or reproduced like icons, expressed with matchless assurance and effect the modern artist's primal claim. Dürer's goal seems obvious: to show in paint that he was an individual, whose gifts and achievements claimed the attention of posterity.

Dürer certainly defined his own reputation in grand terms. In fact, he became the first of painting's secular saints. Protestant collectors who shuddered at the Catholic practice of collecting pieces of the True Cross and the shank bones of the Holy Innocents slaughtered by Herod prized locks of his hair. His students opened his tomb to make a death mask of him. And for the remainder of the sixteenth century, northern artists defined themselves, more often than not, in terms of his achievement—whether they copied it, parodied it, tried to surpass it, or did all at once.

Dürer, after all, had transformed not only the art, but also the artistic life of northern Europe. He mastered and brought north the classical forms that Italian artists and antiquaries had recovered and displayed in modern Europe's first museums. He connected these with a wealth of traditional northern images, some complex and some simple, some theological and some vulgar, which he knew from his own home city of Nuremberg and the others that he wandered through, in the typical way of the craft apprentice, as a young man. His new visual language had unparalleled expressive power and vivid detail. It enabled him to explore both the living detail of the visual world and the hidden depths of the human soul.

Dürer's engravings, which took less time than paintings to produce and which he himself marketed to a wide public, brought his accomplishments into hundreds of shops and collections. They also made him a brilliant artistic propagandist for Charles V's predecessor, Maximilian I, who saw the potential of print media to win the attention and the respect of local elites and noble warriors scattered across Germany's fragmented political landscape. A series of treatises explained Dürer's methods for students and connoisseurs and explicitly staked the claim that art was a classical, theoretical discipline, not a mere craft. By the time Dürer died in 1528, his European fame was unique: the greatest intellectuals of the time, most notably Erasmus, praised the magical powers with which he could conjure up with black lines on white backgrounds not only landscapes, buildings, people and animals, but such shimmeringly ephemeral phenomena as "clouds on a wall." No wonder, one thinks, that his self-portraits made a similar claim in the medium that was most his own.

Koerner has set out not to overturn, but to complicate, this well-established story about the relation between the creation of the modern self-portrait and the portrayal of the creator's modern self. He comes to the task with striking qualifications. At home in the German as well as the American intellectual world, he attacks questions of interpretation with the tools honed by Hans Blumenberg and Hans-Georg Gadamer, and Gotthold Lessing and Friedrich Nietzsche before them. Koerner reads texts well, turns a perceptive eye on images, and writes with unusual energy and wit. He has also managed to induce his publisher to produce his book with a lavish elegance that vividly brings out the qualities of the paintings and graphic works he analyzes. No wonder, then, that he has turned out one of the most compelling, as well as one of the most ambitious, art-historical works of the last decade.

Like his protagonist, Koerner begins by establishing his own position in personal and disciplinary history. The great tradition in the history of northern art—one represented in this book, for the most part, by Erwin Panofsky and Jean Wirth—assumed that the central question posed by northern art was that of meaning. As a young man, Wirth and Panofsky knew, Dürer had had his generation's obsessive interest in the classical past. Throughout his life he read as widely as he could, and worked with scholars who read more, such as the Nuremberg patrician Willibald Pirckheimer, who used a fairly recondite neo-Platonic source in Greek, the *Hieroglyphica* of Horapollo, to help him create an inscription in what they both thought were Egyptian hieroglyphs, in honor of Maximilian. Many of Dürer's images throbbed with detail, not all of it assimilated, from ancient myth, magic, and science. One densely allusive print alone, *Melencolia I,* provoked and inspired three of Europe's greatest cultural historians in this century, Panofsky, Raymond Klibansky, and Fritz Saxl, who devoted years of collaborative research and a magnificent, arcane book to its decoding.

Like a grain of sand lodged under the discipline's collective shell, Dürer found himself buried under smooth and elegant layers of erudition and interpretation. Unfortunately, Koerner holds, much of this activity, elegant in thought and solid in results, was misdirected. Following Panofsky's lead, art historians concentrated on establishing the "meaning" of Dürer's images: in effect, on finding the written text or texts, the ancient anecdote or philosophical tradition, the story or the idea, that each work illustrated. Meanwhile they assumed that they fully understood the visual side of this visual artist's achievement—which amounted, in effect, to reproducing the three-dimensional world of nature more and more accurately on the two-dimensional surfaces of panels and etchings, while also evoking the four-dimensional world of human psychology and character beneath. The richest works displayed both achievements, because Dürer's command of artistic media enabled him to find a mythical hieroglyph that expressed the movements of his own Saturnian, creative soul.

Koerner doubts the possibility of establishing, for any image, a single and exhaustive "meaning." Images have a life and a tradition of their own, which may correspond to, or deviate from, or subvert or explode, the textual story that they supposedly illustrate. Identifying the textual sources of a work of art, in sum, supplies nothing like a full inventory of its contents. Reading cannot take the place of looking.

But looking is not simple, either. Self-portraiture, in fact, poses surprisingly painful analytical problems, which the traditional ways of describing it obscured. Its subject is anything but fixed. Koerner, like many of us, reports that he is anything but sure about what a self is, or what nature is, or how either self or nature can be represented in a simple, definitive way. And the Renaissance no longer appears to him as the age in which the rounded, modern self took shape, the age of Jacob Burckhardt's Renaissance man, who discovered physical and human nature as the veil of medieval culture dissolved before him. Koerner's Renaissance is, to a considerable extent, the one reconstructed in the last decade or so by Stephen Greenblatt and the contributors to the Berkeley journal *Representations.* Like them, Koerner evokes an age of performers brilliantly trying out new roles rather than an age of whole men exerting the full powers of human reason and perception. Koerner's own mastery of the visual material, moreover, reveals just how hard it is, in simple, technical terms, for an artist to carry out the apparently simple task of painting his or her image as seen in a mirror. Exploratory reading in a wide range of sources and inspection of a vast run of images, bewitchingly arranged and reproduced, combine to form a striking new approach to an old subject.

From the start, Koerner interprets his objects with passion and precision. Taking Dürer's Erlangen self-portrait sketch, he shows how it has been read in Romantic terms as a psychological investigation of the artist's profound, melancholy self. He then proposes a different reading of his own, one centered on the drawing's physical attributes rather than its model's spiritual qualities. Lined up against a wonderful series of drawings of pillows, bunched and crumpled, this one seems less a psychological self-portrait than a study in a representational problem: how to show a head propped on a hand. Bold corrections and jumpy movements of the artist's line illustrate his effort to make the image record the work that brought it into being: comparisons underline Dürer's passionate interest in solving challenging problems of representation. The Erlangen sketch emerges not as an emotional sounding of the depths of the creative intellect and soul but as a formal study of the very hand that created it.

Yet Koerner has no intention of replacing what he sees as the reduction-ism of an older tradition with a new reductionism of his own. He insists on the challenge and the novelty of Dürer's images of his self: on the possible rightness of Dürer's claim to inaugurate something radically new in west-ern culture. The pillows with which he compares the Erlangen sketch turn out, on close inspection, to reveal the forms of faces—including Dürer's own. The gesture that the Dürer figure makes reappears in other contexts, illustrating the meditations of Joseph and the contemplations of Dürer's own melancholy angel. Perhaps the Erlangen sketch makes statements about the self, or the soul, as well as about problems of representation.

Koerner sets out, then, not simply to refute a traditional oversimplifica-tion but to explore just how Dürer's repeated efforts to imprison himself in two dimensions came out of a particular, three-dimensional historical experience—while insisting that those efforts cannot be confined to that experience, and that the historian can no more reproduce the three dimen-sions of the past in prose than the artist can in paint. Like all good magi-cians, Koerner keeps his best trick simple. Instead of teasing out what these pictures mean, Koerner asks what tasks they carried out. And not surpris-ingly, in this age of reflexivity, they turn out above all to comment on the work of art itself: on its virtues, its defects, and its status.

The first substantial part of the book concentrates above all on Dürer's painted self-portrait in the Alte Pinakothek in Munich, a startling full-face image, painted in 1500. Dürer catches himself before a dark background, between his own monogram and a Latin caption. The picture will dazzle readers, as it dazzles visitors in Munich, by its meticulous, almost halluci-natory precision in evoking cloth and fur, the artist's long streaming hair, slender, expressive face, and one delicate hand. But Koerner wants it to do more: to testify, as a star witness, to the triumphs and the tragedies of northern art in that moment, around 1500, when German intellectuals suddenly felt that they could challenge the Italians for cultural preemi-nence in every realm from classical scholarship to the visual arts.

His interpretation gains support from the picture's date and the artist's carefully recorded age. At twenty-eight, as Dürer probably knew, he had reached an astrologically defined climacteric year, a multiple of seven; also an age that at least some of the many traditional doctrines about the human lifespan identified as one's prime. As to the year, humanists that Dürer knew, such as the poet Conrad Celtis, saw it as the beginning of a new age in which Germany would begin to play a central position in world history, as, they thought, it had long before. Textual material, some of it quite traditional, thus forms part of Koerner's stage setting. But the image itself—in which, many modern viewers have thought, Dürer deliberately represents himself as the Savior—plays the central role in his argument.

Did Dürer portray himself as Christ? Could an artist of his time do so? To answer these questions, Koerner deploys a technique that he uses throughout the book: systematic comparison of a particularly controlled and penetrating kind. Portraits of Martin Luther—including the famous Catholic polemical image of him as a man with seven heads—suggest that Renaissance portraitists portrayed their subjects not as a single, unchanging essence but as players of varying roles. A seventeenth-century image of Christ by George Vischer, which quotes Dürer's self-portrait to represent the Savior, shows that an artist more than three hundred years closer to Dürer than we are could see the self-portrait as an image of Jesus. "Reception"—an approach widely applied to literature in the last generation, especially in Germany—here shows its fruitfulness when applied to visual images; the use that later artists made of Dürer's work sheds light, again and again, on his enterprise.

But identifying the visual type that Dürer's work belongs to hardly amounts to a full account of the work. What did it mean for an artist to compare himself to Christ? That he practiced the disciplines of late medieval piety and sought to apply the principles of *Imitatio Christi* in his own life? That he saw the proportion and beauty of the human form as an *imago Dei,* in fact as the sharpest *imago Dei* in our imperfect physical world? Art historians have suggested both readings, which in some way tame the image. They use its historical context to explain that it makes no extravagant claims. Koerner, by contrast, insists that a tension lies at the core of the work: a tension between the visual tradition of representing Christ's face and the new enterprise of the autonomous self-portrait "that Dürer can be said to have invented for the north." By juxtaposing the two enterprises, Koerner holds, Dürer tried not to express a stable relationship between his self and Christ but to state a new set of arguments and claims about the nature of the visual arts.

To teach us to see the image as he does, Koerner embeds it in a series of contexts, each of which focuses our attention on a particular feature of the work. Formally, he argues, it belongs to a particular tradition of Christian icons: the faces of Christ, looking directly forward, that supposedly derived from the Veronica, the sweat cloth on which an image of the divine features was imprinted without the work of human hands. Rich visual and verbal material, skillfully mobilized, shows that Dürer knew this tradition of imagery intimately and continued it himself in various forms.

Koerner also points out that Jan van Eyck had already interposed questions about the artist's self into this tradition, with its rhetoric of absolutely faithful reproduction, supposedly carried out by divine intervention rather than by the artist's hand. Van Eyck's *Holy Face,* now in London, uses a painted, three-dimensional–looking frame to set off the image of Christ's face from the onlooker in a coherent space of its own, though the traditional Veronic image floated out of space and time. A signature and the motto *Als ik kan,* "As I can," emphasized the human and creative component in van Eyck's version of icon-making. When Dürer took care to show viewers that he himself had made an image of a traditional kind, the value of which supposedly depended on the fact that no one had made it—when he underlined the modernity and the contingency of an icon, the content of which should theoretically have been dictated by traditional, inviolable rules—he was writing (or rather, painting) himself into a northern tradition.

But Dürer made richer pictorial play of these motifs. Consider, for example, his hands, which were praised in his lifetime for their beauty. Only one hand, at first sight the right one, appears in the self-portrait. It touches the fur border of his robe and points upward. In fact, however, as Koerner shows, the portrait offers a mirror image: the hand shown is the left hand. The right hand, fully occupied with the task of painting, is present also—but implicitly. It is embodied in the matchless, meticulous detail of the work it created, rather than represented. Dürer thus cannot render every detail of the visual field: the working hand is both present and absent, perfection both given and taken away by the same divinely gifted member. But the left hand also makes more than one point. Represented as a member of great beauty, it reflects Dürer's constant, ever-frustrated search for the ideal proportions of the human body. Marked by idiosyncratic details, it embodies the effort to portray the world as it was that also inspired Dürer to produce the dazzlingly soft, strokable-looking fur of his collar (and, as Koerner rightly suggests, his breathtaking images of rabbits, plants, even a clod of earth). The painting thus quotes a tradition of images held to be perfect, inhuman and immortal, to dramatize the efforts of a fallible, human, and mortal artist.

Koerner's close attention to other features of the work—such as the representation of the artist's hair, at once the symbol of his high art and the reminder of his sinful, even wild morality—confirms this reading. So does his rich analysis of Dürer's later efforts to explore the dialectical relationship between ideal beauty and living human flesh, through his engravings and drawings of the nude. A profoundly ambivalent nude self-portrait, brilliantly discussed by Koerner, illustrates Dürer's sometimes shocking modernity—and makes a highly appropriate close to this part of the book. Equally appropriate and telling is a very long second section, a book in itself, about Dürer's student Hans Baldung Grien.

That complex, bizarre artist receives from Koerner his first full-scale interpretation in English. Born in 1484 or 1485 into a cultivated Strasbourg family, Baldung had contact through his relatives with both the traditional learning of the universities and the new classical scholarship of the humanists. He worked and studied in Dürer's studio, which he may even have managed for a time. And his virtually Oedipal relation to his master's brush enabled him to reveal, again and again, the worm at the core of Dürer's Edenic apple, the canker at the center of his complex, perfect rose.

Dürer's range of imagery extended from the ideal and classical forms of his Adam and Eve to the terrifyingly literal detail of his illustrations of the Book of Revelation. Baldung, by contrast, devoted himself above all to the worm that eats and the flesh that corrodes. Dürer's images of Adam and Eve, as Koerner shows, rest on what he (and virtually all other Renaissance artists) saw as the central practice of classical art. By selecting the best possible members from a variety of models and by appropriating poses and forms from classical statues, Dürer made his first man and woman, whom he showed at the very instant of their sin, embody the perfection that came before the Fall. His ability to reconstruct that perfection, on the other hand, asserted that art could momentarily redeem what sin had destroyed.

Baldung painted and engraved Adam and Eve again and again, sometimes copying Dürer directly. But his images differ radically from his master's. The moment of choice has passed. Sly expressions and lubricious gestures show that corruption has taken place. Adam reaches for Eve's breasts, and in one version seems to be entering her from behind. History has begun; and as Mark Twain pointed out, when complaining that God should have put Martin Luther and Joan of Arc in Eden, it looks like a bad idea.

A vast range of Baldung's other works imagine and explore, in lovingly horrified detail, the damage done by death and time, and the horrors that may lie outside both: from a strange engraving of death attacking a knight with a pitchfork, which Koerner analyzes at eloquent length, to a long series of images, complex, sensuous, and powerful, in which Baldung shows witches at acrobatic play, to the famous, manifestly pornographic works in which death or a diabolic figure confronts or attacks a partly draped woman. The fantasy that expresses itself in every detail of these works—from the strange gases that witches produce by farting to the thick sausages they cook and eat, which may just be the penises Germans thought witches liked to remove and hide in birds' nests—rivals Francisco Goya's sheer macabre elaboration of detail. Yet it lacks Goya's humanity. Baldung collaborated in the production of an image of witchcraft, spun by learned lunatics from a few fantastic assumptions and thin air, that would result in thousands of deaths. German lawyers, courts, and ordinary people collaborated for the next century and a half in hunting down supposed witches, using torture as their standard means of inquiry.

Koerner analyzes these works with close attention, great energy and just a dash of late-eighties P.C. Baldung, he argues, gave graphic form to all the confusions of male desire: between making love and doing violence, between male fear of women and female hatred of men, between female seductiveness and male lust. The onlooker is pulled into the image, forced to admit that he—the onlooker is certainly a man—finds the female sexual organs as visually compelling as they are artfully concealed. This pictorial technique, in turn, is suggestively juxtaposed with an analysis of the elder Cranach's religious art. In a Lutheran culture that took as its first article of faith the total depravity of man, Baldung's artistic version of "gotcha" could perhaps perform a theological function as well as a pornographic one. His pictorial traps suggested that high art, like Mosaic Law, presented its high ideals not to save, but to condemn sinners whom only divine grace could redeem.

Baldung also subverted Dürer's self-portrait. In a great engraving circa 1544, Baldung represented himself as a groom, lying flat on a stable floor, his impressively large feet toward the viewer. Baldung drastically foreshortened and flattened his face, which is far less prominent than his feet or the genitals that swell under his codpiece. Behind him stands one of Dürer's powerful horses. Through the stable window a witch looks into the room, gesturing wildly with a torch. Baldung uses a classically simple picture space and a meticulously rendered horse, both taken from his master, to subvert Dürer's hard-won classical decorum.

For, in a famous late engraving, Dürer had represented an artist dealing with a nude in the proper way. On a table, cramped and awkward, lies a naked woman. Separated from her by a screen designed to help lay out the perspective in his picture space, an artist stares decorously, using an instrument that looks like an obelisk, at her genitals. Dürer's professional artist, secure in his code of conduct, studies the female body with masterful calm. Baldung himself, overcome by lust or magic, writhes on the floor and displays his sexuality. He is literally fallen. No redemptive self-portrait can conceal the human sinfulness that leers from every image of a beautiful man or woman—even from Dürer's image of himself as Christ. So much for the calm, unemotional study of naked bodies that Dürer had claimed to practice.

No summary can do justice to the richness of Koerner's pictorial material, or to the pleasure that his deft and eloquent analyses inspire. Yet Koerner is not as generous as he should be to some of his predecessors, the ones he criticizes and the ones he praises. His summaries of Panofsky and Wirth, which serve polemical purposes, do not do justice to the arguments that they wish to dismantle. Though his application of "reception theory" to images draws on the exemplary earlier work of Thomas Kaufmann, Kaufmann is cited only as art authority, not as a model; and as an art historian committed to the close study of form, Koerner could have said more about one fairly obvious formal point, which is the simple fact that very little of Baldung's work can rival his master's, that Baldung's wild horses show less energy than Dürer's tame ones.

More seriously, Koerner's interpretations of written evidence sometimes lack the deftness and the precision that make his readings of images so compelling. This problem becomes particularly acute when he analyzes, at length, the painted, engraved, and written words and letters that appear in many works by Dürer and Baldung. Koerner convincingly argues that this material should play a central role in the interpretation of the works in question. He shows that Dürer used texts not only to date his self-portrait and many other works, but also to assert his authorship of them—a claim that proved especially problematic in the case of graphic works that existed in many copies, and that rivals counterfeited and sold as his. An absorbing chapter describes Dürer's successful effort to defend his sole right to sell copies of his prints with his own authenticating monogram; and an elegant counterpart analyzes Baldung's subversive use of forms of signature that parodied Dürer's. Koerner leaves no doubt that Dürer's written claims to originality as an artist reflected the particular conditions of a new art market that he did much to create, as well as the personal aspirations that gave rise to the Munich self-portrait.

Perplexities arise, however, when Koerner sets out to analyze the intellectual content of Dürer's painted words—for example, the classically elegant inscription on the engraving of the *Fall*, in which Dürer says that he "was making" (*faciebat*) the image in 1504. (A similar formula appears on the self-portrait of 1500.) Koerner rightly connects Dürer's choice of the imperfect tense, rather than the simple past tense, with the practice of ancient Greek sculptors. As he also points out, this had been discussed in the most extended classical work on the visual arts, the long section on sculpture in the elder Pliny's encyclopedic *Natural History*, which Dürer's learned friend Pirckheimer called to his attention. Koerner takes Dürer's revival of an ancient custom as a powerful statement about his modern artistic practice: "Following an ancient practice recorded in Pliny and rediscovered by Pirckheimer . . . Dürer signed his work with *faciebat* to suggest that the making of the work is never fully complete and past but remains always active and ongoing." In quoting this formula and related ones, Koerner argues, Dürer used German classical scholarship to assert that he had reached the highest possible levels of originality and perfection: "though man's moment of perfection has passed, art can reoccupy a space prior to fallen history." Dürer's novel signatures thus formed an integral part of the German "moment of self-portraiture."

Koerner rightly insists on the importance of these written clues, but his sleuthing skills fail him when he tries to trace them to their historical point of origin. Italians, not Germans, were the ones who realized that ancient artists had cast their signatures in the imperfect. The Florentine scholar Angelo Poliziano recorded, in his *Miscellanea* of 1489, that he and a friend had found a pedestal in Rome that bore the words "Lysippos was making this" in Greek. He explained that the ancients had used this formula not to heighten their claims to artistic achievement, but to limit them: as a statement that even their most finished works of art were, necessarily, incomplete. Only three Greek sculptures had been signed in a different way, indicating that they were absolutely finished—and these signatures had made the works in question quite unpopular. Poliziano's book attracted fascinated attention throughout Europe. When Pirckheimer told Dürer to write *faciebat,* he did not claim a discovery of his own but advised his friend to show conformity with the most up-to-date Italian scholarship. Moreover, both of them must have known that Dürer, in doing so, would not be claiming perfection for his work, but admitting its limitations.

Admittedly, Dürer did not always feel modest when a project reached completion. A close analysis of the variant forms of his signature, which Koerner does not offer, would yield a fascinating story of artistic mood swings. While in Venice, for example, where Dürer exulted in the fact that he felt like a gentleman, not a mere craftsman, he wrote on one work: "Albrecht Dürer the German brought this forth [*exegit*] in five months"— an obvious allusion to an ode of the Roman poet Horace, which begins *Exegi monumentum aere perennius* ("I have brought forth a monument that will outlast bronze"). This amounted to the claim—a central one of Renaissance artists—that the visual arts enjoyed the same cultural status as the verbal ones, and the artist himself the same intellectual and social status as a scholar or writer. Nowhere does the distance of Dürer's world from our own come through more clearly than in the great artist's desire to share the exalted status of a classical scholar. He went so far as to describe another image as "the work of five days," a blasphemous allusion to the fact that God had taken five or six days to create the world.

But the existence of these elegant variations only underlines the importance of Dürer's normal practice. The imperfect was his tense of choice, and the attitude it expressed was the one he normally felt (or thought he should feel). These brief, elegant captions reveal both Dürer's pride in authorship and his shame about the incompleteness of his own creations. As vividly as Baldung's parodies, and more directly, they mirror the artist's awareness of the incompleteness of all picturing. Small and subtle, the clues provided by Dürer's signatures are as revealing as fingerprints. They show that the traditions of Italian classical scholarship—as well as those of northern painting—enabled the artist to express the pains and pleasures of his artistic project. Read this way, Dürer looks much more like the figure evoked by Panofsky, who saw *Melencolia I* as the artist's profound analysis of the human creator's necessary and appropriate dejection and Dürer himself as the most creative of intermediaries between Italy and the north, than Koerner would have us think. Thus the best of revisionist scholarship proves closer in results than in spirit to the tradition that it attacks. Koerner's northern "moment of self-portraiture" threatens to dissolve into a richly reimagined, but recognizably high Renaissance, moment of synthesis.

Both the virtues and the defects of Koerner's project reflect the condition of the discipline that he practices so well. Art history has been in a state of excited internecine debate for so long that crisis has begun to look like stasis. A generation ago the zodiacal sign of the iconographer declined and that of the social historian rose. Down with the old, went the cry; we have identified too many obscure myths and scenes from ancient history. The art historian must not grope about, in modern reference works and editions, for the forgotten classical text or motif that an artist's hypothetical scholarly adviser might have had in mind, but reconstruct the precise economic, social, and cultural world within which the artist actually worked.

This program yielded spectacular results. It broadened the interests of many art historians, including those who did not accept it. It stimulated the production of some brilliantly successful experiments in the writing of art history, in works by Svetlana Alpers, Michael Baxandall, T. J. Clark, and Thomas Crow, among others, many of which have become classics. And if it also led to the undervaluing of earlier work and the floating of some balloons that exploded, this was no cause for general dismay. When any discipline takes a new shape, antitraditionalist rhetoric becomes the standard mode for framing one's work as virtuous and innovative, and several *Hindenburgs* are produced for every *Spirit of St. Louis*.

But one feature of the new art history raises serious questions. As schools form, the hypotheses of pioneers have a tendency to become facts for their students. Questions turn into answers, and experimental equipment designed to yield new data metamorphosizes into a sausage machine that makes all data, however discordant, look and taste alike. The practitioners of the new art history insisted from the outset that northern art had distinctive traditions and qualities. They argued, further, that one could not reconstruct its underlying aesthetic from contemporary theoretical texts, since those texts normally took too classical and Italianate a line to shed light on artistic practice. The works themselves—and a rich range of documents establishing their precise, localized social and cultural context—must lie at the center of the inquiry. Sharp breaks, concentrated moments of change, and the northernness of the north called for particularly intense study.

These principles, which began as hypotheses, inspire Koerner's work in large part, and account for much of its excellence. But these same principles—and his reluctance to subject them to sharp critical analysis—also explain his weaknesses: his overinsistence on providing a local, northern genealogy for Dürer's ideas and practices, and his failure to notice the telltale bits of mud and gravel that enabled the detectives of an earlier generation to follow some of these back to Italy. Koerner, in short, reveals some of the strains that characterize his own time in the history of his profession. His book, too, is a moment of self-portraiture.

Koerner's accomplishments are nonetheless remarkable. He sets Dürer into a rich new context that complements and enriches those provided by previous interpreters. He brilliantly explores Baldung's life and work. More generally, he analyzes and dramatizes a fascinating place, time, and culture that is less well known than it should be in America and England. His book should find admiring—as well as contentious—readers long after the particular moment to which it belongs has passed.

4

The Rest versus the West

⟨ಿಯಾಲಿ⟩

This essay was a review of *The Darker Side of the Renaissance: Literacy, Territoriality, and Colonization* (1995), by Walter D. Mignolo, and *Reframing the Renaissance: Visual Culture in Europe and Latin America, 1450–1650* (1995), edited by Claire Farago.

I

*J*OSÉ DE ACOSTA did not mind confronting problems. A brilliant speaker and efficient administrator, he dominated the Jesuits' mission in Peru in the 1570s. Acosta taught, preached, organized church councils, rewrote the liturgy, and went on expeditions into the interior of the country, even though he suffered grievously from the melancholy which, many believed at the time, afflicted men of high talent. Later, back in Spain, he wrote one of the most influential historical works of the later sixteenth century, a *Natural and Moral History of the Indies,* which appeared in 1590. Translated into Italian, French, English, Dutch, and Latin, it found a public everywhere in Europe.

Acosta's historical theories were as bold as his missionary practices. When he realized that the Torrid Zone, declared uninhabitable by Aristotle, had a large population and in many areas a temperate climate, he declared without hesitation that "the philosopher" had been wrong. Aristotle had followed the historians and cosmographers of his time, whose knowledge was limited. Though he was and remained a good Aristotelian, Acosta had the courage to admit that the thinker he most admired, and whose methods he used, did not know everything—still a rare virtue in an age when doctors trained at the greatest medical school in Europe, Padua, had to swear an oath to defend Aristotle's authority.[1]

Acosta produced the first full-scale effort to describe for a wide European public the societies, religions, and cultures of the New World. But even he could not solve all the intellectual problems that his huge tasks of research and writing posed. In particular, he worried about whether he himself really could reconstruct in solid detail the history and cultures of lands that lacked a written tradition like the western one. Would he, like Aristotle, wind up a laughingstock, the helpless victim of unreliable informants?

Acosta's fellow Jesuit Juan de Tovar had sent him an illustrated history of Mexico to use in his own work. Turning to Tovar for advice, Acosta wrote him in 1586 to ask a series of pointed questions. "What certainty or authority," he wanted to know, "does this narrative or history have?" How could the native inhabitants of New Spain, who did not have a system of alphabetic writing, preserve the memory of events over a long period? And how could they preserve the precise wording of the speeches of their "ancient rhetoricians"? Tovar answered in detail and encouragingly. The Mexicas, he admitted, had used images rather than alphabetic script to record their tradition, and images were less precise than words. But their symbols had enabled them to record "all the events and memorable occurrences that they had in their histories"—that is, in their calendar wheels. Tovar enclosed a copy of one of these. At the same time, their highly trained memories preserved their ancestors' eloquent speeches without any deviation, metaphor by metaphor and word by word. Tovar assured Acosta that native sources would yield a proper history.[2] Acosta evidently agreed, since he incorporated parts of Tovar's letter directly into his book.

A generation ago, this exchange seemed to embody one of the great intellectual events of the sixteenth and seventeenth centuries: Europeans' long, slow, painful realization that the world contained civilizations not mentioned in the Bible or the histories of the Greeks and Romans. J. H. Elliott treated the discussion between Acosta and Tovar as one of the more dramatic episodes in this eventful story, which began in the mid-sixteenth century. Apologists for contemporary life insisted that the invention of gunpowder, the compass, and the printing press had made the modern world more cosmopolitan and more powerful than the ancient one. Early Europeans, more and more scholars reflected, must have resembled not the robed sages of Raphael's *School of Athens* but the naked inhabitants of pre-Conquest Virginia and Mexico. They had been not the masters of a universally valid Great Tradition but the prisoners of a little one, not venerable philosophers but blue-painted worshipers of savage gods. Francis Bacon, as always, put the common wisdom with uncommon brilliance: antiquity, he said, was not the old age but the youth of the human race, and had no special claim on the respect of later times. The myth of the ancients' omniscience—the traditional belief that the arts and sciences had existed in their purest imaginable form at the beginning of time—melted, very slowly, into air.

Some observers of keen sensibility, like Bartolomé de las Casas and Michel de Montaigne, came to believe that the discoveries challenged not only ancient Europe's intellectual reputation, but also modern Europe's moral standing. Some of the nations the Europeans had conquered had developed sophisticated arts and crafts, systems of roads, and forms of poetry. Christian colonists had come, moreover, not as missionaries and teachers but as predators. The atrocities such invaders had committed against peaceful Caribbean islanders and Incas suggested that Europeans, not Indians, were the real barbarians.[3] Antiquity lost authority; modern life lost luster; true civilization suddenly proved hard to locate—and might turn out to inhabit Paraguayan forests or Peruvian mountains rather than European cities. Tovar's letter—with its demonstration that a tradition radically different from the European idea of narrative history could still preserve the basic facts—fitted naturally into this larger story.

First published in 1970, Elliott's book—which remains by far the best introduction to the problems posed by discoveries such as Tovar's—was only one of several bold efforts since the 1920s to reconsider the history of Europe's relation to the rest of the world. Scholars broke open new veins in the seemingly exhausted mines of European intellectual history. Sergio Landucci showed that efforts to describe and understand primitive societies occupied dozens of early modern jurists and philosophers—and did so long before the Baron de Lahontan and Joseph-François Lafitau, the

Enlightenment thinkers traditionally singled out, for good or ill, as anthropology's founding fathers, were born or thought of.[4] The late Giuliano Gliozzi combined the erudition of a traditional humanist with the indignation of a sixties radical. Mounting an extensive enquiry into Renaissance efforts to find biblical or classical passages that identified the New World's inhabitants and explained how they reached their homes, he emerged with a fierce denunciation of humanists, historians, and theologians. Gliozzi argued that these intellectuals had prostituted their erudition to the service of their states, tearing passages from ancient texts and twisting them to justify modern empires.[5]

More recently still, scholars have scrutinized the documents of European colonizers with equal intensity, but from different angles of vision. Sabine MacCormack and Fernando Cervantes—to name only two—have concentrated not on scholarly libraries and collections in Europe but on churches, convents, and plazas in the Americas. They have shown in detail how European intellectuals, coming as missionaries, brought with them historical and theological scripts which they tried to make the inhabitants of the New World conform to. And they made clear that many natives rejected these, or insisted on performing them in ways distinctly their own—like those inhabitants of New Spain who drove the Dominican Diego Durán wild with frustration by coming to church only for those feasts that corresponded with sacred dates in their pre-Christian religious calendar, until he shrugged in despair, picked up a feathered staff of his own, and joined their procession.[6] Few fields of cultural history, in short, can rival this one for consistent fertility and compulsive interest.

During the last five years or so, however, the herds of scholars who have browsed in tranquillity for so long among the records of missionaries and inquisitors have been startled to hear repeated critical rumbles. Many of these began as noises off, originating in quite different fields of study. Edward Said's study *Orientalism*, for example, filled many western scholars with disquiet about the ways in which they and their predecessors had spoken for, rather than listened to, those they referred to as inhabitants of "the Orient." The precise and original monographs of historians in the Indian Subaltern Studies school showed that the categories and certainties of empire looked quite different when viewed not from the top of a heap of archival documents preserved in a cast-iron Victorian panopticon in one of Europe's capitals, but from the colonial perspective of the towns where "riots" and "revolutions" took place.

The theorists who dominated so many humanities departments challenged all conventional ways of writing history. And the large numbers of students identifying themselves as Hispanic, Asian, and Native American who entered elite universities demanded courses and textbooks that did not identify with Europeans and conquerors. Specialists in many disciplines began to recast in radically new terms the discussion of the cultural collision between the West and the Rest. The rumbles have begun to sound like thunder—especially during and after the quincentennial celebrations of 1992, when revisionists and their critics, caught up in equal and opposite fits of moral indignation, denounced one another from every pulpit they could reach.

The atmosphere in which these discussions take place is heavily charged. Even the subtlest historians and social scientists tread the bloody crossroads where cultures meet with the breathless caution of soldiers in a minefield. Many seem almost paralyzed with fear at the possibility of exploiting the colonized or colluding with the colonizers. But even the most careful precautions do not ensure safe passage. Grave scholars make comic appearances, belaboring one another with bladders and slapsticks, each accusing the other of speaking for the native instead of hearing the native's voice, of making the native too radically Other or too imperialistically the Same.[7] Others disappear into an almost mystical state of self-scrutiny, indulging to extremes that truly ineffable scholarly pleasure, the public revelation of their own bad faith. The historiography of the discoveries sometimes seems likely to turn from a real library into an imaginary but gruesome butcher shop—rather like the curiously Goyaesque cannibal slaughterhouses, hung and strewn with smoked human limbs, that early sixteenth-century artists and pamphleteers conjured up to adorn a Caribbean of the mind.

Most of the revisionists agree on certain cardinal points. All exchanges of ideas and images, they argue, are conditioned by the situations—the resources and problems, strengths and weaknesses—of their protagonists. In the sixteenth and seventeenth centuries, European scholars spoke from a position of power, native inhabitants of the Americas from one of weakness. European scholars, enjoying the support of powerful states and the conquering Christian church, wrote in the languages and genres that would reach worldwide audiences. Native Americans, by contrast, used languages not designed to be printed or accessible to readers outside their own regions. Inevitably, western voices drowned nonwestern ones in public discussions of society and history.

All too many modern scholars—so the revisionists argued—have forgotten that Europe's intellectual projects won out less for intellectual than for political and military reasons. Often they have ignored texts and images that served the immediate needs of smaller, less powerful publics in the New World itself. Where their predecessors detected the clean, cool odor of ethnographic saintliness in the letters exchanged by Tovar and Acosta, in short, the revisionists detect the putrescence of bad faith. The missionaries' effort to write a new kind of history formed part of an effort to colonize minds as well as lands. Their creation of an anthropological approach to inquiry served to justify a spiritual and political conquest.

At its worst, revisionist work takes the form of Big Red Books: compilations of today's politically acceptable value judgments, compressed to the size of large pills meant to be forced down the throats of fuddy-duddies. More than one of the studies published in the last five years will look as quaint, in a generation or two, as the Social Darwinist beatitudes of the late nineteenth century or the Popular Front verities of the thirties do now. At its best, however, the new scholarship opens windows into lost worlds of thought and experience and restores voices to those long deprived of them. These revisionists, like many others, tend to exaggerate, and sometimes show a complacent ignorance of the older literature they attack. But the new wave of their scholarship now cresting in books and journals deserves serious attention from anyone interested in the problems and prospects of cultural history.

2

Walter Mignolo, an Argentinian scholar who has taught for many years in the United States, has fired a fierce broadside against what he sees as the clichés of a Eurocentric history of cultural contact in *The Darker Side of the Renaissance*. At once a bold theorist and a meticulous philologist, Mignolo attacks older scholarship both implicitly and explicitly. He deliberately refuses to present his material in chronological order, cutting back and forth among periods, places, and peoples, and juxtaposing texts and writers rarely studied together. Instead of telling one story with a neat, dramatic ending—for example, that of how European intellectuals filed those they called Indians neatly away in a drawer marked "Primitives"—he weaves several story lines together. The whole form and tenor of his book strongly suggest that events—as opposed to written histories—rarely have neat climaxes and resolutions.

The suggestion becomes explicit when Mignolo calls for the creation of a "pluritopic hermeneutics." Mignolo's formative intellectual experiences as a young student in Argentina clearly impressed him deeply. He and his friends felt themselves caught for years, like flies in amber, at the margins of modern political life and up-to-date scholarly research. Their sensibilities were sharpened by local and international repression, their minds opened by Antonio Gramsci and other radical thinkers whose work circulated widely in their highly sophisticated milieu. (Paradoxically, in view of Mignolo's present position, the Argentina of his youth impressed many observers as very European.)

They also benefited from the work of local scholars like Rodolfo Kusch and José Cruz, to whom Mignolo pays moving tribute. Kusch, for example, developed an ambitious and sophisticated comparative analysis of Argentinian culture—one that went "beyond a surface of dichotomous oppositions" to "find the seminal pattern that connects the hidden underground of Western thought with explicit Amerindian attitudes, which have resisted the assimilation to causal thinking." Mignolo shows that Kusch and his contemporaries could draw on rich intellectual resources for understanding the hybrid cultures of former colonies, long before Said and the Subaltern School began to have an impact on the historiography of the Americas. But their acute powers of observation earned little credit at home or abroad. To take part in the high talk of the Republic of Letters, they would have to move their site of operations, mentally or physically (in Mignolo's case, even to abandon Spanish for English). Exile was a high price of entrance, and Mignolo has no interest in forgetting that he paid it. Instead, he tries to use his experiences as a source of empathy: to work his way backward from the position he knows in his flesh and bone, that of the modern colonial intellectual, to the position of those he seeks to know, the native wise men and mixed-breed historians of the sixteenth and seventeenth centuries. He pursues a scholarship, as well as a politics, of identity.

The historian, Mignolo argues, must listen as hard to losing narratives as to those that won out. No modern scholar will fully succeed in gaining empathetic understanding of the pre-Columbian civilizations. But it should be possible to master more fully the tales and images, ideas and methods that came into existence after the Conquests. Many texts and maps fused native and European ideas and techniques, imperfectly but richly. Paying close attention to the richness of such hybrid artifacts is a form of moral as well as intellectual discipline. The scholar who does so can learn to push the European books and maps that have always formed the chief objects of scholarly discussion from their unearned position of privilege. All versions of Mexican space and time, society and history—native, European, and hybrid—were produced in situations of inequality and served particular needs. None of them, accordingly, deserves a central, canonical status attained at the expense of the rest. The currently fashionable terminology in which Mignolo casts his argument serves a serious intellectual purpose. It gives him a language in which he can emphasize that the historian needs a new place to stand. Inquiry must begin from the assumption that documents are not organic, ordered parts of a natural hierarchy in which literary works in European languages occupy the pinnacle, but parts of a dialogue, both sides of which deserve close attention.

Mignolo makes good on a number of his theoretical claims, since he shows that they enable him to reframe the precise investigation of the sources. He undertakes precise study of the terms used in Nahuatl, the language of the Aztecs, for books and those who wrote them, and offers a vivid and fascinating account of Inca quipus, the knotted cords whose textures provided Peruvians with records of public events and even, after the Conquest, private sins. By doing so—and then by comparing these sophisticated technologies of the word with the first European descriptions of them—he demonstrates that even the shrewdest Spanish observers never fully understood Americans' radically different experiences of such basic activities as reading and writing. They neither grasped the distance between the specialized work of a Christian *letrado* and that of a Mexican wise man nor accorded the latter equal standing with the former.

When movement from Nahuatl to Spanish is involved, Mignolo turns the sharp eye of a detective on slippages of meaning and implication. Even the supremely well-informed Bernardino de Sahagún, he argues, failed to render precisely the terms in which representatives of the Mexican nobility spoke of their tradition. When they described themselves as literally "unfolding" their texts, which were depicted on a series of hinged screens, Sahagun spoke merely of "reading"—the decoding of a western book, not the physical opening up and traditional, oral exposition of a Mexica codex, during which images served to jog richly stored memories.

Mignolo's interpretations of hybrid texts—texts by authors, some of mixed parentage, who employed mixed genres—deftly explore the ways in which older styles of tale-telling infected and altered formal narratives. His close reading of the *relaciones* of Francisco de San Antón Muñón Chimalpaín, written in Nahuatl but in Latin script, uncovers the lasting presence in Chimalpaín's writing of "the repetitive structure of the oral." Like Serge Gruzinski, a highly innovative scholar on whose work he draws, Mignolo follows the passage from the pre-Columbian form of schooling, "in which a part of learning was to look at and to interpret the books" of images, to "the new one, in which Chimalpaín himself was educated and learned to replace the *pinturas* by alphabetic writing, and to move speech toward written prose."[8]

Any reader who perseveres through Mignolo's sinuous arguments, precise interpretations, and theoretical discussions will emerge with rewards. He provides not only new perspectives, but also fresh encounters with such little-known and fascinating persons as Lorenzo Boturini Benaduci, a peripatetic Italian intellectual who drew on Giambattista Vico's *New Science* to explain the hieroglyphs and other historical records that he avidly bought up in Mexico.[9]

A rich collection of articles edited by the art historian Claire Farago complements Mignolo's work in strategic ways. Like Mignolo, Farago insists that the categories of western scholarship require critical study. In particular, she argues, the interpretative categories of modern art history, as given influential formulation by Jacob Burckhardt, Erwin Panofsky, and others, rest on assumptions about the nature of nations and peoples that no contemporary scholar could accept. Art historians have traditionally drawn a firm distinction, for example, between artifacts, which reveal the nature of lower, alien cultures, and works of art, which give material form to the aesthetic values of high cultures like our own. But this distinction turns out, on inspection, to be itself a historical artifact, and one that embodies questionable assumptions and prejudices.

Farago sees no reason to accept—as many modern scholars have with-out much reflection—the judgment of Giorgio Vasari and other sixteenth-century scholars that the northern Europeans who came to Italy to gain culture were barbarians. By contrast, she sees every reason to connect the Renaissance, as a cultural event, with the vast movement of European images to the non-European world and the accompanying movement of non-European images to Europe: she wants to make "exchange," rather than "revival," the central issue. Neither Farago nor most of her collabora-tors would deny that some objects are more beautiful or more powerful than others. But many of them attack, with erudite and eloquent argu-ments, the well-established ways of sorting the history of art into neat pigeonholes that such traditional categories imply.

Anthony Cutler, who surveys European views of Byzantine art, and Thomas Cummins, who dissects in a series of critical case studies Euro-pean ways of dealing with American records in pictorial form, reveal the size and weight of the conceptual baggage that early modern intellectual travelers dragged behind them. Both scholars show how it hampered efforts to confront and understand foreign visual documents, and ensured that even the images that Europeans most respected—like Mesoamerican calendars—were understood and explained in European terms. Claudia Lazzaro, who analyzes the stone menagerie that the Medici set up in their great garden at Castello, and Pauline Moffitt Watts, who studies the role of gesture in sixteenth-century religious plays in Mexico, delicately trace the interplay, in the Old World and the New, between classical traditions and new social and natural phenomena. Both replace one-dimensional accounts with dialectical analyses, doing justice to both sides in a long and complex cultural exchange.

Thomas Kaufmann's erudite essay on Italian art in central Europe, though dealing with a different part of the world, shows a similar sensitiv-ity to the complex ways in which ideas, images, and techniques are trans-formed when applied in a new context. He challenges traditional ways of discussing the movement of artistic forms—as well as traditional notions about the "vernacular" arts of central Europe, and draws on Marshall Sahlins for a more complex and elaborate model of cultural relations.

Most stimulating of all, perhaps, are the essays of Martin Kemp and Cecilia Klein, both of whom criticize contemporary orthodoxies in com-plementary ways. Kemp shows how the manifold uses of natural objects in the decorative arts of the Renaissance challenge distinctions between "Gothic and Renaissance, classical and non-classical, western and non-western, single style and plural styles, mechanical and intellectual, applied arts and fine arts." The "magical creations" of Renaissance craftsmen incorporated and imitated such marvels of nature as ostrich eggs, wart hog tusks, and coral branches. Kemp rejects the idea that these spectacularly rebarbative objects served only to confirm the prejudices of collectors, who tried to arrange them in neat, orderly systems that mirrored the structure of the whole universe. On the contrary, the objects, in effect, insisted on their own status as exceptions—neither purely natural nor purely artistic, neither purely European nor non-European. And they thereby sapped the foundations of vast structures of traditional natural philosophy. Klein shows that the image of a sharp-toothed, flesh-eating Wild Woman which appears in post-Conquest codices may reflect European traditions and beliefs about cannibals and witches—but it also certainly derives from documented pre-Columbian beliefs and rituals.

Kemp undermines the currently popular but anachronistic thesis that all Europeans were and thought alike—a belief that grossly distorts the divergent local dialects and warring religious beliefs of the fifteenth and sixteenth centuries. Klein powerfully attacks the widespread suspicion that modern scholars cannot know anything of substance about non-European cultures. These noncomformist defenses of tradition do much to make *Reframing the Renaissance* into a real debate.

3

Questions arise nonetheless. Revisionism, as currently practiced, often brings rewards but sometimes exacts a price, a price paid in failures to take account of contexts, to discriminate, to accord to European witnesses the full attention now accorded to non-Europeans. The exchange between Acosta and Tovar—which figures in both Mignolo's book and in Farago's—may provide a small case in point of the pains that accompany revisionism's pleasures.

For Mignolo—as he argued at greater length in an influential earlier article—the Jesuits' letters serve above all as documents of prejudice and Eurocentrism.[10] When Acosta asked whether one could write the history of a people without history, he revealed his sense of superiority to his subjects. And even Tovar, for all the direct knowledge of Mexican life and tradition manifest in his detailed study of the Aztec calendar, condemned Aztec hieroglyphs as inferior to the Latin alphabet. Thomas Cummins, in Claire Farago's book, advances a different, but to some extent a parallel, argument. He shows, most elegantly, how images can serve as a medium of communication between cultures—but also that many forms of intellectual and visual static limit their effectiveness. Tovar, he claims, ascribed as much authority to the illustrated work of an earlier western observer, the Spanish Dominican friar Diego Durán, as he did to the native illustrator whose images Durán had copied—even though he must have perceived the enormous differences between the westernized reproductions Durán provided and their models. Both Tovar and his source, in other words, failed to take scholarly account of the visual slippages that inevitably occurred when texts and images underwent westernization.[11]

Both Mignolo and Cummins direct attention to significant features of the documents, but both of their discussions are also flawed. They suffer from an inattention to the European context of what are, after all, European historical texts. In raising questions about the veracity of indigenous American accounts of history, the Jesuits did something that any well-trained scholar of their time was expected to do—and that had little connection with their position of power or their belief in the superiority of western to nonwestern cultures. At the end of the fifteenth century, the Dominican theologian Giovanni Nanni da Viterbo published a series of works ascribed to ancient historians, such as the Egyptian priest Manetho and the Persian Metasthenes. Both these texts and his commentaries on them denounced Greek historians, like Herodotus, as fantasists, and insisted that only the priests of ancient Near Eastern lands like Chaldea had preserved a full and accurate written record of the past.

Nanni's texts were forgeries, of course, but they attracted a wide and sometimes appreciative readership in the Iberian world.[12] Bartolomé de las Casas, the brave and independent defender of the Indians, began his history of the discoveries with quotations from Nanni's attacks on Greek historians. Melchior Cano, a bitter persecutor of the Jewish converts called New Christians, persecuted new forgeries with equal zeal. But he paid tribute to the widespread interest in Nanni's work when he discussed it at length in his own elaborate work on historians and their credibility.[13] By the middle of the sixteenth century, in other words, any alert scholar knew that the early histories of many nations were open to a great many questions, and that the quality of Greek and Roman records had been sharply attacked by writers who seemed to enjoy some authority.

Many humanists scrutinized the preserved records of Greek and Roman history with as much attention and ingenuity as Nanni had devoted to forging replacements for them. Roman historians knew perfectly well that the early history narrated by Livy swarmed with minor and major contradictions and errors. Worse still, the entire tradition rested on the weakest of foundations. It could not have been transmitted in writing over the centuries, since the Gauls had sacked the city of Rome and destroyed its records.[14] By the 1580s and 1590s, some scholars suspected that the whole story of Roman origins—all those *fabulae faciles* about Romulus and Remus, Numa and Egeria, Horatius and the bridge—owed their origins to the imaginations of late Roman historians. Others, who tried to defend the core of the tradition as historical, argued early in the seventeenth century that Roman banquet songs could have preserved real events. The early history of the greatest of ancient states, the source of a thousand florid paintings of disciplined Horatii, writhing Sabine women, and virtuous Lucretias, owed its survival to memory and performance.[15] When Tovar and Acosta discussed what would constitute a "*historia bien cumplida*" of the New World, in short, they showed their awareness not of their own ethnic superiority but of their contemporaries' methodological debates—an awareness that their recent critics seldom take into account.

Tovar, moreover, did not dismiss the Mexicas' pictorial records so brusquely as Mignolo and Cummins suggest. Cummins complains that Tovar gave Diego Durán's work the status of a preferred native document. In fact, however, Tovar explained that he had had to use the derivative work because his own earlier compilation, the result of direct study of Mexica codices and instruction from their "*sabios*," had been out of reach. Durán's work seemed to him "the closest to the ancient sources that I have seen."[16] Tovar's use of a surrogate source seems reasonable enough in the circumstances. Even his lack of sensitivity to the visual details of native drawings should occasion no surprise. Recent studies of antiquaries working in Europe who copied and interpreted Greek, Roman, and Egyptian antiquities have stressed that very few of them ever managed to reproduce the precise details of an ancient or a foreign style without importing elements of their own style and sensibility.[17] Put into context, what looks like

Eurocentrism may turn out to be the natural deficiencies of a set of historical disciplines still in formation.

The Jesuits' judgments of the Mexicas' records also provoke objections
from Mignolo. He writes that, according to Tovar, "their figures and characters are not as sufficient as our writing." Here he accurately reproduces
what Acosta wrote in his history, summarizing Tovar's letter.[18] Tovar, however, actually said something different: that the Mexicas' hieroglyphs "were
not sufficiently like our writing, so that everyone would report what was
written, without any variation, in the same words. They only agreed on the
general ideas."[19] That explained why the Mexica wise men who traditionally had the task of explaining the codices had to commit ancient speeches
and other traditional materials to memory. Only by doing so could they
explicate and comment on the pictographic codices that alluded to them.
Tovar, in short, tried not to demonstrate the inferiority of Mexica images
but to show that they had formed only part of the Mexica way of preserving the past.

Acosta, to be sure, took a more negative view of Mexica pictographs: but
his views were put forward against a larger intellectual background, of
which Mignolo does not take account. Pamela Jones contributes to Claire
Farago's collection a discussion of the artistic theory of the sixteenth-
century Bolognese prelate Gabriele Paleotti. She points out that he regarded most viewers of sacred art as illiterate, sensual, and unable to tease
out the higher senses of images. Paleotti defended an orthodox position:
Christian art should provide the illiterate with a vivid, accessible Bible. But
he also feared—with reason—that images could easily convey wrong messages. Jones wondered whether Paleotti's views might have had an impact
in the New World, but found no evidence bearing on the point.

In fact, as the Italian scholar Gianfranco Cantelli argued some time ago,
the Counter-Reformation theories of art espoused by Paleotti reshaped
Renaissance views of nonalphabetic writing. Fifteenth- and sixteenth-
century scholars avidly collected information about Egyptian hieroglyphs.
Following a well-established ancient tradition, they interpreted these as
superior to alphabetic writing: as a symbolic language, created by ancient
philosophers, which rested on direct insight into the structure of the universe. Their enthusiasm knew few bounds. Early in the sixteenth century,
the intellectuals of the Roman curia amused themselves by trying to

decode the hieroglyphs they saw on ruins as they picnicked among Rome's deserted temples and colonnades. So did the very different intellectuals of the contemporary Holy Roman Empire. The Nuremberg patrician Willibald Pirckheimer, for example, wrote out a mock-hieroglyphic praise of the emperor Maximilian I; his close friend Albrecht Dürer gave it visual embodiment in his magnificent woodcut *The Triumphal Arch*. Maximilian himself found the idea that hieroglyphs were the earliest form of writing very attractive, as he did the notion that his own family tree could be traced back to ancient Egypt. Hieroglyphs—and the mysterious land of their origin—were in.[20]

Paleotti's doubts about the transparency of images, however, led him to dismiss pictorial writing as primitive, as a crude way of recording facts and ideas, which the alphabet naturally displaced. Acosta followed Paleotti's authoritative lead when he treated hieroglyphs as primitive in his *History*—and when he argued, in the same work, that even the pictographic writing of the Chinese and Japanese was less adaptable and sophisticated than western alphabets. Aztecs and Egyptians soon brushed shoulders in other locales. Michele Mercati's detailed and fascinating study of the obelisks of Rome, for example, mentioned the Mexican hieroglyphs already known to habitués of the Vatican library as well as Egyptian hieroglyphs, treating both as relatively primitive forms of pictorial writing. Counter-Reformation prejudices thus helped to bring about a minor revolution in western thought: the demolition of the belief in the symbolic wisdom of the ancient barbarian sages, a campaign that Vico and others carried to a conclusion in the early eighteenth century.[21]

Any full account of Europeans' efforts to assess, describe, and analyze Mexican codices will have to set them in the wider context Cantelli has laid out—and compare them with the same intellectuals' efforts to deal with the traditions of other "barbarian" nations, like the ancient Egyptians and Chaldeans. This story may provide some intriguing parallels to Mignolo's. It may partly confirm his thesis—one that he develops in what amounts to a dialogue with Jacques Derrida—that western scholars, from the Renaissance to the present, have characteristically seen alphabetic writing as the only true form, and codices as the only true books. But the story will have a complexity his lacks, and will suggest a new range of historical questions in its own right: for example, why the early modern scholars who knew something from Greek descriptions about the forms of Egyptian language and scribal culture seem not to have used these as a model for thinking about Indian images and wise men.

Mignolo denies any desire to criticize his European protagonists for failing to live up to modern scholarly standards (though he sometimes seems to do exactly that). Several of Farago's authors go further, telling the reader that they do not share the prejudices of Hernando Cortés or Paleotti—as if they fear that studying the European conquest of the New World might prove contagious, infecting scholars with Renaissance ideas about religion, race, and rights. Such practices and declarations may worry some readers, who will perceive—rightly or wrongly—a connection between them and the occasional forced readings of European sources that accompany them.

Like other revisionist historiographies, this one will have to evolve further before its full value—and its full compatibility with more traditional forms—becomes clear. The presence of discordant voices in the choir and the high quality of individual results give reason for optimism. So does the appearance on historians' all-too-old-fashioned radar screens of a wide range of new witnesses, new objects, and new problems.

At the moment, however, the more traditional methods of interpretation applied by Elliott and Landucci, MacCormack and Cervantes still afford the best guidance into the minds of the early modern Europeans who tried to understand the societies that had fallen victim to the great inhumanity of conquest. These scholars, for all their differences in method and motive, all separate with a surgeon's delicate care the layers of classical, biblical, and later ideas and of purely local experiences of rites and mores that seem inextricably fused in the finished form of Acosta's work and its competitors. They all concentrate on varieties of religious and practical experience—the varieties that enabled some Europeans to recognize the richness and complexity of certain non-European societies, but allowed others to dismiss them as barbarian creations of the devil. And they insist not only on the prejudices and presuppositions European observers brought with them to their field of work, but also on their remarkable ability to look and record.

Early observers of societies—like early students of physics and biology—could not, as they created the humanities we have inherited, avoid committing many errors that now seem obvious. Surely their occasional successes deserve at least as much attention as their frequent failures. Many revisionists do not willingly concede that much to the European devil, and in failing to do so, they reveal the screen of prejudices that separates them, too, from the objects of their study. It remains to be seen how—or if—another generation will succeed in fusing the methods of traditional crafts-manship with the flamboyant hybrid forms of the new scholarship, to produce wonders which, like Kemp's marvels of nature, can challenge prej-udices instead of reinforcing them.[22]

II

HUMANISM
AND
SCIENCE

෨෩

5

The New Science
and the Traditions
of Humanism

෨෩෨

*C*ONSTANTIJN HUYGENS was one of the most virtuous of the seventeenth-century virtuosi who collected antiquities, devised scientific instruments, and cultivated a taste for natural curiosities. He painted, wrote poetry in several languages, and played the lute for the king of England. The most modern English thinkers and writers appealed to him: he translated John Donne into Dutch and copied out Francis Bacon's theories about progress. He loved the humanist art of Peter Paul Rubens, but recognized the young Rembrandt's supremacy as a history painter. His unfinished classic in Dutch, the *Dagwerck,* celebrated the discoveries of the new science, which he tried to connect with the domestic life of the Dutch Golden Age, the sunny world of scrubbed tile floors, tables covered by rich rugs, and crystalline windows so memorably depicted by Vermeer.

Huygens came honestly by his wide range of skills and interests: he was raised to have them. His father had him taught to speak French by the direct method as a child and encouraged him to study science, music, and painting. As a teenager he enrolled at Leiden, the most modern university of his day. There he attended not only courses in Latin on canonical texts but also courses in Dutch on modern mathematics and military engineering. Even the professors of classical humanities wrote Dutch poetry. Soon Huygens became a habitué less of universities than of courts, ambassadors' residences, and scientific societies. He seems as prototypically modern a figure as René Descartes; and like Descartes, he saw the story of his own progress as worth recording in a carefully constructed autobiography.[1]

At this point, however, the resemblance ends. Descartes described in the *Discours de la méthode* (*Discourse on the Method,* 1637) the formation of a revolutionary, one who had deliberately turned away from the humanist learning and scholastic philosophy of the colleges and built the world anew. Huygens, by contrast, described the formation of a moderate, one who combined humanist and scientific interests, classical and modern tastes without strain. He was as delighted to remember how he learned to write Latin verse as how he learned to use the microscope. He saw no opposition between his up-to-date and his traditional endeavors. And he wrote his memoirs in what he still considered the language of science and learning: not French or Dutch but Latin, and not plain Latin at that but an elaborate, formal prose studded with allusions and quotations. Even when Huygens wished to praise a quintessentially modern enterprise—like Hugo Grotius's treatise in the vernacular on the principles of Dutch law— he did so as a classicist, remarking that Dutch farmers would be most grateful to Grotius "sua si bona norint"—"if they knew their own good." He rightly assumed that his contemporaries would recognize his quotation from Virgil's *Georgics* (II.458).

An active command of elegant Latin still mattered deeply in the Holland of the Golden Age. It gave those who possessed it an entrée to the international Republic of Letters. It expressed ideas and reported events with a precision that the vernacular lacked. And it proved perfectly adequate for dealing with the most modern concepts and inventions—at least if, like Huygens, the Latinist was willing to ransack texts and lexica for plausible ways of referring to "military engineers" *(architectones castrenses)* and other nonclassical beasts. Latin eloquence, the core skill and mental discipline of the Renaissance humanist, lived.

For a variety of reasons, until the last generation or so most historians of civilization, literature, and art assumed that Renaissance humanism died as the sixteenth century wound to a close. On the one hand, the cutting edge of change in early modern literature did not seem to belong to the Latin language, whose elegances the humanists cultivated with so much painstaking attention. By the sixteenth century, after all, Italian had become not only a literary language but a classical one in its own right. The young aristocrat had to read, speak, and write it as well as Latin, and its canon of once smooth-hulled classics, from Dante, Petrarch, and Boccaccio down to Ludovico Ariosto and Torquato Tasso, had developed a thick new barnacling of literary and philological commentary. The French poets of the Pléiade, the tragic and comic playwrights of the London theater, and the young Dutch poets in the circle of the University of Leiden all showed in their turn, to widespread satisfaction, that one could imitate, emulate, and satirize the ancients in their languages as well. Just as close imitation of Greek models had turned the primitive babble of early Rome into a language of high literature, so close imitation of Greek, Latin, and Italian precedents could make any modern vernacular a vehicle fit for epic or lyric, history or tragedy. The easily imitated oxymorons and exclamations of Petrarch's lyrics, for instance, found creative imitators in every European language. Latin was still needed, at least by professional intellectuals.[2] But the age of creative writing in classicizing modern Latin—the age that stretched from Petrarch to Erasmus and a little beyond—had presumably reached its natural end.

On the other hand, it also seemed reasonable to infer that the content of the humanist curriculum had become either elementary or sterile—or both—by the turn of the seventeenth century. True, the creators of the Scientific Revolution enjoyed in almost every case that fine classical education, based on a thorough study of Greek literature, which, according to Thomas Gaisford's famous remark, "not only elevates above the vulgar herd, but leads not infrequently to positions of considerable emolument."[3] But a standard genealogy of modern thought, one inherited from its seventeenth-century creators, suggested that the new philosophy that called everything into doubt grew in soil fertilized by the ashes of the humanist tradition. Montaigne, himself the beneficiary of an idiosyncratic but excellent humanist training, showed in his last essay (III.13: "On experience") that the whole enterprise of trying to find guidance for modern behavior in classical texts required readers to rip their supposed authorities out of time and context. Individual lives and situations, societies, and religions differed so radically that one could not reasonably hope to make the past shed light on the present.[4] He also subjected the wasted time required by a normal humanist education to a searching critique, which reformer after reformer would paraphrase or quote.

Where Montaigne questioned and subverted, two of his faithful readers inserted dynamite and lit the fuse. Francis Bacon—himself a humanistic rhetorician—treated many of the characteristic pursuits of Renaissance humanism as fatal diseases of learning. The humanists had failed to see that the world had changed, that modern voyages were more extended, modern empires more far-flung and modern technology more powerful than those of the ancients. They had confused the "antiquity" of the Greeks and Romans—the fact that their texts had existed for a long time—with the authority that human beings gain as they age—an authority that can be invested only in people, who continue to learn as they age, not in books, which are impervious to experience (if not to damage). The philology of the humanists, with its obsessive citation and imitation of authorities, had been an intellectual distraction from the thinker's true mission of extending man's empire. The humanists had entirely failed to see how much they could have learned from the practical men of their own day, whose theories about the natural world rested on experience, not mere textual exegesis—and who lived their intellectual lives, with every appearance of satisfaction, in the vernacular.[5] Descartes, for his part, admitted that the historical learning he had acquired at the Jesuit college of La Flèche had a certain value: it had taught him that values and behavior differed from place to place and age to age. But travel could have taught the same lesson, and probably in a fresher way. As for the study of past philosophers, it showed only that—as Montaigne had already seen—they disagreed with each other on so many central points that none of their systems could claim the status of offering certain knowledge.

Many other prophets of the new science joined the chorus of those who groaned at the thousands of hours they and others had lost scribbling halting verse in a dead language or hoping vainly to find solid knowledge in antiquated books. Galileo used his brilliant Italian to present the results of his investigations to a wide public. He made wicked fun of those who "think," as he wrote to Johannes Kepler, "that philosophy is a sort of book like the *Aeneid* and the *Odyssey*, and that truth is to be found not in the world or in nature but in the collation of texts (I use their terminology)."[6] The members of the Oxford Experimental Philosophy Club and the Fellows of the Royal Society, the Paris Académie des Sciences, and the Roman Accademia dei Lincei agreed that the results of experiments and voyages were most clearly and plainly presented in the vernacular. A host of proposers tried to make up for the one great problem that the downfall of Latin posed—the loss of an international language—by devising universal symbolic or hieroglyphic or pictorial languages, not to mention methods for learning all European vernaculars in a couple of weeks each.[7] Even Sir Isaac Newton, who used his fluent Latin as the appropriate dress for the great baroque world picture of the *Principia,* used English for the pullulating experimental details of his *Optics.* Even G. W. Leibniz, who corresponded in Latin with half of learned Europe, chose French to develop his modern metaphysics. These examples—and many more could be cited—suggest that in the seventeenth century Latin humanism played the crowd-pleasing role of the star in a dramatic execution scene. Just when the humanists had rediscovered most of the ancient texts that would see the light before the second Renaissance of the papyrologists, captured the new medium of printing, and established their position at the start of the educational food chain, the basic futility of their central disciplines was publicly exposed and denounced—and by the most authoritative voices of their day.

Many humanists, finally, admitted, if not that their studies were useless, at least that their age had run its course: "the age of criticism and philosophy," said the classical scholar J. F. Gronovius in the 1650s, "has passed, and one of philosophy and mathematics has taken its place."[8] Even those who continued to insist on the possibility of and the need for historical knowledge generally accepted that the forms of argument and presentation needed updating. Thus Pierre-Daniel Huet tried to make his anti-Cartesian *Demonstratio evangelica* (1679), in which he revealed the biblical origin of the ancient myths, rigorous and convincing in a way that could meet the criticisms of the Cartesians, convinced as they were that all philology was a waste of time.[9] He also tried to make the vast echo-chamber of the accumulated humanist commentaries on classical texts coherent and accessible by editing a series of editions of the classics, in the first instance for the French dauphin, in which only the notes that remained of interest were reprinted, after being boiled down. If humanist scholarship was to survive, in short, it needed to adopt at least the protective coloring of philosophical rationalism. Richard Bentley, Master of Trinity College and master of textual criticism, insisted, in a famous phrase in his commentary on Horace, that "ratio et res ipsa" ("reason and the case in point") mattered far more to him than the testimony of a hundred old manuscripts. He also devoted a famous series of Boyle Lectures to arguing for the philosophical and theological advantages of Newton's cosmology—which, he clearly saw, was no revival of an ancient theory but a new creation with no ancient counterpart.[10] No wonder that most standard narratives of the intellectual history of early modern Europe insist on the transition "from the humanists to men of science," or on the change from a principle of authority to one of free investigation. This modern periodization has ample period support.

In fact, however, humanism long survived the sniping of its critics and the depression of its advocates—and even contributed a surprising amount to some of the intellectual enterprises that eventually replaced it. During the last generation, intellectual historians have come to see more and more clearly that late sixteenth- and seventeenth-century announcements of the death of humanism were a considerable exaggeration. Characteristic humanist enterprises, both philological and philosophical, continued to be carried out, sometimes on a grand scale, throughout the age of the new science. If some of them showed evidence of wear, and their advocates signs of edginess, others revealed a clear capacity to serve modern needs.

Throughout the late sixteenth and early seventeenth centuries, the need for young men trained to work in government expanded. From the ever larger courts of late Elizabethan and early Stuart England to the little police states of the Holy Roman Empire, bureaucracies grew, paper circulated in larger quantities, and monarchs demanded more and more detailed advice about political options and social policies.[11] The humanist curriculum continued—so most teachers and most government officials agreed—to provide the skills and qualities young men needed to carry out these vital tasks. Across Europe, educational theorists continued to argue with unmistakable energy and conviction that the best formation for a young man lay in the close study of the same classical disciplines that Leonardo Bruni and Guarino of Verona had defined, following Cicero and Quintilian, as key skills for one who hoped to lead an active life. The young man who wished to serve his prince as a judge or an ambassador, so the influential Helmstedt scholar Arnold Clapmarius explained, must begin by attaining real mastery of Latin, even if he could already read the language and had only three years to spend on all the disciplines: "you need to possess it in a polished and elegant form, unless you want to philosophize in the way of vulgar writers. I approve entirely of their intelligence, so long as they produce their ideas in an eloquent form. But they do the reverse, and instead of shedding light on their learning, they obscure it with their awkward brushwork." Real mastery, in turn, meant not only a written command of the language, but oral fluency: "It is my advice that you should always speak Latin with your roommate. If either forgets, let him pay a penalty." Only those who had attained this level—which required systematic reading of the comedies of Plautus, to amass a store of colloquialisms—could hope to avoid the humiliation suffered by many Germans, who, since they normally spoke no Latin, found themselves crippled by nervousness when they had to do so, because they had to take such scrupulous care to avoid solecisms.[12]

Clapmarius's belief in the need to immerse oneself in Latin, to strain for active command of a dead language, was not unusual: G. J. Vossius, the influential teacher of rhetoric at the Amsterdam Academy, also wanted his students to begin their studies by mastering as pure a Latin as possible. Though he admitted that no ancient author had treated all subjects and found all the writers of Golden Latin prose acceptable models, he urged them to concentrate on systematic—though not slavish—imitation of Cicero, the greatest single master of Latin eloquence and the only master of the highest, periodic form of Latin prose.[13] The Jesuit colleges that began in the mid-sixteenth century to offer such successful instruction that they won the children of many Protestant noble families for their curriculum (and for Catholicism), even in parts of the Holy Roman Empire and Poland that had threatened to adopt the new religion permanently, adopted similar ideals. Like the Protestant academies, they specialized in active mastery of Latin poetry and history, and imposed the speaking of Latin as a vital scholastic discipline. But their curriculum was no more strictly classical and rhetorical than that of the influential Protestant academies in Strasbourg and Altdorf or of the English public schools, all of which offered their pupils much the same mix of Latin grammar, rhetoric, and prosody, spiced with historical examples and moral lessons.[14]

The curriculum that young men were advised to undertake in the six-teenth and seventeenth centuries embraced many subjects. Grotius urged a prospective diplomat to devote himself not only to the arts, but also to logic, physics, and even to parts of the scholastic theology of Thomas Aquinas. This demand perhaps reflected unusually—and unrealistically—high standards. Grotius had himself been a brilliant prodigy at Leiden, where he mastered textual criticism, under the tutelage of Joseph Scaliger, at the ripe age of twelve, and became one of the most original intellectuals of the time, the writer of massive treatises on Christian theology and international law. But Grotius stood in the main line of educational writing when he defined the small core of subjects that the young politician absolutely had to study. Vossius maintained that the future "politicus" must master rhetoric above all: only with the help of this instrument of persuasion could he hope to win friends and influence people in private or to address them effectively in public. Grotius agreed absolutely: the young man should begin by studying Cicero's letters, which showed "how to fit the general precepts to particular topics." Then he must read Aristotle's *Rhetoric* in the light of his ethical and political works, which showed "how streams of moral and political wisdom should be gently drawn down to form the craft of persuasion." Study of the orations of Cicero and Demosthenes would provide worked examples of these more sophisticated precepts.[15] Clapmarius also recommended the study of rhetoric in this sophisticated form, sternly insisting that his young men must learn ethics and politics, as well as Latin, before they could venture to compose anything so demanding as an oration. Close study of moral philosophy and rhetoric, attentive reading of the central ancient texts, carried on in an orderly and systematic way, would make the young man virtuous and eloquent—a "vir bonus dicendi peritus," just as Roman and Italian educational theorists had always said. These doctrines have the ring of familiarity: *mutatis mutandis,* Bruni or Erasmus could have advanced similar arguments for making the study of ancient literature and the classical discipline of rhetoric the core of an education for civil life. It is not surprising, then, that Bruni's *De studiis et litteris* (1424) and Erasmus's *De ratione studii* (1511) were reprinted, along with more up-to-date texts, in seventeenth-century collections on educational theory.[16]

The production of classicists naturally required close study of the classics. Like earlier humanists, those of the late sixteenth and early seventeenth centuries were certain that classical texts embodied ethical and prudential principles of eternal value. Grotius, for example, advised his mature students to study the tragedies of Euripides, the comedies of Terence, and the *Satires* of Horace. The young, he admitted, would see in such works only "the purity and brilliance of their language." Older students, however, would appreciate these texts' more important quality—their provision of ethical lessons as valid now as they had been in antiquity: "they will regard there, as in a mirror, the life and conduct of humanity."[17] Caspar Barlaeus, a brilliant neo-Latin poet, agreed as he recommended that the young try to transform the best of Horace's *Odes* into their "blood and marrow," finding in them not only the beautiful language that naturally appealed to boys but also incomparably sound doctrines on piety, morality, and the disasters that ensue after civil war, which only mature men could hope to appreciate.

Most of the methods that teachers recommended were as traditional as these justifications for reading the classics. They had read their Montaigne as well as their Cicero and Quintilian, and emphasized the need to make the classical curriculum practicable for young men born to high political and military rather than a purely literary and philological life. Promising young men must not be overworked: they must—as Vittorino da Feltre had shown long before—be allowed time for physical exercise and other honest forms of leisure. More important still, they should not be "dried out" and transformed into desiccated pedants. The teacher should not, for example, expect the ordinary young scholar to commit long works in Latin prose—as opposed to verse, more easily remembered—to memory.[18] Often this meant that reading the classics had to become a collaborative enterprise: a young scholar by profession must help the young nobleman to gain access to the elements of classical culture. Like Guarino of Verona, who had advised his patron and star pupil, Leonello d'Este, to find a poor but able lad to help him compile systematic notebooks on his classical reading, Grotius advised his prospective diplomat not to study a logic text himself, but to have his "study helper, who has more free time, read some outstanding expert on this art and remember to report to you anything worthy of note that he finds." This *coadjutor,* not the young noble, should also undertake the tedious but necessary task of working through the ancient and modern commentators on Aristotle's *Ethics* and *Politics* and abridging their remarks for his pupil.[19] The tutor, who accompanied his young charge to school and university, went over lessons with him, and took him on travels later on, was a familiar figure in noble families across Europe.

So was the professional *anagnostes,* or reader, who read classical texts with the mature king or nobleman, explaining the continued relevance of classical precepts and examples for the modern active life and helping in the compilation of study aids. Sir Philip Sidney, for example, told his brother Robert in a famous letter on the study of history that that "excellent man," Mr. Henry Savile, could help him—thereby giving a glimpse of the humble tasks which could occupy, in his earlier years, a man who later rose to be provost of Eton College, the creator of a magnificent edition of the works of Chrysostom, a great book-collector, and an original mathematician.[20] To this profession belonged Henry Cuffe, whose lessons on Aristotle's *Politics* were blamed by Essex for having brought him to rebel against Elizabeth; not to mention Thomas Hobbes, who carried out similar jobs for no less a patron than Francis Bacon.[21]

Reading had to be systematic as well as collaborative. The young man should learn as early as possible—so Barlaeus explained—to keep careful notes on what he read: "Meanwhile, as they read, they should have notebooks at hand, in which they may copy out the more elegant phrases and sentences; or let them have some blank pages bound in at the end of the books they read, and on them they may note down the number of the page in question and the heading of some remarkable topic. Then, when need arises, they will be able to make reference to it."[22] Meticulously kept notebooks on the graces of Latin style, in which classical ways for beginning and ending a sentence, making a transition, or quoting an authority were organized by type, Vossius explained, could produce real copiousness in Latin, preventing the student from revealing the poverty of his linguistic resources by repetition.[23] And equally meticulous notes on historical reading—as Jean Bodin taught in his influential *Methodus ad facilem historiarum cognitionem* (*Method for Readily Attaining Knowledge of History*, 1566)—would provide the knowledge of peoples and customs, constitutions and laws that the jurisconsult or politician must have at his fingertips.[24]

In every case, the categories into which the student divided the matter he collected were essential: only these would enable him to impose a logical order on the spiraling mass of details he would gather as he read any major classical text—not to mention enabling him to find them again when necessary. As Sidney told his brother: "but that I wish herein is this, that when you read any such thing, you straight bring it to his head, not only of what art, but by your logical subdivisions, to the next member and parcel of the art. And so, as in a table, be it witty words, of which Tacitus is full, sentences, of which Livy, or similitudes, whereof Plutarch, straight to lay it up in the right place of his storehouse, as either military, or more especially defensive military, or more particularly defensive by fortification, and so lay it up. So likewise in politic matters."[25]

The late humanist and his pupil—like the humanists of the fifteenth and early sixteenth century—trained themselves to read with their pens ever ready in their hands. Word-for-word paraphrases of set texts, entered by hand between the lines of specially printed school editions, made them readily accessible. So, even more, did the longer remarks that teachers dictated and that students recorded in the wide margins or on interleaved sheets of their texts. And all this material, endlessly sorted and copied, processed and reprocessed, moved inexorably from margins to notebooks and back again into school compositions and formal treatises. When the natural philosopher John Jonston described the work that had gone into his *Thaumatographia naturalis* (1630), he claimed not to have explored the natural world but to have done an immense amount of reading and excerpting, drawing on both the ancient *Natural History* of the elder Pliny—itself avowedly a work of compilation—and the great modern texts of Georgius Agricola and Girolamo Cardano.[26] In doing so he merely described more explicitly than usual a method of intellectual work adopted by generations of writers and readers—from the political thinkers Bodin and Lipsius to the great essayist Montaigne, who published not only his essays, laden with artful quotations, but also the formal summary judgments that he had entered, like a good pupil of his humanist masters, in his copies of ancient and modern historians. The literary methods of Guarino and Erasmus, in short, survived and flourished: the student, armed with a notebook and a set of *loci,* places or categories, in which to store material for rapid retrieval, set out as confidently in 1630 as his counterparts had one or two centuries before to break the classics up into bite-sized segments and organize them for aggressively confident reuse.

Naturally, this literary regime could easily reduce itself—in uncreative hands—to a sterile exercise in *bricolage,* the endless recycling of the same commonplaces to no creative effect. Even the ablest students spent a vast amount of time and energy on meticulous, almost verbatim adaptations of particular classical texts. Johannes Kepler, for example, while a student at Tübingen in the 1590s, spun a laboriously clever epithalamium for a law student out of the ancient *Laus Pisonis:* parts of his work, as was common, effectively amounted to a patchwork of lines from the original.[27] Textbooks often provided little more than lists of ways to perform a particular literary task—quoting an authority, for example—in a suitably classical way.[28] And even loyal believers in the value of classical learning complained bitterly of the length of time it took to be initiated into the mysteries of artistic Latin. Jan Amos Comenius, for example, devised his celebrated *Orbis sensualium pictus* (*The Visible World,* 1666), in which simple pictures directly expressed the meanings of the words that referred to them, not to replace but to abridge the rule-based teaching of the humanists.

If the framework of humanist pedagogy was astonishingly traditional, however, its content was both contentious and protean. Controversies continued to rage about every element in the humanist curriculum. Marc-Antoine Muret and Justus Lipsius argued that the Latinist of the later sixteenth century should find his models not only in the oratory of the Roman republic but also in the close-knit, sententious writing of Tacitus and Seneca. Lipsian Latin, in particular, became a fad in Protestant and Catholic Europe alike: but it also came under sharp attack. The great Calvinist scholar Joseph Scaliger was appalled by Lipsius's numerous abrupt phrases and minimal use of conjunctions: "I do not know," he plaintively told the students who lodged with him, "what sort of Latin this is."[29] Scaliger set out systematically to extirpate trendy Tacitisms from the Latin written by students at Leiden—and thereby found himself in agreement, unexpectedly, with the Jesuit pedagogues he loathed, who insisted that Lipsius's "Laconism" was not the right way to attain the stylistic qualities of wit and paradox that they thought students should strive for.[30]

Not only the niceties of style, but also the structure of the curriculum as a whole, came in for sharp debate. Reformers like the Protestant martyr Peter Ramus and his followers, who attained considerable influence in Cambridge as well as Paris, urged educational authorities and students to take up a new, pragmatic version of dialectic and rhetoric. The teacher should treat every literary text, including the poems of Horace and the Psalms of David, as a systematic argument, which could be reduced in principle to a series of logical statements. Regent masters in Paris collèges and continental universities found this a splendid way to teach the skills of argumentation through the literary classics. They presumably considered it useful, as well as witty, to treat "Dulce et decorum est pro patria mori" ("It is sweet and fitting to die for one's country"), Horace's often-quoted exhortation to spill one's gore in a patriotic way, as simply one move in an argumentative game.[31]

But the Ramists also ran into opposition in many quarters, in part from Aristotelians who detested Ramus's effort to alter the traditional structures of dialectic and rhetoric. Many humanists insisted that literary texts should be analyzed in a literary way, that the teacher should pay more attention to metaphors and turns of speech than to structure and forms of argument. The pamphlet wars that blazed up wherever Ramus and his followers went illuminate their progress rather as exploding land mines illuminate the progress of an army attacking entrenched positions: resistance almost everywhere was vigorous. The survival of the ideal of eloquence, in short, did not remotely imply unanimity about its content. Indeed, the heat and extent of the debate are the best indicator of the vitality humanism retained, especially in those cases, as in France around 1600, when divisions about the nature and purpose of eloquence corresponded to a large extent with political and religious divides. When the Gallican lawyers of the Paris *parlement* and the Jesuits they briefly drove from Paris disagreed about the proper models of Latin prose, they also debated alternate political and social ideals of life. Not even the sharpest humanistic debates of the fifteenth century over the virtues of republics and monarchies reveal deeper divisions over principle than those that took place, still in Latin and still taking classical writers as their main figures, two centuries later.[32]

For all the range of argument that attended problems of style and substance, however, a single, visibly homogeneous model for the core of humanistic learning took shape in institutions as apparently different as the medieval colleges of the University of Paris and the new Protestant "illustrious academies" that sprang up in Strasbourg, Altdorf, and other cities that wanted the prestige and income that an institution of higher learning could bring, as well as a safe and reliable training for their sons. In most of these institutions—as opposed to new environments like the French court, where new models of vernacular eloquence flourished—the teaching of rhetoric centered, much as it had in the fifteenth century, on the analysis of works of Cicero. Within his canon, however, the emphasis shifted, moving from the orations which had fascinated the civic humanists of fifteenth-century Italy to the letters. Written rather than oral texts, apparently personal and informal rather than public and theatrical, these offered the student a vast range of models of prose rather than the highly formal one of Cicero's oratory. They also seemed more appropriate models for young men whose future tasks would involve far more document preparation than public speaking. Accordingly, students at early stages of their education, from Strasbourg to Rome, spent large amounts of time reading, translating, and imitating Cicero's letters. Humanism modernized itself, responding to practical needs with pragmatic, sensible solutions.

One side of this modernization took the form of an increasing attention to material objects, both as found in nature and as reworked by man. This interest grew in part from classical texts. No text fascinated the humanists more, from the fifteenth century onward, than Pliny's *Natural History,* and this great encyclopedic work, though itself mostly compiled from written sources, offered a wealth of information about the development of sculpture and the range of natural objects and species. Though Pliny remained the richest source of information about the arts in antiquity, Aristotle's works on animals and Theophrastus's on plants, translated into Latin in the mid-fifteenth century, complemented it with further material, much of it derived from direct inspection of the natural world. Humanists collected gems, fragments of ancient sculpture, and modern art objects, shells and fossils. Connoisseurship became almost as central a skill of the educated young man as Latin eloquence.[33]

By the middle of the sixteenth century, humanist households regularly contained not only a library but a collection, the contents of which were as painstakingly sorted and labeled as the contents of the owner's schoolbooks had been sorted and copied into notebooks: in 1543, for example, the historian and collector Count Wilhelm Werner von Zimmern showed Sebastian Münster, who visited him in his castle of Herrenzimmern bei Rottweil, "an enormous treasury of texts, especially the historians, an almost infinite number of antiquities, golden and silver vessels shut away in a niche in the wall, a stock of simples adorned with varied confections."[34] The Paduan antiquary Lorenzo Pignoria was one of relatively few Italian scholars of the period around 1600 to enjoy the whole-hearted respect of humanists throughout the Protestant north as well as patrons in his own region. He had not only a fine library, which included manuscripts of Dante and Boccaccio, humanist Latin poetry, and a treatise on pumping machines, but also a museum stocked with coins, medals, shells, busts, papyri, and a whole "iconotheca," or collection of paintings of illustrious men—not to mention a graphic work by Dürer "showing the image of a woman, of wonderful skill"—*Melencolia I,* perhaps?[35] His collection differed only in extent, not in character, from that of his older contemporary Joseph Scaliger, who doted on the headless bird of paradise he had been given by Dutch merchants in an uncharacteristic fit of generosity, used drawings he had made as a young man in Italy and southern France to introduce his students to the study of antiquities, and found mummies and papyri rivetingly interesting. The better-endowed or better-supported colleges had museums of their own. The Jesuit Collegio Romano of the mid-seventeenth century, for example, swarmed with the giant bones and wooden model obelisks collected or fabricated by its dominant intellectual figure, Athanasius Kircher. Not only the critics of traditional book-learning, in sum, took a serious interest in the material world. Humanists did so as well. They ventured, with varying success, to interpret relics of the ancient world, like the Egyptian cult object known as the *Mensa Isiaca* and the pagan temples of ancient Scandinavia, which were not explicitly described in preserved texts. And they compiled exhaustive studies of the development of the visual arts in antiquity, which made clear their belief that the educated young Latinist must be able to discuss the work of artists as well as that of writers, in detail and with a sophisticated conceptual apparatus. In this belief—if not often in their own abilities as draughtsmen and architects—the late humanists showed themselves the direct heirs of Leon Battista Alberti.[36]

No single discipline shows the interplay of tradition and innovation in late humanism more clearly than history. On the one hand, humanist teachers and historians around 1600 clearly saw themselves as the heirs of the Greek and Roman statesmen who had defined what history should be. They agreed, that is, that the historian should try to form readers for public life. To that end he should deal, above all, with political events of great importance. From these he should extract for especially precise treatment examples of good and evil, effective and ineffective conduct, which his readers would be able to imitate (or avoid) in their turn. The way of precepts, so the humanists endlessly repeated, was long and winding; but the way of examples was short and direct. *Exempla* not only revealed which principles worked and which did not, but impressed them on the malleable mind and memory of the young reader with a force no general presentation could attain—and gave him a stock of quotations and allusions which would serve him in good stead when he had to speak or write on public issues.[37]

These convictions, firmly based on Livy and Polybius, echoed from one end of the humanist Republic of Letters to the other. Philip Sidney expressed them with characteristic force in the letter to his brother Robert: "In that kind you have principally to note the examples of virtue and vice, with their good or evil successes, the establishment or ruins of great estates, with the causes, the time, and circumstances of the laws then written of, the enterings and endings of wars, and therein, the stratagems against the enemy and the discipline upon the soldier; and thus much as a very historiographer. Besides this, the historian makes himself a discourser for profit, and an orator, yea a poet, sometimes for ornament."[38] Sidney took his own advice: to prepare for his embassy to the court of the Holy Roman Emperor in 1577, he spent some time reading the first three books of Livy with the erudite Gabriel Harvey. Harvey later recalled that "the courtier Philip Sidney and I had privately discussed these three books of Livy, scrutinizing them so far as we could from all points of view, applying a political analysis . . . Our consideration was chiefly directed at the forms of states, the conditions of persons, and the qualities of actions."[39] In doing so he showed himself, for all his renowned dash and spontaneity, as docile a follower of humanist tradition as the Nuremberg scholar Philip Camerarius, son of the famous Joachim, who liked to tell the students of the Altdorf Academy that "when one considers the past and pays attention to the present, one can draw reasonable conclusions about the future. The present is a riddle, which time solves."[40] In offering this advice, so everyone knew, Camerarius simply gave voice to the traditional beliefs of the Roman historians about the value of their craft. "Historia magistra vitae" ("history, the teacher of life")—the age-old doctrine, expressed with matchless clarity by Cicero, that the texture of human life remained fundamentally the same through the centuries, so that examples from any good historian should serve for imitation by an intelligent later reader—lived on in the lecture courses about how to read the historians held by thinkers who diverged as radically as Agostino Mascardi, ex-Jesuit professor of eloquence at Genoa and Rome, and Degory Wheare, professor of history at Oxford.

Yet the study of ancient history was anything but static in the crucial years around 1600. In fact, it underwent a series of changes, as scholars and teachers made a deliberate effort to adjust their practices to fit the immediate needs of their pupils and patrons. Already at the beginning of the sixteenth century, Niccolò Machiavelli and Francesco Guicciardini had called into question the traditional humanist justifications for studying history. Both had insisted that one should draw only pragmatic, not moral lessons from the ancient past. Machiavelli had implicitly questioned the ability of modern readers to follow even the former, since all individuals tended to follow one line of behavior, even if it proved unproductive, and to misread their own situation as well. Guicciardini explicitly complained that even Machiavelli had gone wrong by concentrating so exclusively on the lessons of Roman history, since the modern world hardly resembled the one the ancient historians had described: "How wrong it is," he complained, "to cite the Romans at every turn."[41]

Two generations later, many humanists adapted as their own the fundamental points of what had been intended as a critique of their predecessors. Marc-Antoine Muret, whose lectures on classical texts at the Collegio Romano attracted as much attention as his influential earlier ones had in Paris, admitted that "there are very few republics in our days." From this, however, he drew a novel conclusion: not that one should cease to study Roman history, but rather that one should transfer one's interests from the lost republic, evoked with such nostalgic eloquence by Livy, to the early empire, analyzed with such searching irony by Tacitus. In the empire, as in the modern world, he reasoned, most states were ruled by an individual: to that extent at least, he told his pupils in 1580, the "state of affairs under the emperors comes closer to resembling our times than that which obtained when the people ruled. Though, thanks be to God," he went on with his characteristic irony, "our age has no Tiberiuses, Caligulas, Neros, it is still useful to know how even under them there lived good and prudent men." After all, he reflected, the art of dissimulation was essential to anyone living in a modern court: "Princes often have many qualities which a good man cannot praise, but can conceal and pass over in silence. Those who do not know how to wink at these both endanger themselves and generally make the princes worse."[42] Tacitus, in short, could teach the art of silence so essential to life in the court of a Philip II or the curia of a Gregory XIII. More generally, close attention to the context in which a given historian had written could overcome the objection that examples were too generalized to be instructive.

What Muret offered as the justification for lecturing on Tacitus became the program for two generations of politically minded humanists. Justus Lipsius, the brilliant young Fleming who learned—and plagiarized—much from Muret during his early years in Rome, brought back with him to the Low Countries the notion that historical training must rest on "similitudo temporum"—on the careful, analytical establishment of parallels between countries and periods. He made it the foundation of his brilliant courses on Roman history and antiquities, in which he explained exactly how one could and should revive the secrets of the Roman army in modern times. Lipsius's most brilliant pupil, Maurice of Nassau, Prince of Orange, put these lessons into practice as he created the disciplined, professional land army that kept the northern Netherlands free from Spain—even though his teacher had to explain to him, repeatedly, that he had in mind not a slavish revival of Rome's now obsolete military technology, but a systematic effort to drill soldiers to the same level of discipline and cohesion, in small units, that had made the Romans so formidable. Lectures and disputations on pragmatic politics, centering on Tacitus and emphasizing how hard it was to draw the marrow from the bones of his uniquely clipped style, made Leiden the largest and most fashionable university in northern Europe for the first half of the seventeenth century.[43] Even after Lipsius himself moved to Louvain and returned to the Catholic faith he had been born in, the tradition of politically engaged, contextually sensitive teaching of history that he founded was carried on by men like Daniel Heinsius, who deeply appreciated Tacitus's ability, comparable to that of Thucydides, to grasp and express the real secrets of state action. Throughout Europe, humanist historians could claim to be the reigning experts in a subject of immediate and obvious contemporary relevance. They had better access than anyone else to the *arcana imperii* of the ancient world, the secret rules by which—as Clapmarius explained in his most famous book—the Roman Empire had really functioned.[44] It is not surprising, therefore, that Kepler, when called upon to offer precise political advice to erudite, touchy patrons like the Emperor Rudolf II, preferred to do so not as an "astrologus" but as a "politicus"—an experienced reader and interpreter of Tacitus and other classics of political history.[45]

Late humanist students of history, however, did not confine themselves to pragmatics, to meeting the charge of statesmen that their ways of reading were too innocent. In the first place, they also set out to make the study of the ancient historians methodical and systematic, in ways that Machiavelli and Guicciardini—and perhaps Muret as well—never anticipated. Alongside the study of historical texts flourished a second branch of humanist scholarship, equally classical in origin but often far more technical in character: antiquarianism, the systematic effort to reconstruct the institutions and mores, religions and rituals of the Greek and Roman world, which Alberti, Flavio Biondo, and others had refounded in the fifteenth century. The antiquaries of the sixteenth century compiled enormous corpora, of ancient objects and inscriptions, which they organized not in chronological or geographical but in systematic order. Inscriptions were arranged, first in notebooks and then in printed editions, and carefully indexed, to illustrate not examples of good and evil conduct but permanent features of ancient societies: religion and ritual, family relations and parental affection, styles of patronage and forms of priestly brotherhood. Antiquities became essential to the study of ancient history, which they enlivened and enriched. Illustrations of objects could give a vivid, almost three-dimensional reality to what would otherwise have remained pale and unconvincing descriptions of gladiatorial combat or the making of encampments.[46]

The antiquarian enterprise became a standard support to historical research and teaching. Lipsius, for example, not only lectured on Tacitus at Leiden, but drew from Polybius's famous analysis in Book VI of his *Histories* and a wealth of complementary sources a coherent reconstruction of the Roman army, which he presented first to his Leiden students, as well as to his pupil Maurice of Nassau, and then to the readers of his *De militia Romana* (1596). The French jurist François Hotman urged his students to learn Roman antiquities by studying Cicero, whom he explicated to them with such success that a German baron who came to him in 1557 barely able to utter a word of Latin produced his own book on Roman families two years later.[47]

Though the marriage between history and antiquarianism proved hard at first to consummate, it was eventually more fertile than those who served as witnesses had expected. Traditionally, humanists saw the ancient historians as privileged witnesses to the history of Greece and Rome. They offered corrections for textual errors and even, occasionally, for factual ones, but made no effort to replace the narratives of Livy or Tacitus with new ones. But the antiquarian looked for kinds of information about the past that ancient historians had offered only in passing. The categories he used in compiling a collection of inscriptions, for example, were systematic rather than moral or pragmatic, and aimed at reconstructing the basic institutions of a past society rather than emulating the great deeds of its leaders.[48] Gradually, however, some Renaissance antiquaries came to see that this approach represented something of a challenge to the reigning one. Lipsius, for instance, urged the student to make himself notebooks for reading history, which he should divide into the same categories as he would have divided a notebook of inscriptions: everything that he read which bore on the beliefs or rituals, magistracies or priesthoods, military insignia or gladiatorial games of the Greeks or Romans should be entered under those heads. He also suggested that the student compile notes on fine examples. But this bow to tradition does not conceal the radicalism of his approach. In effect, Lipsius accepted that the ancient historians should not enjoy a more privileged status than other remains of the ancient world. All of them, literary texts and stone inscriptions alike—should be submitted to the same forms of analysis. All of them should be forced, that is, to yield an analysis of ancient history quite unlike that to be found in any ancient writer. For only thus, said Lipsius, anticipating the much later scholars who spoke of a "hermeneutic circle," could one hope to understand texts that merely referred to, but did not explain in detail, the mores and institutions of the societies they described.[49]

Other humanists challenged the limits of traditional historical method at other points. The Roman antiquaries Carlo Sigonio and Onofrio Panvinio and northern polymaths like Scaliger and the well-named chronologer Joannes Temporarius agreed that one could not derive a full and accurate chronology of ancient history, a firm backbone of facts and dates, from any preserved source. They set out to use Roman monuments, the fragments of Greek and Jewish historians, and the data of the new astronomy to rebuild this lost structure. And they succeeded not only in creating a new and fashionable discipline—one known for making bold hypotheses about history and myth, Egyptian dynasties and Jewish kingdoms—but also in calling into question the accuracy and authority of the traditional narratives of biblical and classical history.[50] In the hands of Scaliger and Temporarius, Romulus disappeared from world history, and Moses threatened to follow him.[51] Still others, like the influential satirist John Barclay, argued that the historian should concern himself not with technical details but with the larger question of identifying the "genius," or spirit, which had inspired the writers and artists, politicians and generals of each distinct historical period—much as a different natural "genius" should be identified and studied by the well-informed and intelligent traveler.[52] History, in other words, a preeminent discipline of the Latin-writing, learned citizens of the late humanist Republic of Letters, was alive, flourishing and even rife with sophisticated discussion. No wonder, then, that other disciplines flourished as well: that the Latin writers of a relatively backward country, England, produced substantial contributions to virtually every literary and scientific, philosophical and historical genre known in the time of Elizabeth I and James I.[53] Humanism lived, deep into the age of science.

6

Civic Humanism and
Scientific Scholarship
at Leiden

ℐN 1619 that intrepid traveler James Howell visited Leiden to see the university. He was not impressed. True, he appreciated the faculty, with its many scholars of European reputation. "Apollo," he admitted, "hath a strong influence here." But he found the buildings laughable by comparison with the great stone colleges that had transformed Oxford since the mid-sixteenth century: "Here are no Colleges at all, God-wot . . . nor scarce the face of an University." And he found the climate and situation no laughing matter: "The Heaven here has always some Cloud in his Countenance, and from this grossness and spissitude of Air proceeds the slow nature of the Inhabitants."[1] Thirty years before, Fynes Moryson had been more impressed by the lectures, but he too had criticized the "ruinous College" where the estates of Holland maintained poor scholars and public plays and festivals "poorely" represented the Spanish siege that preceded the founding of the university.[2] Twenty years later, John Evelyn found even more to say against the "college and schools, which are nothing extraordinary," and the so-called magnificus Professor who accepted a fee of one rixdollar for taking Evelyn's oath and entering him as a student of the university.[3]

Yet the view from England was parochial, then as now. Throughout the seventeenth and eighteenth centuries most continental scholars saw Leiden as the greatest of their universities. German polyhistors wrote doggerel about that Parnassus of late humanism:

Wo der Phoenix aller Zeiten
Scaliger, der Wunder-Mann,
Und der ihm stund an der Seiten,
Lipsius hat viel gethan,
Und auch derer Creaturen,
Mehr als Menschliche Naturen.[4]

Even French *philosophes* respected this one institution of the ancien régime. The *Encyclopédie* itself called Leiden "the first Academy in all of Europe."[5] And students from the entire Protestant world—England and Scotland as well as Sweden and Prussia—ignored the snide English travelers and crowded into Leiden's few lecture halls and cramped lodging houses.

It is easy enough to account for individuals' divergent reactions. All universities are Rorschach blots. Their buildings, their statutes, and their customs evoke radically different evaluations from their visitors. Take, for example, the Leiden anatomy theater—that famous circular room, decorated in lurid Mannerist style with articulated skeletons and grinning skulls, where sixty human bodies, male and female, were dissected publicly in the twenty-two years after it was built in 1593. The English Baconian Evelyn saw this as an agglomeration of interesting natural objects and man-made implements, rich in that fascinating detail which obsessed philosophers of his ilk:

I was much pleased with a sight of their anatomy-school, theatre and repository adjoining, which is well furnished with natural curiosities; skeletons, from the whale and elephant to the fly and spider, which last is a very delicate piece of art, to see how the bones (if I may so call them of so tender an insect) could be separated from the mucilaginous parts of that minute animal. Amongst a great variety of other things, I was shown the knife newly taken out of a drunken Dutchman's guts. . . . The pictures of the chirurgeon and his patient, both living, were there.[6]

The German poet Andreas Gryphius, later to be celebrated for his tragedies, those magnificent six- and seven-hour spectacles of dazzling erudition and ghoulish obscurity, read a different lesson into the natural wonders that the Dutch displayed: "He found such delight in the study [of anatomy] that he himself undertook some dissections. And who would not be delighted to see in the human body a quintessence and model of the great world?"[7]

The English vision of a cosmos ruled by law and accessible to human intervention and the German vision of a cosmos ruled by sympathies made visible by physical resemblances could both be projected into the same display, seen in the same year. And while modern prejudices may lead us to imagine that Evelyn's vision reproduced that of his Dutch hosts, recent research has shown that Gryphius in fact teased out the moral and cosmological lessons that the designers of the theater had meant to teach.[8]

But the difficulties of interpreting Leiden University are even more substantial than these first soundings suggest. The further one plunges into early sources and modern histories, the more one despairs of ever emerging from the depths of detail. It seems impossible to lay out a panorama of the university's life and thought that does not falsify perspective and proportion. I do not refer to the difficulties that confront all historians of universities—the clouds of flatulent rhetoric in which administrators hide like squids projecting ink; the taciturnity of teachers and students alike about just what they do all day in study and classroom. Nor do I refer to the standard period problems of the late Renaissance—the sheer obscurity and appalling variety of the curriculum with its efforts to include all texts, all subjects, and all periods in a single vast encyclopedia, and its heroes who could, as Gryphius did while a Privatdozent at Leiden, give a single course that covered "metaphysics, geography, and trigonometry, logic, physiognomics, and tragedy." These obstacles rise up in changing form to terrify any traveler hardy enough to make the voyage up the river of sources and opinions to the dark and lurking realities of the early modern university.[9]

Leiden presents its own special obstacles to the historian's progress. The sources are so rich, the conclusions that historians have drawn from them so varied, that the scholar is more likely to feel surfeited than satiated after making a meal of them.[10] Most historians have singled out the modern and progressive aspects of the university for emphasis. They have pointed to its botanical garden, its anatomy theater, its observatory, and its laboratories. They have emphasized the university's desire to foster advanced research as well as traditional teaching—its willingness to pay two great scholars, Joseph Scaliger and Claude Saumaise, not to teach but simply to give "reputation and luster" to the university's name by their presence and their publications. And they have zealously collected rich evidence to suggest that the faculty was as innovative in its thinking as in its institutional setting. They have called attention to the development of new subjects with a bearing on Holland's commercial expansion—above all, Oriental languages and international law. They have laid great stress on the faculty's sympathy for liberal traditions in thought and research—above all, the efforts of Paul Merula and Dominicus Baudius, guided in part by Scaliger, to publish vital documents about Erasmus's life, to defend his Christian orthodoxy, and to perpetuate his brand of Christian humanist scholarship.[11] They have savored the satires on orthodox bigotry and simple dullness that Leiden professors produced in some abundance. And indeed, one can still derive amusement from Petrus Cunaeus's rich mockery of the theologians' efforts to impose dogmatic positions about unknowable points on all other scholars and Daniel Heinsius's imaginative parody of the grammarians' pedantic concentration on minute points of grammar at the expense of larger ones of meaning (the latter takes the form of an imaginary confrontation between the Athenians at the time of the Persian Wars, trying to make sense of the Delphic oracle's instruction to trust their wooden walls, and a grammarian who offers to clear the oracle up by parsing it, word for word).[12] And they have enumerated dozens of the most innovative Europeans of the late sixteenth and seventeenth centuries, from the lawyer Hugo Grotius through natural scientists such as Willebrord Snellius and Simon Stevin, Descartes and Galileo, to poets such as Gryphius and Heinsius, who lived, taught, or at least published their works in the Batavian Helicon.[13] Such evidence, all of it valid, seems to substantiate Wilhelm Dilthey's imposing judgment: "Leiden became the first university in a modern sense. For the distinguishing mark of such a university is the combination of teaching with independent research as an express purpose of the university's operation. . . . More was done for the progress of the sciences here than in any other place in Europe."[14]

But historians of a different and newer stripe have hacked quite different paths through the facts and documents. They have drawn attention to the fencing school that occupied as much space as—and was probably open more hours a week than—the legendary library on the floor above it; to the vernacular-language engineering school opened by Stevin in 1600; to the strong curricular emphasis on politics and warfare. Leiden was less a unique center for advanced research than a supremely successful late Renaissance academy of the type run by every pedagogue from the Jesuits to the Puritans—the pragmatic upper-class academy designed to turn out tough, literate, new-model officers for the new-model armies and states of the seventeenth century. They have used these severely practical considerations to explain the vast numbers of otherwise ordinary young men—11,076 between 1626 and 1650, more than half of them foreigners—who chose Leiden rather than the physically grand but intellectually old-fashioned colleges of Oxford and Cambridge.[15] And they have identified as the normal Leiden student not the eager young intellectuals such as Gryphius, who stayed for years, read widely, and even taught, but those anonymous and boisterous young German students of applied mathematics who celebrated the Dutch defeat of the English fleet in 1666 by sailing through the town's canals on a barge, setting off ingenious fireworks, and shouting "Vivant Batavi." Normal Leiden students very likely took as much interest in their individual duels and drinking sprees as in intellectual pursuits.[16]

Still others have battered their way into the forbidding premises of the theological faculty. They have discovered that most Hebrew and New Testament scholarship in Leiden was designed not as an inquiry into "wie es eigentlich gewesen" but as a set of tools for training orthodox theologians.[17] They have listened with admirable patience to the debates of Arminians and Gomarists about the being and nature of God and man's ability to know him, and they have discovered a substantial persistence of Thomist and Scotist methods and attitudes, especially among those who held some natural knowledge of God to be allotted to rational adults.[18] They have found allies among the historians of the liberal arts—notably the historians of science, who have revealed that the Aristotelian cosmos was alive and well in seventeenth-century philosophy teaching—and have shown that by no means all Leiden scientists promoted observation and experiment.[19] They have suggested, accordingly, that Leiden and Oxford were not all that far apart in the intellectual map of Baroque Europe. And it is hard to resist their contentions wholeheartedly when one eavesdrops on the massed sages of the faculties of philosophy and medicine debating about whether suspected witches should be tied up and thrown into bodies of water—and condemned if they floated. True, one constantly sees the telltale signs of Dutch calmness and humanity even among the theologians. They explained the tendency of suspected witches to float in simple, natural terms. Many suspects suffered from melancholy and were therefore flatulent; the gases they produced, rather than the repugnance of the water into which they were thrown, were what made them float.[20] But most of these men clearly still lived in a solid and comfortable Aristotelian universe, perfect above the moon's sphere and corruptible below, with four elements, seven planets moved by solid spheres, and scripture a full and perfect source of information about life, the universe, and everything.

Thanks to this realization—and to the growing reaction against Whig histories of ideas—a number of Leiden scholars have been reevaluated by historians of the disciplines they practiced. Georg Hornius, for example, an influential historian, appears as a prototypically modern thinker in Adalbert Klempt's influential book of 1960, *Die Säkularisierung der universalhistorischen Auffassung*. After all, Hornius's *Arca Noae (Noah's Ark)* of 1666, a tiny but elaborate manual of world history, included not just the traditional four ancient monarchies but also China and the Meso-American civilizations. Evidently this Latin-writing professor had learned much from the Dutch sailors whose exploits he praised in his dedicatory letter—so Klempt argued. In fact, however, Erich Hassinger has pointed out that Hornius drew his information from classical writers wherever possible, even where the merchants had refuted or amended what they had to say and the Amsterdam atlas makers had incorporated the newest information in their maps. His history, moreover, enfolds even its novel contents in the traditional story of Noah's ark and Noah's progeny—as is clear from its title page, where the four beasts of the book of Daniel, the traditional symbols of the Four Monarchies, engage in a scramble for possession of the globe, which hangs illogically but vividly in the sky above Noah's ark. Not all the news was fit to teach, then, even in mid-seventeenth-century Leiden.[21]

In recent years, happily, both Dutch and foreign students of the university have tried to synthesize these different interpretations fairly—to accept the apparent paradoxes and contradictions rather than to explain them away. In the splendid quatercentenary festschriften of 1975 and in numerous monographs, they have begun to portray an institution at once cosmopolitan and provincial, oriented toward research and dedicated to pedagogy, innovative and traditional. It is in this revisionist spirit that I try to put some of Leiden's early teachers and institutions back into the busy streets in which they flourished.[22]

To begin with the city and its larger setting, the province of Holland, both were caught up in one of the greatest—and longest—political upheavals in modern European history. The provinces of the north, with Holland as their leader, slid into revolution against their Spanish overlord, Philip II, from the 1560s onward. The bitter and self-assured Calvinist missionaries detested the equally bitter and self-assured Catholic king, who hoped to use his inquisition and his superb armies to wipe them out. The aristocrats and urban patricians, rich and tolerant, were as often Catholic as Calvinist in their sympathies, but they too loathed Philip, for the style as much as the substance of his regime. They disliked the rising toll of burned heretics, the imposition of new taxes, and the violation of old privileges. And they hated the austere and distant demeanor of that overlord who never left Spain, never laughed, and built his castle in the image of the gridiron on which his favorite saint was fried. The urban poor, periodically reduced to desperation by economic hardships and food shortages, were ready to riot when provoked or repressed. Unstable alliances took shape, never crystallizing, never quite dissolving. Cities were forced into rebellion, and in Holland, above all, they proved able to resist Spanish sieges. Leiden's university, the first in the north, was founded in 1575 as part of the rituals of celebration that attended the citizens' hard-won victory over the Spanish—a victory obtained by opening the dykes and flooding the fields. The founding, then, was a political as well as an intellectual event, even though the edge was slightly taken off it by the fact that the university was at once equipped with a forged charter in which King Philip was made to express his pleasure in the new enterprise—and to authenticate it with a genuine-looking seal.[23]

After 1575, immigrants poured in, particularly Protestant refugees from the south. Capital and skill came with them. The population of Leiden rose from around 12,000 in 1581 to around 45,000 in 1622. The city became one of the industrial centers of Europe, rivaling Lyons in manufacturing productivity and threatening Amsterdam's commercial hegemony. Leiden was the center of the Dutch wool industry. It made clocks and lenses. It supported fifty to sixty printers at a given time. In short, it was new, rich, and vulgar. And this peculiar combination of circumstances also helped to shape the new university.[24]

On the one hand, the city did not expand beyond its medieval walls until 1610, and despite that and later expansions it remained desperately crowded. The price of land became extortionate, and space for new buildings was almost impossible to obtain. No wonder, then, that Leiden professors bitterly complained about the noise, squalor, and crowding of their surroundings—so inadequately represented by the contemporary engravings, which show an orderly, cultivated agrarian world outside the walls and an equally orderly inhabited world of houses within them.[25]

No wonder, either, that the university never tried to assume a physical form as grand as those of the late Renaissance colleges of Oxford and Cambridge—or, indeed, Altdorf and Helmstedt. Leiden had impressive buildings—the city hall with its richly decorated facade and its churches with their vast windows, fanciful spires, and chimes carefully not synchronized, so that some Leiden church rang the quarter-hour at any moment—as they still do. But educational funds were spent on salaries, which could win results and thus enhance the university's standing, rather than on bricks and mortar, which could not be effectively deployed.

On the other hand, the fact that students and faculty had to lodge in the town rather than live in separate quarters—the fact that university life could never be sealed off from urban life—had radical consequences of a different sort. A third of the professors, often the most prominent ones, came from foreign countries, above all France and Germany. Yet they had to deal with Dutch culture and society. Teaching in Leiden required learning of an informal but hardly unimportant kind, an involuntary Berlitz immersion course in the mores of a very unusual society, one that struck many outsiders as riven by tensions and contradictions. The Dutch houses, still familiar to us from the painted world of Vermeer, gleamed with the paint and varnish needed to protect them from the corrosive moistness of the air. But Dutch bodies went unwashed even at meals. And the Dutch way of handling human waste seemed to flout the otherwise basic preoccupation with keeping public and private spaces clean. According to Moryson, "At Leyden young wenches of 12 or 13 yeares age, after 9 of the Clocke in the morning, shamed not ordinarily to doe those neceessityes of nature in the open and fayre streetes, which our women will not be seene to doe in private houses."[26] The men, for their part, disfigured the town's two great churches by urinating at their doors, twenty at a time, while the congregation left on Sundays.[27] Dutch commercial honesty put the rest of Europe to shame; Dutch greediness and reserve made relations between sons and fathers, husbands and wives take place in what seemed a colder and less intimate key than anywhere else. The Dutch saved something every year, whatever hardships they had to undergo in order to do so, and they thus sustained their heavy taxes. But half the population of Leiden lived by seasonal work and needed a dole of food every year to survive. No European society set more store by reserve and decorum in adults. But Dutch children ran wild in the streets, howling insults at the students, and their parents would beat anyone who resisted them.[28]

The confrontation with this alien society naturally left indelible marks on the university and its members. The heavy drinking normal in Holland, for example, depleted the ranks of the faculty in both the short term (as when Daniel Heinsius's students had to post a sign reading *Heinsius non legit hodie propter hesternam crapulam*—"Heinsius is too hung over to teach today") and the long term (as when alcoholism killed off Gerard Tuning, who died of apoplexy while riding his carriage *bene potus, ut dicebatur,* and Dominicus Baudius).[29] It also shocked foreigners. Scaliger, attending a doctoral promotion only a month after his arrival in Leiden in 1593, had as a colleague Everard Bronckhorst, who recalled, "I drank rather a lot, so much that I vomited; may God forgive me." (Three months later Bronckhorst suffered a three-day-long hangover after another party; he did not swear off drinking with students until the city guards shot a fellow partygoer at his side in 1607.)[30] No wonder that Scaliger, for all his love and admiration for Leiden, bitterly complained about the drunken Dutchmen who disturbed him at work and at rest: "my neighbors shout, I can't hinder them; they drink from early morning on a fast day."[31]

More serious shocks arose from the fault lines where different cultural and economic groups rubbed against one another in city and university, each trying to establish control, if not hegemony. The power of the predikants made itself felt in the university's emphasis on theology, the only field whose students had two tiny colleges to live in, the States' College and the Walloon College, and scholarships to live on. The provision of theologians and preachers to serve the Protestant cause—so one local official said in the 1590s—was the secret purpose for which the entire university was founded.[32] Yet the power—and very different goals and desires—of the local patriciate had as great an impact. Janus Dousa, a local nobleman who had made a great splash in the bracing waters of Parisian literary circles, knew the high talk of the great world, and had an international reputation as poet and philologist, led the city's defense against the Spanish. He and the other curators made certain to appoint scholars of distinction, from other countries when they had to. They resisted the clerics' demands for control over every level of schooling and insisted that the arts faculty must offer the high level of training in history and rhetoric needed to fit the local elite for its political and military functions. And even the earliest sketches of the university's curriculum reflect the strong desire of these patrons to produce statesmen as well as clerics.[33] Thus some of Leiden's apparent contradictions can be economically explained, though not in economic terms. They stem from the conflict of well-defined groups, all powerful but none dominant, all wishing to manipulate the curriculum and appointments.

Naturally, neither preachers nor patricians can simply be dismissed as simpleminded followers of a group line. They were complex individuals, whose decisions cannot be accounted for by simple schemata. More important, they gradually influenced one another in complicated and subtle ways. The patrician humanists who defended scientific independence and theological diversity as curators also pored over the university's accounts with what now looks like a fine lower-middle-class attention to petty details. They demanded that professors of great distinction account for every absence from class and pay fines for those unexcused by vital business elsewhere, admittedly a reasonable course of action when the cause of the absence was a hangover. At one point they even censured a famous and well-established professor, Johannes Meursius, because his "writing of many books" *(het schrijven van veel boucken)* had interfered with his teaching and caused enrollments in his Greek course to fall.[34] Meanwhile, predikants took as much pride as curators in the addition of great men such as Scaliger and Claudius Salmasius to the faculty.

The most violent interaction between the two sides took place during the religious crisis of 1618–19. Two of the three curators were dismissed and replaced by men who favored the predikants and Maurice of Nassau. Arminian professors were also dismissed, though some—such as Cunaeus—rode out the storm by promising insincerely to apologize for their errors, and others eventually found themselves restored to grace—and jobs. The "Genevan Inquisition," as earlier curators called the Calvinist system of control by ministers and lay elders, never won total control, to be sure. But the new Leiden was a quite orthodox institution and, as such, represented a partial victory for what had been only one party in the university's early years.[35] When the young German intellectual Hermann Conring came to Leiden on scholarship in the 1620s, he learned an enormous amount about politics and medicine from his formal teachers. But it was in Amsterdam, not Leiden, that he sensed the existence of a unique *"ingenii libertas"* that made him long to resist his *Ruf* back to Germany and stay forever in Holland.[36] Such experiences warn us not to overestimate Leiden's hospitality for varieties of conduct and opinion.[37]

The most profound interactions between university and city, however, took place at a less formal level. The university always remained—at least in the ideals of its professors—a cosmopolitan institution, part of the Europe-wide, Latin-speaking Republic of Letters. True, from Johan Huizinga on, historians have emphasized that the university helped Holland become the great intellectual intermediary between northern and southern, eastern and western Europe. But they have sometimes done less to follow the impact of this very international university on its very provincial setting.[38] In many ways the university acted as a great cultural syringe, injecting new ideas and cultural forms into what had previously been a narrowly traditional culture. The university was the center of sustained efforts to develop classical genres in Dutch poetry as the French had already done.[39] It was the center of efforts to replace the crude vernacular chronicles of the later Middle Ages with a critical and reflective historiography in Latin. It was the center of efforts to devise a new system of international law to support the commercial and military expansion of Holland in Asia and the New World. A private scholar intimately associated with the university, Petrus Scriverius, offered crucial support to Rembrandt during his early career as a painter in Leiden. Scriverius's learning provided Rembrandt with the first of those classical themes and biblical subjects that set his artistic enterprise off so sharply from the better-known Dutch project of describing man and nature in all their insignificant but gloriously profuse detail.[40] Like patricians and predikants, university and society were locked together in a symbiosis that enriched both parties.

The cross-fertilization of city and university could be traced on many levels and through many sources. But to watch the process at its most complex, we should attend to what the university and most of its visitors agreed was its intellectual core: the work of its great classical philologists, whose rather forbidding portraits—and entirely terrifying bibliographies— are the chief adornment of Meursius's commemorative volume of 1625, *Athenae Batavae*.[41] Justus Lipsius, professor of history and law from 1578 to 1591, and Joseph Scaliger, research scholar from 1593 to 1609, gave Leiden the distinctive reputation it enjoyed until after 1800 as the greatest center in the world for classical studies. We turn now to watching them at work in their chosen city.

Lipsius was himself a Dutchman, from the south. Educated at Louvain and in Italy, he had made his name by the early 1570s as an expert on Roman history and the possessor of an incandescent Latin prose style. In particular, he had made himself *the* expert on the greatest Roman philosopher of the first century C.E., Seneca, and the greatest Roman historian, Tacitus. He had seen that the Roman empire they had known offered a vivid premonitory image of his own time, with its monarchs absolutely corrupted by absolute power and its revolutionaries bent on turning the world upside down. He had shown that sensitive young patricians could learn from Tacitus's cynicism how to read the motives of their masters, and from Seneca's Stoicism how to put up with the situations that resulted. And he had set himself what turned out to be his lifelong tasks: editing these texts critically and explicating them effectively.[42]

In Leiden, Lipsius saw that his palette of skills could make one crucial addition to local resources, cultural and political. He realized that the Dutch, though far superior in seamanship to the Spanish, were inferior on land. Ordinary soldiers lacked skill and discipline, and their leaders, though brave, knew far too little about strategy and tactics. Lipsius decided that his brand of scholarship could supply exactly the tools that the Dutch needed. Going back to Greek texts—above all Polybius's history of Rome—he reconstructed those features of military organization and discipline that made the Romans so superior to their opponents. He praised their uniforms, their diet, their harsh code of military justice, and their clear chains of command. But above all he singled out their ability to deploy their soldiers flexibly in dozens of small cohesive units that could respond rapidly to changes in the situation of a battle.[43]

Lipsius urged the Dutch to adopt the Roman order of battle (and even some features of Roman arms). And his audience took him very seriously indeed. Maurice of Orange, who studied with Lipsius at Leiden, disciplined his soldiers sternly, made them spend their winter months in training, and became the first Dutch commander who could beat the Spanish in the field. The Estates General of the Netherlands took Lipsius's advice and made their soldiers dig their own ditches and raise their own palisades, as the Romans had done. As late as 1595–96, when Lipsius had left Leiden and returned to his original Catholic faith, Maurice was still experimenting with what he had learned from him. Maurice made a troop of soldiers armed as Romans fight another troop armed as Spaniards, to see who would prevail—and then received a sharp message from Lipsius criticizing this absurdly mechanical application of his precepts.

At the same time, Lipsius continued his work in history and philosophy. His *De constantia* of 1584 summed up Stoic ethics for the young aristocrat. His *Politica* of 1589 summed up the lessons of Stoics and historians about politics and warfare. And as a brilliant lecturer as well as a fashionable writer, he did more than anyone else to attract students to the fledgling university (which had started, three years before his arrival, with an enrollment of two!). Leiden, in short, enabled Lipsius to update the enterprise of Renaissance humanism both intellectually and pedagogically, to show that classical sources still provided sure guidance for practical action in this world.[44]

Yet relations between Lipsius and Leiden were more complex than this simple list of facts may suggest. After all, Lipsius himself was no straightforward Protestant academic. In fact, recent work has revealed that he stole others' intellectual property and—worse still by the standards of the time—was a heretic.[45] He changed his religious practices and professions almost as rapidly and easily as he changed his academic jobs. And he saw the last practice as justified, we now know, because for a long time he belonged to a heretical sect, the Family of Love. This group included rich merchants, learned scholars, and illiterate but charismatic prophets. It centered in the great printing and publishing house of Christopher Plantin, who himself lived in Leiden during the 1580s. Its members spread in thin but strangely powerful streams across geographical and confessional borders. One tiny group flourished under the nose of Philip II in the Escorial, a second in Leiden, the intellectual citadel of his Calvinist enemies. All members claimed a direct access to God's commandments. All felt that they could take part in the public ceremonies of any Christian church, since all external acts were secondary to the illumination that burned within them. In Leiden, Lipsius and Plantin heard their prophets explicate the dreams and visions of the Book of Revelation. They went on long walks in the country, and in those private moments they admitted to each other that all religions "have a lot of simulation and concealment, but they are not to be despised, provided they involve no crime, since they are useful to feebler minds. The common people have need of such elementary aids."[46] By coming to Leiden, then, Lipsius not only did his bit to add more stonework to the intellectual fortress of Calvinism but also carved a private niche within it for himself and other spiritualists.

The idyll did not last. Lipsius gradually lost faith both in the military abilities of his aristocratic pupils and in the spiritual powers of Plantin's unlettered prophets. He came under powerful attack from the predikants, who thought that his *De constantia* took a pagan view of providence, and from a noisy liberal, Dirck Volckertsz. Coornhert, who attacked his *Politica* for urging that religious dissenters who disturbed the peace be restrained by force. Lipsius, the moderate and spiritualist, became notorious as the man who told religious and lay authorities to "burn and cut" *(ure et seca)* when confronted by contumacious heretics. Alleging the failure of his health, Lipsius left for Germany in 1591. Soon he reappeared as a Catholic professor in Louvain, where he spent his declining years purging his earlier books to get them off the *Index of Forbidden Books* and writing tracts about wonder-working shrines of the Virgin Mary that had cured pious invalids of such minor ills as blindness and having one leg shorter than the other.[47]

If we now tried to cast a balance—to weigh up the effects of the scholar on the city and the city on the scholar—we would, I think, run directly into difficulties. Was Leiden a favorable or an unfavorable environment? Did it do more to shape or to distort Lipsius's thought? Which was his real self—the secret Leiden liberal or the overt Louvain reactionary? I have no firm answer to these hard questions. And my second exemplary figure, Joseph Scaliger, poses even harder ones.

In some ways, to be sure, Scaliger's case seems the simpler of the two. From his early twenties on, he was a strict and devout Calvinist, closer in theology to the rigorist Franciscus Gomarus (who became his literary executor) than to the liberal Jacobus Arminius.[48] His coming to Leiden marked a natural transition, from private Protestant intellectual (he had taught for only two years at Geneva, long before) to public Protestant leader. And his qualifications for his post were as patent as his religious views. He was a great master of Latin and Greek textual criticism. He was the greatest master of historical chronology, that strange Mannerist discipline, now almost forgotten, that used both astronomical and philological techniques to establish the armature of dates on which all the exemplary events of biblical and classical history must be properly spaced and ordered like beads on a string.[49] Dousa invited him to restore to the university the "noise and brilliance" it had lost when Lipsius departed. When he refused to teach, Dousa and his colleagues gave Scaliger a permanent research fellowship, inviting him to stay in Leiden, supported by a lavish salary, a housing subvention, and tax concessions, while he pursued his research untroubled by the need to give lectures.[50]

Like other high-priced professors, Scaliger proved a disappointment at first. The first book he wrote in Leiden, a Latin panegyric to his supposed ancestors, the della Scala of Verona, backfired; it provoked his Catholic enemies to dig up the documentary evidence to prove that he was no della Scala, despite the purple robe he liked to wear, but the grandson of a manuscript illuminator and scribe named Benedetto Bordon.[51] The book he had brought with him and published with much fanfare after arriving, a treatise on the squaring of the circle, electrified the small and hypersensitive community of mathematicians by claiming that every one of them from Archimedes on had misunderstood the problem and the nature of their science. This too had unexpected—and unfortunate—consequences, since the specialists found it easy to show that many elementary mistakes vitiated Scaliger's arguments.[52] Even Scaliger's well-known aristocratic manners did not always win respect. One early observer wrote to Lipsius, no doubt hoping to please him, that "he is vehement both in praise and in abuse, and often of the same man or thing. Those he calls scoundrels, asses, beasts and ignoramuses today, will be gentleman, learned and erudite another day. And he makes both the praise and the abuse public. Many would be offended had he not become more a figure of fun than a cause of hatred."[53]

Yet Scaliger soon became one of the stately humanists of Leiden. With extraordinary energy, he put out twenty-five hundred folio pages on chronology, which more than restored his eminent position as a scholar. With even more extraordinary prescience, he chose disciples from the native and foreign young. Hugo Grotius had Scaliger's aid when he published—at the age of fifteen—his first major work, an edition of the hideously obscure late-antique encyclopedia by Martianus Capella. Other students included Daniel Heinsius, the most influential critic of Greek tragedy of the seventeenth century; Philip Cluverius, the first great historical geographer; and Thomas Erpenius, the Arabist.[54] Scaliger never did lecture. But he became a well-known figure in Dutch political and cultural life and a celebrity among Leiden students and visitors, just the sort of imposing person who had to be wheeled out when the city guard shot and killed a student in December 1607, and Scaliger's presence—along with a three-hour speech in Latin by his colleague Dominicus Baudius—helped to calm the rest of the students.[55]

Scaliger's most original Leiden creation was a unique but ambitious kind of teaching. What he offered was a direct initiation into research. The signs of this are everywhere evident. In the edition of the fragments—all that survive—of the Roman satirist Lucilius that Dousa's son Franciscus prepared, Scaliger pops up on every other page. He amended verbal corruptions. He explained difficulties of diction and content. He requested what amounted to brief seminar papers which Dousa meticulously produced. In a characteristic passage, Dousa says, "Scaliger suggested to me that this very fine line too should be assigned to Lucilius (its author has hitherto been unknown). Many things conspire to make me agree. First there are traces of archaic Latin . . . like the use of the dative for the ablative. Then there is the matter of chronology."[56] In Scaliger's letters to another favorite student, Janus Wowerius, we see him keeping the firm hand of a dissertation director on a particularly erratic doctorand. When Wowerius proposes to edit the ancient Latin translation by Germanicus of the Greek astronomical poem by Aratus, Scaliger steers him elsewhere at once. His other student Grotius, he explains, has already done a perfect job, and Wowerius's samples of his new text "offer nothing better than or different from Grotius's edition."[57] But Scaliger, like a good Doktorvater, did more than steer his pupil away from terra already cognita. He helped Wowerius enter one of the roughest but richest territories known to early modern or modern philology, the history of scholarship itself—a subject on which Wowerius published an elaborate treatise two years later, which both followed Scaliger's general approach and incorporated his specific suggestions. And like a good doctoral student, Wowerius showed his appreciation by giving Scaliger no credit at all where it was due.[58]

In normal Protestant universities, professors lectured on set texts and students disputed on set questions. Even those students who tried to prove their learning in the humanities normally did so by defending in public a printed dissertation written by their professor, who collected a fee for providing it and often reprinted his students' collected dissertations under his own name. In Leiden, where he had an elite to teach, an assured income, and no trivial lectures to give, Scaliger could cut new pedagogical paths as he liked. No wonder that Dilthey stressed the modernity of the world Scaliger helped to build.

If we examine the preeminent source for Scaliger's informal teaching, the table talk recorded by two of his students between 1603 and 1607, we will see that he did more than assign specific technical tasks. He also presented a new cumulative ideal of knowledge itself. He forecast the great collaborative enterprises of modern classical scholarship, such as the Corpora of Greek and Latin inscriptions, with their epoch-making recovery of the day-to-day life of the ancient world: "There are so many splendid wills and ancient documents in inscriptions . . . if some young man would take the trouble to collect them, and all the letters dispersed everywhere, he would do well. There is a lot in inscriptions."[59]

He suggested some of the deep intellectual problems that the study of the New Testament would pose in the centuries to come, as it established the later origins and undermined the textual reliability of the canon in its received form: "There are more than fifty additions or changes to the New Testament and the Gospels. It's a strange thing, I don't dare to say it. If it were a profane author I would speak of it very differently."[60]

It was Scaliger's work as a chronologer that led him to these conclusions. He assumed, as a good Calvinist, that the chronology in all the Gospels must originally have been the same, that the chronology of Acts must match that of Paul's Epistles. He discovered, as a good scholar, that the texts lacked the harmony that his prejudices had wrongly led him to expect. Accordingly, he came from dogmatic premises to the historically correct conclusion that the New Testament had not been transmitted intact (naturally, he did not guess that the texts had originally disagreed). Teaching by hint and indirection in his chimney corner, Scaliger adumbrated many of the fierce debates that would rend the Republic of Letters for the next century and more.

Yet Leiden provided more than a fertile germ plasm in which the bacilli Scaliger injected could grow and multiply. He took as well as gave. One of his many Leiden projects—to take a simple case first—was a vast index, more than one hundred folio pages long, to the greatest corpus of Greek and Latin inscriptions published in his time (a project in fact carried out by a Heidelberg scholar, Janus Gruter, with Scaliger's epistolary support and direction). Scaliger's meticulous and elegant tool for retrieving the vast banks of information assembled by his colleague gave a clear and systematic order to the religious, historical, and antiquarian contents of thousands of documents. His work has long been praised as the first really modern work of epigraphy. Yet, in fact, Scaliger took both the general form of his indices and much of their specific content from an earlier work that he never mentioned, a manuscript index to an earlier corpus that happened to wind up in Leiden because Dousa bought it in time for Scaliger to use it. Thus very local resources inspired a great international project.[61]

Some of Scaliger's debts to his Dutch milieu were both deeper and more complex than this one. From 1600 to 1606 he worked at the greatest of his historical enterprises, the *Thesaurus temporum (Chronological Treasury)*. In compiling this, he stumbled across a Byzantine world chronicle that yielded up the first genuine sources ever discovered for the history of the ancient Near East. Scaliger became the first scholar for centuries to read the accounts of Babylonian antiquities and Egyptian dynastic history written in Greek in the third century B.C.E. by the Babylonian priest Berosus and the Egyptian priest Manetho. Both works posed serious problems to a good sixteenth-century Calvinist like Scaliger. Berosus made civilization begin when a great fishlike monster, Oannes, climbed out of the ocean and taught men the arts and sciences. Manetho made his thirty-one Egyptian dynasties begin not just before the Flood but before the Creation.[62] Yet Scaliger saw that neither text was simply fraudulent, even if both seemed impossible to explicate. He insisted that both refracted, in mythical form, the true events of early human history that the Bible and the Greek historians had not recorded. And he included both sets of sources in his great book.

Scaliger's new sources sent violent waves rolling across the normally placid waters of European scholarship. For the next century and more, philosophers like Spinoza, theologians like Simon, and scholars like Vico would debate the veracity of these strange texts. The notion that they offered a mythical account of real events—in essence, Scaliger's original solution—gradually prevailed. As Paolo Rossi has shown in a recent book of great importance, these debates provided both much of the impetus and much of the matter for Vico's *New Science* as well as for many lesser books now justly unread.[63]

The curious fact in this sequence of debates is the position Scaliger took in it. For in his earlier chronological work he had devoted almost no attention to figures (like Theseus) and writers (like Hermes Trismegistus) who flourished in what he called the "mythical" period before the Olympic Games began in 776 B.C.E. Unlike most of his contemporaries, he seems to have had little hope of giving such events and people firm dates and places. Myths, accordingly, received almost no attention in his chronological scholarship until be came to Leiden.

What sensitized Scaliger to the historical uses of myth was a local controversy. Throughout the sixteenth century the intellectuals of nearby Frisia had developed an astonishingly detailed and dramatic early history for their province. They argued that three Indian gentlemen, Friso, Saxo, and Bruno, had left their native country in the fourth century B.C.E. They studied with Plato, fought for Philip and Alexander of Macedon, and then settled in darkest Friesland, where they drove off the giants who had previously inhabited northern Europe and founded Groningen. The legend was not unusual, in an age when every monarchy claimed Trojan descent. But around 1600 it sparked criticism, like its British cousin.[64] Ubbo Emmius, whom Scaliger knew and respected, attacked these tales as fabulous.[65] And Suffridus Petri, who had given these stories currency in learned Latin, mounted a brilliant defense. He claimed that the early history of Frisia could have been transmitted in genuine ancient texts now lost and in popular songs—such as the famous *carmina* that had preserved the tales of Roman and German origins in antiquity. And he insisted that even if such sources contained fables, they should be analyzed and purified, not abandoned: "Antiquities are one thing, the fables mixed up with them are another. A good historian should not simply abandon the antiquities because of the fables, but should cleanse the fables for the sake of the antiquities [they contain]."[66] From Petri's wrong but admirably ingenious defense of Frisian legends, which came out just as he attacked Berosus and Manetho, Scaliger took the tolerant and eclectic analytical principles that he applied. Thus a debate literally provincial to the point of marginality—one that Scaliger encountered only because members of the Leiden elite took part in it—produced a vital element of the vast historical structure Scaliger reared. Vico owed something of his concept of the aboriginal giants to the Frisian antiquaries Scaliger had read as well as to the Neapolitan *lazzaroni* he himself knew. For, as Rossi's evidence shows, it was Scaliger's new evidence and his insistence that it be taken seriously that shook European intellectuals' confidence in the primacy of the Bible as an account of man's early history. Had Scaliger not compiled, Vico would never have distilled his peculiar and visionary concoctions; and as we can now see, Scaliger's work rested in a fundamental sense on that of Petri and others.

Scaliger's case also shows the futility of trying to impose neat causal schemes on this crowded but vital city and its learned but lively professors. Only a few morals emerge. In each case interaction took place in two directions, the city shaping its professor and the professor his city. In each case we can trace the interaction only if we abandon the registers of matriculated students and accounts of extracurricular high jinks that preoccupy most historians of education and plunge into the vast and terrifying Latin books that reveal these teachers' goals and methods in detail. In each case, in the end, we learn more from a complex image than from a deceptively simplified road map. City and university, scholar and society, come together in a constantly changing pattern that requires the skills of a choreographer rather than a cartographer to record it. The steps of the dance are complex and involuted, the tune so faint that not all its notes can be recovered. Yet our only hope of understanding the formal intellectual life of early modern Europe in its urban context is to abandon prejudices and formulas, plunge in, and join the dance ourselves.

III

COMMUNITIES
OF LEARNING

7

Printers' Correctors
and the Publication
of Classical Texts

Ꮯᴍᴍꜱ

*I*N THE SPRING of 1585, Henri Estienne took a mournful pleasure in recalling life in the *familia* of his father, Robert. For all his accomplishments as a learned publisher, his recent life had been hard. In the 1550s and 1560s, he had worked, in collaboration with a galaxy of brilliant young poets and scholars, to create a second Hellenic Renaissance. The first edition he published, the *Anacreontea* of 1554, inspired Jean Dorat and others to create a new lyric poetry.[1] His critical text of Aeschylus, produced in collaboration with the great Florentine Hellenist Pier Vettori, had transformed the study of Greek tragedy—and that at a time when critics of many schools were trying with obsessive energy to recreate the ancient theater.[2] His editions of the fragments of Latin poetry and of Greek poetry in dactylic hexameter had revolutionized the study of ancient literature. More recently, however, he had had to witness all the horrors of the French wars of religion. His own safety in Geneva—and the considerable skills he developed as an anti-Catholic polemicist—could not assuage the rage and sorrow he felt when his co-religionists died in their hundreds, while old friends and acquaintances like Jean Dorat denounced the Protestants as ungodly. His magnificent five-volume *Thesaurus* of the Greek language, which remains the foundation of classical Greek lexicography, drove him into bankruptcy. Estienne quarreled with many of the scholars who had once been closest to him, like Joseph Scaliger, and found himself, already aged, compelled to print works on commission for other publishers and to make constant trips in search of business. He became so used to misfortune, in fact, that he developed a discipline for dealing with it: he read letters that he expected to contain bad news only long before or long after he slept and ate.[3]

It is hardly surprising, then, that Estienne's mind turned back to the heroic days of Parisian humanism in the 1530s and 1540s. As he prepared a new text of Aulus Gellius's description of learned life in the Rome of the late second century C.E., he found himself stirred to record, like a modern Gellius, the learned circles he himself had known as a teenager.[4] In those days, he told his son Paul, the female as well as the male members of his father's household had spoken Latin: "Even most of the serving-maids understood most Latin words, and could say many of them (though they sometimes got them wrong). Your grandmother understood anything said in Latin almost as easily as if it had been said in French, unless someone used a relatively rare word. And then here is my surviving sister, your aunt Catherine. She does not need anyone to translate Latin for her. And she can say a good deal in that language herself, and well enough that everyone understands her, even if she sometimes stumbles."[5] None of these women had studied Latin as boys did, with a teacher. Instead, they had learned it "as the French learn French and the Italians learn Italian"—by immersion.[6]

Robert Estienne's publishing house, Henri went on to explain, had provided a unique linguistic and cultural experience for everyone who inhabited it:

> There was a time when your grandfather, Robert Estienne, had a literary team with ten members in his house—and one made up not only of representatives of every nation, but also of speakers of every language. These ten men, some of whom were cultured and some highly cultured, were in part employed as correctors—especially those who prefaced Robert's last edition of his Latin *Thesaurus* with their poems. As they came from various nations, and had a variety of native languages, they used Latin as their common medium of discussion. The serving boys and girls heard some of them at one time, some at another, discussing things which they either knew about or could guess; they also heard them at table, discussing a wide range of things, including those that normally come up at meals. Accordingly, little by little they accustomed themselves to hearing their words, to

such an extent that they could not only understand the majority of the things the correctors said, but also say some things themselves.[7]

Henri and his brother Robert had learned their Latin by the same direct method, since their father and his erudite employees spoke Latin with them, encouraging them to "stammer out," as Henri said, their own first words in the language of learning.[8]

Pure spoken Latin—as Françoise Waquet has recently shown in a remarkable book—was a rare attainment in the sixteenth century, rarer than humanist teachers sometimes liked to admit. Montaigne frightened his famous teachers at the Collège de Guienne in Bordeaux by the precocious fluency he developed as a small child, when his father had decided to have him learn, also, by the direct method. Yet in Estienne's printing house, Latin was as much the common language as in the nearby colleges of the University of Paris. Robert Estienne genuinely was a great printer, one who, according to report, not only employed ten correctors, but also hung his proofs up in public, promising a reward to anyone who could detect typographical errors in them.[9] Henri's account, moreover, rested on his own experience. He had begun to correct Greek texts as a teenager, working with his father on the proofs of Robert's magnificent edition of Dionysius of Halicarnassus, a spectacular example of "les grecs du roi" which appeared in 1547.[10] And Robert Estienne's Parisian printing house, for all the high quality of its staff and the Latinity of their daily conversation, was not the most erudite one of the Renaissance. That title must go to the earlier house of Aldo Manuzio. Aldo's erudite Greek correctors went so far as to constitute themselves the members of a Neakademia, a Greek-speaking learned society. Any lapse into Latin or Italian would have to be made up for by the payment of a fine into a common fund, which would eventually go to cover the costs of a splendid meal.[11] These rules, as Martin Lowry has shown, indicated aspirations, not realities: but they also reflected the accomplishments of a genuinely remarkable group of scholars.[12]

Cases like these, well known to historians of the book, have long served to underline the historical novelty and significance of the Renaissance printing house. A commercial enterprise, designed—and required—to make money, the publisher's shop was also the locale of learned activities. Early illustrations show correctors—learned men, able not only to read but also to correct classical and modern texts in Latin—working alongside craftsmen, ignoring noise, dirt, and ink in order to concentrate on the word.[13] The society of the ancien régime distinguished sharply between those who worked with their hands and those who worked with their brains.[14] But in the printing house, the work of craft required the presence of intellectual supervisors. And the supervisors, in turn, could not avoid getting their hands dirty, at least from time to time. Martin Sicherl, a pioneering student of the Aldine press, used the inky fingerprints still present in manuscripts of the Greek texts Aldo printed as vital clues. They identified the *Vorlagen,* or base texts, from which Aldo and his correctors worked. More remarkably still, they also established the scene of the crime, showing that scholars really studied and corrected texts, as had long been suspected, in the workplace.[15]

Historians have not contented themselves with recreating the work done by individual correctors. They have also argued that the corrector represented a new social type: a phenomenon brought into the world by printing. Mechanical reproduction by print, after all, severed the process of copying texts from that of studying and correcting them. An early fifteenth-century humanist like Poggio Braccolini could be both a pioneering scribe, one of the creators of the new humanistic script, and a serious textual critic, one who systematically tried to improve the texts he discovered and copied.[16] An early sixteenth-century humanist like Erasmus or Beatus Rhenanus, by contrast, could only supervise and correct the work done by the printers' journeymen and apprentices.[17]

Printing, moreover, brought new tasks into being. The printer had to compete with many rivals in the marketplace. To do so successfully, he had to show that his product was superior to those of his rivals. One way to do so—as printers rapidly decided—was to emphasize, in the colophon or, later, on the title page, that learned men had corrected the text. In Italy and Germany alike, books printed in the fifteenth century promised their readers not just texts, but texts "corrected" *(emendata)* by a particular scholar— or even by a whole group of them, such as "the learned masters of the University of Tübingen."[18] Hiring someone to correct a text—or claiming to have done so, as many printers did, even though they had not— represented a rational way to claim market share.

Another way was to produce a more accessible and attractive product. A publisher could have a text divided into neat sections, equipped with marginal summaries, or furnished with systematic indices. Regularization and standardization became preeminent features of the modern, uniform, printed text. In the course of time, correctors assumed responsibility for providing all of these services.[19] The corrector, accordingly, seems a pre-eminently modern figure, one brought into being by the requirements of a new technology, rather like the Webmasters and Web-page designers of the 1990s. As the bright creatures of the ocean bottom can exist only in their special, dark environment, which would destroy all other forms of life, so the corrector, it seems, could live only in the printing house. Like the new intellectual crafts demanded by the Internet, moreover, that of the correc-tor took shape with what now seems breathtaking rapidity. Within a few decades after the invention of print, correctors had devised the system of marks to indicate corrections that authors still use, on the rare occasions when they still have the chance to correct the proofs of their work.[20]

The corrector seems a preeminently modern figure in other ways as well. For the modern literary system, as Michel Foucault and others have taught us, is collaborative. It takes the work of many intermediaries—publishers, printers, editors, advertisers, journalists, booksellers, and more—to create a single "author." And the corrector was present at the creation of this modern form of textual production. For correctors did not only take responsibility—as in the cases of Estienne and Manuzio—for improving the texts of ancient and medieval authors, who could not fight back. Nor did they limit themselves to the task which even contemporaries saw as their central, defining one: scanning the proofs of a text as an assistant, appropriately called a "lector" or "reader," read the original copy aloud.[21]

From very early times, correctors were also expected to prepare the copy produced by their own contemporaries. Jerome Hornschuch, who pub-lished the first manual for proof correctors, the *Orthotypographia,* early in the seventeenth century, made clear that he and his colleagues spent most of their time deciphering, punctuating, and annotating the texts submit-ted by modern writers—whose handwriting often proved so illegible that they found themselves reduced to asking "Do hens have hands?"[22] And preparation of copy required not just the elimination of scribal errors, but also that of authorial ones—at least of those "which are of no great importance, in order to avoid doing any harm to the author's reputa-tion."[23] J. C. Zeltner, the early eighteenth-century historian of proof cor-rection who wrote these words, did so with strong personal feeling. He felt mortified, he explained, when he saw that the printer or corrector of his own book on proof correctors, who "though not unlearned, was also not ripe for this task," had left the verb *extollerunt* on page 16 of his book, even though Zeltner had clearly meant to write *extulerunt*. Zeltner admitted that he did not know if the corrector's blunders resulted from incompetence or illness. In either event, he found it necessary to add five closely printed pages of errata to his book on proof correction—pages in which, no doubt to his profound disgust, still more typographical errors occurred.[24] Even when correctors did not deliberately alter the texts entrusted to them, moreover, the tasks they carried out substantially affected the meaning and reception of the works they prepared for print. For centuries, correctors—rather than authors—inserted marks of punctuation. Some of these, like the semicolon, they actually invented. All of them, as Paolo Trovato has shown in a classic study, immediately affected the way that texts were understood, and gradually changed the habits of writers themselves, as they began occasionally to employ in composition the semicolon and other signs originally devised to be added in the course of printing.[25] As Trovato has also shown, correctors regularly ignored the question of authorial intention on these and related points—even when doing so clearly implied a change in the meaning of a text.

The presence of the corrector did more than interpose another individual into the social processes that constitute authorship. Correctors inspired anxiety. Most of them were the social inferiors of their authors. Hornschuch, for example, admitted that he had taken up the trade only to escape the still worse one of the private tutor.[26] Yet they ventured to correct better-born and supposedly better-educated writers; indeed, as we have already seen, correctors were criticized when they failed to make corrections that an author saw as necessary. Anecdotes circulated about the radical alterations that correctors introduced, sometimes on religious grounds. Zeltner told the story of "a certain corrector in the famous Franconian episcopal see [of Würzburg], who was beaten publicly, some time ago, and expelled from the city, because he allowed a disgusting word to be substituted for the *Schweiss-Tuch* of Veronica, omitting the letter *w*, as though out of carelessness."[27] Henri Estienne complained bitterly that illiterate correctors had ruined the reputation of printing. He himself—he claimed, satirically—had observed one of them operating like a mad counterpart to the goddess Circe, removing the unusual word *proci* (suitors) from a Latin text and inserting the more common *porci* (pigs).[28] Yet Scaliger singled

Estienne out as an example of the bad sort of printer who changed the texts of his authors' works without consulting them. Struggles for literary power, slippages of meaning, uncertainty about where the authorship of a text actually rests—all of these preeminently modern features of literature as a social world made their appearance in the locales inhabited by Renaissance correctors.

Artis Typographicae Querimonia: Correctors and the Classics

The correctors who produced the first editions of classical texts, as Trovato has recently shown, were rarely full-time specialists in Latin (or Greek) textual criticism. In the fifteenth century, many of them were priests, often members of religious orders: Giovanni Andrea de' Bussi, who corrected texts for Conrad Sweynheym and Arnold Pannartz, was bishop of Aleria and governed the Vatican Library. But laymen also corrected texts, and their numbers apparently increased in the sixteenth century. What linked both sorts of corrector—and empowered them to do their job—was normally a humanistic formation, a general training in the art of Latin grammar and the study of the classics. Many correctors also worked, like Aldo Manuzio himself, as private tutors or schoolmasters. Correction, in other words, represented, in the first instance, a new employment opportunity for humanists—a highly rational way to employ their knowledge to improve the classical texts in circulation while earning payment, often substantial, by dedicating the works in question to a patron of learning or by receiving a fee from the publisher.[29]

The economics of publishing, as we have already seen, created the demand which these correctors supplied: correction, in the full range of its senses, produced a better, more desirable product. But the structure of the industry, as many historians have emphasized, also exercised powerful pressures on the work correctors did. Printing required a large initial outlay on equipment, paper, and labor. But it did not produce income until finished books became available for sale. Publishers, accordingly, had a strong incentive to limit the amount of time that a corrector could spend on a given piece of work. Many correctors complained that they had had far too little time at their disposal to work carefully. Girolamo Squarzafico explained that he began one demanding editorial project "when the printers asked me very pressingly, one day ahead of time, to edit

Cicero *De oratore.*"[30] Giovanni Andrea Bussi, as E. J. Kenney has shown in his classic study *The Classical Text,* and Massimo Miglio has confirmed with his edition of Bussi's prefatory letters, worked as hard and well as he could on his remarkable series of *editiones principes.* These finely printed texts included Apuleius, Gellius, Caesar, Cicero's *Familiares,* and Livy. But time always flew. Bussi had only two weeks to produce his text of Silius Italicus; he lost the copy of Caesar which he had carefully corrected for the press, so that he had to execute his edition rapidly and without due care; and he edited the letters of Cyprian only because the printers "suddenly demanded" that he produce a work in small format, which could keep their presses busy in a period when they lacked "charta maior." Even when Bussi saw that more complex and expensive measures were necessary—as when he wished to add marginal glosses to the difficult text of Gellius— Sweynheym and Pannartz could not oblige.[31] Some of those who produced early editions offered their readers detailed information about the texts they had used: Giorgio Merula, for example, made clear that his text of Plautus rested, for the most part, as all others, on the celebrated Orsini manuscript, Vat. lat. 3870, a ninth-century codex well known to be the only source for twelve of the sixteen plays.[32] But for the most part, early editors chose a base text, more or less at random; made little or no use of earlier manuscripts, even when they knew about their existence; and offered little precise information about the nature of what they had done in preparing any given text for publication.

The first editions of the classics represented, in Kenney's eloquent terms, a "more or less random dip into the stream of tradition," which then became "frozen" in place, as later scholars and editors based their work of collation and emendation not on the earliest recoverable stage of the tradition, but on readily available printed texts.[33] Insofar as the texts were altered in the course of printing, moreover, the changes reflected the tastes of their correctors rather than a sustained effort to recover, from historical and philological evidence, what the author might have written. In the circumstances, it could hardly have been otherwise. Some correctors' complaints about the speed with which they had had to work were exaggerated; some printers worked slowly and precisely. The 1467 Subiaco edition of Augustine's *City of God,* for example, reveals on every page the care its printers took to reproduce the manuscript they used as a base text— down to the corrections, entered in pen in copy after copy, which reflect that a final stage of verification took place even after the type had been definitively set.[34] But the basic economics of book production, which required correctors to take as little time and cost as little money as possible, would rarely have allowed them to do more. After all, their agreements with publishers sometimes gave them only a day or two to go over each gathering they printed.[35] The prefaces in which correctors described how they had prepared their texts, moreover, were primarily designed to serve practical ends. These rhetorical set-pieces advertised the virtues of the ancient author in question and appealed to the patrons to whom the editions in question were dedicated, in the hope of attracting buyers on the one hand and a larger individual payment on the other. Detailed descriptions of editorial method would have been as rhetorically incongruous in this context as more scrupulous methods would have been economically incongruous in printing shops organized to make money.

The few precise studies of how correctors actually prepared texts for publication confirm the gloomy picture drawn from their own writings. When Bussi, for example, prepared his 1470 edition of Pliny's *Natural History* for the press, he knew that he was dealing with a spectacularly rich and difficult text, which offered a vast range of information on matters as varied as the history of the arts in antiquity and the nature of modern medicine. "Difficillima Plynii absoluta recognitio est," he wrote in the manuscript he prepared for the printer, part of which survives as Vat. lat. 5991: "A really good edition of Pliny is a very challenging task." Nonetheless, he based his work chiefly on what is now MS 1097 of the Biblioteca Angelica in Rome—a codex written only ten years earlier by the scribe Ieronimus de Botis, whose own knowledge of Latin was notably weak. Bussi made only unsystematic efforts to improve the text by collating the other manuscripts at his disposal, and when he entered emendations in the text, he sometimes explained the thinking that had generated them in the margin—and sometimes simply entered them, in exactly the same way that he entered manuscript variants. Often, he left problems unsolved, reminding himself in the margin that he should find a better solution or chase up one of Pliny's sources. Yet he devoted himself energetically to what now seem elementary tasks, many of them more appropriate to a copy-editor or desk editor than a textual critic: correcting errors of spelling and word division, reordering parts of the text that had fallen out of order, and reworking the division of the text into books and chapters.[36] All of this, in turn, preceded the creation of the printer's copy, and was followed in turn by further efforts at revising the text in proof. Bussi may not have spent as long as he boasted on the *Natural History*—he claimed to have devoted nine years to the text—but he certainly worked hard.

Bussi devoted part of his dedicatory letter to this edition to a celebration of the virtues of printing: "Is there anything in the whole annals of human invention," he asked rhetorically, that can claim to be comparable or superior to our printers' art of writing?"[37] But few of his readers agreed. Within only a couple of years after his edition appeared, a series of sharp commentaries by Niccolò Perotti and others subjected both Bussi's Pliny and the art of printing to a withering critique. Though Pliny remained the object of passionate debate throughout the fifteenth and early sixteenth centuries, moreover, even as Ermolao Barbaro, Nicolò Leoniceno, and others did their Herculean best to cleanse the Augean stable of the *Natural History,* no editor found it possible to base a new text strictly on a better manuscript than those used by Bussi and his colleagues. The economics of correction, in short, not only constrained the individual, but shaped the results of the system as a whole. The same, basically materialist explanation accounts for the defects not only of individual works like Bussi's Pliny, but also of the larger critical enterprise of early printers.

No wonder, then, that as John Monfasani and Martin Davies have shown, the appearance of Bussi's edition of Pliny and the other *editiones principes* provoked, within months, not only debate, but also a demand for public regulation—censorship—of the press.[38] In a long letter to the Roman humanist Francesco Guarneri, secretary to the papal nephew, Cardinal Marco Barbo, Niccolò Perotti denounced correctors, like Bussi, who "insert their prefaces in the books of the most eminent men; for nothing could seem more shameful, more unworthy, than joining a sewer to an altar."[39] He devoted some scathing—and in this case fairly accurate—words to Bussi's methods, which he described as normal. And he wound up by urging the creation of an official system of textual criticism, a sort of philological censorship:

> The easiest arrangement is to have someone or other charged by papal authority to oversee the work [of printing classical texts], who would both prescribe to the printers regulations governing the printing of books and would appoint some moderately learned man to

examine and emend individual formes before printing. Furthermore, [the appointed corrector] should take meticulous care that the primary correctors [employed by the printers] do not indulge in reckless advertisement [in their prefaces] but keep to the just measure we described before. The task calls for intelligence, singular erudition, incredible zeal, and the highest vigilance. If this is done, we will have not only many books, but also unmutilated ones.[40]

Perotti, in other words, stated the principle that correctors needed to work slowly and systematically, to change only what was manifestly false in the texts entrusted to them, and to record explicitly what they had done. But he also saw that in practice, in many cases, and perhaps in most, they could not. The market, he argued, not only would fail to ensure the preservation of the classical heritage, but would ruin it. Printing had to be removed from the hands of entrepreneurs and placed under the control of enlightened patrons and officials. Only disinterested rulers, not greedy printers, could preserve the stream of tradition from contamination. Perotti's remarks seem as timely—as sharp a reaction to the moment—as Bussi's boasts. Once again, modernity emerges as the most striking characteristic of the corrector and his enterprise.

Manuscript Origins of Print Culture

In fact, however, a look at the context yields a more complex story than this. Perotti, as Monfasani has shown, exempted one corrector, and one preface, from his condemnation. In the same year that Bussi edited Pliny, 1470, Giannantonio Campano had overseen an edition of Livy for the German printer Ulrich Han. Like Bussi, Campano had celebrated the powers of printing. From now on, he exulted, texts would no longer appear riddled with errors. Previously, every scribe had felt free to make— or ruin—his copy of a given text in his own way. The printers, by contrast, "produce as many copies as they want, all uniform, from a single exemplar which has been scrutinized and corrected." All readers of his Livy—and of faithful reprints of it—could depend upon it: they would have access to a text with no arbitrary changes and, he thought, few errors—except perhaps in place names. Once, classical texts had been accessible only to the rich; now, rich and poor alike could buy a good version of Livy.[41]

But Campano also recognized that it was not easy to produce a critical text. For copyists continually intervened in and altered the texts they were employed to reproduce: "They think what they do not understand is superfluous, or what they do not grasp is obscure, or what the author deliberately inverted is corrupt. Turning themselves from scribes into correctors, they apply their own judgment most stringently where they understand the least." Campano, accordingly, had set himself to produce a critical text by choosing an entirely different method. He had "relied on many exemplars." He had refrained from unnecessary changes: "I was never," Campano insisted, "a curious interpreter or diviner." Instead of being clever at the expense of his author, he had brought to his task "nothing but my efforts and my diligence," and had tried not to change the text but to stabilize it, "to remove the errors of the scribes." Perotti not only praised Campano, he borrowed the other man's explanation of scribal error, extending it to printers' correctors. They too, he insisted, went wrong above all because "they think what they do not understand is false."[42]

Both Campano and Perotti, moreover, drew on and rethought existing institutions from the world of manuscripts as they tried to understand and correct the world of printing. Campano, for his part, worked as a corrector in two distinct period senses. In the fifteenth century, as Paul Oskar Kristeller established long ago, humanists who wished to produce works in Latin that met a high standard of classical correctness and intelligence generally submitted them to the judgment of a friend—someone capable of assessing and correcting both substance and content. Ideally, the author would not send presentation copies of his work to patrons and colleagues, or allow a *cartolaio* to make and sell further copies, until it had undergone this process of purgation (in practice, of course, copies of uncorrected texts also entered circulation).[43] Individual humanists, like Niccolò Niccoli and Antonio Panormita, became famous for their skill at identifying others' errors and correcting them. Niccoli edited the works of Poggio Bracciolini, and many others demanded his help—even though, or perhaps because, he notoriously thought most of the writings of his contemporaries more fit to be used in the toilet than to be read.[44]

The humanists who edited others' works were, in a genuine sense, correctors. They called the stylistic and substantive changes they suggested "emendations," and referred to their own activity as "emendatio."[45] And the work they did closely resembled—in both its relatively banal character and its sometimes radical proposals to violate authorial intention—the work that printers' correctors later did on classical texts. Surviving printers' copy of modern Latin works with corrections—like the manuscript of Pius II's work *De statu Europae* which Michael Christan prepared for the press—closely resemble printers' copy for classical texts.[46]

Campano himself, moreover, served as a corrector in this first sense before printing reached Italy. Michele Ferno, his biographer, records that "everyone brought him whatever they had created, as if to a common censor and supreme oracle. No scholar would have dared at that time to publish anything before he had investigated his critical judgment. Anyone who obtained his commendation thought that it brought his work immense glory."[47] The brilliant writer and humanist pope Pius II gave Campano "the power to remove what I found superfluous, to correct what seemed problematic, and to explicate what seemed rather obscure"—though, to be sure, Campano found Pius's *Commentaries* so purely and vividly written "that they not only require no one else's hand to enhance their worth, but are clearly such as to make would-be imitators despair."[48] According to Ferno, Campano's skill as a corrector of modern Latin texts that circulated in manuscript actually won him his employment in the printing house: "That was why no printer in Italy in those days apparently wanted to undertake a publication which did not have one of his prefatory letters to illuminate its path."[49] The connection between manuscript correction and print correction seems clear.

Equally clear, however, is the difference. Campano clearly realized that classical texts, in his time, were unstable. Every time a scribe who thought himself learned copied a text, he "corrected" it, usually on poor grounds. And the "corrector" who set out deliberately to improve a text naturally affected it even more radically. Printing, by contrast, offered a chance to stabilize texts: to establish texts that rested, ideally, only on the best manuscripts, accurately reproduced; or, to put it another way, that represented honest labor rather than dishonorable ingenuity.

Campano left unclear how printers and correctors could accomplish this transformation in their methods. He was a conservative editor. Publishing the first substantial collection of the Latin translations of Plutarch's *Lives,* also in 1470, he admitted that not all the versions he had used were equally good: "I wish that all of these translations had the artistry of the originals. True, the majority of them, thanks to the intelligence of their translators, have both retained their original elegance and received the same quality in Latin. But a few of them, which had the bad fortune to fall into less skilled hands, are rather roughly translated."[50] But he preserved the texts as he had received them, arguing that the accuracy (*fides rerum*) rather than the style (*verborum copia*) of a historical account determined its value. Here, as in the case of Livy, Campano not only struck a conservative pose, but adopted a conservative method, reproducing texts he could have edited quite radically.

Perotti, clearly stimulated by Campano's suggestions, also developed them further. A public authority could ensure that correctors worked as Campano claimed he had. In making this proposal, Perotti certainly had in mind the predatory, competitive world of print that was taking shape before his eyes. But he also drew—more systematically than Campano— on existing precedents. Almost a century before, the Florentine chancellor and humanist Coluccio Salutati had deplored the corrupt state of the classical and patristic texts in circulation. Like Campano and Perotti, he blamed scribes and readers who "arbitrarily changed texts they did not understand," omitted passages as they copied, or transposed glosses into texts.[51] And like Perotti, he urged that public institutions be created to regulate the quality of texts: "Public libraries should be established, with complete collections of books. And men of the highest competence should be set in charge of the libraries, so that they may revise the texts by collating them very carefully with others and remove all the textual variants by accurate judgment and resolution."[52] This proposal was either remembered or reinvented, moreover, in the middle of the fifteenth century—and in precisely the world of learning Perotti knew best. In 1452, when the scribe Ioannes Lamperti finished a splendid copy of Lorenzo Valla's Latin translation of Thucydides, Valla deposited it in the then new Vatican Library. In a holograph subscription, Valla wrote that he wished this manuscript "to be the official master text [*archetypus*] of my translation, against which other copies could be corrected."[53] Valla, in other words, saw the Vatican Library as an official collection, which could preserve official copies that would have a stablizing effect on the texts they contained. Nicholas V very likely shared this view. When Perotti called for an official system for control of the press, to be based in the Vatican, he did not devise his plan from whole cloth. Rather, like Campano, he rethought ideas and institutions that had already taken shape in Roman manuscript culture, reshaping traditions in the light of the new conditions imposed by printing.

Coda: A Partial Correction

The corrector and his critics were not, then, such radically new creations as historians of the book have sometimes held. The arbitrary method that the first correctors of printed editions of the classics applied to their texts derived from scribal tradition and the methods that earlier correctors had used on contemporary Latin works. Even the most sophisticated criticisms of these procedures formulated in the first decades of printing, moreover, were constituted in large part from existing cultural and scholarly resources. Campano and Perotti reimagined the existing practices and revived the existing polemics of the manuscript book world. The material conditions normally cited to explain the rise and progress of the corrector—if progress is the right word—are necessary, but not sufficient, to their task. It remains to be seen if the new social and intellectual types that flourish on the World Wide Web will also draw effectively on the resources that exist in the world of the traditional printed book.

8

Those Humanists!

⚬⚭⚬

This essay was a review of *Impolite Learning* (1995) by Anne Goldgar.

*T*HE SIGHT that confronted the French Protestant minister d'Origny Delaloge when he left his London house at nine o'clock one morning in 1707 struck him as out of the ordinary. A fellow Huguenot, wearing a blond wig, a black suit with a damask vest, and a hat with a rose on it, stood before the house and addressed him, first in English and then in French. He identified himself as Jean Le Clerc, the celebrated philologist and theologian from Holland who had edited the complete Latin works of Erasmus, produced a widely read periodical, and written the first systematic modern manual of critical method, the *Ars Critica.* Explaining that he was traveling incognito, he nonetheless managed to reveal that he had come to occupy a chair in Oriental languages at Cambridge, his Latin inaugural lecture in his pocket. When Delaloge, who clearly found him impressive, invited him to dinner, Le Clerc spread himself in literary gossip, talking freely of the publishing houses and periodicals to which he enjoyed access. He even tried to appropriate a manuscript by Delaloge, which he promised to print in the *Bibliothèque choisie.* Only when foiled in this effort did Le Clerc finally leave, and even then he behaved oddly, insisting that he would walk after his puzzled host had called him a coach.

In the days that followed Le Clerc appeared at the houses of other ministers, who received him warmly and fed him well. Politely, the distinguished foreign savant invited his benefactors to a fine dinner at an inn in Romford, where he lavishly returned their hospitality. But when the bill came, he had vanished, leaving his fuming guests to pay up. The internationally famous scholar had apparently unmasked himself as a vulgar conman.

The grubby final chapter of this episode confirmed what Delaloge already suspected. This "Le Clerc" was not the literary celebrity he claimed to be, but an impostor: a former monk named Frédéric-Auguste Gabillon. While in England Gabillon not only fooled the clergy, whose readiness to extend charity perhaps resulted from a professional deformation: he also succeeded at the harder task of cheating a bookseller out of a substantial amount of money, and misbehaved in public in ludicrous ways, making wild offers to the queen, the bishop of London, and the Hanoverian envoy. The episode deeply pained the genuine Le Clerc, whom Delaloge and others kept apprised of the situation. Though in public he professed to feel only amusement at his impersonator's antics, in private he organized a propaganda campaign to ensure that his name would not fall into discredit.

The story is typical of the world of the French Protestant intellectuals who went into exile throughout Europe after Louis XIV revoked the Edict of Nantes in 1685. It suggests the extent of the personal and intellectual networks these industrious, attractive refugees spun. By implication at least, it conveys something of the inexhaustible energy they lavished on making contacts, soliciting manuscripts, and winning publicity. And it indicates, as well, some of the conflicts that proved inevitable as they tried to create and sustain an international scholarly community.

Both the black-coated, industrious Huguenots and their calf-bound, erudite writings circulated from darkest Berlin to coldest Scotland. In due course they became, if not the sole founders, at least the main pillars of the late-seventeenth-century Republic of Letters. This was a sort of literary European Union which drew its citizens from every civilized country, used French as its literary *écu*—and took Holland, land of tolerance and good publishers, as its capital. Within this efficient and cosmopolitan country of the mind, communications were remarkably good. The stock of a young author from a small provincial town in Brandenburg or Zeeland, once he published in the right places and attracted the benevolent attention of the journals, could rapidly become a known quantity on the bourses of celebrity from Posnan to Portsmouth. He would then have the power to offer favors to other men of letters, and the right to make claims in his turn on their friendship and hospitality: the false Le Clerc did both in London.

The communications networks of the Republic of Letters carried powerful charges. Intellectuals of very different origins and interests—like John Locke and Giambattista Vico—cared deeply about the French versions and summaries of their ideas which could bring them to, or distort them for, a European public unwilling or unable to read English and Italian. Unfortunately, like more modern literary circuits, those of the Republic of Letters often shorted. Prominent scholars refused to conduct their polemics in the courteous manner dictated by good taste. Young upstarts behaved bumptiously toward their elders and betters—or even, like Gabillon, appropriated their identities. Nonetheless, this French-speaking, Europe-wide literary community existed for decades and continues to command the interest of literary and intellectual historians. Its citizens included the great philosopher and dictionary maker Pierre Bayle as well as his enemy Le Clerc. Its new language of reasoned criticism eventually developed into the polemical medium in which the *philosophes* of the Enlightenment waged their wars against superstition and *l'infâme*. The Republic of Letters—as Paul Hazard argued long ago in a classic book—provided the stage on which the crisis of the modern European mind was enacted.

In a more recent study, Anne Goldgar has mapped this imaginary state, offering precise surveys of its borders and colorful sketches of its local topographies and communities. Instead of analyzing the content of late-seventeenth- and early-eighteenth-century thought, she reconstructs its contours and contexts, the personal relations and professional institutions within which intellectuals lived and worked. She enables the reader to see, for the first time, exactly how the citizens of the Republic of Letters went about the business of pre-Enlightenment. And she brings to light a gallery of unjustly forgotten Grub Street characters whose eccentricities and exploits she describes with infectious zest. No reader will forget "the ultimate *demi-savant*," the crazed Prussian cavalry officer Christoph Heinrich Oelven, crippled by unsuccessful mercury treatments for venereal disease, who began writing vicious satires against his betters and wound up raving;

or the short, fat, gouty corrector Charles de la Motte, described as a "pygmy," a "Lilliputian," and "that little figure of papier-mâché" by the contemporaries who hurled epithets at him with all the glee and accuracy of a literary darts team aiming at a target adorned with the face of a too-successful colleague.

Lively in style and sometimes hilarious in content, Goldgar's book has a perfectly serious purpose. She seeks to show how the literary and intellectual system of the Republic took shape and functioned. To that end, she has spelunked in dozens of archives across Europe, reading hundreds of unpublished letters that record the unrequited loves and unremitting hatreds of authors, reviewers, editors, and publishers. Deft use of these vivid and often unguarded texts enables her to give voices and qualities to scores of forgotten intellectual hacks and more than a few highly creative thinkers. More important still, by putting shrewd new questions to her rich sources, Goldgar draws from them the forgotten rules and practices of a lost world of literature and scholarship. It looks, in more than one respect, surprisingly—and depressingly—familiar.

Goldgar explains for the first time, for example, just how authors from all over Europe managed to have their books published by the French-speaking *libraires* of Holland. The Lilliputian de la Motte, the better-known Prosper Marchand, and other correctors served as the intellectual and commercial intermediaries who kept the publication system open and mobile. Receiving a manuscript from a distant author, sometimes a friend or acquaintance but often a complete stranger, they would search for a printer willing to bring the text out. At the same time, they would advise the author on whether or not to accept the format and type fonts that the printer suggested and the honorarium he offered, which could consist of money, copies of the book, or both. While savants usually knew little about publishers' interests, methods, and standard terms for publication, the corrector could give expert advice on all these points. And while savants could easily find themselves frustrated by the widely noted decline of interest in learned books, which led many publishers to abandon the heavily annotated works of the learned in favor of more salable plays, novels, and accounts of voyages, the corrector could find the most amenable *libraires* and address them more persuasively than any stranger.

Once author and printer had reached their agreement, moreover, the corrector often continued to play a vital role in the drama of publication.

He might well put the manuscript into better order, improve its spelling and punctuation, and make final decisions about its content. In return for all this formally unpaid assistance, the corrector received praise from the author, a copy of the resulting publication, and, if all went well, a commission. He also hoped to correct the proofs of the work in question, a service normally provided not by the author but by a professional, and one for which the printer would pay a set fee. Something between an agent and a desk editor in modern terms, the corrector greased the squeaky gears of literary commerce, enabling authors to escape or mitigate what some already called the "Despotique Tyranny of Booksellers"—though at the price of subjecting them to what modern authors often revile as the triumphant idiocy of copy-editors.

The existence of these figures, whom Goldgar describes, quite reasonably, as the first literary agents, points to the increasing specialization and professionalization of the world of letters. By contrast, the many widely read review journals which also came into being around 1700 show that ideals of cosmopolitanism and amateurism also continued to flourish in the Republic. By the later years of the seventeenth century, the streams of literature that had issued for more than two centuries from Europe's presses had swelled and merged in an irresistible flood. Scholars found themselves increasingly hard pressed to read all of this material, much less to cite it appositely and critically. The enormous older printed literature swarmed with multiple, divergent editions of crucial literary, historical, and theological texts. Bibliographical ghosts and legends—like that of the famous, but nonexistent, work of libertine thought, the *Book on the Three Impostors*—haunted collectors and libraries. At the same time, each year's Frankfurt fair brought vast quantities of new texts and theories onto the market. The sprawling footnotes of Bayle's *Dictionary* give a sense of the immense range of textual and bibliographical information which one had to master simply in order to follow the debates of the learned. The price of entry to the intellectual games of the Republic was very high.

In Holland, high incomes, cosmopolitan booksellers, and good libraries enabled established literati to own the basic equipment of erudition and find more recondite or expensive materials when necessary. But in many poor and remote areas, young writers had no direct access to a large, up-to-date library. In the Holy Roman Empire, which the Thirty Years' War had reduced to poverty, a curious form of oral performance often took the place of direct reading. Professors used the printed auction catalogues of great Dutch private libraries as the outlines for lecture courses on "Literary History," in which they told their students a bit about each title listed and provided agreeably nasty gossip about each author. The students who took down at dictation speed hundreds of pages of minutely detailed bibliographical notes on books they had never seen could afterward appear knowing even if they could hardly become knowledgeable. The basic poverty of this and similar expedients reveals how desperate readers had become. In much of Europe, apprentice literati who believed they had a duty to familiarize themselves with the entire encyclopedia could afford to buy and read only a few set texts. Even mature, well-to-do scholars found themselves doomed to fall behind in those fields which lay outside their special interests. In any event, a book trade fragmented by hundreds of customs barriers and forced to adapt to all the vagaries of local tastes could hardly bring the latest in physics or philology to isolated readers scattered across Europe's provincial cities.

Eventually, as Goldgar shows, a new form of publication took shape, one which could carry the literary news efficiently and affordably from Ghent to Aix and beyond. Periodicals popped up, designed to offer a broad readership summaries and criticisms of new literature. Origins and staffing methods varied. Some journals were organized and largely written by a single editor, like Pierre Bayle, others by a sort of cooperative—such as the group of young Huguenots in Berlin who decided, in 1720, to create a *Bibliothèque germanique* in order to inform a European public of the many interesting works that appeared every year in barbarous German. Copy varied also: some journals concentrated almost exclusively on *extraits* or reviews, while others gave large amounts of space to articles and letters.

In every case, however, the journal's existence depended on the cooperation of a publisher willing to obtain books for review, publish the resulting copy, and pay for the privilege of doing so. In almost every case, the editor or editors took all or most of the *libraire*'s fee for themselves, even as they trawled the waters for gullible collaborators. In many cases, outside reviewers proved willing to turn out large amounts of copy in return for a free copy of the journal, some exposure to the public, and warm personal letters from the editor. These told contributors how urgently their unfinished work was needed, how long it would take before their previous submissions could possibly appear, and how sadly the life of an editor lacked beer and skittles. And in almost every case editors tried to give their periodical a clear personality, something like—but not identical to—a modern editorial line. Each editor tried to show that his journal was—like himself—a model citizen of the Republic of Letters. Editorial statements regularly insisted that a given journal would not encroach on territory already well covered by another journal, would not allow reviewers to insult authors, would stand above religious and political parties, and would judge—if it judged at all—by impartial standards of taste and accuracy. The journals, in short, stood in theory against party and competition, for an ideal of cosmopolitan cooperation—even if their practices rarely lived up to these high ideals, and their all-too-rapid expansion and all-too-common gaffes attracted the bent nibs of satirists, one of whom claimed that he planned "to put out on Tuesdays and Fridays a *Gazette des ignorans*."

This was the terrain that many young intellectuals wanted to bestride. The means they chose were as varied as the resources at their disposal. One could provide texts or inscriptions for a more important savant, edit the letters of a departed celebrity, or translate the works of a living one into French. In any event, the celebrities of the Republic could count on regularly hearing the noise that F. A. Cornford described in a famous passage: the strange sound of young men in a hurry—in a hurry to get their elders out of the way. Goldgar describes the tactics of these ambitious climbers and celebrity hunters in vivid detail: for example, the way in which Pierre Coste, who translated Locke, gradually claimed more and more space in his versions for notes of his own, in which he qualified or even controverted the philosopher's views. Such passages will strike a hauntingly familiar note for any senior scholar who has ever received a flattering letter inviting him or her to comment, at a conference, on the exciting new research of three or four younger colleagues.

For all their sophisticated design, the gears and flywheels of the Republic's machinery often turned anything but smoothly. Religious and political divisions continually threatened the cosmopolitanism which intellectuals professed to believe in; greed and ambition continually challenged their claim to cooperate in the public service. These quarrels do not, in themselves, disprove the existence or refute the ideals of the Republic. Goldgar rightly argues that the historian reconstructing an organization may find its malfunctions more informative, in crucial respects, than its blueprints.

But many debates proved impossible to resolve. Even within the world of the Huguenots, disagreement raged—for example, on whether local churches had the right to demand a standard of orthodoxy from Protestant writers or to impose censorship on them. Between Catholics and Protestants, of course, walls of principle were even higher and thicker. New institutions of learning, like journals, academies, and the system of literary agents, promoted more efficient communication, but did so at the expense of fostering an impersonality and professionalism that could clash with the traditions of amateurism and literary friendship. Many of the Republic's most prominent citizens feared that its own success in treating new literary forms might doom it to extinction. For example, the Catholic bishop Pierre-Daniel Huet, no Huguenot but the pupil and friend of Protestants, denounced the new review journals. Such short-cuts, he insisted, like the manuals and encyclopedias of late antiquity, would eventually induce readers to ignore full texts in favor of abridgments and thus prove fatal to accurate learning.

External threats also loomed. After 1700 the appeal of Latin publications rapidly declined. Scholars' social prominence was challenged by the rise of a *mondain* culture, whose representatives mocked the pedantry and unworldliness of savants. Scholarly privileges became hard, or impossible, to enforce, even within the Holy Roman Empire, where Latin was still spoken and degrees and titles mattered a good deal: in Hessen-Kassel in 1762, "doctors" were relegated to the same social rank as valets and pastrycooks. Huet lamented, early in the eighteenth century, that his one (admittedly long) lifetime had seen both the rise and the fall of letters.

To meet these challenges, so Goldgar argues in the most ambitious— and contentious—pages of her book, the citizens of the Republic adopted a coherent strategy: they made the cultivation of politeness in the world of letters into the core of their enterprise. As good letters found less support in the outside world and consensus proved elusive even within the calf-lined libraries of the learned, it became clear that form—good form— must take precedence over content. The savants of the early eighteenth century spent enormous time and effort on exchanges of courtesies and information that now seem devoid of serious intellectual content. They developed elaborate strategies for the exchange and presentation of books. They sent florid letters, largely made up of exaggerated compliments, to total strangers. They made long literary voyages, meticulously recorded in thick diaries, in the course of which they tried to visit the library of every literatus in every small town in the empire or the Low Countries. As often as not, their reward for these civilities seems small to the modern historian. A morning's call on a given pastor or professor might well be repaid with nothing more than a cup of chocolate or coffee, a chance to handle two or three rare editions, and some bibliographical chat of stunning dryness.

Goldgar finds these activities as bizarre and meaningless as Alice's caucus-race. But she also sees them as the central activities of the Republic. Their very sterility shows how important they must have been: otherwise they would have been dropped. They expressed a widespread and passionate concern to preserve the social networks of learning from inward corruption and outward assault: to show that letters, like military service, conveyed nobility. Like some recent historians of the scientific revolution, in short, Goldgar invokes the ideals of civility and gentlemanliness, the civilizing process, to explain the origins of vital early modern practices and institutions.

But the decision to separate social from textual realms causes problems. The substance of more than one of the late seventeenth century's debates probably contributed at least as much as the social conditions Goldgar invokes to her savants' pervasive sense of unease. Both the new philosophy of Descartes and the new philology of Richard Bentley, who sided with the moderns in the Battle of the Books, called into question the perennial value of the ancient writers that the savants loved, studied, and edited. The rise of a new religion of intellectual progress, a passionately expressed faith in the value of the modern, must have had more than a little to do with the status anxieties that these classicists' letters and quarrels reveal.

Goldgar's general assessment of the enterprise of the seventeenth-century savants, in sum, carries less conviction than her particular analyses of their experience as authors and climbers. It will take studies based on the matter as well as the manner of the late-seventeenth-century intellect to reveal exactly what formed the core concerns of the French-speaking, Huguenot-dominated Republic of Letters—as well as to clarify its relation to the Latin-speaking Respublica literarum of the early seventeenth century, from which it arose, and the Enlightenment of the mid-eighteenth, into which it evidently devolved. But Goldgar's particular observations, her meticulous and craftsmanlike accounts of how publishers, authors, and editors operated, stand even if her larger analytical structure fails. Her remarkable erudition, exhibited on every page of this book, marks her out as the lineal successor of the seventeenth-century savants she knows so well. And her witty style shows that she also has learned a good deal from their *mondain* opponents. The Republic of Letters lives.

9

The World of the Polyhistors:
Humanism and Encyclopedism

⟨〰〰〰〰⟩

*I*N 1713 AND 1715 Johann Burkhard Mencke subjected the scholars of the Holy Roman Empire to a searching examination. They failed it. His two speeches "On the Charlatanry of the Learned"—best sellers wherever they were not banned—ridiculed the minds and the mores of the polyhistors with equal zest. Mencke anatomized their love for overblown tides: "Today . . . you see many demanding to be called *Clarissimus* who are absolutely unknown outside the walls of their city; *Magnificus,* who have scarcely any dignity at home; *Consultissimus,* who have little or no advice to give: and *Excellentissimus,* who do not know as much about anything worth knowing as the veriest tyro."[1] He savaged the equally fatuous titles that they assigned to their books—for example, "Public Law; that is, a Medical Treatise on Headache." He demolished their ridiculous efforts to capture all knowledge in single encyclopedias or treatises—"Golden Keys, Royal Methods, . . . Oceanic Macro-Micro-Cosmicos, . . . and other such grandiose works that are put out to ensnare buyers."[2] He heaped special scorn on their belief that their scholarship could recover an ancient, perfect philosophy, encoded by the wise priests of ancient Egypt in their mysterious hieroglyphs:

> Some mischievous youths of Rome, hearing that a building was to
> be erected on a certain site, resolved to put [Athanasius] Kircher's
> ingenuity to the test. So they secretly buried there a rough stone on

which they had designed some appealing voluptuous figures. When the foundation of the new structure was being dug, the stone was found . . . At once an interpreter was sought, and Kircher was chosen. As soon as he saw the stone, he began to leap and dance for joy—and to give a beautiful interpretation of the circles, the crosses, and all the other meaningless signs.[3]

So much for the efforts at deciphering hieroglyphs that had fascinated humanists from Cyriac of Ancona to Nicolas Caussin. So much for the belief in a *prisca theologia* that had deluded neo-Platonists from Marsilio Ficino to Robert Fludd.[4]

An early *philosophe,* Mencke found the erudite compilers who had loaded seventeenth-century bookshelves to breaking point with their huge folios to be figures of fun rather than types of learning. And many contemporaries shared his views. Vernacular writers joined him in satirizing the pedantry of the old scholarship—one of the best was Gottlieb Wilhelm Rabener, who wrote a mock dissertation entirely in footnotes.[5] Educational reformers joined him in attacking the sterility of the old curriculum—one of the most effective was Christian Thomasius, who tried to replace scholastic with modern philosophy and Latin with German in university teaching.[6] Such critics of the old system seem sympathetic figures even now, and they have had at least their fair share of attention from modern scholars. But the objects of their abuse, the men whose ideals and practices dominated the schools, academies, and universities of the old empire from the mid-sixteenth to the mid-eighteenth century—these men have had not only little sympathy but little attention of any kind. To the exploration of the obscure, forbidding territory that was theirs I now turn.

It is not surprising that the world of the polyhistors has attracted few explorers in recent times. Its inhabitants wrote at fantastic length in barbarous Latin about tedious and terrifying subjects. Caspar Barth's *Adversaria* was one of their most quoted and best respected products. Of it A. E. Housman wrote: "to read 3000 tall columns of close print by a third-rate scholar is no proper occupation for mortals."[7] What could be more dismal than 3,000 columns too crabbed even for Housman? Yet Barth, a great manuscript hunter and pioneering student of medieval Latin, has more to offer modern classicists, at least, than does Daniel Georg Morhof, with whom he shared intellectual preeminence in the seventeenth-century empire.[8] True, a few hardy souls have tried to work out the lay of this unpromising land. Erich Trunz surveyed the polyhistors' whole territory in one brisk essay seventy years ago, achieving clarity and broad coverage but losing detail and local color in the process.[9] More recently, some literary and intellectual historians have traveled on foot through individual provinces, enriching Trunz's sketchy geography with rich if isolated chorographies.[10] Wilhelm Kühlmann has distilled an imposing synthesis from these monographs and dozens of primary sources; and more recently, Hans Bots and Françoise Waquet have laid out the topography of the whole Republic of Letters in a brilliant sketch map.[11] But all too many regions lie untraveled and uncultivated. The survey that follows, though produced after some long tramps through the *Respublica litterarum,* is offered with many reservations.

The general shape of the map we need to draw seems as clear as its details are elusive. For if the polyhistors bewilder any modern scholar by the breadth of their interests, almost all of their intellectual activities nonetheless fall within a well-defined area, bounded by the two enterprises mentioned in the title of this essay. Humanism and encyclopedism, eloquence and erudition—these were the pursuits that the polyhistors made their own.

Humanism is not difficult to define. For the intellectuals of the empire it retained until deep in the eighteenth century the original form that Erasmus and his contemporaries had given it. It meant the cluster of disciplines that trained a scholar to interpret and produce literary texts in Latin. Above all, it meant rhetoric—the art of arts and science of sciences, which took as its lofty goal the production of the eloquent and effective citizen, the *vir bonus peritus dicendi,* and imposed as its humble task the memorization of hundreds of examples, aphorisms, and tropes, the *copia rerum ac verborum.*[12] Latin schools, academies, and universities throughout Germany forced their inhabitants to speak and argue in Latin on everything from metonymy to Mersenne.[13] More ambitiously, they offered the art of rhetoric, with its clearly defined goals and methods, its five major subdivisions, and its three (or four) general types of speeches, as the model for any other discipline that aspired to be a liberal art. The intellectual who wished to praise painting claimed that it too could "kindle its audiences to seek glory and virtue"; that it too had to seek subjects out, arrange them attractively, adorn them appropriately, and give them life with "motion and gesture"; that it too had to rest on knowledge of the ideas and material realities of the ancient world.[14] The painter, in short, had to be a *vir bonus peritus pingendi;* and other disciplines from theology to sculpture were envisioned in analogous terms.

For the most part rhetoric was far more a matter of practice than of theory. The learned man had to be just as deft in 1700 as his forebears had been a century and a half before at speaking Latin on public occasions, writing Latin about official business, composing poems in Latin on demand and treatises in Latin on subjects the ancients had never imagined—like the compass, the barometer, and the properties of Iceland spar. Such skills were not easy to attain.[15] Marc-Antoine Muret and Jacques-Auguste de Thou, the masters to whom the polyhistors looked back, achieved their eloquence by direct study of the ancients. But the young German student in search of a career in the *Gelehrtenstand* had too little leisure to devote himself to digesting the classics themselves. Hence the presses remained busy producing the old-fashioned but still useful short-cuts to eloquence that Renaissance humanists had devised, as well as newer additions to the stock of teaching aids, distinguished less by high ideals or deep learning than by their austerely practical character.

One typical collection of rhetoric texts, aimed at the learned young of the 1650s, begins with that shortest of all short-cuts to loquacity in Latin, Erasmus's *De copia*. The book is justly famous for its exuberant pursuit of synonyms and metaphors, its table of 150 ways to say "Thank you for the letter" in good Latin: "Tuis literis nulla res unquam accidit mihi festivior: nihil unquam vidi tuis literis lubentius: haud est quicquam, quod gaudentiore acceperim animo, quam proximas Fausti mei literas: quo me credis affluxisse gaudio, cum tuum animum tuis in literis agnoscerem? cum tabellarius tuam mihi traderet epistolam, statim animus mihi laetitia ineffabili prurire coepit."[16] If Erasmus's mastery of classical literature and sheer joy in the accumulation of words sometimes suffused his dry instructions with a curiously poetic character, his seventeenth-century successors had far lower ends in view and applied far lower means to attain them. The work that follows Erasmus in the corpus I describe bears the title "Marrow of the Transitions Most Used in Orations."[17] Written for the gymnasium students of Livonia, it offers not guidance in independent composition but model exordia, transitions, and conclusions, in which the student had only to fill in the blanks as his occasion dictated: "Though our ancestors ordained many splendid things, none of these was more splendid, more useful, more prudent, more carefully adapted to preserve scholarship, more efficiently designed to promote the studiousness of the young, more brilliantly appropriate to preserving the authority of ranks and orders in society and enlarging the prestige of letters, than_____."[18] What could be more practical than this? Or further from Erasmus's spirit?

The search for *eloquentia* occupied a prominent place even in the interests of mature scholars. Seth Calvisius, professor of music at Leipzig and a highly proficient chronologer in his own right, corresponded extensively about the latter field with the greatest expert in the world, Joseph Scaliger. The drafts of his letters, preserved in Göttingen, record not merely some heated arguments about the dating and order of the kings of ancient Israel, but also a passionate search for the proper Latin adjectives and turns of phrase. Each paragraph is a little set-piece: "Your *Elenchus* [of Christopher Clavius] has also reached me . . . I read it with great pleasure, because you lay him out and overwhelm him with such manifest [lined out: arguments] proofs and such vigorous [later amended to: severe and vigorous] prose that he seems quite defeated. Therefore, though he wrote against me, I think I should remain silent now, lest I seem to insult a dead dog and write an Iliad after Homer."[19] Clavius's self-conscious effort to accumulate laudatory terms and parallel clauses, his overuse of classical proverbs, his very emphasis on Scaliger's virtuosity as a stylist—all these traits of the mature scholar were acquired at the schoolboy's desk, and firmly internalized.

Yet even this apparently atavistic obsession with good Latin had its uses in the seventeenth century. It meant that Latin remained up to date and accessible—and thus preserved it as a means of winning advancement (and, of course, of keeping those unfitted by birth and position from winning advancement in their turn). It inspired some polyhistors to make real additions to the expressive possibilities of Latin (as they did with those strange compositions, half poem and half inscription, that became the fashionable way to write political lampoons in the 1660s, and the textbook for which was written by a Jena professor of eloquence in 1670).[20] And it made the rulers of the *Kleinstaat* far more cosmopolitan than they would have been had they not had immediate access to the normal language of European science and learning. We customarily take our cue from Descartes and Christian Thomasius and denounce the schools' obsession with blowing artificial life into a dead language. In doing so we forget that there was no alternative save French—and that to accept that would have made Germany a cultural province of France instead of an independent member state of what Germans always insisted on seeing as a Europe-wide, Latin-speaking Republic of Letters. To that extent the pursuit of eloquence was still a coherent and plausible as well as a pragmatic and useful enterprise.

Encyclopedism is harder than humanism to define. It refers not only to the specific effort to organize knowledge in systematic compendia but also to the more general intellectual aspirations of the polyhistors—aspirations so sweeping as to boggle the modern mind.[21] The polyhistor was a figure very alien to us, with our close-fitting specialties and our contented refusal to have anything to do with our intellectual neighbors (except the occasional pleasure of denying the value of their pursuits). He wanted to cover every base on the intellectual field. His ideal was embodied in the great polymaths of the years around 1600, like Claudius Salmasius, "a man from whom one could cut three specialists." The scholar had to know the structure and relations of all disciplines, the titles and contents of all books, the character traits and oddities of all significant earlier scholars. Given the proliferation of books since 1450 and of new knowledge since the Renaissance the ideal had become desperately hard to realize by the time that Morhof gave it an appropriately ambitious name and an appropriately chaotic handbook with his *Polyhistor* of 1697.

The polyhistors hit on a variety of expedients for setting in order and passing on the universal knowledge they needed. They did produce some genuine encyclopedias—like Johann Heinrich Alsted's, which rammed together introductory works from a variety of disciplines, and Theodor Zwinger's, which amassed passages on all subjects from over 500 authors on over 5,000 folio pages.[22] They charted the relations of the disciplines to one another, laying these out in tables that always differed from one another and generally revealed no great measure of internal coherence.[23] They tried to force the basic content of individual disciplines and the basic rules for studying any subject into concise introductory textbooks. A standard collection of tracts by G. J. Vossius and others covers these topics (I keep the original order): a survey of the legitimate disciplines, chronology, history, imitation in oratory and poetry, history again, public speaking, ancient shorthand, letter writing, punctuation, the organization of libraries, the study of law, the study of law again, the method of study in all fields, theology, theology again, Hebrew and Aramaic, law again, medicine, natural philosophy, music, and ethics—all in 720 small pages.[24] It is more orderly than some of its competitors.

Such compendia neither reflected any clear idea of the hierarchy of the liberal arts, professions, and philosophies nor offered any serious grasp of their content, methods, and data. The object of the exercise was at best the lexical one traditional since Martianus Capella and Isidore of Seville: to acquaint the student with the names and terminologies of disciplines so that he could recognize them when he encountered them in his reading.[25] At worst it degenerated into mere quackery. The ears of the seventeenth-century student rang with promises to teach him "Latin in eight months, Greek in twenty days, astronomy in eight or ten days, philosophy and music in a month or less."[26] Bartholomaeus Ernestus promised his readers that his methods would enable them "to teach an art and language in an orderly way and learn it at a moderately high level, by means of reasonable diligence, in 8 or 14 days"; that he could train "city-dweller and peasant to be able to fill some 100 sheets with correct Latin verses."[27] Even Andreas Gryphius, a genuinely learned man as well as a gifted poet, can hardly have been competent to deal with all the topics encompassed by the "Collegium Metaphysicum, Geographicum & Trigonometricum, Logicum, Physiognomicum & Tragicum"—"Course on metaphysics, geography, and trigonometry, logic, physiognomics, and tragedy"—that he gave at Leiden—not to mention his further lectures on peripatetic and modern philosophy, Roman antiquities, and astronomy.[28] And even Leibniz, certainly no charlatan, chased all his life an ideal as alluring and unattainable as Jan Amos Comenius's: the creation of a survey of all knowledge, derived from the best books and encoded in a universal language.[29]

The polyhistors, though quixotic, were not in all respects divorced from the reality around them. Much of their effort was carefully directed at meeting specifically modern needs. For example, they took account in everything they did of the revolution in the dissemination of knowledge brought about by printing. Unlike most earlier encyclopedists, they did not have to try to preserve all of learning between two covers, since the printers ensured that every necessary book and many others existed in thousands of copies. On the other hand they did feel an irresistible pressure to survey the literature of every field as well as its structure, since the very richness of the available offerings meant that readers and students needed guidance in the choice of books.

Gabriel Naudé showed how to meet this need. His sprawling works on how to organize a library and on the bibliography of politics provided a rich mix of book chat, bibliophily, and ill-considered advice for the student. Here are his instructions on where to look for competent help in reading Aristotle's *Politics:*

> Thomas Aquinas . . . was followed by Nicole Oresme . . . [His] books are now very hard to find and accordingly much esteemed by connoisseurs, since they were printed 120 years ago at Paris in Lombardic script . . . the special commentators Camerarius and Giphanius rarely put a foot wrong; and more or less consonant with them are Antonius Scainus . . . and that very eloquent Jesuit Tarquinius Gallutius, who interpreted the first five books of the *Politics* so learnedly as to be far more of a polymath than the rest. But he who chooses Daniel Heinsius's paraphrase with the commentaries of Zwinger and Vettori as the basis of his studies—he, I think, will have done well as regards both ease of learning and the utility of his studies.[30]

Naudé's ideal scholar was the late sixteenth-century humanist and lawyer Jean Bodin, "who vanquished the difficulties of almost all languages and sciences, built the theater of nature on new principles, and systematized the kinds, laws, institutions, secrets, virtues, and vices of all the world's past and present kingdoms."[31] And his ideal public filled the universities of contemporary Germany, where Hermann Conring and others reprinted his books and expanded on them in lectures.

Such courses in general literature became the rule throughout Protestant Germany. The teacher would print and distribute an outline of his system of knowledge or have his students buy the printed catalogue of a great private library. He would then expatiate, offering information about the best editions of texts and textbooks, describing the styles and virtues of ancient and modern authors, and enlivening the hour with curious anecdotes about the lives and fortunes of men of letters. The student would scurry to keep up, often copying the teachers' words verbatim page after page.

The results have a certain pathos. Often their level of analysis is terrifyingly meager and superficial: "*Plato.* His style is not philosophical but swollen and declamatory, and furthermore allegorical and hieroglyphical. But his *Republic* and *Laws* have a more philosophical style. Aristotle excelled at this, and sticks to the austere and accurate philosophical style."[32] So much for the great debate between Platonists and Aristotelians. Yet at the same time teachers could make the most extravagant demands on their students' willingness and ability to buy, borrow, or steal expensive books: "In the history of antiquities we indicate the following: Franciscus Ferrarius *De veterum acclamationibus libri VII*, Milan 1627; on the ancients' rings see Ioannes Kirchmannus, Lübeck 1623, Fortun. Licetus, Udine 1646, Georgius Longus on the ancients' signet rings, Milan 1645; on the ancients' bracelets see Thomas Bartholinus, Amsterdam 1676; on the Roman toga Hieronymus Borsius, Amsterdam 1671; on the ancient and mystic boot Benedictus Balduinus, Paris 1615; on the ancients' crowns Carolus Paschalius."[33] Few university libraries would have offered this wealth of ore to a student's spade, even if they had been open to students (or to anyone for more than a few hours a week). And few inhabitants of an ordinary city could have hoped to taste more than a spoonful or two of this spicy stew of erudition.

The intent was clear; just as textbooks acquainted their readers with the basic terms of the arts, so lectures on literature acquainted their hearers with the basic titles and authors, giving a vision of the whole compass of learning that must have been at once inspiring and deeply frustrating. Yet they did offer the student some sense of the European world of learning, as one which he could enter by reading even if he lacked the means to travel to such capital cities of the *Respublica litterarum* as Leiden or Paris. And they were literally all that Germans could afford, given the poverty of the country and the high price of books. Hence this oral and disorderly mode of imparting information remained standard through the eighteenth and nineteenth centuries. J. M. Gesner, F. A. Wolf, and August Böckh, now remembered as the reformers of classical scholarship and teaching, offered to students who had never seen the books in question exactly this traditional form of schematic bibliographical comment—and found auditors loyal enough to copy out and publish what they had to say.[34] In this and other respects the polyhistors laid the foundations of the new historical curriculum that replaced theirs—and that is often seen, unfairly, as the antithesis of all that they held dear.[35]

We find it easier to laugh at the polyhistors than to understand them. Our ideal of scholarship is no longer encapsulated by Morhof's hero Julius Caesar Bottifanga, who knew all the arts and sciences, played—and built— all the musical instruments, and embroidered more deftly than any woman.[36] We find it easy to see that Peter Lambeck could never have finished the work a sketch of which he published in the 1650s: "A literary history, containing a general narrative of the origin, rise, transformation, fall, and restoration of all the languages, sciences, faculties, and liberal arts, in chronological order through all the centuries, with a special account of famous men and women."[37] Yet we should not mock the polyhistors without acknowledging their merits. Their broad interests did not lead only to chaotic or superficial work. In history, for example, they enlarged both the range of subjects and the range of nations that the discipline studied. Universal history as treated by sixteenth-century teachers had confined itself to a political narrative of the fortunes of the four biblical monarchies. But universal history as treated by Georg Hornius in his *Arca Noae* included Egyptians, Chinese, and American Indians as well as Assyrians, Greeks, and Romans, and dealt at length with religious ritual, literature, and art as well as with the deeds and deaths of kings. The result was a history curriculum far richer than anything a Renaissance university had provided. Hornius's work lacked the sharp concentration on drawing moral and political lessons from the past that had given shape to late Renaissance historiography. But in its cosmopolitan breadth and richness it looked forward to the innovative historical school of eighteenth-century Göttingen.[38]

The general borders of the country that the polyhistors inhabited are now clear. They were citizens less of a terrestrial empire than of an imaginary republic—the *Respublica litterarum.* They felt more at home in its artificially preserved Latin than in their native German. They prized the *alba amicorum* and letters from distinguished strangers that served as its badges of citizenship as highly as their local distinctions. And their desperate efforts to preserve its traditions of universal curiosity and eloquent rhetoric linked them to spiritual compatriots throughout Europe. In Scotland and Poland, Holland and Italy, many intellectuals resisted the transformation of the Latin-speaking *Respublica litterarum* into a French-speaking *République des lettres,* the turn from a humanism bound to the past to a philosophy intent upon the future. They kept one another informed of literary and scientific news by the old-fashioned means of formal Latin correspondence; they helped one another gain access to the old materials from which new works of erudition were to be constructed; they formed societies to distribute the best new Latin books from northern Europe in the south, and vice versa. The Germans who shared these tastes and interests saw themselves as threatened by the new French ideal of the cultivated but unscholarly *honnête homme. But* they did not stand alone against the French. Antonio Magliabechi and Ludovico Antonio Muratori, Peter Burman and Thomas Ruddiman shared their tastes and interests.

The problems that remain are easy to state if difficult to answer. How far were German polyhistors peculiarly German? And how far did they—could they—respond to the challenge of the new philosophy by updating their own tools and interests?

The best way to answer the first question is to exchange the telescopic lens we have been using for a microscopic one. A single case study in *Polyhistorie* will add some color, relief, and detail to our outline map. And a singularly curious specimen is available to be its object: Conrad Samuel Schurzfleisch (1641–1708), the most distinguished Wittenberg professor of the generation after the Thirty Years' War. Schurzfleisch deserves attention less for the lasting distinction of his thought than for the richness of the evidence he left behind and the vividness with which it reveals the impact of *Kleinstaat* habits of life and thought on a cosmopolitan and idealistic man. We have several hundred pages of his letters, several hundred more of his Latin orations, and two collections of his informal lectures on general literature—one euphoniously entitled *Schurzfleischiana* and uneuphoniously couched in a hideous mixture of Latin and German that bears the clear hallmark of informal delivery. Taken together, these enable us to see the polyhistor, as it were, in his shirt-sleeves—and thus to identify some highly localized elements in a cosmopolitan style of life and thought.

In many respects, to be sure, Schurzfleisch was a traditional figure whose duplicates could be found across Europe. He loved to whip his Latin rhetoric up to a fine frenzy of high-sounding phrases quite devoid of sense: "[Frisia (he wrote to a young lady whose Latin prose and German modesty he admired)]: You have joined the ranks of the learned Heroides . . . You have imitated the imperial virago Alexia Comnena. You have equaled Hroswitha, once the ornament of all Saxony. You have vanquished the rest, or at least made the decision a close one. There was nothing left for you save to transfer those incomparable virtues to the wedding bed, and spread [them] among your children and grandchildren."[39] He took pride in his mastery of the traditional but taxing craft of writing pure Latin: "I would find it difficult to maintain a consistent style had I not worked hard at it when I was young."[40] He gave his students careful instruction in the avoidance of solecisms—even those that had the sanction of great humanist names behind them: "Among words we must distinguish those that are Roman from those that are used in a Roman way . . . they commonly say that *deputare* someone means the same as *delegare, abschicken;* even de Thou used it in this sense, 'He was *deputatus* by him,' when the Latin way to say it is '*delegatus.*' For example, if our academy sends someone to Dresden . . . , then don't say, he was *deputatus,* but he was *delegatus.*"[41] He agonized over those apparent correspondences between vernacular and Latin words that often trap students of composition. No student of Schurzfleisch's left Wittenberg thinking that Latin *circulus* was the proper term for a *Kreis* of the Holy Roman Empire.[42]

Schurzfleisch treated the pursuit of Latin eloquence as an enterprise whose moral worth was too obvious to need defense, and whose practical value was enormous. Its possessor could win high position and wide reputation in the many parts of Europe where really good metaphors still mattered: "In Germany the humanities are taken very seriously, as in Sweden and Denmark. I praise the King of France too. The Saxon court is especially dextrous in German style, and has men highly skilled in Latin style as well. This they esteem highly in the (Saxon) court at Weimar. Even in Vienna they pick up Latin and German writings from our Elector like a Gospel, and they say there, 'Herr Secretair, lernts auch'—'Mr Secretary, you too should learn how to do this.'"[43] Schurzfleisch looked back to the happy days before his time, when really great scholars like Scaliger and Isaac Casaubon had flourished, as superior to his own time in learning and literacy. He deeply admired the earlier humanists' ready wit and command of Latin: This was what had enabled Nicodemus Frischlin to cap a faltering Latinist's effort at extemporaneous verse address, "Tu, Frischline, vates" with the perfect complement—"Tu mihi lambe nates." "He was so witty," Schurzfleisch sighed. Yet he saw no reason to think that the earlier humanists' values and interests need be abandoned. No one had told him that the age of Latin eloquence was over.

Schurzfleisch's curiosity was as boundless as his definition of correct Latin was strict. He read with pleasure the great compendia of seventeenth-century lore like Samuel Bochart's *Phaleg et Canaan* and Huet's *Demonstratio evangelica*. He discussed for his students questions as varied as the dating of medieval diplomas and the probability that men had drunk wine before the Flood. He took as much interest in Leibniz's discoveries in algebra as he did in Scaliger's principles of chronology. He met even the most bumptious manifestos of the new philosophy with calm charity, assimilating the new data and methods that they offered and ignoring or rejecting their critique of the aggregate of old-fashioned scholarly disciplines with which he occupied himself. No passage in seventeenth-century literature makes a more memorable assault on humanism than the early sections of Descartes's *Discourse on the Method,* in which we learn that the study of rhetoric, history, and traditional philosophy had served only to teach Descartes the limitations of his range of experience and the bankruptcy of the traditional curriculum. No reaction to Descartes could seem more bizarre than Schurzfleisch's: "I tell all students to concentrate on that study for which they feel a special aptitude . . . Thus Descartes began as a rhetorician, but, ceasing to make progress, applied his mind to the study of physics."[44] Schurzfleisch's very calmness—his willingness to accept the new Cartesian science without becoming hysterical about the challenge it posed him—marks him out a German, for whom the new philosophy meant the renovation, not the destruction, of the old encyclopedia.

A less pleasing set of stigmata is also visible on closer inspection. Schurzfleisch and his brethren were after all men of the German *Kleinstaat,* their vision of the world narrowed by a cramped and ossified Protestantism. The tolerance they showed for philosophical speculation did not extend to matters of morality and behavior. And that explains why even the broad-minded classicist Schurzfleisch could not recommend all the classics to his pupils with an easy mind. He felt impelled to warn them that "Tibullus wrote a pretty elegy, and purely, but with too many foulnesses mixed in; but Catullus is an arch-pig and buffoon, who offers wagonloads of obscenities for sale."[45] True, he was not so intolerant of all the controversial pagans. He carried his Epicurus with him everywhere, finding him a rewarding and spiritual philosopher.[46] But when sex became the topic Schurzfleisch shuddered and withdrew. This lover of good Latin found only one justification for the study of Catullus—"one can learn from him the many rituals of the ancients."[47] And this warning, for all its antiquarian sensitivity, in turn warns us not to overestimate the humanity and open-mindedness of the polyhistors. On social and sexual matters they were as small-minded as their neighbors—and thus good citizens of the old empire.

This map of the polyhistors' world must remain sketchy and incomplete. To perfect it we would need to weave diachronic threads that do not now exist across the synchronic ones that I have traced here—to show how individual sectors of the polyhistors' culture shifted over time and across distances. It would be most revealing, for example, to draw the complex and jagged path by which the discipline of hermeneutics evolved from the time of Martin Luther to that of Johann Salome Semler two centuries later. This would reveal how German professors of biblical interpretation could teach, in the sixteenth century, that the central message of the Bible was to be found in the teachings of a few select books, while the rest were to be played down or even excised from the corpus; in the seventeenth century, that the central message of the Bible was to be found in every book, every word, and every mark of punctuation in the Old Testament as well as the New; in the eighteenth century, that each book of the Bible had been written for a specific audience and must be in interpreted in accordance with the values, beliefs, and assumptions of its original readers.[48] Modern accounts hardly suggest the richness of the polyhistors' work in this central field—far less the diversity of their conclusions. Yet a final assessment of their work must take account of changes as radical as these in half a dozen other fields as well, from classical philology to music.[49] Perhaps that is enough to show that much more exploration is still needed in the regions we have traveled through so rapidly.

In the end, we may well share Mencke's amusement at his predecessors. We cannot fail to see the comic side of men like "Johann Seger, rector of the University of Wittenberg and imperial poet laureate. He had an engraving made on copper, showing the crucified Christ in the background and himself in front. From his lips came the words 'Lord Jesus, do you love me?', and from the lips of Jesus came the answer 'Yes, most eminent, excellent and learned Master Seger, imperial poet laureate and worthy rector of Wittenberg, I do love you.' "[50] Yet we should not assume that Mencke is telling the whole story. After all, it will go hard with our memory if historians two centuries from now rely solely upon our critics. If we can muster energy, sympathy, and a willingness to read some unpromising sources, we can find as much that is solid as is funny in the world of the polyhistors. Schurzfleisch himself would have had enough of a sense of humor and self-mockery to find that an appropriate epitaph, for himself and for his culture.

10

Jean Hardouin:
The Antiquary
as Pariah

〇〇〇

*I*N OCTOBER 1678, Leibniz surveyed the antiquarian learning of his time. Writing to Pierre-Daniel Huet, whose *Demonstratio evangelica* he eagerly awaited, he emphasized the vital importance of the antiquaries' preferred studies. The tasks they attacked, while difficult, mattered greatly. The material remains which they collected and analyzed—manuscripts, coins, inscriptions, and other "treasures"—proved the historical *fides* of the Christian religion. But for all his massive erudition, Leibniz admitted that he found it hard to master all these diverse forms of evidence. Indeed, he had often wished that "someone would lay out for us an inventory, so to speak, of this precious treasury, and of all the remains of antiquity that survive today, so far as that is possible."[1] Fortunately, a number of scholars had intensively cultivated individual sectors of this enormous field. Leibniz saw reason to hope that they would soon supply authoritative surveys: "We await something of this sort, with regard to inscriptions, from that great expert in this field, Marquard Gude; and Ezechiel Spanheim and other men of worth will certainly offer their services for coins—especially your friend Pierre de Carcavy, the admirable guardian of such treasures in this realm."[2]

Areas of ignorance naturally remained, and Leibniz's discussion of one of these reveals his erudition and prescience as clearly as his correct prediction that Spanheim would revolutionize the study of ancient coins. "I still regret the lack of a history of manuscripts," he confided to Huet, "one which lists the best codices that are extant in Europe today, especially the ones on which the editions of authors rest, and the unique ones."[3] Only three years later, Jean Mabillon would publish *De re diplomatica*, the first systematic effort to provide criteria for authenticating charters and manuscripts.[4] In 1709, Mabillon's fellow Maurist Bernard de Montfaucon would provide, with his *Palaeographia Graeca*, something very much like the critical "history of manuscripts" Leibniz had wished to read.

Huet's own *Demonstratio*, which Leibniz had hoped would contain "the entire apparatus needed to confirm sacred history," in fact proved to be a controversial effort to identify traces of biblical history in myths and legends drawn from a vast range of ancient literature and modern travelers' accounts.[5] But Leibniz's more general optimism was justified, as Arnaldo Momigliano demonstrated half a century ago in an essay that has become a classic of modern historical writing. The antiquaries, he showed, helped to carry out a "revolution in historical method." Instead of relying on the historians of Greece and Rome, they "subordinated literary texts to coins, statues, vases, and inscriptions," compiling and analyzing so much evidence that they refuted the doubts of historical Pyrrhonists about the possibility of knowing the past. Instead of writing narratives, they crafted analyses of customs and institutions, rituals and beliefs. Though the antiquaries eventually disappeared from the historical scene, their work remained, as a vital part of the modern historian's method and "ethics" alike.[6]

Momigliano emphasized that some of the antiquaries, carried away by enthusiasm for their discoveries, raised more questions than they answered—especially those who thought that the material evidence of coins and inscriptions could infallibly solve all historical problems. It was only in this larger context, he wrote, that one could understand "the extraordinary story" of that "pathological case," the Jesuit Jean Hardouin, who "found contradictions between coins and literary texts and slowly reached the conclusion that all the ancient texts (except Cicero, Virgil's *Georgics*, Horace's *Satires* and *Epistles*, and his beloved Pliny the Elder) had been forged by a gang of Italians in the late fourteenth century." It was only in this context, too, that one could understand why Hardouin's "contemporaries did not laugh. They answered at length."[7] Hardouin's work—though it went "well beyond the verge of madness"—drew on and developed the same forms of scholarship which were being practiced by his contemporaries, the very men whom Leibniz—and Momigliano—acknowledged as the founders of a new kind of historical scholarship. Not for the last time in the history of European culture, the ravings of a mad outsider revealed much about ideas and practices central to the culture that rejected him.

Fifty years on, Momigliano's essay remains the most authoritative account of the antiquaries and their world.[8] The present essay—which offers a second look at Hardouin—is meant not to contest his diagnosis, but to amplify it: to look more closely at Hardouin and his context, and by doing so to suggest some further ways of understanding how his work sheds light on the cultural situation of Europe in the years around 1700.

To begin with the wider world: antiquaries like Hardouin inhabited one province of a larger intellectual society, the Republic of Letters. As Elizabeth Eisenstein and Françoise Waquet have shown, the Italian humanists of the early fifteenth century, men like Francesco Barbaro and Poggio Bracciolini, called this imaginary community into being.[9] Humanist intellectuals, who lacked a firm institutional base in cloisters or universities, conjured a new, international social system from the air and endowed it with substance. By the later sixteenth century, the Republic had taken shape. Huge folios in Latin, often packed with quotations in other, more obscure languages, provided its favoured currency. The public economy by which these and lesser goods were exchanged was governed by the publishers and booksellers of Rotterdam, Neuchâtel, and other strategic entrepôts where censors' edicts did not run. Multivolume editions of texts and ambitious journals that specialized in providing summaries and reviews carried the literary news from Cracow to Cambridge and beyond. Around and beneath this public sphere, an efficient system of private correspondence connected all the Republic's citizens—a varied body, which included Huguenot refugees, members of half a dozen Catholic religious orders, and even a few Jews.

Personal ties, rather than professional associations, linked the citizens of the Republic. The *voyages littéraires* that well-to-do young men routinely undertook provided a ready way to forge these. Anyone who turned up in a Parisian abbey, a Berlin parsonage, or a London library with the right letter of introduction could depend on it: he would be invited to enter a florid signature and an appropriate sentiment in Latin, Greek, or Hebrew in his host's *album amicorum,* to engage in a morning's book chat, and to

carry away with him introductions to other humane and erudite gentlemen, whose libraries and cabinets of curiosities he would explore in their
turn.[10]

The denizens of this Republic, historians have recently argued, created
the first modern institutions of learning. They were confronted, as their
own testimony shows, by what they saw as particularly grave problems:
certainties had vanished, agreement on the central problems of theology
and history seemed impossible to reach. They met this crisis with energy
and resourcefulness, trying to forge a new standard for public discussion,
one that could accommodate their disagreements on principle without
forcing them to cut off social ties. Many of these scholars insisted on their
own duty to rise above religion and party when judging the work of others.
Protestants generously praised sound works of erudition by Catholics.[11]
Frenchmen welcomed news of the German literati, as long as they could
read it in French in the *Revue germanique.* Together they created rules for
civility in intellectual life—rules which proved vital in the formation of the
modern natural and human sciences—and by doing so laid the foundations of the Enlightenment itself.[12]

Like the larger world of learning which the Republic fostered, the special pursuits of the antiquaries have come in for renewed scrutiny in recent
years.[13] Some recent scholarship has celebrated the originality and power
of antiquarian learning: Krzysztof Pomian and Antoine Schnapper, for
example, have argued that it grew from a new "culture of curiosity," one
that focused on the material rather than the textual and liberated itself
from the ideologies and methodologies of an older humanism.[14] Paula
Findlen and Horst Bredekamp, by contrast, have emphasized the roots of
early modern antiquarianism in earlier forms of learning: even the most
spectacular Renaissance museums, they argue, rested in part on the very
classical ideas about classification that their massed contents often seemed
to challenge.[15] Still others, like Francis Haskell, have taken a more equiv-
ocal position, suggesting that most antiquaries saw the objects they
interpreted through a haze of textual evidence that determined their interpretations. When Montfaucon worked on Greek manuscripts, he showed
a keen sense of discrimination and took meticulous care in reproducing
and analyzing his sources. But qualities like these were less apparent when
he discussed visual evidence about the past.[16] In fact, the ideal antiquary
should be able—as Gisbert Cuperus wrote of Enrico Noris—"to work

effectively at interpreting the Fathers, the Greek and Latin authors, inscriptions and coins." But few attained this ideal—as Cuperus himself conceded when he remarked that Noris's achievement represented "a great adornment to this age."[17]

These studies raise new questions about Momigliano's "pathological case." What do the controversies Hardouin provoked reveal about the manners and morals of the Republic of Letters? How unusual were Hardouin's "extravagances?" Exactly what made his work stand out as bizarre? Certainly, his early career followed more or less normal lines. Born in Brittany in 1646, the son of a bookseller and printer, Hardouin distinguished himself as a pupil in a Jesuit collège, entering the novitiate in 1660. He taught philosophy, belles-lettres, and theology, served as librarian of the Jesuit Collège de Paris, and early won a reputation for wide learning, acute critical sense, and prodigious energy. By the early 1680s, he was beginning to contribute to the Parisian *Journal des sçavans*. His five-volume edition of the elder Pliny's *Natural History* with commentary—which formed part of the famous series that Huet supervised, purportedly for the education of the dauphin—appeared in 1685. It made him famous overnight. Even in that age of incredibly hard workers, readers marveled at his ability to complete in one year a five-volume edition based on collations of twenty manuscripts and including six hundred pages of brand-new indices. These tasks could well have cost a team of normal collaborators a decade. For the rest of Hardouin's long life, which lasted until 1729, his energy never flagged. A long series of treatises on ancient coins, dynasties, and patristics made him a major scholarly figure in that great age of numismatics, epigraphy, and chronology—as well as the opponent in controversy of such formidable, and very different, scholars as Cardinal Ezechiel Noris and the Calvinist statesman and numismatist Ezechiel Spanheim. Only a selection of Hardouin's many shorter treatises figured in the two stately volumes of his miscellaneous works that appeared in 1709 and 1733. This immensely learned and argumentative man seems at first sight characteristic of his age.[18]

For many years Hardouin's main energies went on a literally monumental task assigned by the general assembly of the French clergy: a comprehensive edition of the acts and decrees of the councils of the church, designed to be published with great splendor by the royal presses. The compilation of and commenting on conciliar documents had been a major task of Catholic scholars since Jacques Merlin produced the first printed collection in 1524. From early in the seventeenth century, it preoccupied the Jesuits: members of the order like Jacob Gretser, Antonio Possevino, and Robert Bellarmine contributed materials lavishly to Severinus Bini's editions of 1606 and 1618. And it was naturally a matter of the utmost scholarly and theological delicacy, since even small additions to or excisions from a conciliar text often bore immense implications for church discipline and doctrine. But Hardouin, far from treading lightly, did his best to stir up controversy. The Archbishop of Reims tried to suppress Hardouin's work, arguing—so Bernard de Montfaucon reported—that he had produced nothing but "libri stravaganti e pieni di spropositi."[19] Though greatly delayed, the edition reached completion in 1714–15, in the imposing form of eleven folio volumes in twelve, amounting to almost 22,000 pages. It did not go on sale, however, until ten years later, since the Parlement of Paris prohibited the work's distribution. And the condemnation occasions little surprise. In a time of sharp public controversy between Gallicans and Ultramontanes, Hardouin unequivocally took the side of Rome. A frontispiece dramatized the editor's allegiance to Saint Peter and his see; the last volume included the text of *Unigenitus*.[20] The assembly of the French clergy had clearly had something quite different in mind.[21]

For all its polemical edge, Hardouin's *Concilia* rested on massive critical and scholarly foundations. As a critic, he was a committed modern. In the age of the variorum editions, which piled commentary on commentary until the text to be explicated almost vanished from sight, Hardouin ruthlessly pruned away the excess scholarly apparatus that earlier editors had preserved: "It seemed useless to print the prefaces set out by those who edited the Councils before us. They basically confine themselves to praising the Councils, as if everyone did not know that these were holy; or they praise their own hard work and meticulous care, as if everyone did not willingly admit that they deserve the highest praise for that."[22] Hardouin also excluded all documents that did not formally belong to the records of the councils. In place of these extraneous materials he provided a fair number of variant readings, sometimes relying on the earlier work of Jacques Sirmond, Philippe Labbe, and Etienne Baluze, but also making extensive use of manuscripts in Paris, among which he preferred those in the Jesuits' own library to what he regarded as the basically similar ones in the collections of the king and Colbert.[23] Hardouin did not consistently ask after the descent of the manuscripts he followed. These self-imposed limitations on his search for evidence enabled him to cherish the illusion that the manuscripts of the councils varied less than those of other texts.[24] But he argued explicitly that the manuscripts he followed for the *subscriptiones* of the Council of Nicaea "can be seen to be copied from the original exemplar."[25] Unlike previous editors, he stated clearly that the Latin and Greek texts of the councils often varied, and that the critical editor must preserve the variations rather than seeking to harmonize them.[26] Hardouin's work reached a new level of critical precision. Ironically, it received little appreciation and had almost no impact, since the theological controversies which surrounded its reception distracted many early readers from his philological accomplishments.[27]

Clearly, Hardouin was no ordinary scholar. But even the originality of his editorial work pales by comparison with that of his effort to retrace the transmission of the classical tradition as a whole. Within five years of the beginning of his literary career—so he later recalled—he had already developed what became the core of a unique theory, a literary heresy that its opponents ridiculed as "Harduinismus." "It was in the month of August, 1690," he wrote much later, "that I began to scent fraud in Augustine and his contemporaries." By November he suspected that all the ancients were as problematic as Augustine. In the course of the next two years, he made "long extracts from particular Greek and Latin writers," his feelings veering between "disgust and weariness" and "moments of great delight in the discovery of the truth." In May 1692 he "detected the whole fraud."[28]

"The whole fraud," as Hardouin first revealed it in a short treatise of 1693 on the coins of the dynasty of Herodiads, took many readers' breath away. "I will adduce," he wrote there, "in this place the conjecture of someone never given to idle conjecture, but who is now possibly more suspicious than he should be and indulges his cleverness too much. Let each person take it as he will. The critic I refer to has found out, as he lately whispered in my ear, that a certain band of fellows existed, some centuries ago, who had undertaken the task of concocting ancient history, as we now have it, there being at that time none in existence; that he knew their exact period and workshop; and that in this matter they had as aids the works of Cicero, Pliny, the *Georgics* of Virgil, the *Satires* and *Epistles* of Horace. These alone—the critic considers—as I fear he will find it hard to persuade anyone else to believe—to be genuine monuments out of the whole of Latin antiquity, apart from a very few inscriptions and some *Fasti*."[29]

The whole range of written texts from antiquity, which modern critics strove so desperately to reconcile with one another, Hardouin's imaginary friend dismissed as fakes. The architects of this great deception had possessed, he thought, a "great supply of ancient coins."[30] To their chief, who guarded this treasury with the ferocity of a dragon, they had given the comic double name Severus Archontius: the first name described his censorious character and the second his role as the director of their project. (One of Hardouin's critics cleverly deciphered this particular riddle: Severus Archontius had, of course, been that scourge of the papacy and the orthodox, Frederick II of Hohenstaufen.)[31] Using their hoard of coins and the few genuine ancient texts as their basic source, the *impia cohors* had forged the entire literary heritage of the west; they had given themselves away by the mistakes they committed, most of which resulted from lacunae in their coin collection. Hardouin, the first to detect these, argued that the classical and patristic heritage was not only incomplete, but largely spurious.

Hardouin's first readers were divided in their response to his ideas. On 1 November 1692, Louis Genevrat, Jesuit provincial in France, gave written permission for the book to appear. But on 7 January 1693 another Jesuit, Father Hurault, rector of the Jesuit Collège de Louis le Grand, went with some other members of the order to the workshop of the printer, Jean Anisson. There they confiscated all copies of the text, provoking some Protestants to suspect an underhanded effort to give an impression of rarity and drive up the book's price. Léonard de Sainte-Catherine, the admirably well-informed librarian of the discalced Augustinians of the Place Notre-Dame-des-Victoires, remarked that Hardouin "dares not say everything he thinks. He promised to have his dissertation on the coins of the Herodiads reprinted. But if he does it, he will be forced to cut out everything that was most curious in it."[32] Other friends and correspondents were more sympathetic. Hardouin exchanged detailed letters, for example, with Georges d'Ballonffeaux, an erudite antiquary from Lorraine who lived in Luxemburg. He warmly encouraged Hardouin to develop his full theories about the later history of the Roman empire.[33]

Encouraged by his friends, undisturbed by his opponents, Hardouin continued to work out the implications of his theories in detail. What he eventually made clear—as he had not in his first, short revelation of his ideas—was that the forgers had left in their work a whole series of clues, some inadvertent and others deliberate. In a long series of Latin treatises on history and chronology, Hardouin showed that ancient texts on which scholars had relied for centuries, when properly analyzed, revealed the forgers' hand everywhere at work. Josephus's history of the Herodiad line—the subject of Hardouin's first published exposé—swarmed with errors, as surviving coins clearly proved. Herod the Great had never, for example, restored the Temple at Jerusalem, as Josephus claimed, since no coin commemorated his action. Antipas could not have belonged to the same lineage as Herod the Great, since no coin referred to him as Herod Antipas. The list of ancient Egyptian rulers which Joseph Scaliger had discovered and published, the work of an Egyptian priest named Manetho, was also clearly a fake. Manetho, after all, was not a real Egyptian name but a composite. It referred, like the other falsified proper names found in ancient and medieval histories, to the Savior: "it is composed of the Germanic word *man,* which means man, and then of *et,* with, and *on,* strength. 'Man,' then, or 'son of man with strength,' as we read in Matthew 24.30, is Christ."[34] These falsifications seemed to prove that pagans and Jews had had foreknowledge of the coming of Jesus: accordingly, they did not need the Christian revelation. Medieval history had just as many obvious flaws. Aelfric, for example, clearly came from *el* and the verb *paraq*; it was not the real name of a Saxon king but "God the redeemer."[35] Dynasties fell before Hardouin's criticisms like dandelions before a sickle.

Literary texts proved equally vulnerable. In a long commentary Hardouin proved, beyond doubt, that "the thought of writing the *Aeneid* never entered Virgil's mind."[36] The real author of the *Georgics* could never have produced so footling a poem. It violated the unities of plot and time, contained obviously awkward digressions like the story of the death of Palinurus, and openly incited its readers to viciousness. Virgil would never have made Homer's gods into papier-maché figures: "quite theatrical and fabulous, like wooden and animated effigies of men, little puppets."[37] Certainly, a real poet of high stature could not have committed so many obvious errors of logic. Hardouin scrutinized the ancients as Mark Twain would later scrutinize James Fenimore Cooper. "I noted my tracks and followed them back through the night," says Aeneas, recounting to Dido his terrible experiences on the night when Troy fell. "How," asks Hardouin, "could he see or observe tracks, especially in the dark?"[38] The real Virgil would never have used so many inappropriate words simply in order to make his verses scan. When the author of the *Aeneid* wrote, in Book II, that the Dardanian shore "was bathed in a sweat of blood" ("sudarit sanguine"), he did so only because the constraints of dactylic hexameter did not allow him to say what he meant: that the shore "was wet" ("maduerit").[39] Above all, the real poet would never have composed so many strange and obviously silly phrases. Aeneas's often-quoted words "Sunt lacrimae rerum," "Tears are in the nature of things," were nothing more than "a very abnormal way of saying, simply, 'here we should feel sorry for those poor wretches to whom bad things have happened.' "[40]

Equally devastating was Hardouin's critique of Horace, whose "Integer vitae" ode (I.22) he unmasked as an obvious Christian allegory. Using the same method, he identified Horace's laughing girlfriend Lalage as "Christiana pietas." Hardouin's detailed, line-by-line commentaries on Virgil and Horace probably give a good sense of the long extracts he made as he first worked out the details of his theory. The controversy that attended Hardouin's earliest effort to publish his theory did not discourage or distract him, moreover. He worked systematically through the classical corpus, showing that the philosophy of Plato, the tragedies of Aeschylus, Sophocles, and Euripides, and the poems of Pindar were as spurious as the classics of Golden Latin poetry.[41]

Some of Hardouin's methods for detecting signs of spuriousness belonged to the normal repertoire of techniques for literary study—though he stretched them far past their normal limits. Many texts—like the *Aeneid* and Horace's *Odes*—revealed themselves as fake because their authors violated the rule of decorum that every great writer should have followed. The author of Augustine's *Confessions,* for example, gave the game away when he played on words and put into the mouth of his adolescent self the unworthy prayer to be granted chastity at a later date.[42] In applying this severe literary standard, Hardouin revealed himself as a tasteful Frenchman of the classic age, one who saw the Song of Songs, for example, as a dramatic poem in seven scenes—and was shocked by Hugo Grotius's idea that it recorded an actual dialogue between Solomon and the daughter of the king of Egypt, in which the king used far-fetched metaphors to praise the woman's body.[43] In many other cases, Hardouin's sensitive ear detected the creaking of the forger's stage machinery. He thus identified in Augustine's dramatic account of his conversion experience in the garden a transparent effort to shore up the *fides* of the life of Antony by Athanasius.[44] Hardouin resembled his predecessors, Lorenzo Valla and Joseph Scaliger, and his contemporary Richard Bentley, when he treated forgery as a literary genre with a well-established set of tricks and tropes.[45]

Hardouin shared his dislike of metaphor and other forms of stylistic variety and play with at least some of his contemporaries. Huet—another polymath who, like Hardouin, took an active role in critical discussions of modern as well as ancient literature—condemned the French public, which had shown itself unable to appreciate Jean Chapelain's epic poem, *La Pucelle.* Judging an epic by the tight, precise standards that ruled the writing of sonnets and songs, they had condemned the whole work because it contained a few forced expressions—enough to ruin an epigram, but not a narrative poem on the grand scale. "How," Huet asked, "would these finicky critics judge the *Iliad* of Homer, if it had never appeared, with its careless verses, tedious repetitions, and all the failings that have been pointed out in it?"[46] The Jesuits, in Huet's view, showed the same error, dramatically, in what they wrote. He described their bad habit of always writing Latin "too oratorically." "This results," he argued, "from the fact that they are made to serve as regents from early youth." Since they had "to speak incessantly in public," they grew accustomed to dealing with every subject in the same elevated, flamboyant style, even when writing personal letters, which called for the simple tone of Cicero or Joseph Scaliger. Huet could have explained Hardouin's inability to accept the many styles of classical Greek and Latin as a case in point of a deformation normal among what he called "les gens de Collège."[47] Even Hardouin's wildest errors in the evaluation of style would not have surprised Huet, who maintained that "good judges of poetry are rarer than good poets."[48]

Still, the sheer scale of Hardouin's enterprise was extraordinary. For all his commitment to the Catholic church and the Jesuit order, he condemned not only Augustine, but the other early Christian writers and Fathers of the church—the central sources for orthodox tradition—as clear fakes. Eusebius, in the *Ecclesiastical History,* cited a document in which the clerics of Antioch denounced Paul of Samosata. Among many other failings, they criticized the arrogance that made him wish to be called *ducenarius* (a procurator who enjoyed the high salary of 200 sesterces) (vii.30.8). Hardouin insisted that no such Greek word existed. Clearly, the man in question had demanded to be called *duceparius,* "duc et pair"—a palpable anachronism which only the forger's change of *p* to *n* had concealed.[49] Equally palpable Gallicisms bespeckled every text from medieval chronicles back to Thucydides (whose use of *ho megas* to refer to the elder of a pair of brothers, Hardouin thought, clearly reflected a literal translation of the French "le grand"). Bold theories about the origins and relationships of the European languages flourished in the sixteenth and seventeenth centuries; and though the sort of wild philology Hardouin practiced was already coming under attack in his time from Leibniz and others, who hoped to set etymology on solid historical foundations, many of his contemporaries linked word to word and language to language with just as much inventiveness.[50] But few used them to rewrite the history of the world with quite so much abandon.

Never daunted by the scale of any scholarly task, Hardouin attacked the entire written record, western and nonwestern alike. He demolished the supposed works of scholastics like Thomas Aquinas and Thomas Bradwardine.[51] He revealed that the so-called writings of the rabbis were also spurious. The very language of the Talmud and the Targumim, Aramaic, was in fact nothing but Hebrew: "The words in Esdras and Daniel that are labeled as Chaldean seem to me every bit as much Hebrew words as those which we now use are French, even if they did not exist yet in the time of François I."[52] Even the acts of the councils, which he himself had edited, aroused his hypercritical spirit. In a long series of unpublished commentaries, Hardouin pointed out how absurd it was to imagine that anyone could ever have believed in the Arian heresies condemned by "le prétendu Concile de Nicée."[53]

Each mistake that Hardouin identified might seem trivial in itself. But he insisted on their cumulative as well as their individual weight. The historian, he argued, must imitate the rigor of the officers of a court: "if there be but one faulty notation of time in any instrument, a court will decisively and with great and just indignation reject and repudiate the instrument. How much more vehemently should we vociferate, and how much more justly, when our holy Religion is assailed and undermined?"[54] The *impia cohors* of forgers, Hardouin argued, had deliberately set out to create a coherent web of mutually corroborative documents. They had known—

as he showed, quoting from the letters of Lupus of Ferrières and Jean Mabillon's *De re diplomatica*—that scripts should vary from place to place and time to time. They had used parchment, which would last, as their writing material of choice. They had even mustered the patience to develop both the core classical texts and a vast range of collateral evidence, in the form of apparently genuine later works that referred backward to them.[55]

Hardouin admitted that to prove the *Aeneid* spurious, one must also dismiss as fakes "innumerable testimonies, Ovid, Juvenal, Statius, Silius Italicus, Martial, Propertius, Quintilian, Asconius Pedianus, Tacitus in his *Dialogue on Orators,* and others"—not to mention the Virgilian commentator Servius, the neo-Platonist Macrobius, who compared Virgil to Homer, and a slew of church Fathers.[56] He did so without reservation. In fact, he argued that the *impia cohors* had salted whole libraries across Europe with books of every imaginable kind, expecting readers to take centuries to find them all. "The impious coterie," he said, "had in their service mathematicians who computed eclipses, lawyers who framed codices and laws, medical men who wrote on medicine, poets who put forth their poems, linguists and interpreters of great skill, who turned their Latin writings chiefly into Greek."[57] Their ingenuity knew no bounds: they even succeeded in convincing the inhabitants of Constantinople, who had previously used the Latin Vulgate Bible and a Latin liturgy, to speak Greek, to adopt the Greek Septuagint, and to accept a spurious Byzantine tradition of historiography as their own. Hardouin's polyglot, erudite, cohesive gang of forgers resembled nothing so much as the Jesuits, as their many enemies saw them.

In dissertation after dissertation, Hardouin dwelled with special persistence on one strategy pursued by "la secte athee."[58] They had filled every work they invented, from Plato to Bradwardine, with proper names which they had created artificially by combining Hebrew words. These anagrams described in detail how Jesus would return, in his wrath, to punish the Jews who had spurned and killed him. Unlike the cross references and parallels designed to bolster the authority of the forged texts, these riddles were designed to be noticed and solved. Readers, learning that Jews and pagans had known the whole story of Christ's mission to humanity and the crucifixion in advance, would see that one had no need for the Bible. The forged record represented a massive effort to destroy the foundations of Christianity. Tradition was not the basis, but the antithesis, of true religion.

Two sets of related questions obviously arise: what led Hardouin to advance his strange theories, and how did others receive them? Or, to put it more generally, how did the antiquarian tradition bring forth these strange fruits, and how did the Republic of Letters deal with them? Momigliano long ago suggested an answer to the first question. Many of Hardouin's contemporaries agreed with him in principle: they too considered nonliterary evidence the strongest foundation on which historical scholarship could rest. But he took this argument so far that he reduced it to absurdity—and by doing so seemed to call the whole antiquarian enterprise into question.

The new scholarship on coins and inscriptions represented the scholars' response to what they perceived as the brutal challenge of the New Philosophy. Descartes defiantly told traditionalists that the study of the past could prove, at best, only that ideas and values differed in different times and places. One could learn as much, more agreeably, by traveling. Too much time spent in the past—like too much time spent on travel—could make one "a stranger in one's own country." And the traveler was perhaps less likely than the reader to be confused by the fables, errors, and exaggerations that necessarily clouded the historical record. These made the imitation of historical examples not a rational way to improve one's conduct but a path that led straight to the follies and fantasies of a Don Quixote.[59] Many humanists sadly agreed, lamenting in their letters that the age of philology had ended, and one of philosophy had taken its place. But the philosophers did not see these gestures of submission as a reason to cease flagellating their victims. In the second half of the seventeenth century, Sebastien La Mothe le Vayer and others attacked history even more aggressively than Descartes had. Rigorously considered, they argued, texts and documents could give no certain knowledge about the past. After all, historical narratives often contradicted public records such as inscriptions—as well as one another. The historical record was full of mistakes, many of them obviously caused by historians' fears or desires. But no historian could hope to write without fear or ambition: hence none could avoid error. In any event, it was impossible to prove that even an uncontradicted witness accurately described a time and place that no one could now visit. History based on ancient texts lacked verifiability.[60]

Yet antiquarian studies flourished in the teeth of the philosophers' abuse—and their practitioners even learned to turn some of the philosophers' language against them. Specialists in coins and inscriptions boasted regularly that they too had a contribution to make to what Jacques Spon called, in 1683, a "century of new inventions." The physicists, he acknowledged, had learned how to weigh the air and measure heat, and the doctors had traced the circulation of the blood. Theologians, historians, and jurisconsults all had discoveries and innovations to their credit. But the antiquaries, he argued, "had taken just as many pains to make discoveries in the vast and curious country of antiquity. We have excavated ancient medals of all the kingdoms and the empires; we have deciphered a thousand curiosities of the ancient Romans, which our fathers saw only as mute letters, devoid of spirit and mystery."[61] Modern scholars used unimpeachable records, records produced in the periods to whose events they attested, and produced under public scrutiny at that: the very monuments, Spon explained in his *Miscellanea eruditae antiquitatis* of 1685, with which the ancients "tried to spread and to pass on to posterity the religion, history, and politics, and other arts and sciences, of their time." Ancient historians and orators like Suetonius and Demosthenes had recognized the *auctoritas* of such monuments when they cited them at length to prove points in contention. In short, they offered both rich information about ancient institutions and beliefs and a verifiable record of the most important ancient events. History based on ancient inscriptions and coins had what text-based history lacked: an epistemologically secure foundation.[62]

Hardouin, Momigliano argued, went wrong because he did not realize that the antiquaries had an answer for the skeptics.[63] Passionately convinced of the superiority of coins to texts, he failed to see that the numismatic evidence generally confirmed the transmitted written record. His shattering historical nihilism, which left room for nothing but certain church traditions (and Virgil's *Georgics*) in the record, marked a diversion from the normal development of historical thought and writing in his time. Less hypercritical scholars like Johann Burkhard Mencke and Johann August Ernesti reacted more reasonably when they tried to lay out the reasons for having *fides historica,* at least to a certain extent. Mencke showed that one could reasonably explain the divergence of eyewitness and historians' accounts of the death of Gustavus Adolphus. Ernesti argued that one could tease out, beneath the narrative facade, the content and something of the form of the official documents on which Suetonius had drawn, and which made his account more reliable than the more suspicious Johannes Georgius Graevius had realized.[64] Antiquarianism mitigated, and eventually defeated, skepticism. Hardouin's inability to grasp this point was only the sort of eccentricity natural in the development of new intellectual techniques. The defeat of his extreme historical and literary Pyrrhonism exemplifies the high quality and sophistication of the conflict-resolution techniques that the Republic of Letters had developed.

Hardouin certainly learned and borrowed from the antiquaries of the generation just before his. Jacques Basnage, the Protestant historian of the Jews, advanced one of many attacks on Hardouin's "overturning of all the ideas about [the genealogy of the Herods] that had been held until now." Hardouin's crisp reply made clear that he had learned from Spon and other numismatists to trust objects. For him the authority "of a public testimony, like that of medals" outweighed that of literary documents—even the official ones Josephus quoted, which could just as well be forged as any other part of his text.[65] Hardouin won wide recognition for his skill in this technical and combative field. Spanheim disputed Hardouin's conclusions on many points. But he also took care to acknowledge his adversary's great learning, his membership in the community of competent numismatists and the humanity he had shown toward Spanheim himself.[66]

Indeed, Hardouin shared what seems his largest obvious failure of historical imagination with almost all contemporary numismatists, even those who rejected his theses.[67] He assumed, without debating the matter at length, that coins and medals told the truth about the events they recorded. Yet Hardouin knew perfectly well that medals had other functions too. Sixteenth-century numismatists like Sebastiano Erizzo, whose work Hardouin knew, speculated that some imperial coins were actually celebratory medals. Though Antonio Agustín succeeded in refuting their arguments, they might have raised some doubts about the absolute reliability of numismatic evidence.[68] Hardouin, moreover, praised in phosphorescent Latin the scholarly achievements of the Academy of Inscriptions and Belles-Lettres—a body that existed not only to study such ancient monuments as the coins in the royal treasury but also to create modern ones. The members labored incessantly, as he knew, to design spectacular emblematic medals commemorating the achievements of Louis XIV. These celebrated his assumption of personal rule, his attacks on Algiers and Genoa, and, with special fervor, his destruction of France's Protestant churches and forcible reconversion of two million Calvinists. Peter Burke has shown that the medalists' biased formulations and distortions of the facts were well known—to, among others, the Huguenot pamphleteers who created parodic medals emphasizing the king's greed and cowardice (a notable specimen bore the motto "venit, vidit, sed non vicit").[69]

Blatantly propagandistic, the medals also regularly displayed errors of date and fact—which was only natural, as they were often struck in advance of the occasions they were meant to commemorate and these did not necessarily take place exactly as planned. When Mabillon set out to formulate rules for historical criticism in *De re diplomatica,* he asked his readers above all not to be captious—not, for example, to take the script of a document alone, or any other isolated characteristic, as an adequate reason for rejecting it as a fake.[70] A thought experiment about coins—one clearly based on actual practice—supported his plea that numismatic and epigraphic evidence should not always override that of written documents: "Anyone who set out to fix the day when Louis the Great, our present king, was anointed, would reasonably prefer the *fides* and authority of the coins struck to commemorate the event to any other monuments. And yet the day originally fixed for the celebration was changed, and the royal coronation took place four or five days later, as everyone knows. Accordingly, one should not always cite historians and inscriptions—even authentic ones— against documents."[71] Mabillon, in other words, argued that the historian must weigh all forms of evidence in any given case before deciding which of them deserved credence. He also evidently worried that some— unnamed—antiquarians inclined to give coins and medals a disproportionate amount of *fides historica.* His testimony suggests that Hardouin's theses amounted, just as Momigliano argued, to an extreme form of a fashionable way of using—or misusing—evidence.

But Hardouin's ways of working with evidence were not uniform, and did not all reflect his general claims about the central role of coins in his arguments. Hardouin, as we have seen, made direct use of material evidence when he wanted to. When he set out, for example, to argue that the antiquities found in a tomb at Tournai in 1653–64 were not the royal treasure of King Childeric, as Jean-Jacques Chifflet had thought, he took care to show that he himself had seen and touched the objects in question: "The ring found there is neither that of a king nor Childeric's. It is too heavy to be worn easily on a finger. In fact, it is the kind of ring that noble women used to award to the winners at the tournaments which they attended and watched . . . It is, I say, that sort of ring, and in the Royal Library, where it is kept, I have often marvelled at its weight."[72] He showed equal attention to material detail when he compared the craftsmanship and script of coins struck under Pipin and Charlemagne, in order to establish that the latter directly succeeded the former.[73]

Yet Hardouin did not make a consistent practice of studying the coins and inscriptions that he cited directly. Jean-François Simon, *commis à la garde* of the Cabinet des Médailles from 1712 to 1719, admired Hardouin's skill as an antiquary—but also noted that he often described coins which did not even belong to the Cabinet as if they formed part of its collection.[74] And when Hardouin criticized Mabillon and Montfaucon, he did so solely on the basis of the materials they themselves had assembled, as if the facsimiles and quotations in their books—rather than the years they had spent examining originals in library after library—represented the whole basis of their arguments. He claimed that he was too old to study the documents themselves.[75] In fact, however, Hardouin seems never to have shared Montfaucon's belief that only continual exposure to the brute material sources could enable a scholar to assess them. His approach to historical evidence represented something more complex than an acute form of the professional deformation which claimed so many numismatists.

Hardouin's work, in fact, grew in large part from older, and other, roots—roots that lay entirely outside the antiquarian tradition. When he attacked the credibility of Josephus, for example, he criticized an ancient writer who had not only cited, but celebrated, archival sources—and whose own remarks about the evaluation of documents served as a chief source for all early modern discussions of historical research. His reply to Jacques Basnage's critique of his work on the Herodiads made clear his central reasons for doing so. Hardouin felt the irritation natural in anyone who tries to make sense of Josephus's sums of regnal years. More important, however, he sought to defend an older tradition of Catholic humanism. Cesare Baronio had based his *Annals* of the church on the *Ecclesiastical History* of Eusebius. The *dioscuri* of Protestant erudition, Joseph Scaliger and Isaac Casaubon, attacked Baronio severely on this point. Scaliger declared that Josephus seemed to deserve credibility even when he disagreed with the Bible, as he did on Herod's wife, Herodias. A faithful historian, Josephus had probably drawn his information directly from the *Acta Herodis:* Scaliger characterized the disagreement between this official source and Scripture as "une chose terrible," but did not lose faith in Josephus.[76] Casaubon built his famous critique of Baronio, the *Exercitationes,* around the principle that Josephus, "a most noble historian," deserved credence in most cases.[77] Hardouin, by contrast, declared that he himself said of Josephus only "what Cardinal Baronius and a good many others have already said: [he was a] *scriptor mendacissimus.*"[78] To some extent, then, the sources of Hardouin's polemic against texts trusted by most other scholars lay in the secular struggle of Catholic against Protestant historiography—by his time no recent phenomenon, and not one directly connected with secular antiquarianism. He differed from other Catholics not in his general plan to use the weapons of history to save tradition, but in the particularly ferocious way that he wielded them.[79]

On other occasions, however, Hardouin drew directly on the very Protestant and *politique* scholarly traditions that he attacked in this case. He himself insisted, in his commentary on Virgil, that he had found a precedent for his stinging attack on a supposed classic in the manuscript notes of the early seventeenth-century scholar François Guyet, whose papers Gilles Ménage had given to the Paris *domus professa* of the Jesuits. Guyet frequented such centers of the Parisian erudite scene as the cabinet of the brothers Dupuy.[80] Pierre Bayle says that he "struck out many verses in his Virgil, pretending that they were supposititious, and that the poems of that great poet were like those troops, among which there are many false musters; so that he acted like a rigid commissary, who musters none but true soldiers." A nervous soul despite his iconoclasm, Guyet feared to publish his theories—especially after the notoriously prolific Claude Saumaise promised to write a whole book denouncing him if he did so. ("Salmasius," says Bayle, "would have proved too hard for him; he would have printed a hundred sheets before Guyet had been able to send four to the press.") In private, however, Guyet attacked Horace as well as Virgil, as Hardouin certainly knew.[81]

In doing so, moreover, as the nineteenth-century scholar Otto Friedrich Gruppe pointed out, Guyet imitated none other than a man Hardouin loathed, Scaliger himself, the Huguenot arch-fiend. Scaliger had notoriously transformed the order of Tibullus's distichs, rewriting the transmitted text, and had condemned the letter of Aristeas as a forgery.[82] Guyet continued this radical form of criticism, as Richard Bentley would after him. Each of these critics referred self-consciously to his predecessors. In following their general approach to secular literary texts—if not in the details of his criticism—Hardouin aligned himself with the very modern, mostly Protestant critics whose approach to the early history of the church he tried to refute.[83]

Sometimes Hardouin's allegiances and intentions harbor even more mysteries. One of his most wonderfully eccentric attacks on Virgil deals with the poet's reference to the closing of the gates of the Temple of Janus (*Aeneid,* I.293–296). Hardouin insisted that pseudo-Virgil had gone wrong here by misreading coins. True, coins of Nero supposedly celebrated peace by depicting the Temple of Janus with the motto "pace p.r. terra marique parta janum clusit." In fact, however, the word "janum" did not refer to a god named Janus. It was, rather, a set of initial letters, each of which stood for a whole word. The coins said that Nero had enclosed "imperii armamentarium narbone urbis muris": that is, that he had transferred the imperial armory to Narbonne from Tarragona. The Augustan universal peace that supposedly accompanied the birth of Jesus was only another invention of the impious coterie.[84]

Here too, the appearance of eccentricity masks Hardouin's real conformity, and to an unexpected model. In the late seventeenth century many Protestant scholars, especially in England and Holland, tried to save religion from what they saw as the assault of Hobbes and Spinoza, but also insisted on the conformity between religious truths and those of reason. David Blondel, for example, argued in public lectures that the late antique church historian Orosius had been the first to spread the idea that a miraculous universal peace coincided with the birth of Christ. The Gospels, and other early sources, did not support this claim. Neither, argued John Masson, did the pagan historians, who provided exhaustive information about when the Temple of Janus had actually closed its doors in the reign of Augustus.[85] Unexpectedly, Hardouin reveals himself as a Catholic counterpart to these Protestant defenders of enlightened Christianity. Like them, he wanted to expunge forged and faulty testimonies from the Christian record.[86] Evidently antiquarianism was not a radically modern enterprise, consistently object-oriented and divorced from the concerns of earlier forms of humanism. Committed to traditional ways of studying texts and stimulated by new and radical theologies, antiquaries like Hardouin still lived in a world of encyclopedic humanism that their predecessors from decades—even a century—before would have recognized. Like Vico, they were not simply creating a "New Science," but updating problems, questions, and methods that originated long before their time.[87]

Hardouin's case also sheds new light on the Republic of Letters as a whole. Recent scholarship has emphasized less the intellectual issues that citizens of the Republic grappled with than the formal and informal institutions within which they worked. Hardouin—like many other Jesuits—belonged as firmly as any Huguenot to an international scholarly community. He corresponded with friends throughout Europe and reached a large public by writing for the new French-language scholarly journals. He depended on the kindness of strangers, as well as friends, for the usual sorts of scholarly aid and comfort. Several of his *confrères* collated manuscripts of the elder Pliny on his behalf. Ballonffeaux, in Luxemburg, made extracts from Basnage's critique and sent them to Hardouin so that he could read them at a point when no printed copy of Basnage's history of the Jews had yet reached Paris. He also supplied his Jesuit friend with literary news—like that of the appearance of George Hickes's *Thesaurus,* which included a devastating critique of Hardouin's etymology of Aelfric.[88] Like many other citizens of the Republic, Hardouin proved capable of ignoring or transcending confessional lines to help a fellow scholar. In 1715 and 1716, when the young Johann Jakob Wettstein, a Protestant from Basel, worked in Paris on manuscripts of the New Testament, he rapidly established warm relations with Montfaucon and other Catholic scholars. The Dominican Father Michel le Quien professed himself unable to intercede with his friend Hardouin to gain access for Wettstein to the Jesuits' "very ancient codex of the four Gospels." Since the Jesuits had become embroiled in their controversy with Mabillon, Le Quien explained, they refused to lend their manuscripts to anyone. But he urged Wettstein simply to ask Hardouin directly. True to the best ideals of scholarly cosmopolitanism, Hardouin treated the young Protestant very kindly, giving him free access to the Jesuits' treasures.[89]

At the same time, though, the treatment that Hardouin's theories received in public debate confirms what Anne Goldgar has suggested about the literary system of the Republic as a whole. It was, in the end, a code invoked at times of crisis rather than one followed every day. Rules were usually stated, in fact, precisely when X thought that Y had violated them. Hardouin's case shows that this could happen all too easily when readers were confronted with genuinely new ideas. Citizens of the Republic were supposed to eschew confessional and institutional loyalties when discussing scholarly questions. Hardouin himself, for example, made a point of visiting Mabillon when the Jesuit Barthélemy Germon issued his critique of *De re diplomatica*. He assured the Benedictine that he had had no part in his fellow Jesuit's hopeless effort to show, against Mabillon, that all Merovingian and Carolingian *diplomata* were faked (true, he himself, as we have seen, eventually became convinced that they actually were forgeries).[90]

When Hardouin's theories reached print, however, such attitudes were rarely in evidence. Many *érudits* seemed to find their loyalties as Protestants or Catholics far more compelling than their identities as tolerant, open-minded citizens of the Republic of Letters—especially when these different identities clearly seemed to demand conflicting forms of loyalty and conduct. Hardouin himself took no prisoners when engaged in ecclesiastical controversy. His edition of the councils, for example, began with blistering attacks on Huguenots and Jansenists—whom Hardouin represented as a Huguenot fifth column within the church.[91] Reasonably enough, unsympathetic readers often responded to Hardouin as if he meant all his scholarly work to serve the ends of theological polemic. Mathurin Veyssière de Lacroze, who began life as a Benedictine novice in France and ended it as a Huguenot refugee in Berlin, denounced Hardouin's work at length in both a Latin treatise and a short French text. He insisted that Hardouin was not an individual with idiosyncratic views but the representative of the Jesuit order, out to undermine true religion and spread atheism in its place by destroying trust in the literary tradition. After all, he pointed out, Hardouin's works seemed to have undergone preliminary examinations before they appeared, and by established principle every Jesuit who wrote for publication regarded himself as speaking for the order as a whole. Hence the Society's curious failure to suppress Hardouin's work effectively.[92] Here, as connoisseurs of invective will recognize, Lacroze revived arguments put forward half a century before by Blaise Pascal in the *Provinciales*—a text designed to unmask the hypocrisy of all members of the order and defend the integrity of the Jansenists.[93] The recurrence of the argument suggests yet another motive for Hardouin's attack on the authority of the ancients, which included Augustine among its targets. But such *ad hominem* and *ad societatem* abuse had little to do with the professed ideals of the Republic—even if Lacroze's criticisms on points of detail sometimes struck home.[94]

More serious still, much evidence suggests that Hardouin stirred up opposition not only because his ideas seemed silly but also because they seemed so new. Hardouin's friend Ballonffeaux, who published extracts from their correspondence, celebrated his friend's historical hypotheses as further evidence that the arts and sciences were reaching perfection at the end of the *grand siècle*. And Hardouin himself emphatically agreed. "Eh," he asked, "do you think that I rose all my life at 4 o'clock every morning only in order to say what others had already said before me?"[95] But novelty threatened. The Rotterdam publisher Jean Louis de Lorme, who collected and published Hardouin's *Opera selecta* in 1709, supposedly against Hardouin's will, wrote in the broadsheet with which he advertised the project that many readers would denounce Hardouin's work unread, as a collection of paradoxes and an effort to undermine religion. He appealed to the work's dedicatee, Jean-Paul Bignon, who directed the Academy of Belle-Lettres and much else, to judge this hard case—just as Grotius had appealed to Bignon's grandfather in the dedication to his similarly innovative treatise *De veritate religionis Christianae*.[96] It seems highly appropriate that a publisher—one of those whose work created and sustained the international community of scholars—called attention to and tried to remedy the lack of institutions which could adjudicate the supposed Republic's most serious quarrels.[97]

Not everyone who rejected Hardouin's innovations and those of similar enthusiasts did so simply out of confessional loyalty or committment to the scholarly status quo. Cuperus, for example, welcomed many new finds and new arguments. But he reacted with sharp skepticism when the young Jean-Baptiste Du Bos, later to become famous for his study of Romano-Gallic society, used numismatic as well as textual evidence to argue that there had been four, not three, Roman emperors named Gordian. He complained to Huet that the study of medals would do more harm than good if numismatists began to ignore the testimony of good ancient historians in their favor.[98] And he clearly saw Hardouin as very similar to Du Bos: a learned man, and a skillful student of some forms of material remains, but too clever by more than half: "Certainly, Hardouin is most skillful at explicating ancient coins, but every scholar knows how many paradoxical theories he puts forth, which have not been subjected to expert scrutiny." Writing to the Jansenist Benedetto Bacchini, Cuperus professed his "great admiration for the man's learning" while still insisting that "I do not know how he can manage to reject the testimonies of so many ancient authors." For Cuperus at least, the rejection of Hardouin's theories seems to have involved nothing more than principled weighing of the evidence.[99]

Hardouin's case suggests that many citizens of the Republic were intellectual conservatives who reacted with distaste to any unfamiliar hypothesis. What energized much of the resistance to Hardouin was not reasoned resistance to his theories but unreflective objections to any radically new idea. Richard Bentley, unlike Hardouin, is a hero of modern philology. Eighteenth-century German scholars such as Friedrich August Wolf saw his exposure of the forgery of the epistles of Phalaris as the first truly modern work of historical criticism, and his edition of Horace is still regularly celebrated as the first historically grounded edition of a classical text. His project of restoring the New Testament to the condition it had been in during the early fourth century C.E.—and his insistence that no more perfect text could be attained—seems a model application to religion of the canons of early Enlightenment rationalism.[100]

Yet most contemporary scholars denounced Bentley as a profaner of sacred ancient texts. John Arbuthnot, a member of the circle of Jonathan Swift and Alexander Pope, composed a short Latin commentary on Virgil which appeared in the variorum *Dunciad.* In this text Martinus Scriblerus, who stood for Bentley, altered Virgil at will, changing the best-known lines without reflection: "Italiam fato profugus," for example, became "Italiam flatu profugus," and "terris jactatus" turned into "terris vexatus." Arbuthnot's satirical *Virgilius restauratus* strikingly resembles Hardouin's then unpublished and much longer commentary on Virgil.[101] It seems at least possible that the Scriblerians meant to compare Bentley to Hardouin. And it is certain that Gruppe had a point when he argued, more than a century ago, that Hardouin and Bentley should be bracketed as the first critics really willing to rethink and remake ancient texts in a radical way if the evidence demanded it. By contrast, the Dutch scholar Jacobus Perizonius, who held strictly to the *via media,* insisting that one should neither accept nor deny the historical content of any given text as a whole, gained a great reputation for judiciousness—even when he defended the historical credibility of Quintus Curtius.[102] Many provinces of the Republic of Letters around 1700, in short, fostered a kind of regression to the cultural mean, an easy acquiescence in accepted truths, which contrasts sharply with its recent reputation for maintaining a set of intellectual free ports in which divergent ideas could find expression without censorship.[103]

Like Bentley, Hardouin gave his critics plenty of ammunition—especially when he refused to publish more than oblique remarks and brief hints about his thesis. Like Bentley, too, he often received unfair criticism. Believers in the free and rapid flow of information found Hardouin's taciturnity infuriating. Johann Burkhard Mencke, editor of the Leipzig *Acta eruditorum,* included Hardouin, along with Athanasius Kircher, in that rogue's gallery of credulous and fantastic scholars, his first oration *On the Charlatanry of the Learned.* He devoted a long passage to denouncing the Jesuit's coy refusal to make the grounds of his theory public. But he also speculated meanly, and without citing evidence, about Hardouin's motives.[104] In this and other cases, attacks on Hardouin stemmed from prejudices at least as strong as his own.

One small incident will make the implications of this point plain. In 1707 Hardouin published in the *Journal des Sçavans* a discussion of a coin of Louis XII, struck at Naples and bearing the inscription "perdam babylonis nomen" (I shall destroy the very name of Babylon).[105] Jacques-Auguste de Thou had mentioned this coin at the outset of his great history of France in the religious wars. He interpreted it as evidence for Louis's hatred of Pope Julius II, citing it to show, in still more detail, how France had suffered at Ultramontane hands.[106] Hardouin pointed out, briefly and sharply, that this interpretation was implausible. The coin referred not to Louis's plan to destroy the papacy but to his plan to call a Crusade—an enterprise which, as Hardouin knew, was still flickeringly alive in the early sixteenth century.

Protestant scholars attacked Hardouin's little note with a zeal worthy of a better cause. Earlier publications of the coin were studied. Every collection of coins in the Holy Roman Empire, from the imperial treasury in Vienna to the Gazophylacium Ducale Saxo-Gothanum in Jena, was ransacked. Coins were measured, weighed, and sketched. Leibniz himself took a hand in promoting the collection of accurate information about the various extant specimens of the coin. For all their efforts at precise measurement and weighing of the evidence, however, not one of the Protestants who involved themselves in the dispute seems to have considered the possibility that Hardouin might just be right. Instead, they dismissed his view, in private letters and published treatises alike, as obviously wrong. The Eisleben scholar Christian Sigismund Liebe, who gathered and published all of this material, admitted that Hardouin had a remarkable gift for making ingenious conjectures. But he dismissed Hardouin's explication of the coin as an obvious product of bias: "driven by his zeal for the religion which he professes, Hardouin could not stomach it when an excellent prince ridiculed Rome and made the city abhorrent with the name of Babylon." In this case at least, hatred of new theories and dislike of Catholics combined: and they enabled intellectual bad money not just to drive off the good, but to prevent it from ever entering the marketplace of ideas.[107]

Hardouin's story reveals much—as Momigliano saw—about the condition of antiquarian learning in the years around 1700. But it also reveals much about the more general conditions in which scholars worked, about the formal and informal institutions they created, about the conflicts between their precepts and their practices—and about the difficulty of establishing exactly which of the Jesuit's many curious traits led to his exclusion from the capacious late-seventeenth-century world of learning. Over time, Hardouin exhibited plenty of obsessions and pathologies. In a later age, he might well have written interminable commentaries in order to prove the Baconian authorship of Shakespeare's plays or the authenticity of the *Protocols of the Elders of Zion*. But some of his methods and arguments met the normal standards of the world in which he practiced his scholarly craft, and some of the rebuttals which his contemporaries directed at his work were motivated by confessional animosity, not scholarly rectitude. Indeed, Hardouin's enemies did much to make him the paranoid he eventually became.

Until recently, historians have been tempted to dismiss the Republic of Letters as an ideal construct, something more purely imaginary than the states of Europe. But Benedict Anderson and others have taught us that all communities are imaginary. Creations of the orator and the historian, rather than *das Volk,* they are constituted in large part by shared myths about customs and traditions.[108] The citizens of the Republic of Letters were certainly linked by powerful myths. But they could also combine—

like the citizens of less ethereal republics—to condemn individuals, for real or invented violations of real and imagined traditions, and even to send them into a kind of exile. In that sad sense, Hardouin's case helps to show that the Republic of Letters had more than an ideal existence. It had enough weight to shape—and deform—the recondite scholarship to which its most learned citizens devoted their lives. At the same time, it lacked institutions which could resolve the inevitable conflicts between its citizens—conflicts which their membership in other, more visible communities did much to exacerbate. Learning, like science, has a social history. In the period from the late sixteenth to the early eighteenth century, the society most relevant to it was the international world of polymathic erudition and interdenominational sociability to which Leibniz and Mabillon, Huet and Hickes pledged their loyalty—the world which became Hardouin's paradise lost, as he became its brilliant, baffling Lucifer.

II

Petronius and
Neo-Latin Satire:
The Reception of the
Cena Trimalchionis

☙

*I*N 1603 Bartholomaeus Schöbinger wrote an eloquent letter to Melchior Goldast about Petronius's *Satyricon*. Schöbinger—a St. Gall patrician who had been educated in Italy—often had occasion to write to his German friend. For it was he who had won access for Goldast to such treasures of the St. Gall library as Notker Labeo's translation of the Psalms, a favor Goldast repaid by taking as many manuscripts as he could away with him and clinging to them despite Schöbinger's ardent pleas for their return. Many of the books—like Notker Labeo—never came back. But this was only the dark side of a relationship that also had its bright one; the two men joined in a magnificent collaborative effort to draw up accurate transcripts and editions of early German texts. The letter on Petronius also belongs to the bright side. It reads: "I received Petronius's *Satyricon* and read through it with the greatest pleasure and eagerness. It called back to mind all those things I did and heard in the same infamous way when I spent time in Italy. If I were to recall what I know is done in Rome, you'd say that the times of Petronius have been reborn, and the Encolpii and Ascylti have come back to life. But shame forbids it . . . Alas, how great is the disgrace, and the corruption of our chaste youth."[1]

I begin with this passage because it is one of the relatively few early modern responses to Petronius that make any sense at all now. Schöbinger's Petronius—like that of Goldast, who used the *Satyricon* to explain what Saint Paul had had in mind when he complained of the unnatural vices of Roman women—is a lurid text that extracts good fun from bad behavior.[2] He read more or less the same text that delighted and absorbed J.-K. Huysmans's Baron des Esseintes centuries later with its vivid, level, and amoral pictures of "les aventures de gibiers de Sodome . . . les vices d'une civilisation décrépite"; the same text that still more recently inspired Federico Fellini's *Satyricon, Petronius's Guide to New York,* and other modern classics.[3] But the apparent modernity of Schöbinger's response, as we shall see, makes it unusual, and even bizarre for its period. Though the *Satyricon* seems likely to manipulate the literary and sexual responses of its readers in uniform and obvious ways, in fact it struck what now seem curious and unexpected sparks from the wits of the late Renaissance scholars who first studied it in detail.

The afterlife of the *Satyricon* has been rich and varied. Many topics still demand study, including the manuscript transmission of the text, its literary appropriation, and its artistic representation—if that is not too lofty a term for the visions of what Lucky Jim called "Sex Life in Ancient Rome" that adorn Petronian title pages, from the genial Baroque orgy that begins Adrien de Valois's edition, to the flaccid Dutch party at the start of Peter Burman's variorum, to the spewing rakes who welcome readers to the early-eighteenth-century English translation with a strong and appropriate whiff of Gin Lane. Here I shall record only one short chapter of this long and complex story: the recovery and early reception of the section of the *Satyricon* now known as the *Cena Trimalchionis.* Preserved in the unique manuscript of Petronius copied for Poggio Bracciolini in 1423, the *Cena* wound up in the fifteenth century in Trau, in Dalmatia. There it escaped scholarly attention for a long time, only to create a scandal when Marino Statileo finally unearthed it. It reached print in 1664, unleashing a flood of scholarly invective against text and discoverer alike. The dramatic circumstances attending its rebirth, as we will see, were only one of several factors that made it seem a modern forgery.[4] The *Cena,* now known to be genuine, is one of the most amusing and rewarding bits of the *Satyricon.* It has been mined by lexicographers for its record of the Latin language as it was spoken by ordinary people, and by historians for its reproduction of Roman life as it was lived. Whatever their debates on date, authorship, and intent of the text, modern scholars have agreed on at least one point: the many obsolete or unique words, grammatical and syntactical errors, and other curiosities that characterize its Latinity are not textual errors but literary devices. Petronius used them to imitate the speech of men and women of low origin:

> Caussam enim, cur hic plures plebeiorum idiotismi et graecismi offendantur, esse hanc, quod plures liberti, homines plebeii et semi-graeci in coena Trimalchionis colloquantur, quam in aliis locis, facile intelligitur.

> The Debochee e'ry where maintains his *Character,* and the *Whores* are always of a piece; the *Freed-men* always speak like Men without Education; and the Slaves ne'r lift their Thoughts or Expressions above the humble level of their condition.[5]

So concurred the English translator William Burnaby at the beginning of the eighteenth century and the Wittenberg Hebrew professor C. G. Anton, editing the text for fun in 1781. Evidently the nature of Petronius's Latinity was critical and scholarly common ground in the Enlightenment. But if we move backward into the age of late humanism, the ground shifts. What seemed obviously deliberate errors to the most ordinary eighteenth-century scholars seemed clear evidence of forgery or gross corruption to the most perceptive and experienced Latinists of the 1660s and 1670s.

Unmodern reactions to Petronius, like the condemnation of the *Cena,* have usually seemed more puzzling than interesting to modern scholars. K. F. C. Rose made especially devoted efforts to locate perceptive remarks and valid discoveries in the early treatises and commentaries, and showed only contempt for those nineteenth-century *Philologen* who failed to see that Renaissance scholars had often anticipated or refuted their hypotheses. Yet even he saw the early commentaries, with their rejection of the *Cena* and other disposable theories, as a vast maggot heap of pullulating error, a record of the crimes and follies of the humanists. "To those who may in the future desire to add to the roll of folly recorded in part above"—so he wound up one magnificent diatribe—"this imprecation: perish, don't publish."[6]

To be sure, the scholars of the mid-seventeenth century came to the *Cena* with expectations that we no longer share, and accordingly bounced off the strange language and stranger action of the text in directions a respectable scholar would not now follow. But these actions and reactions invite understanding rather than horror. We must record these motions and decode their hidden logic; and as this becomes familiar to us, the text itself will become strange—strange as it seemed to those who read it first. Thus we can make the apparent errors in the textual record the evidence of a deeper, lost history that the surface of the sources conceals.

The *Cena* did not fall on obviously stony intellectual ground when the first texts came off the presses. It certainly found plenty of interested readers in the salons and libraries where the senators of the Republic of Letters assembled. J. C. Wagenseil, for example, first heard of the discovery in Rome, where he was told that a complete *Satyricon* had come to light. He learned in Turin that only a fragment had actually been found. And he finally discovered at one of the weekly meetings of the learned "in the museum of the distinguished M. Menage" at Paris that the text in question had been printed in Italy and was being reprinted in Paris at that very moment. He hurried off to the bookseller, hoping to find a fragment as precious as that ancient torso Michelangelo had once prized above all other ancient works of art in Rome; he paid the full price asked; and only then did he realize, as he read, that the style lacked the characteristic flavor of Petronius's Latin. Equally exciting scenes were played everywhere from Rome and Florence to Uppsala and Leiden, and those who acted the most prominent parts in them were textual critics eminently qualified by talent and experience alike to bend their effort and ingenuity to the tasks the *Cena* posed. After all, they included Nicolaas Heinsius, the most gifted Latin textual critic before Bentley; Thomas Muncker, whose edition of the *Mythographi Latini* made a mighty contribution to the study of Latin prose as well as that of classical myth; and J. F. Gronovius.[7]

For all their powers of analysis and digestion, however, these men found the *Cena* impossible to swallow. "I fear Dalmatians as well as Greeks, even bearing gifts," Gronovius dourly wrote to Heinsius—though he admitted that the author of this "cento" had seen a bit more Petronius than was extant in the seventeenth century. Heinsius at first agreed: "The jokes mostly fall flat," he wrote to an Italian friend, "the pointed remarks are so blunt that they hardly strike the reader's palate"—though he too found in some bits of the text a sophisticated knowledge of the ancient world unlikely to be possessed by a modern forger.[8] Joannes Schefferus, editing the text with Heinsius's advice, argued in his edition that the *Cena* must be a late reworking of a genuine body of material. But Heinsius found even this *via media* unpersuasive when he first heard it proposed in 1664. Only in 1672 did he relent, writing to Schefferus that he now believed "that the [fragment] was the legitimate offspring of the Arbiter."[9] Schefferus no doubt received this belatedly decisive statement with mixed feelings. Modern scholars often attribute the reluctance of their early modern colleagues to accept the *Cena* to the corruptness of the text in print, at least until the appearance of the first careful transcript in 1670.[10] True, the 1664 edition and the first reprints were corrupt, like the Trau manuscript they inaccurately represented. Schefferus and the rest had to turn an unreadable mess into recognizable Latin even as they quarreled about its authenticity. But they did not conflate problems of higher and lower criticism. Heinsius, above all, objected not to the wrongly transmitted pure Latin of the *Cena*—that he was used to—but to its correctly transmitted mistakes. He complained in his early letters on the *Cena* that "a good many solecisms and barbarisms occur: heaven forbid that we should believe them to be the utterances of Petronius"; that the "barbarisms" and "solecisms" of the *Cena* could not belong to the brilliant Latin of a great ancient writer.[11]

For the *Cena* to become genuine, Heinsius's and others' beliefs about what was possible in Latin had to change. This they did; but the process was bumpy and sometimes painful, as one episode will suggest. In Chapter XXXIX Trimalchio gives a long astrological explication of the effects of the zodiacal signs, as represented on a dish. Virgo produces women and runaway slaves, Sagittarius cross-eyed men who take the bacon while looking at the vegetables, Aquarius innkeepers and men with water on the brain. Of Capricorn he says:

> In capricorno aerumnosi [sc. nascuntur], quibus prae mala sua cornua nascuntur.

> In Capricorn wretched men [are born], who grow horns because of their evil.

The grammar here was puzzling. The preposition *prae* takes the ablative, but *mala* seemed to be a neuter accusative plural. How could the critic account for so gross a mistake in a classic? Or did it prove the text unclassical?

Every editor in turn had a go at this intractable puzzle, some more than once. Schefferus suggested emending *prae mala sua* to *prae mole sua:* Capricorn produces men who are wretched "because of the [figurative] weight on their backs." This rid the text of the offending accusative but did not give it a very satisfactory sense. So Schefferus tried again after consulting the Blaeu edition, which showed that the manuscript read not *prae* but *pre mala*. He stuck to the *ductus litterarum* and turned *pre* into *per*, which properly governs the accusative *mala*.[12] Muncker, writing to Heinsius in late 1676, tried *per malas*, "through their cheeks," and took the phrase as describing the deep, visible facial wrinkles of emaciated paupers. In reply Heinsius suggested changing plural *mala* to singular *malo*, grammatically correct but still substantively awkward. He also argued that Trimalchio's astrology was as faulty as the text's grammar: "It is ridiculous, and in keeping with his ignorance in other respects, that he says that wretched men are born under Capricorn; in fact very successful men were born under it."

Four days later the denarius finally dropped. Heinsius saw that the grammatical error fitted Trimalchio as perfectly as the astrological one. He sent off a second letter to Muncker in pursuit of the first, a wonderful exercise in intellectual honesty as well as textual exegesis. He declared that his earlier solution had been quite wrong and defended the transmitted text, bad grammar and all, as part of Petronius's effort to portray his characters with graphic fidelity to their ungrammatical habits of speech: "Our author frequently commits solecisms when he represents Trimalchio and his fellow freedmen, those ignorant men." "Nihil," he now concluded, "est mutandum." Muncker took his point at once: "One must entirely agree with you," he wrote, "that Trimalchio and his fellow freedmen are deliberately represented as speaking barbarously"—an insight he rapidly applied to other passages as well.[13] Heinsius and Muncker evidently had expected Petronius to write pure Latin. But the idiosyncrasies of the *Cena* were too glaring to be reconciled with this expectation or removed by emendation. Great scholars that they were, Heinsius and Muncker did what only the greatest scholars can: they sacrificed their assumptions to save their text.

If the difficulties Heinsius and others had to surmount are now clear, their origin is not. Why did the most proficient Latinists of an age still in touch with Latinity work from historically and stylistically incorrect assumptions in this one case? The answer, I think, lies both in the nature of this particular text and in the wider literary context within which it was read. By following the view of Petronius that Heinsius rejected back to its origins, we may come to understand not only this single episode, but some of the dynamics of literary history and scholarship in this period.

Petronius was never an ordinary classic. The sexual license of his characters, the difficulty of his vocabulary, and the many out-of-the-way objects and customs he described all called for commentary. After 1587, when the brothers Pithou published their brief, anonymous textual annotations, scholar after scholar explicated the text. In the next few decades, rank clumps of annotation grew up around the *Satyricon,* and many a Petronian chapter of *Variae lectiones* rose in the distance. Though these early crops were periodically harvested and rid of chaff by editors—like Janus Wowerius in 1596 and the house of Raphelengius in 1604—the still compact early variorum editions were soon dwarfed by the vast second-growth erudition of the seventeenth century. It is easy to scoff after inspecting any given page of Burman's 1709 variorum, where two stout columns of notes in small print may support one or two lines of the original text at the top of the page. This seems a classic case of the situation so often described by practitioners—and satirized by critics—of modern literary studies. Interpretation has begun its dreadful work. The text is mute, and the only voices to be heard are those of professional scholars carrying out the rituals of their trade. Even Burman, himself both a commentator and a compiler, complained, as Gronovius had before him, that the mass of notes made it harder, not easier, to tease out the real meaning of the text—or even to identify its author's normal stylistic devices.[14]

In fact, however, the efforts of early scholars to scale and master the mountain of problems with which Petronius presented them were neither trivial nor pointless. The *Satyricon* swarmed with formidable linguistic and textual difficulties, which any reader had to try to solve before he could hope to feel any deeper or more direct reaction to it. Moreover, the early readers did not confine themselves to minor questions of textual criticism and lemmatic exegesis, though they expended much effort on those vital enterprises. They also directed much of their effort to stating and solving the largest problems any text can pose: reconstructing the author's historical and biographical situation, identifying the literary genre within which he worked, teasing out the reactions that he meant to evoke from his readers. In raising these questions, the sixteenth- and seventeenth-century humanists took as literary an approach as their culture allowed to the *Satyricon.* Paradoxically, it was by doing this that they blinded themselves to the true nature of the text—and especially to that bit of it they could not read until 1664, the *Cena*. To understand their misunderstanding we must see it as a sophisticated literary and historical enterprise. There is no other way to grasp how learned men could impose a voice of their own on the magnificently articulate Arbiter.

The interpreters first of all found a historical home for both the author and the text. Around 1570 Joseph Scaliger noticed in Tacitus's *Annals* the story of one Caius Petronius. A cultivated man, he rose to high station under Nero, fell from favor as the emperor fell into debauchery, and eventually enjoyed a long and dignified suicide while under arrest at Cumae—but only after sending Nero sealed *codicilli* in which he castigated the emperor and his favorites for their crimes. This elegant courtier must have written the elegant *Satyricon*. Scaliger made his discovery known subtly but influentially. He added the initial C. to the name Petronius in the heading of his manuscript of the text. The jurists in his immediate circle, who edited the text again and again in the 1570s and 1580s, made Scaliger's connection explicit in print. Pierre Pithou quoted the Tacitus passage in his account of Petronius's life, and Pierre Daniel raised the question—long to dog students of the *Satyricon*—whether the text might be the very *codicilli* Tacitus mentioned. Jacques Durant de Chazelle assumed that Petronius satirized Nero's misdeeds, and excused the foulness of his language on that highly moral ground. Janus Dousa scraped hard for textual evidence to nail home Petronius's Neronian date—though he, like his successors, turned up only a parallel with Martial that proves nothing about the relative chronology of the two men. Goldast, just after 1600, agreed that the whole text was "an attack on Nero, whose example shaped the entire Roman world of the time, proving the truth of the saying *Qualis rex, talis grex*." A quarter of a century later, Gonzales de Salas argued at even greater length that the *Satyricon* was written during Petronius's time in Cumae, and that every linguistic and historical detail in the text confirmed its Neronian date and moral purpose.[15] The text was dated, ascribed, fixed to a milieu and a culture.

As the *Satyricon* was fitted into its historical niche, it was also assigned a clear literary genre. Using the testimony of Quintilian and that of Varro himself (the latter as presented by Cicero), Pithou, Daniel, and Isaac Casaubon identified the *Satyricon* as the foremost extant specimen of Menippean satire—the mixed form of satire, composed of prose and verse interspersed, in which Varro had treated philosophical topics in an accessible, popular way. The commentators read their scanty and indirect evidence all too literally. If Varro said, in Cicero's *Academica*, that he had dealt with learned matters, then Casaubon took him exactly at his word: "Hoc autem sine dubio voluit *Varro*: ita se, cum Satiras componeret, philologiam philosophia temperasse, ut mixta ex utroque genere scriptio dici potuerit." This was already to go beyond the evidence he had. And when he asserted that "Petronii libellus mera est Satura Varroniana," he not only piled one assertion on another but also suggested something almost certainly false: that the *Satyricon* was not just a work that required learned commentaries but a learned work in its own right—a book as laden with philosophy and philology as Varro's lost work—or, indeed, Casaubon's own treatise on Greek and Roman satire.[16]

Meanwhile a complementary development—perhaps the essential one—took place outside the narrow realm of philology, in that of imaginative literature—where, of course, many of the most original Renaissance readings of classical texts took shape. From the 1580s onward, humanists began not only to edit but to write Latin prose satires. The genre came back to life with Justus Lipsius's *Menippean Satire* of 1581 against contemporary textual critics, and reached maturity with John Barclay's *Euphormionis Satyricon* in 1605.[17] All the works that fell within it shared certain characteristics. They were academic to a fault: written in deliberately difficult Latin, they followed the doings of characters whose polysyllabic Greek names did more to conceal than to reveal their allegorical meanings. They often explicitly parodied academic customs and follies. Many of them took shots at such sitting ducks as the professional textual critic, that doyen of obsessive pedants, or offered set-piece parodies of university lectures and disputations. They were written, by and large, by the same sort of person who studied the *Satyricon*: Lipsius, himself a great critic of Latin prose; Barclay, friend and correspondent of Scaliger; François Guyet, habitué of the salon of the brothers Dupuy. And as one might expect, they often turned out so difficult and obscure that they could not be read at all without help. Manuscript keys to Barclay's *Satyricon* circulated along with the published book; Pierre de l'Estoile copied them into his vast diary. And Isaac Casaubon wrote to Daniel Heinsius— intending praise, not criticism—that he had had to help his son read Heinsius's satire on Caspar Scioppius, *Hercules tuam fidem*.[18]

These erudite texts set out not only to amuse but to teach. In fact, they really were just the sort of pedagogically designed, obnoxiously informative book that a great scholar would want to read with his son. Most of them, for example, have plots not so much picaresque as berserk. The protagonist, pursued by fate, a magician, or the gods, is hurried from country to country, courtroom to prison cell, sinking ship to pillory, without reason or time to relax. Chaos seems to have dominion over all. Yet a higher purpose inspired all this violent, apparently random movement. While describing his protagonist's adventures, the author had ample opportunity to give the reader detailed lessons about the characters of the different European peoples. Barclay, for example, offers elaborate treatments in his *Satyricon* of the effusive, hypocritical courtesy of the Italians and the filthy tobacco smoking, and extreme religious fanaticism, of the English. These were exactly the observations that cultivated young men were supposed to make as they traveled in or read about other countries. Barclay, indeed, made them all over again in his collective portrait of the natures of the European nations, the *Icon animorum,* which he meant as a serious guide to learned travel. No wonder, then, that early editors treated the informative—but hardly comic—*Icon* as an integral part of the *Satyricon,* labeling it Book IV of a single work that began as fiction. After all, the work as a whole was meant to inform and instruct—as Leibniz made clear when he included it among the *Moralia* in his 1689 sketch of a *Bibliotheca universalis selecta.* It hardly needs saying that he put Petronius's *Satyricon* in the same category—though he did not fully share his contemporaries' admiring view of the work.[19]

The neo-Latin satires were not only ponderously informative in content but demandingly purist in style. They described the customs of modern nations and even the products of nasal passages and bowels in an elevated Latin that greatly detracts from their comic effect. Here, for example, Guyet lists the ingredients of the concoction that the protagonist of his novel was made to drink as a parody of Communion: "illata est immensa pelvis indomito Falerno plena . . . Hilario iussit statim ad se transmitti: cumque in ea sudantem vultum lavisset et manus, bis terque ructu violenter emisso, quidquid stomacho infuderat iniecto in os loro vomitorio toto gutture ad oculorum horrorem egessit . . . Haud mora, hic viscosa narium purgamenta, hic olidissimum sputum, ille fluentem de sebaceis liquorem . . . plurimi stercoris canini foeditatem et, si quid foedius verrentium ancillarum incuria transmiserat, intulere. Nec defuere qui exonerata vesica illic obscaena intingerent."[20] The Latinate *Verfremdungseffekt* that one experiences in reading this passage was not only intended, it was prized. One could offer no higher praise for one of these productions than the statement that it seemed a genuine classic; no more searing criticism than that the author's vernacular had infected—and made unclassical—his Latin prose. If Barclay—a Scot educated in France—committed Gallicisms, as Scioppius claimed he did, they were not charming slips but outward and visible signs of lack of grace.[21]

Literary historians have treated neo-Latin satire as a sign of rising scholarly interest in Petronius.[22] It would be nearer the mark to see the rising scholarly interest in Petronius as a sign of the impact of neo-Latin satire. For once the editors had worked out Petronius's date and intent, they set about the real task for which the Latin literature they knew best had prepared them: turning his work into a neo-Latin classic, the sort of thing that one of them would have written had he lived under Nero. They read Petronius's *Satyricon* as a heavy-handed political allegory like Barclay's work of the same title. Like the editors and authors of the modern satirical novels, they drew up formal keys to disclose the real identities of Petronius's characters. One of them, François Nodot, even forged extra scenes for the *Satyricon* to make it a better seventeenth-century novel. In one of these, which provoked much scorn from his critics, a beautiful woman entertains gentlemen callers, "la gorge découverte," at her "ornamentum matutinum"—or toilette.[23]

Admirers of Petronius, like those of Barclay, insisted above all on the purity of Petronius's style. Even an early-sixteenth-century scholar like Battista Pio had marveled at Petronius's ability to avoid "verborum vilitas" and use only "voces plebe summotas," "so that he seems to realize the famous phrase 'Odi profanum vulgus et arceo.'"[24] At the end of the century Lipsius deplored Petronius's obscenity—though claiming it left no more mark on him than a boat did on the water it passed through—but praised his stylistic "purissima impuritas."[25] And as the seventeenth century wore on, editors insisted on his elegance with ever greater enthusiasm, even when they had to come to terms with his difficulties and idiosyncrasies—as Pierre Bourdelot did when he drew up a *Glossarium Petronianum,* the key to which began with a frank admission that asterisks identified some words and phrases as inexplicable.

The humanists' vision of what was and what was not possible in classical Latin covered a multitude of sins in grammar, syntax, and usage. A few Ciceronians, to be sure, tried to confine modern Latinists to a single style and lexicon. But anyone who studied and taught the ancient writers knew that the greatest Romans had often violated important canons of good Latin. When Erasmus set out his prescriptions for good usage, for example, he could sound as resolute a purist as any Ciceronian:

> *Quisque* [every] is connected with superlatives, not positives or comparatives. Virgil: "Optima quaeque dies miseris mortalibus aevi / Prima fugit [*G* 3. 66–67]." Every grammarian of the best sort teaches this [*Eruditissimus quisque Grammaticus haec tradit*].[26]

But he knew perfectly well that his well-tended grammarian's garden did not closely resemble the jungles of linguistic reality. After all, he was summarizing longer passages in Lorenzo Valla's *Elegantiae* and *In errores Antonii Raudensis adnotationes,* in which Valla not only asserted the rules for using *quisque* but admitted that Sallust had apparently, and later writers like Macrobius had definitely, broken them.[27] The humanists' realization that Virgil, for example, had committed solecisms should not occasion surprise. The Roman grammarians and their Alexandrian predecessors had had both to establish their own institutional authority over the language they studied and taught, and to explicate texts written some centuries before their own time, in a language that often violated the "good usage" of their day. No wonder that Servius and others spent so much time defending—and warning pupils not to emulate—Virgil's solecisms; no wonder either that most humanists both replied systematically to these criticisms of their canon and assimilated the critical standpoint on which they rested.[28] They knew that even the most polished of classics did not amount to a body of perfect examples of grammatical and syntactical rules perfectly followed. But they still could not enfold the *Cena* within the most capacious vision they could frame of classical Latin; it seemed not to contain individual minor "barbarisms," as any text must, but simply to be one.

A complex of interlocking ideas had taken shape, one which held scholars' imaginations and perceptions in its clutches. Petronius was Nero's Arbiter. His *Satyricon* portrayed Nero's court—and did so as a good humanist satire, moral in purpose, learned in content, and classical in style. Individuals rejected one or another of these theses, as Lipsius did when he expressed discreet doubts in his commentary on Tacitus about whether C. Petronius really wrote the text. But no one could escape the fence of connected assumptions that philological tradition and literary practice had erected. Like barbed wire, it was so tough, flexible, and self-reinforcing that it could restrain its inmates even if one section failed.

These humanist preoccupations, still flourishing in the 1660s, prevented readers from welcoming the *Cena*. The two scholars who attacked the text most heatedly, J. C. Wagenseil the Hebraist and Adrien de Valois the classicist, both did so because it was not what they expected of its author. Both drew up impressive lists of words Petronius could not have used and solecisms he could not have committed—for example, making *prae* govern the accusative in the phrase *prae mala sua*.[29] Wagenseil accepted the normal view that Petronius had attacked Nero. Hence he made content the basis for his criticism. The *Cena* could not be part of the *Satyricon* because the ill-mannered and ignorant Trimalchio could hardly represent a young and cultured—if debauched—emperor.[30] De Valois, by contrast, denied that the author of the *Satyricon* had even lived in Nero's time. But he too agreed that the *arbiter elegantiarum* who wrote the main text could not have committed prose like that of the *Cena*.[31] Both men, finally, used the very technique by which critics had assessed the quality of neo-Latin satires to measure—and find wanting—that of this classical text. They looked for and found evidence of vernacular idioms underlying the Latin of the *Cena,* just as Scioppius had found Gallicisms in Barclay (and Nodot's critics would find Gallicisms in his supplements to Petronius).[32] Wagenseil showed that the author of the text must have thought in Italian; the phrase "unus servus Agamemnonis interpellavit," for example, was not proper Latin but Italian translated word for word—"Un servidore d'Agamemnon ci interruppe." De Valois used the same method to prove that the author was French: "Habuimus in primo porcum" (for "habuimus primum") irresistibly recalled the French phrase that must have been in the writer's mind, "Nous avons eu en premier lieu un cochon."[33] The *Cena* could not be by Petronius, because it did not belong in a proper neo-Latin novel.

The distorting lens through which almost all scholars read the text was clearly thick. It sufficed, in the first place, to prevent them from juxtaposing the *Cena* with a different tradition of modern prose satire, one more than a century old and rather out of favor by 1600, which would have provided a far better analogy than Barclay for the *Cena*. This was the multilingual, vulgar prose satire of François Rabelais and the *Epistolae obscurorum virorum,* which had deliberately manipulated different languages and levels of speech to comic effect, and had never shied from committing deliberate solecisms in the good cause of exposing a real person's or imagined character's ignorance. This tradition of genuinely Menippean satire was still flickeringly alive in the world where Petronian studies flourished. In 1593–94 the younger Pithou, Florent Chrestien, and other habitués of politique circles wrote the *Satyre Ménippée,* a brilliant attack on the Catholic League and its allies.[34] They made the papal envoy declare in mock Italian that hearing talk of peace makes him feel as though he is being given "un servitiale d'inchiostro," and a cardinal pompously insist in the Latin of the Obscure Men that "est enim operae pretium ut nos praecipue qui studuimus in celeberrima Academia Parisius, et sapimus magis quam fex populi, habeamus aliquid secreti quod mulieres non intelligant."[35] The text winds up with a mock note from its printer energetically praising the fine French of a work in several languages. Self-conscious use of low language to characterize low people—this was Heinsius's key to the *Cena,* and it seems a shame that others had not already discovered it in the *Satyre.*

The lens Heinsius and Gronovius looked through also prevented them from seeing that the true nature of the *Cena* had already been discovered by at least one reader before them. The Parisian doctor Pierre Petit published a pseudonymous reply to Wagenseil and de Valois in 1666. He argued brilliantly that the language of the *Cena* was not modern but unclassical; it was, in fact, the Latin of low society, of "plebeian and ignorant men," women, and provincials. He pointed out, with an insight sometimes not found in his modern successors, that any argument that the text could not be Neronian must beg the question, since much Neronian literature had not survived; and Seneca's extant satire on Claudius resembled it.[36] He did not anticipate every detail of Heinsius's work on the text. *Prae mala sua,* for example, he took as a grammatically correct phrase about the jaw *(mala, malae);* those born under Capricorn seem to grow horns, he thought, because the rods which hold their bundles together project like horns past their heads.[37] But he did make the same basic historical and literary points that Heinsius would, and gave careful arguments and full documentation for them. Yet the reign of prejudice was so strong that Heinsius could not accept Petit's thesis until he had arrived at it himself by many more years of direct tinkering with the details of the text.

The general lessons of this story are obvious. Modern literature really does alter the classics; Barclay really does shape Petronius. Awareness of this fact can help us to use our texts as the basis for our hypotheses instead of making our hypotheses the basis from which we read our texts. But another, narrower point also emerges, one more strictly relevant to the study of Latin literature and scholarship in early modern Europe. In perhaps the quaintest comment on *Satyricon* XXXIX, Schefferus explained the *cornua* of those born under Capricorn as separate, hornlike growths caused by the active *spiritus* of the burdened melancholics whom that sign of the zodiac produced. He took Petronius's children of Capricorn, that is, as genuinely horned individuals. Whether he was right I do not know. But I do know that his comment applies with curious felicity to the situation of modern students of late humanism. This field has recently expanded in two directions, like Schefferus's two horns. Scholars now work actively on both the history of classical scholarship and the production of Latin literature in early modern Europe. Yet these have become largely separate enterprises, carried on with little mutual interest or concern. And that separation of studies, as our story shows, imports an alien dissociation of sensibilities into an early modern past where eloquence and erudition were still closely linked. The traditions of Latin scholarship and literary artistry still formed a whole in the age of Barclay and Heinsius, and it is worth following the intricate process by which the *Cena* was finally digested if by doing so we can rekindle our own desire to connect.

Appendix:
Making Petronius Classical—and Making Him Petronius

Muncker to Heinsius, 30 November 1676; *Syll.* 5.370:

> Non minus vexatus est ille locus: Quibus prae mala sua cornua nascuntur. divinavi aliquando: Quibus per malas cornua nascuntur. Ut per cornua intelligi velit genas extantes, quales videmus esse macilentis illis et monogrammis.

Heinsius to Muncker, 1 December 1676; *Syll.* 5.371:

> In altero loco legebam, quibus prae malo suo cornua nascuntur. Ut
> denuo hic lateat adagium plebejum, prae malo suo videtur requiri,
> ut ad aerumnosos referatur. Ridicule autem et pro caetera sua in-
> scitia sub Capricorno monet nasci aerumnosos, cum nascerentur
> felicissimi.

Heinsius to Muncker, 5 December 1676; *Syll.* 5.372:

> Vix ultimis meis tabellario traditis, dum recogito, quae ad te scripsis-
> sem, serius agnovi errorem meum: nam in Petroniano loco, quibus
> prae mala sua cornua nascuntur nihil est mutandum. Frequenter
> enim soloecissat noster, quoties Trimalchionem aut collibertos ejus
> homines inscitos introducit loquentes.

Muncker to Heinsius, 21 December 1676 [dated 1675 by Burman]; *Syll.*
5.360:

> Barbare loquentes induci de industria Trimalchionem et ejus colliber-
> tos, omnino tecum statuendum, nequis cum Patavino editore mire-
> tur, Cap. 44. Futiles aediles male eveniat.

IV

PROFILES

12

Portrait of
Justus Lipsius

֍

*J*USTUS LIPSIUS survives, barely, as a fading figure on the periphery of our mental panorama of Renaissance culture. We are amused at his famous offer to recite the text of Tacitus while his listener held a dagger to his belly—and to allow the listener to plunge the dagger in if Lipsius stumbled on a word. We are amazed by his early career as a prodigy, one that made him the proverbial perfect schoolboy as late as the nineteenth century, when King, the classical master in Rudyard Kipling's *Stalky & Co.,* still plagued his boys with anecdotes about "the learned Lipsius, who at the age of. . . ." We have admired the public image that he wished to leave behind him, as projected in a painting by his friend Peter Paul Rubens, *Four Philosophers:* a quiet, contemplative gentleman, one who was happiest when reading books or cultivating his legendary tulip garden while his dog, Mops, barked at his heels. We have even heard his voice. Lipsius, as Morris Croll showed many years ago, did more than anyone else to popularize the Senecan, pointed prose style that so delighted the strong wits of seventeenth-century Europe. When we read the epigrams of Francisco Gómez di Quevedo or the essays of Francis Bacon, we can detect many echoes of that pointed Latin prose, poor in verbs but rich in inkhorn terms, that enchanted students in Leiden and Louvain, inspired the great scholar-printer Henri Estienne to write a whole book, *About Lipsius's Latinity*—and provoked Lipsius's Leiden successor Joseph Scaliger to cry, "Je ne sçay quel Latin c'est."

Yet recent scholarship has revealed another Lipsius as well, a figure both more flamboyant and more alienated than the stately icon that Rubens created and many later historians have helped to gild. Lipsius was no retiring academic who wrote for his colleagues in the "community of the competent." In fact, he was a best seller. He took an active and often unattractive part in the great debates of his day about civil war and religious liberty. More dramatic still, he was a plagiarist, a liar, and a heretic. He changed churches in pursuit of sanctity—or safety—almost as easily as he changed jobs in the course of his dazzling academic career. His contemporaries knew him not as *Lipsius philosophus,* the Stoic unmoved by pain or fear, but as *Lipsius Proteus,* one of the most puzzling and unnerving intellectual celebrities of a time that included such rivals as Giordano Bruno and Tommaso Campanella. And we must come to terms with this second Lipsius, as well as with the first—and, finally, with the full range of paradoxes and enigmas that we are posed by the existence in one man of these two personae—before we can leave Lipsius in his garden and conclude with some reflections on the larger meaning of his case.

First, Rubens's Lipsius, the sage and scholar. There is no doubt that Lipsius ranked with the most learned and creative members of his generation—itself, perhaps, the most learned generation in European history, that of Joseph Scaliger and Isaac Casaubon. His first book, a miscellany of short essays on technical points of textual criticism, written in phosphorescent Ciceronian Latin, he finished in 1566, when he was all of nineteen years old. His edition of Tacitus, which marked a radical improvement in a notoriously difficult text, appeared in 1574, when he was not yet thirty. And throughout his life, which extended from 1547 to 1606, he issued a powerful stream of editions, commentaries, and monographs. These culminated in 1605 in a second magnificent edition, that of Seneca, and won him preferment in the academic centers of Lutheran Europe (Jena), Calvinist Europe (Leiden), and Catholic Europe (Louvain).

How can we judge Lipsius's achievement in the technical and rebarbative fields he liked to cultivate? We can turn for some enlightenment to modern classical scholars who have replowed his furrows. Elaine Fantham, for example, has recently confirmed the excellence of Lipsius's critical judgment as applied to Seneca. Presented with a late and not completely accurate manuscript descended from the famous *codex Etruscus* of the *Tragedies,* Lipsius realized that he was dealing not just with scribal errors but with a previously unused branch of the textual tradition. Accordingly he made so many valid changes in the text then standard that the discoverer of *Etruscus* itself, J. F. Gronovius, had little to do save confirm from the original source the justness of Lipsius's choices and emendations. J. Ruysschaert and C. O. Brink have subjected Lipsius's corrections of the text of Tacitus's *Annales* to even more searching scrutiny. The results are striking. In *Annales* I, modern texts contain some 130 emendations of the text transmitted by the *codex Mediceus*. Eighty of these, many obvious, were made by the first editor, the younger Filippo Beroaldo, who prepared the manuscript for the press in 1505 with great skill and tact. Lipsius comes next, with 20 to his credit. The competition lags far behind; indeed, the combined efforts of nineteenth- and early-twentieth-century scholars have resulted in 2 emendations generally accepted. Statistics, admittedly, tend to glaze the reader's eye; but these few numbers do suggest just how gigantic an effort Lipsius made to improve the texts he worked on, and how secure his mastery was of the historical background and the historian's language. Most impressive, perhaps, are the fairly numerous passages that Lipsius left unchanged, that later scholars emended, and that modern scholars—catching up with their sixteenth-century predecessor—now take as Tacitean rather than corrupt.

Yet numbers tell an austere and limited story. To grasp a scholar's characteristic working methods, we must catch him in his study (or his garden), applying his favorite tools to his chosen raw materials. And we must compare his work systematically not to that of his modern successors but to that of his predecessors and contemporaries. We can spy on Lipsius as he attacks one of the many attractive complex problems posed by one of his favorite authors: the perennial question of which Seneca wrote what. In the Middle Ages, more or less everything that circulated under the name Seneca was attributed to the philosopher who suffered under Nero. But the fourteenth century saw the awakening of a new historical curiosity and a new stylistic sensitivity. In many cases, Renaissance humanism appeared and all was light; it took only one scholar of the new brand to read the younger Pliny's letters and notice that this Pliny could not very well be the author of the *Natural History*, since he vividly described that other Pliny's death. But in Seneca's case the humanist confronted a pullulating mass of disparate materials: letters, essays, tragedies, rhetorical exercises, works on natural philosophy, and a correspondence with Saint Paul. He also knew, from ancient testimony, that two writers named Seneca had flourished under the early Roman empire. And he saw that no single man could have written this entire discordant corpus. No wonder, given this range of evidence and problems, that the new Senecan scholarship served to transmute the simple assumptions of the medieval scribe into an unbearable cacophony of contradictory hypotheses.

We can begin by following a learned man of the early fifteenth century, Sicco Polenton, as he worked at solving these problems in his pioneering history of Latin literature. Sicco knew from the play *Octavia*, so he thought, that the author of Seneca's tragedies had outlived Nero and described his death. But he also knew that Seneca the moral philosopher had died before Nero. He knew that Seneca the creator of rhetorical exercises had had three sons, one of whom was also named Seneca. And he tied all of this information together with a neat philologist's clove hitch. One Seneca had written the rhetorical and philosophical works and died a Christian; his son Seneca had written the tragedies. Naturally, this solution not only solved problems but raised them. But Sicco was equal to the challenge. When (unnamed) detractors suggested that the *Octavia*, the keystone of his argumentative arch, was not by the author of the other plays, he buried them under a flood of smug rebuttal of a kind unhappily still to be found in philological argument: "Any expert can see that these tragedies reveal no variety, but that all of them have one and the same tenor of style, eloquence, dignity; thus all of them, as they are, seem the product of one source, one parent, one mind." No one with insight, he concluded, could deny the plays' unity of authorship. This argument, which makes the one play all modern scholars have thought spurious the companion and even the touchstone of the rest, seems strange enough. But it is not half so curious as Sicco's other daring hypothesis. In the rhetorical work, Seneca mentions that he could have heard Cicero speak had the civil wars not made it impracticable. Accordingly, he must have been fairly mature—Sicco suggests fourteen years old at least—before Cicero died in 43 B.C.E. Yet Seneca the philosopher died in C.E. 65, and some humanists denied that he could have heard Cicero at all. Sicco, however, cut this knot as elegantly as he had tied the other. His opponents, he asserted, simply failed to see the obvious truth—Seneca must have lived to be 118 years old. Anyone who failed to accept this view "would rather quarrel than accept the obvious truth."

Erasmus, a hundred years later, saw far more sharply than Sicco had that not everything that glittered with Seneca's name was Senecan gold. For the correspondence of Seneca with Saint Paul he had only contempt, and he disproved its authenticity with an elegant piece of historical reasoning: "There is nothing in the letters from Paul worthy of Paul's spirit. One hardly hears the name of Christ, which normally pervades Paul's discourse. [The author] makes that powerful defender of the Gospel cowardly and timorous. . . . And it's the mark of really monumental stupidity when he makes Seneca send Paul a book *De copia verborum* [*On Building Vocabulary*] so that he will be able to write better Latin. If Paul didn't know Latin he could have written in Greek. Seneca did know Greek." But Erasmus made little effort to separate the rest of the Senecan corpus into its original components. He did doubt that one man could have written all of the tragedies. But of Cicero's contemporary, Seneca the rhetorician who died under Nero, Erasmus said only that he wished that his *Declamationes* had survived in their entirety, "for they would have been a great help in [learning rhetorical] invention and judgment."

With these efforts of earlier humanists we may now compare what Lipsius had to say in the set-piece chapter, sharp and concise, with which his *Electa* of 1580 begins:

The *vulgus* holds that books entitled *Controversiae* and *Suasoriae* were written by the Seneca known as the philosopher, who was Nero's tutor. The *vulgus* holds this, and therefore it errs. That opinion is refuted by Seneca's period, his life, his style. I explain the problem of period in detail. Whoever wrote these books lived in the time of Augustus and Tiberius, not that of Claudius and Nero. I infer this from a number of passages where he speaks about himself. He says at one point that he knew Cestius Pius, Portius Latro, Valerius Messalla [minor rhetoricians who lived under Augustus]; at another that he heard the poet Ovid declaim; and that he knew Asinius Pollio [d. C.E. 5] both as a robust man and as an old one. I know that all these lights illuminated the middle of the principate of Augustus. But Seneca [the philosopher] flourished in the time of Claudius and Nero.

Lipsius easily disposes of his predecessor's effort to make Seneca the classical prototype of the two-thousand-year-old man. After all, he points out,

Tacitus treats Seneca's last years and death in detail, and describes him as fairly vigorous. He could hardly have applied such terms to a slippered pantaloon of 118. After dispelling this and other errors, the result of which had been to confuse the two Senecas as thoroughly as the two Menaechmi in Plautus's play, Lipsius sets out his own lucid hypothesis. Two writers named Seneca must be distinguished. The older lived in the days of Augustus and wrote the rhetorical works; the younger, his son, lived under Claudius and Nero and wrote philosophy and tragedy.

Clearly Lipsius's philology was dramatically different from that of Sicco or Erasmus. What strikes the reader most sharply is not that Lipsius's solution is basically the modern one, but that his methods are so professional. He does not examine isolated passages or data as though a few bits of evidence could decide the case. Rather, he pulls from the rhetorical works every passage that mentions a contemporary, lines them up, and then draws from them a plausible and coherent theory. He does not refute his adversaries by claiming a superior sensibility, as though the ability to date a text were something as ineffable as a sense of smell. Rather, he gives all the relevant evidence and shows that no hypothesis but his can be reconciled with it. Above all, he establishes his point simply because he knows the history of Rome, civil and literary, year by year and almost day by day, and can thus make what had been mere names to his predecessors into unbreakable links in the chain of his arguments. This combination of learning and precision marks Lipsius as a member of that great generation that set the history of the ancient world itself, as well as that of ancient literature, into its proper order.

Lipsius's virtuosity as a scholar enabled him not only to restore texts but also to reconstruct lost customs and institutions. His works on such topics have more virtues than a sample can reveal. He had the imaginative ability to see in disparate and difficult texts the traces of what he liked to describe as an ancient custom "fleeing into oblivion." He had a detective writer's gift for charging obscure subjects with excitement, so that the reader too becomes eager to know how long you had to serve in the Roman army before you could become a *veteranus,* or who the *iuvenes* were who made trouble at games and chariot races. And he had a dedicated scholar's willingness to work through any text, however unattractive; to nail down every detail, however obscure; and to use every possible device—including elaborate illustrations—to clarify his descriptions. His profusely illustrated and elaborately documented books marked a new stage in the development of historical research.

In one respect, to be sure, Lipsius tried to spoil the gleaming perfection of his own achievements. He stole emendations of the texts he worked on from any book and any person that could provide them. He gave little or no acknowledgment of his debts. And when these surfaced—as when his former friend Claude Chifflet protested that his own proposals to emend passages in Tacitus's *Annales* were presented as Lipsius's in the latter's commentary—he held his peace, ignored the fuss, and carefully effaced from his working copy of Tacitus—which still survives in Leiden—the references to Chifflet's name that he had neatly entered by Chifflet's proposals in his notes. Yet plagiarism of this kind, though ugly, was not unusual. Both Scaliger and Casaubon played down the merits of their predecessors and claimed others' achievements as their own. As Brink points out, in an age when few scholars fully identified the sources of the texts they printed, it was only natural for conjectures, too, to be passed on from hand to hand without full identification. Given the peculiar nature of conjectural emendations—which, like some sorts of scientific discovery, become private property only when they are published for the first time—it is not hard to see why even a brilliant and learned man might steal a few extra jewels to add to the vast piles that he had excavated, cut, and polished on his own.

Yet—and yet—this story is not the whole one. Lipsius's attitude toward the technical skills he deployed in editions and monographs is unexpectedly complex and ambivalent. On the one hand, he repeatedly mocked the scholars of his time for their perverse obsession with the details of scholarly problems. In an influential little dialogue dedicated to Scaliger, for example, Lipsius portrays himself attending, in a dream, a meeting of the senate of Roman writers. One after another, Cicero, Sallust, and Ovid, Tribonian and Pliny denounce the critics who have mutilated their texts and call for extreme punishments: "Have we no Cornelian law to deal with assassins? And are these men not assassins? How often have they been caught, pen and sword in hand, as they set out to kill a word?" Lipsius trembles in terror, and escapes punishment only when Varro, the greatest Roman scholar, persuades his colleagues that they owe some debt to modern printers and critics. And though the whole exercise ends with a set of rules—not very penetrating ones—for proper textual criticism, it leaves the reader with the impression that critics are intrinsically absurd creatures, who inflict wounds on the very texts they seek to heal. No wonder that Lipsius's *Dream* became the model for a whole subspecies of Latin satires of scholars and scholarship.

Yet Lipsius went further still. In his scholarly works, as well, he repeatedly expressed reservations about the ultimate value of philology. His first edition of the commentary on Tacitus, the greatest of his scholarly feats, carries a stern warning against excessive indulgence in conjectural emendation: "I have confirmed some old emendations and added new ones, but have not done either with great zeal. For this is the sin that besets us Critics, and Tacitus nowadays suffers as much from remedies as he once did from errors." Elsewhere he put the point more cogently: *non ad ista sed per ista,* textual criticism is a means not an end. And he added an extensive treatment of this theme to the unannotated edition of Julius Caesar's *Commentaries* that he prepared for use by gentlemen in schools—and that remained standard long after his death.

Lipsius's ambivalence, moreover, is the direct result of a characteristic of his work that is as important as its solid basis of learning. Lipsius saw the real end of scholarship not as scientific but as practical. He chose the texts he edited and the issues he studied with his attention fixed above all on the needs of his own time. He concentrated on Tacitus and Seneca not simply because he esteemed their prose but because he felt that they had lived in, analyzed, and could help the careful modern scholar to put up with an age of despotism and rebellion. In Tacitus, he told his readers, they would find not useless stories about the austere early days of the Roman republic but cold and practical analysis of a world in which power was concentrated in the hands of a small group:

> Tacitus doesn't present you with showy wars or triumphs, which serve no purpose except the reader's pleasure; with rebellions or speeches of the tribunes, with agrarian or frumentary laws, which are quite irrelevant to our time. Behold instead kings and rulers and, so to speak, a theater of our modern life. I see a ruler rising up against the laws in one passage, subjects rising up against a ruler elsewhere. I find the devices that make the destruction of liberty possible and the unsuccessful effort to regain it. I read of tyrants overthrown in their turn, and of power, ever unfaithful to those who abuse it. And there are also the evils that accompany liberty regained: chaos, rivalry between

equals, greed, looting, wealth pursued from, not on behalf of, the community. Good God, he is a great and useful writer! And those who govern should certainly have him at hand at all times.

If Tacitus cast the most searching light on the chiaroscuro political scene of the late sixteenth century, Seneca taught those caught up in such events how to survive them with their dignity intact. In the philosophy of later Stoicism, in fact, Lipsius found a simple guide to life, one that would enable the young aristocrat to purge himself of fear and anger, to master his passions, and then to instill discipline in himself and in his soldiers. This was the message that Lipsius made popular in his brief and vivid dialogues *On Constancy*, in which, as he said, he taught subjects their duty: that of suffering what their lords inflicted on them. This was the message, on a grander scale, of the Senecan commentary and the two great manuals of Stoic philosophy that occupied Lipsius during the last decade of his life, and that remained standard works until the nineteenth century.

Antiquarianism, finally, proved to be the most practical of all Lipsius's studies—a conclusion that may seem surprising, given the pejorative sense in which we nowadays use the term in English. In the detailed study of Roman institutions, Lipsius found solutions to the most pressing problems of military and political organization. For example, in the detailed accounts of Roman military organization and tactics given by Polybius and others, Lipsius thought that he could find the model for a military machine more effective than anything in existence. He reconstructed and recommended Roman soldiers' customs: their Spartan habit of living on bread and water in the field, their acceptance of a stern code of discipline enforced by condign punishment, their willingness to dig ditches and build palisades. He praised their weapons, their formations, their uniforms, and their chains of command. And though he admitted that some modern weapons, like the pike, had their place in the military order, he urged the commanders of his time to combine these with "ancient arms and the ancient order and line of battle"—and promised that if they would do so, their armies would give them a monopoly of violence in their states and enable them to create vast empires.

Lipsius, in other words, created a brand of philology that was entirely relevant to current and practical problems. No wonder, then, that his studies attracted the attention of his rivals—like Joseph Scaliger, who was still making sketches of the Roman *pilum* on his deathbed in order to show where Lipsius had gone wrong. No wonder, either, that his works reached generals as well as scholars. Maurice of Nassau, the most competent commander the Dutch had, studied with Lipsius at Leiden and put his lecture notes into practice afterward. In 1595 a friend reported to Lipsius that "Count Maurice, while encamped at the Hague, has taught his soldiers to fight like Romans. There were 60 footsoldiers with spears on the one side, 40 on the other armed by ancient custom with the Roman shield. The fight took place, and the men with shields stood firm for a long time despite the opposition of those with spears, which had no effect. In the end, the men with shields were driven off thanks to the violence and agility of a few of the others—yet in such a way that they retained much dignity and praise."

It is bemusing to see scholarship so firmly in possession of the role that science enjoys now, the source of the powerful knowledge that statesmen most need. Yet the spectacle helps us to understand why Lipsius's work found a market. It shows that military leaders were predisposed to follow ancient precedents and models. And it shows that Lipsius really could interpret these far more subtly than professional soldiers. In this case Lipsius wrote back to explain that Maurice had chosen the wrong way to imitate the Romans: "The experiment is a good one, but in my opinion should be carried out differently. One should not set one company, that is, 60 soldiers, against another 60, but several companies at once. It is that conjoining and mutual help which give strength, as beams do in buildings. The Roman legions always beat the phalanx—but together. Had you set a few Roman soldiers against a few Macedonians, things might have gone quite differently."

The cloistered scholar had to teach the general, then, that the shape of Roman shields mattered less than the cohesion of Roman armies as a whole. Lipsius, as Gerhard Oestreich, Wilhelm Hahlweg, and Geoffrey Parker have shown, provided Maurice and other influential military thinkers with the basic ideas from which they created the seventeenth-century Military Revolution, with its disciplined professional armies and elaborate chains of command. No wonder that Maurice seemed "to fall in love" with Lipsius's book on Roman arms, the *De militia Romana*. This great book not only brought lost aspects of antiquity back to life but reshaped the face of battle.

Lipsius did not only study war. In fact, he tried to distill the wisdom of the ancients on all political and military subjects into a single, accessible whole, and did so in a book that reached a public even larger than that of the *De militia Romana.* Lipsius's *Six Books of Politics,* published in 1589, guided the early modern monarch through the whole grim array of tasks and duties that confronted him. It told him how to raise an army, how to quell dissent, how to impose discipline. It told him which tricks against enemies were licit and which (those that involved the breaking of oaths) were not. And it did all of this in a couple of hundred uniquely pithy pages. For in the *Politics,* as Lipsius pointed out in the preface, he brilliantly mixed entirely traditional, even classical, ingredients in such a way that they made an ultra-modern concoction. One sample will give a taste of Lipsius's creation. Should a state, he asks, tolerate religious dissent? To begin with, one must distinguish between public and private dissent. Then one can lay out the opinions of the ancients in a coherent and useful way:

> I say that they sin publicly, who both entertain wrong opinions about God and the traditional rites and induce others to do so by making disturbances. Privately, who entertain the same wrong opinions, but keep them to themselves. As to the first, the question is, should such men get off scot free? No! "Let them be punished by you lest you be punished in their place."   (Cyprian)

> Especially if they create disturbances. "Better that one perish than that unity perish."   (Augustine)

> "The penalty for profanation of religions varies from place to place, but there always is one."   (Seneca)

> There is no room for clemency here. "Burn, cut, so that a member perish rather than the whole body."   (Cicero)

> "For crimes against holy religion amount to crimes against everyone." (Justinian)

Lipsius, in other words, created not a smooth fresco of his own devising but a brilliant mosaic of classical sentiments, astutely chosen and arranged.

In this case, his assemblage of authoritarian *sententiae* draws on pagan and Christian, legal and oratorical texts. Nothing could seem clearer than that all wise men, at all times and places, have called for the suppression of public religious dissent. And Lipsius, drawing heavily on his wonderfully stocked memory, found and assembled quotations of equal brevity and pith on every subject from the need of real soldiers to dig their own ditches to the need of real tyrants to be punished.

This recipe for political discourse tickled even more palates than Lipsius's military cookbook. The *Politics* went through a staggering fifty-four editions in Latin and twenty-two more in vernacular translations. Statesmen read the book as eagerly as professors. Even a hard-bitten professional like Bernardino de Mendoza, a cavalryman under the duke of Alba in the 1560s and the Spanish ambassador to France in the days of the Holy League, took time off between efforts to assassinate Queen Elizabeth to translate the *Politics* into Spanish. Lipsius's new way of teaching politics induced thousands of foreign students to come to Leiden, which became for a time the largest university in Europe. His grim political maxims became the staple of political thought in much of Europe. They were vulgarized by the writers on state secrets, *arcana rerumpublicarum*. They were cannibalized by commentators on Tacitus and students writing dissertations. They were even satirized by the great opponent of centralized monarchy and religious repression, Traiano Boccalini, in his bitterly comic *Newsletters from Parnassus*.

It is not hard to account for the success of *Politica à la mode de Lipse*. Humanists of the generation before Lipsius's had also seen philology as the one tool that could deal constructively with civil and religious war. But the great jurists of mid-sixteenth-century France, François Baudouin and Jean Bodin, had envisioned a philology very different from Lipsius's. They held that the young leader must begin by reading all significant historians (Bodin provided a helpful list of several hundred titles to be getting on with). He must next evaluate each historian in the light of his original situation and assumptions. He must then study the events the historian recorded in the light of his nation's experience as a whole—in the light, in fact, of every available fact about the physical setting, climatic conditions, and political institutions that had shaped the individuals and the nation. Bodin knew that peoples migrated, and thus insisted that his future leader not only study the nations as the historians described them, but also pursue them back to their origins, however distant. In order to locate these he made magnificent use of etymology—arguing, for example, that the Belgian term for the Gauls, Walloons, was most informative; in its Latin form, *Ouallones,* it revealed that they were a French tribe that had wandered about saying "Où allons-nous?" Only after every battle and every institution had been set like a jewel into a context fully reconstructed by up-to-date scholarship could one hope to assess its value and write beside it, in one's notebook, CTV (*consilium turpe utile*—a vile plan, but a useful one) or CH *(consilium honestum).*

In theory this program realized the highest ideals of humanism. In practice it resulted in utter intellectual chaos. No one could hope to find straight answers to practical questions in Bodin's mistitled masterpiece, the *Method for the Easy Comprehension of History.* Bodin himself abandoned historicism and philology and found in conversion to Judaism and the persecution of witches an intellectual and emotional security that his scholarship had not afforded him. By contrast, Lipsius's *Politics* offered authoritative maxims stripped of context and complication. No wonder that these won the day, and held the high ground until they were replaced around 1650 by the new theories of Hermann Conring and William Petty, with their emphasis on economic and demographic problems. To be sure, Lipsius's synthesis was not his own invention. He owed his basic assumptions, at least, to the teacher he encountered in his early years in Rome, Marc-Antoine Muret. But Muret's Roman superiors never let him develop his views at any length—and at first would not let him lecture on an author so hostile to Jews and Christians as Tacitus. The details and the literary form at any rate were Lipsius's own.

It is just here, in Lipsius's most successful works, that the paradoxes seem most glaring. Lipsius was a professional student of the ancient world. He based his claim to provide modern rulers with powerful knowledge on his supreme ability to interpret ancient texts. And yet, to make his texts useful in the age of Philip II, Lipsius constantly had to interpret them not as his sense of their authors' views suggested but as his own requirements dictated. To recreate the Roman military order as a whole he had to use texts from many different periods as if they described the same institution—a practice that provoked Scaliger to enter many critical marginalia in his copy of the *De militia Romana.* To construct a Stoic ethics for the modern warrior, Lipsius had to pretend, far more strongly than the evidence warranted, that the writings of Epictetus and Seneca "secretly lead one to Christian doctrine and to piety"—and to support this view not with the evidence of the texts but with an anecdote about how useful Epictetus had been to the pious Cardinal Cesare Baronio. To construct his politics for the modern governor, finally, Lipsius had to banish all thought of literary or historical context from his mind. He himself compared his enterprise to the making of a poetic cento, and argued that in that genre one was not only free but obliged to twist lines from their original senses. This comparison is eloquent. The poetic cento Lipsius's readers knew best was perhaps the nuptial one by Ausonius, in which innocent lines and half-lines from Virgil are twisted into a splendidly obscene epithalamium complete with a section on the taking of virginity. In comparing his *Politics* to such works, Lipsius made clear that he saw himself less as a scholar collecting data than as a writer continuing—and reshaping—a literary tradition.

By the end of his life Lipsius readily admitted that his chief aim had been not to interpret the ancient world but to exploit it. He described the *Politics* and *Constantia* as the natural culmination of his life's work. And he described that as an effort to make philology useful: "I was the first or the only one in my time to make literature serve true wisdom. I made philology into philosophy." In this comment, as Renaissance readers knew, Lipsius was appropriating one of his favorite ancient texts, the 108th letter of Seneca. This described the reverse of the process Lipsius claimed to have brought about. It complained, that is, that in Seneca's time philosophy had degenerated into philology. Everyone was disputing about details and ignoring the main points. Future scholars were reading Virgil for merely scholarly ends: "The future grammarian studying Virgil does not read that incomparable phrase, *fugit inreparabile tempus,* in order to reflect that "we must be on our guard; swift time drives us onward, and is driven . . ." but to observe that whenever Virgil describes the speed of time's passage he uses the verb *fugio.*"

Seneca and Lipsius prefer the productive, "philosophical" interpreter who appropriates his text to some moral end to the passive, "grammatical" interpreter who merely wants to know how and what his author meant. We must admire the ancient and the Renaissance writer's prescient insight into the methods readers use to construct meanings from their texts. But we must also be depressed by Lipsius's willingness to abandon the core of the humanistic enterprise, the effort to understand the past on its own terms, in his desire to make ancient experience accessible. Here, as well as in his thoughts on religious dissent, we see a humanist at his most inhumane. Lipsius was willing to crush the individuality of Tacitus or Cicero as ruthlessly as that of an Anabaptist; and it is hard to find his posture in either case an attractive one.

How then do we come to terms with Lipsius? Recent scholarship has provided two powerful and exciting ways of doing so. In the first place, Bernard Rekers and others have shown that Lipsius belonged to the Family of Love—that strange sect of spiritual reformers that stretched like a shadowy wheel across mid-sixteenth-century Europe, its hub in Christopher Plantin's printing shop in Antwerp and its spokes reaching London, Prague, and even Madrid (where a tiny group of disciples in the Escorial itself eagerly awaited each new batch of commentaries on the Apocalypse in code). The members of this group saw all formal religions as equally valuable for instilling discipline in ordinary folk and as equally irrelevant to themselves. Thanks to their prophets and their inward voices, they enjoyed a direct access to religious truth. They were independent of the organized churches, which they joined only out of prudence, and of the Scriptures, which they allegorized very freely. And they considered themselves free to conform to the ruling faith of any land they might settle in. At the same time, though, they laid great stress on the need for peace and order, and urged political authorities to enforce religious unity on the many-headed mob. Knowing that Lipsius belonged to this group, we can understand his willingness to play the Lutheran in Jena, the Catholic in Italy, the Calvinist fellow traveler in Leiden, and the Catholic once again in Louvain. Such changes in external practice and allegiance affected only the outward and visible husk of what was to Lipsius an inward and spiritual experience.

In the second place, Dutch and German scholars like W. Kühlmann and H. Wansink have found the key to Lipsius in his profession. He was a rhetorician by trade. He used the rhetorician's normal methods to determine the topics of political discourse, to find its verbal and argumentative content, and to adorn it. And he made his *Politics* as much a treasury of sentences to be quoted by other rhetoricians—rather like Erasmus's *Adages*—as a work of analysis. Rhetoricians, of course, seek to persuade their listeners rather than to provide absolutely valid proofs. They can do without convictions. And Lipsius, accordingly, could happily aim all his life not at knowledge of the true and the good but at his own immediate advantage. This body of literature represents Lipsius as a man with little individuality but great will to succeed—a young upwardly mobile philologist, one might say, who sold his matchless skills to a succession of higher bidders.

These two theories, unfortunately, are hard to reconcile with each other, and neither can account for all the facts. If Lipsius was above all a spiritual reformer, he did not have to become an enthusiastic Lutheran pamphleteer at Jena (where he praised the dukes of Saxony as the race chosen by God to chastise the papacy) or an enthusiastic Catholic pamphleteer in his last years at Louvain (where he applied his philological skills to proving that Flemish shrines of the Virgin had produced miraculous cures for blindness, running sores, and diabolic possession, to the distress of his Catholic as well as his Protestant friends). If he was a pure pragmatist, on the other hand, he did not need to write a provocative argument for centralized monarchy and religious repression while teaching in decentralized and tolerant Holland. Nor did he have to defend the liberty of the individual conscience against princely efforts to read men's souls, as he consistently did, even while insisting that heretics who disturbed the public peace deserved punishment—a point well made by Gerhard Güldner in a penetrating study of Lipsius's debate with Coornhert.

Moreover, neither of these theories helps us to understand Lipsius the interpreter of texts; yet interpretation was the center of his intellectual life. In this area, what strikes the modern student most forcibly are the paradoxes I have already identified. Admittedly, humanists had always had to separate philology from pedagogy. Erasmus the scholar knew a great deal about Greek and Roman homosexuality. But Erasmus the teacher, as Jacques Chomarat has recently reminded us, gave instructions on how to teach the first line of Virgil's second *Eclogue* ("Corydon the shepherd was hot for pretty Alexis") in such a way as to distract the student from realizing what the poem was about. And Erasmus the translator, as Erika Rummel has shown, carefully fudged references to pederasty and homosexuality when rendering decently obscure Greek into worrisomely accessible Latin.

But by the end of the sixteenth century, the paganness of the pagans, their historical and cultural distance from modern Europeans, had become impossible to ignore. Montaigne had proclaimed the bankruptcy of any branch of thought that assumed—as humanism must assume—clear resemblances between ancient examples and modern imitations. And Lipsius can perhaps best be seen as the last serious scholar who tried to rebut these objections and to prove that the ancients still could offer detailed models and instructions for modern actions. The price he paid for splitting scholarship from practice, for insisting that the student keep separate notebooks for political and historical learning, was a high one. He had to transform humanism itself from a device for criticizing the world as it is by comparing it to an ideal past into a device for leaving the world unchanged while learning from the past how to cope with its defects. Where earlier humanists like Erasmus and More had criticized the militarism and greed of the fledgling New Monarchies, Lipsius collaborated in the creation of the far more powerful and less humane states of the seventeenth century. Yet no other solution could have preserved the apparent utility of classical studies for so long against the corrosive attacks of skepticism and the New Philosophy. And no gentler doctrine could have met the needs of that cruel age, when even Hugo Grotius would defend as legal the destruction of civilian property and the execution of hostages.

In the end, though, explanations like this operate on too general a level to satisfy. Lipsius's achievements can be described and his historical situation can be analyzed. But his personal motives and emotions remain obscure. And perhaps we should be willing to leave them so. It somehow seems appropriate that the man who unveiled the secrets of generals and emperors should preserve his own more modest—but more complex—philologist's secrets intact.

13

Descartes
the Dreamer

〰️

ALL PHILOSOPHERS have theories. Good philosophers have students and critics. But great philosophers have primal scenes. They play the starring roles in striking stories, which their disciples and later writers tell and retell, over the decades and even the centuries. Thales, whom the Greeks remembered as their first philosopher, tumbled into a well while looking up at the night sky, to the accompanying mockery of a serving maid. His example showed, more clearly than any argument could, that philosophy served no practical purpose. Those who take a different view of philosophy can cite a contrasting anecdote, also ancient, in their support: after drawing on his knowledge of nature to predict an abundant harvest, Thales rented out all the olive presses in Miletus and Chios. He made a fortune charging high rates for them; better still, he showed that scholar rhymes with dollar after all.

At the other end of western history, in the twentieth century, Ludwig Wittgenstein held that propositions are, in some way, pictures of the world: that they must have the same "logical form" as what they describe. He did so, at least, until he took a train ride one day with Piero Sraffa, an Italian economist at Cambridge. Making a characteristic Italian gesture, drawing his hand across his throat, Sraffa asked, "What is the logical form of that?" He thus set his friend off on what became the vastly influential *Philosophical Investigations,* that fascinating, endlessly puzzling text which the American philosophers of my youth took as their bible, and to the exegesis of which they brought a ferocious cleverness that would do credit to any seminarian. If Helen's face launched a thousand ships, Sraffa's gesture launched at least a hundred careers.

In each case—and in dozens of others—the story has passed from books to lectures to articles and back, becoming as smooth and shiny in the process as a pebble carried along by a swift-flowing stream. In fact, these stories have become talismans of sorts: evidence that the most profound ideas, the most rigorous analyses, have their origins in curious, human circumstances and strange, all-too-human people. Such anecdotes accessibly dramatize the heroic originality and rigor of philosophers—qualities that one cannot always appreciate only by studying their texts, slowly and carefully.

It seems appropriate, then, that no philosopher in the western tradition has left a more fascinating—or more puzzling—trail of anecdote behind him than the Frenchman René Descartes. Like Wittgenstein's philosophy, Descartes's began from curious experiences; but in his case the provocation was—or was remembered as—nothing so banal as a train ride.

Early in his life, Descartes became a soldier, serving two years in the Dutch army before joining the Bavarian service. He writes that in the late fall of 1619, while stationed in the German city of Ulm, he "was detained by the onset of winter in quarters where, having neither conversation to divert me nor, fortunately, cares or passions to trouble me, I was completely free to consider my own thoughts." He refused all company, went on solitary walks, and dedicated himself to an exhausting search for . . . he did not quite know what. Suddenly he stumbled on what he called "the foundations of a marvelous science." After an almost mystical experience of deep joy, Descartes fell asleep, in his close, stove-heated room. He then dreamed, three times.

In the first dream, terrible phantoms surrounded him. His efforts to fight them off were hindered by a weakness in his right side, which made him stagger in a way that struck him as terribly humiliating. Trying to reach a chapel that belonged to a college, he found himself pinned to the wall by the wind—only to be addressed by someone who called him by name, promising that one "M.N." would give him something (which Descartes took to be a melon from another country). The wind died, and he awoke with a pain in his left side. Turning over, he reflected for some time, slept again, and dreamed of a clap of thunder. Waking, he saw that his room was full of sparks. In the third dream, finally, he found two books, which he discussed with a stranger. The second book, a collection of poems, included one about the choice of a form of life—as well as some copperplate portraits, which seemed familiar.

Waking again and reflecting, Descartes decided that these dreams had been divinely sent. He connected them, both at the time and later, with the discovery of the new method that would ultimately enable him to rebuild philosophy from its foundations. Paradoxically, Descartes, the pre-eminent modern rationalist, took dreams as the basis for his confidence in his new philosophy—a philosophy that did more than any other to de-animate the world, to convince intellectuals that they lived in a world uninhabited by occult forces, among animals and plants unequipped with souls, where the only ground of certainty lay in the thinking self.

Like Wittgenstein, Descartes enjoys a tribute that modern philosophers rarely offer their predecessors. He is still taken seriously enough to be attacked. Courses in the history of philosophy regularly skip hundreds of years. They ignore whole periods, such as the Renaissance, and genres, such as moral philosophy, since these lack the qualities of rigor, austerity, and explanatory power that win a text or thinker a starring position in the modern philosophical heavens. But Descartes continues to play a major role. In histories of philosophy, he marks the beginning of modernity and seriousness; he is, in fact, the earliest philosopher after ancient times to enjoy canonical status. Students of Descartes can rejoice in the existence of an excellent *Cambridge Companion to Descartes,* edited by John Cottingham, two helpful Descartes dictionaries, and even a brief and breezy *Descartes in Ninety Minutes*—as well as a jungle of monographs and articles on Descartes's epistemology and ethics, physics and metaphysics, through which only the specialist can find a path. (One standard anthology of modern responses to Descartes's work extends to four thick volumes.) Descartes still provokes.

In a sense, moreover, he provokes more now than he did twenty years ago. In the last generation, developments in a wide range of disciplines—computer and software design, primate research, neurology, psychology—have made the question of how to define human consciousness more urgent, perhaps, than it has ever been. What would show that the computer or an ape thinks as humans do? Can one prove that the measurable physiological phenomena that accompany mental states should be identified with them? How can physical events cause mental ones, and vice versa? And who should settle such questions: philosophers, or scientists, or both in collaboration? New interdisciplinary programs for the study of consciousness or artificial intelligence provide forums for the debate— which remains fierce—on these and other issues. And the debates are, if anything, becoming fiercer. Successes in solving particular problems— such as the creation of a machine genuinely able to play chess, rather than the man disguised as a machine unmasked by Edgar Allan Poe—excite some of the specialists responsible for them to declare victory: if a computer has a mind, then the mind is a computer. Stalwart opponents swat these optimists with rolled-up newspapers, insisting that vast areas of mental and emotional experience—like the pain caused by the rolled-up newspaper—undeniably exist and matter even though they have no counterpart in computer models. From whatever side they come, a great many of the contributions to these debates start with a reference to, or amount to, a sustained attack on Descartes.

It is not hard to explain why this Frenchman, who has been dead for three and a half centuries, still seems modern enough to interest and irritate philosophers who otherwise feel contempt for most of their predecessors. He felt and wrote exactly the same way about his own predecessors.

Descartes, as is well known, began his career as a philosopher in a state of radical discontent with the resources of the intellectual disciplines. He described this state with unforgettable clarity, moreover, in the autobiography with which he began his most famous text, his *Discourse on the Method* (1637). Born in 1596, Descartes lost his mother as a baby and saw little of his father, a councilor in the *parlement* of Brittany at Rennes. For almost a decade, beginning around the age of ten, he attended the Jesuit college of La Flèche at Anjou. Here, he recalled, he made a comprehensive study of classical literature and science. He read—and wrote—much fine Latin, debated in public, learned how to produce an *explication du texte*. He knew all the clichés that humanists used to defend the classical curriculum, and he recited them with palpable irony: "I knew . . . that the charm of fables awakens the mind, while memorable deeds told in histories uplift it and help to shape one's judgment if they are read with discretion; that reading good books is like having a conversation with the most distinguished men of past ages."

But all this contact with traditional high culture left Descartes unconvinced. Knowledge of literary traditions and past events might give a young man a certain cosmopolitan gloss, but it could not yield profound and practical knowledge: "For conversing with those of past centuries is much the same as traveling. It is good to know something of the customs of various peoples, so that we may judge our own more soundly and not think that everything contrary to our own ways is ridiculous and irrational, as those who have seen nothing of the world ordinarily do. But one who spends too much time traveling eventually becomes a stranger in his own country; and one who is too curious about the practices of past ages usually remains quite ignorant about those of the present."

The humanists of the Renaissance had praised the Greeks and Romans, who did not waste time trying to define the good but made their readers wish to pursue it with their powerful rhetorical appeal. Descartes recognized fluff when he heard it: "I compared the moral writings of the ancient pagans to very proud and magnificent palaces built only on mud and sand. They extol the virtues, and made them appear more estimable than anything else in the world; but they do not adequately explain how to recognize a virtue, and often what they call by this fine name is nothing but a case of callousness, or vanity, or desperation, or parricide." So much for the soft, irrelevant humanities—still a popular view in American and English philosophy departments. Descartes, in other words, was the first, though hardly the last, philosopher to treat his discipline as if it should have the austere rigor of a natural science.

Even the study of mathematics and systematic philosophy, however—at least as Descartes encountered them in his college—had proved unrewarding. The mathematicians had missed "the real use" of their own subject, failing to see that it could be of service outside "the mechanical arts." And the philosophers had created only arguments without end: "[philosophy] has been cultivated for many centuries by the most excellent minds, and yet there is still no point in it which is not disputed and hence doubtful." All previous thinkers, all earlier systems, seemed to Descartes merely confused.

He thought he knew the reason, too. All earlier thinkers had set out to carry on a tradition. They had taken over from their predecessors ideas, terms, and theories which they tried to fit together, along with some new thoughts of their own, into new structures. Predictably, their results were incoherent: not lucid Renaissance palaces, in which all surface forms manifested the regular and logical structures underneath them, but messy Gothic pastiches of strange shapes and colors randomly assembled over the centuries. Such theories, "made up and put together bit by bit from the opinions of many different people," could never match the coherence of "the simple reasoning which a man of good sense naturally makes concerning whatever he comes across."

Descartes's "marvelous science" would be, by contrast, all his own work, and it would have the "perfection," as well as the explanatory power, that more traditional philosophies lacked. To revolutionize philosophy, accordingly, Descartes "entirely abandoned the study of letters." He ceased to read the work of others, turned his attention inward, and created an entire philosophical system—and indeed an entire universe—of his own. He hoped that this would make up in clarity and coherence for what it might lack in richness of content. And the first publication of his theories, in the form of the *Discourse* and a group of related texts, made him a controversial celebrity in the world of European thought.

As Wittgenstein, three hundred years later, cleared the decks of philosophy by insisting that most of its traditional problems had no meaning, so Descartes insisted that most of philosophy's traditional tools had no function. Like Wittgenstein, he became the idol of dozens of young philosophers, who practiced the opposite of what he preached by taking over bits of his system and combining them with ideas of their own. Unlike Wittgenstein, however, he also became the object of bitter, sometimes vicious criticism, from both Protestant and Catholic thinkers who resented the threat he posed to theological orthodoxy or simply to the established curriculum. No wonder that he, unlike his opponents, remains a hero in the age that has none. What characterizes modernity—so more than one philosopher has argued—is its state of perpetual revolution, its continual effort to produce radically new ideas and institutions. Modern heroes—from Reformation theologians such as Martin Luther to political radicals such as Karl Marx—established their position by insisting that traditional social and intellectual structures that looked as solid and heavy as the Albert Memorial would dissolve and float away when seen from a new and critical point of view. The Descartes who wrote the *Discourse* belongs to this same line of intellectual rebels, and in this sense he is deservedly regarded as the first modern philosopher.

Again like Wittgenstein Descartes refused to take part in normal or in academic high society. Though he devoted a period at the University of Poitiers to study of the law, he made little effort to follow a career as a lawyer—a path chosen by many intellectuals at the time. Though admired by patrons and intellectuals in France and elsewhere, he took little interest in court or city. He did not spend much time in Paris, where in his lifetime the classic French literary canon was being defined on stage and in the Academy and where the fashionable gossiped brilliantly about literature, history, and sex.

Descartes, who contributed so much to the development of that classic French virtue, clarity, kept aloof from his colleagues in the creation of the modern French language. He lived most contentedly in Holland, sometimes in relatively sophisticated towns such as Leiden and Deventer but often in the deep country, where he had at most one or two partners in conversation—one was a cobbler with a gift for mathematics—and led an existence undisturbed by great excitements. He only once showed great sorrow, when his illegitimate daughter, Francine, who was borne by a serving maid named Hélène in 1635, died as a young child. And he only once departed from his accustomed ways: when he moved to the court of that eager, imperious student of ideas, texts, and religions, Queen Christina of Sweden. There he became mortally ill when she made him rise at four in the frozen northern dawn to give her philosophy lessons. He died at the age of fifty-three, a martyr to intellectual curiosity, in February 1650.

Descartes's "marvelous science" portrayed a whole new universe: one that consisted not, like that of traditional philosophy, of bodies animated by a number of souls intimately connected to them, and related to one another by occult influences, but of hard matter in predictable motion. He cast his ideas not in the traditional form of commentary on ancient texts and ideas, but in the radically antitraditionalist one of systematic treatises that did not cite authorities—other than that of Descartes's own ability to reason. He said that he saw no point in weaving together chains of syllogisms, as the Scholastics of the Middle Ages had, in the vain hope that major and minor premises of unclear validity, drawn at random from old texts and swarming with unexamined assumptions, could somehow yield new and important conclusions. He did not try to protect his weaker arguments from attack by covering them with a thick, brittle armor plating of quotations from ancient and modern sources in the manner of the Renaissance humanists, who saw philology as the mainstay of philosophy.

Descartes, instead, claimed that he could build entirely on his own something new, coherent, and symmetrical. He liked to compare his work to that of the great town planners of his time, who saw the ideal city as a lucid walled polyhedron surrounding a central square, rather than an irregular, picturesque embodiment of centuries of time and change. The "crooked and irregular" streets and varied heights of the buildings in old cities suggested that "it is chance, rather than the will of men using reason, that placed them so," he said. Coherence, uniformity, symmetry attracted him: the Paris of the Place des Vosges rather than the palaces and alleys of the older parts of the city.

Descartes saw mathematics as the model for the new form of intellectual architecture he hoped to create. For he himself, as he discovered later than stereotypes would lead one to expect, was a very gifted mathematician, one of the creators of modern algebra and the inventor of analytical geometry. Like a mathematician, he tried to begin from absolutely hard premises: ideas so "clear and distinct" that he could not even begin to deny them. In these, and only in these, he found a place to stand. Descartes could imagine away the physical world, the value of the classics, and much else. But he could not deny, while thinking, the existence of his thinking self. Cogito, ergo sum.

From this narrow foothold he began to climb. He proved the existence of God in a way that he himself found deeply satisfactory though many others did not: the idea of God includes every perfection, and it is more perfect to exist than not to exist. Hence God must exist—and be the source of the innate faculties and ideas that all humans possess. He worked out the sort of universe that God would have to create. And he devised, over the course of time, a system that embraced everything from the nature of the planets to that of the human mind, from the solution of technical problems in mathematics to the circulation of the blood.

Wherever possible, precise quantitative models showed how Cartesian nature would work in detail: he not only devised laws for the refraction and reflection of light, for example, but also designed a lens-grinding machine that would apply them (and prove their validity). Parts of his system clanked and sputtered. His elaborate cosmology—which interpreted planetary systems as whirlpools, or vortices, of matter in motion—was technically outdated before it appeared. It could not account for the mathematical details of planetary motion established by Tycho Brahe and Johannes Kepler. Nonetheless, the rigor and coherence of his system inspired natural philosophers on the Continent for a century and more after his death.

The reception of Descartes's philosophy was anything but easy or straightforward. At the outset of his career as a published writer, in the *Discourse on the Method*, he invited those who had objections to his work to communicate them to him for reply. He circulated his *Meditations* for comment before he published them in 1641, and printed them along with systematic objections and his own replies. Thomas Hobbes, Marin Mersenne, Pierre Gassendi, and others now known only to specialists pushed him to define his terms and defend his arguments. At the same time, his thought became controversial in wider circles. Descartes long feared this outcome. Both a good Copernican and a good Catholic, he was appalled by the condemnation of Galileo in 1633. This led him both to delay publication of his treatise *The World* and to try to devise a metaphysics that would prove his natural philosophy legitimate.

But once his work reached print, Descartes could not avoid controversy. In 1639, his supporters in the faculty of the University of Utrecht began to praise his new philosophy, holding public debates about his theories. The influential theologian Gisbert Voetius defended traditional theology, not only against Cartesianism but against Descartes, whose beliefs and morality Voetius attacked. Descartes found himself forced to defend himself in a series of pamphlets. He lost some sympathizers—such as the scholar Anna Maria van Schurmann, one of a number of women with whom he discussed theological or philosophical issues.

In the 1640s, Descartes's political and legal situation became extremely serious, and his life in the Netherlands increasingly exhausting and disturbing. Nor did he always agree with those who considered themselves his followers. Ironically, if inevitably, Descartes's philosophy mutated into Cartesianism—one more of the philosophical schools whose competing claims had driven the young Descartes to try something completely different. Some academic Cartesians—as Theo Verbeek and others have shown—even used his philosophy along with others in a deliberately eclectic way their master would have condemned.

Nonetheless, until recent years philosophers generally thought they had a clear idea both of what Descartes meant to do and about why he framed his enterprise as he did. The question of consciousness, of the nature of the mind and its relation to the body, provides a good example of how Descartes has generally been read. Earlier philosophers, drawing on and adding to a tradition that went back to Aristotle, explained life and consciousness in a way that varied endlessly in detail but not in substance. A whole series of souls, hierarchically ordered, each of them equipped with particular faculties, accounted for organic life in plants, movement in animals, and consciousness in humans. The number and quality of faculties possessed by each being corresponded to its position in the hierarchical chain of being, which determined the number and kinds of souls that being possessed. And the well-established nature and location of these faculties in the body could be used to show how body and soul were intimately and intricately connected. It made perfectly good sense to assume—as the astrologers, then almost as fashionable as now, regularly did—that celestial influences, acting on the four humors in the body, could affect the mind. No one could establish an easy, clear division between mind and body, man and nature.

Descartes, by contrast, drew a sharp line, here as elsewhere, both between his views and traditional ones and between physical and mental processes. He proved, as he insisted he could, that mind and body were in fact separate. Descartes could imagine that he had no body at all, but he could not imagine that he, the one imagining, did not exist. The mind, in other words, was fundamentally different from the body. Bodies had as their defining properties hardness and extension. Their other attributes—such as color and texture—were merely superficial, as one could see, for example, by melting a lump of wax. The material world, accordingly, could be measured, divided, cut. The mind, by contrast, was clearly indivisible; when conscious, one always had access to all of it. Descartes divided human beings, accordingly, into two components: a material, extended body, mobile and mortal, and an immaterial, thinking soul, located somewhere within the body but at least potentially immortal. He redefined the struggles between different souls which Saint Augustine had so influentially described in his *Confessions* and of which others regularly spoke as struggles between the body and the soul. These took place, Descartes argued, in a particular organ: the pineal gland, within the brain, the one point where soul and body interacted. He held that animals could not have minds, at least in the sense that human beings do. And the firm distinction he made between the physical plane that humans share with other beings and the mental operations that attest to their existence on more than a physical plane continues to irritate philosophers—just as his sharp distinction between the real world of solid matter in motion and the qualitative, unreal world of perception and passion once enraged T. S. Eliot and Basil Willey, who held him guilty of causing the seventeenth century's "dissociation of sensibility."

Descartes's position in the history of thought has seemed, in recent years, as easily defined as his innovative contributions to it. By the time he was born, in 1596, intellectual norms that had existed for centuries, even millennia, were being called into question. The discovery of the New World had challenged traditional respect for the cosmology and philosophy of the ancients. The Protestant Reformation had destroyed the unity of Christendom, offering radically new ways of reading the Bible. The Scholastic philosophers who dominated the faculties of theology in the traditional universities, though all of them worked within a common, basically Aristotelian idiom, had come into conflict with one another on many fundamental points, and some humanists claimed that their vast Gothic structures of argument rested on misunderstandings of the Bible and Aristotle.

Some thinkers looked desperately for moorings in this intellectual storm. Justus Lipsius, for example, tried to show that ancient Stoicism, with its firm code of duties, could provide an adequate philosophy for the modern aristocrat and military officer. Others began to think that there were no moorings to be found and even to accept that fact as welcome, since it undermined the dogmatic pretensions that led to religious revolutions and persecutions. The philosophy of the ancient Skeptics, in particular, offered tools to anyone who wished to deny that philosophers could attain the truth about man, the natural world, or anything else.

Skepticism, as Richard Popkin and Charles Schmitt have shown, interested a few intellectuals in the fifteenth century, such as Lorenzo Valla. But it first attracted widespread interest during the Reformation. Erasmus, for example, drew on skeptical arguments to show that Luther was wrongly splitting the Catholic church on issues about which humans could never attain certainty. The major ancient skeptical texts, the works of Sextus Empiricus, appeared in Latin translation late in the sixteenth century—just as the Wars of Religion between French Calvinists and Catholics were reaching their hottest point. Michel de Montaigne, the great essayist whom Descartes eagerly read and tacitly cited, drew heavily on Greek Skepticism when he mounted his attacks on intellectual intolerance. To some—especially the so-called Politiques, such as Montaigne, who was not only a writer but one of the statesmen who negotiated religious peace in France at the end of the sixteenth century—Skepticism came as a deeply desirable solution to religious crisis. To others, however—especially to Catholic and Protestant philosophers who still felt the need to show that their religious doctrines not only rested on biblical authority but also corresponded to the best possible human reasoning—Skepticism came as a threat to all intellectual certainties, including the necessary ones.

Descartes tried on principle to doubt everything he knew. (He called his method, eloquently, one of "hyperbolic doubt.") But he found, as we have seen, that there were some things even he could not doubt, and many others found his arguments convincing. Accordingly, Descartes appears in many histories of philosophy above all as one of those who resolved a skeptical crisis by providing a new basis for physics, metaphysics, and morality. Similarly, he appears in many histories of science, alongside Francis Bacon, as one of those who created a whole new method for studying the natural world.

For the last twenty years or so, however, this view of Descartes's place in the history of thought has begun to undergo scrutiny and criticism. Not only students of consciousness but historians of philosophy and science have begun to raise questions about Descartes's isolation in his own intellectual world. For all his insistence on the novelty of his views and the necessity for a serious thinker to work alone, he always looked for partners in discussion.

And this was only natural. "Even the most radical innovator," write the historians of philosophy Roger Ariew and Marjorie Grene, "has roots; even the most outrageous new beginner belongs to an intellectual community in which opponents have to be refuted and friends won over." Descartes, moreover, not only belonged to a community, as he himself acknowledged; he also drew, as he usually did not like to admit, from a variety of intellectual traditions.

For example, Stephen Gaukroger, whose intricately detailed intellectual biography of Descartes elegantly balances close analysis of texts with a rich recreation of context, finds an ancient source for Descartes's apparently novel notion that certain "clear and distinct" ideas compel assent. The core of the Jesuit curriculum Descartes mastered so well was formed by rhetoric, the ancient art of persuasive speech. Quintilian, the Roman author of the most systematic ancient manual of the subject, analyzed extensively the ways in which an orator could "engage the emotions of the audience." To do so, he argued, the orator must "*exhibit* rather than *display* his proofs." He must produce a mental image so vivid and palpable that his hearers cannot deny it: a clear and distinct idea.

Gaukroger admits that Roman orators saw themselves first and foremost as producing such conviction in others, while Descartes saw his first duty as convincing himself. But Gaukroger elegantly points out that classical rhetoric, for all its concern with public utterance, also embodied something like Descartes's concern with the private, with "self-conviction." The orator, as Quintilian clearly said, had to convince himself in order to convince others: "The first essential is that those feelings should prevail with us that we wish to prevail with the judge."

Descartes's doctrine of clear and distinct ideas is usually described as radically new. It turns out, on inspection, to be a diabolically clever adaptation to new ends of the rhetorical five-finger exercises the philosopher had first mastered as a schoolboy. Gaukroger's negative findings are equally intriguing: he interprets Descartes's famous dreams as evidence not of a breakthrough but of a breakdown, and he argues forcefully that Skepticism played virtually no role in Descartes's original formulation of his method and its consequences.

Several other studies have revealed similarly creative uses of tradition in many pockets of Descartes's philosophy. As John Cottingham has shown, Descartes more than once found himself compelled to use traditional philosophical terminology—with all the problematic assumptions it embodied. Despite his dislike of tradition, he also disliked being suspected of radicalism, and claimed at times not to offer a new theory but to revive a long-forgotten ancient one—for example, the *"vera mathesis"* ("true mathematical science") of the ancient mathematicians Pappus and Diophantus. No one denies the substantial novelty of Descartes's intellectual program; but students of his work, like recent students of Wittgenstein, show themselves ever more concerned to trace the complex relations between radicalism and tradition, text and context.

Descartes's dreams—and his autobiographical use of them—play a special role in this revisionist enterprise. His earliest substantial work, composed in the late 1620s but left unfinished, takes the form of *Rules for the Direction of the Mind;* his great philosophical text of 1641 bears the title *Meditations.* In structure as well as substance, both works unmistakably point backward to his formation in a Jesuit college. There he had not only to study the classics and some modern science but to "make" the *Spiritual Exercises* laid down for Jesuits and their pupils by the founder of the Jesuit order, Ignatius Loyola. These consisted of a set of systematic, graded exercises in contemplation, visualization, and meditation. Students—and candidates for membership in the order—had to reconstruct as vividly as they could in their minds the Crucifixion, Hell, and other scenes that could produce profound emotional and spiritual effects in them. These exercises were intended to enable those who did them to discipline their minds and spirits, to identify and rid themselves of their besetting weaknesses, and finally to choose the vocation for which God intended them. Visions—and even mystical experiences—regularly formed a controlled part of the process, as they had for Ignatius of Loyola himself. The similarity between these exercises in spiritual self-discipline and Descartes's philosophical self-discipline is no coincidence. Here too Descartes transposed part of the education he thought he had rejected into the fabric of his philosophy.

In seeing visions as a form of divine communication—evidence of a special providence that singled recipients out as the possessors of a Mission—Descartes remained firmly within the Jesuit intellectual tradition. He was, in fact, far from the only product of a good Jesuit education to trace his own development in minute interpretative detail. Consider the case of his near contemporary Athanasius Kircher—another mathematically gifted young man, who studied in Jesuit schools in south Germany before becoming the central intellectual figure in baroque Rome. Kircher's interests were as varied as Descartes's were sharply defined: he spelunked in volcanoes, experimented with magnets, reconstructed the travel of Noah's Ark, and studied languages ranging from Coptic to Chinese, with varying degrees of success. But he defined the core of his enterprise with Cartesian precision, if in totally un-Cartesian terms, as an effort to decipher the ancient philosophy encoded in the hieroglyphic inscriptions on Egyptian obelisks. This effort attracted much criticism but also received generous papal support. Ultimately it inspired some of Giovanni Lorenzo Bernini's most spectacular Roman works of sculpture and architecture, in the Piazza Navona and before the church of Santa Maria sopra Minerva.

Descartes would have found most of Kircher's project risible. Yet they had something vital in common. Kircher, like Descartes, tried to prove the rigor and providential inspiration of his work by writing an autobiography.

Kircher's dreams and visions played as large a role in this work as his colorful and sometimes terrifying experiences. Like Descartes, he saw his
unconscious experiences as evidence that God had set him on earth to
carry out a particular plan. His accidental encounter with a book in which
Egyptian hieroglyphs were reproduced and discussed exemplified—he
thought in retrospect—the sort of special providences by which God had
led him in the right direction. Evidently, then, Cartesian autobiography
was actually Jesuit autobiography. Brilliant style, concision, and lucidity
set off the beginning of the *Discourse on the Method* from Kircher's Latin
treatise. But the enterprises were basically as similar as the larger enterprises they were meant to serve were different. And Descartes's dreams not
only make a nice story to adorn the beginning of a lecture but actually
shed light on the origins of his central intellectual enterprise.

In effect, then, Descartes has come back to new life in recent years—in
two radically different ways. The Descartes who appears in so many studies
of the philosophy and physiology of mind—the radical innovator, owing
nothing to his predecessors, who devised the brutally simple theory about
"the ghost in the machine"—seems hard to reconcile with the Descartes
now being reconstructed by historians: the complex, reflective figure,
whose relation to tradition took many different forms, and whose system
embodied foreign elements even he did not recognize as such. Gaukroger's
book marks a first and very rewarding effort to bring the two Descartes
together. But the task will be a long one. It may prove impossible to fit
Descartes the dreamer into traditional genealogies of modern thought—or
to establish a simple relation between his theories of intelligence and current ones. Descartes lives, a troubling ghost in the machine of modern
philosophy.

14

An Introduction to the *New Science* of Giambattista Vico

⊙ⅢⅢ◎

GIAMBATTISTA VICO bestrides the modern social sciences and humanities like a colossus. Historians, anthropologists, and philosophers around the world agree in seeing his *New Science* as a work of dazzling prescience. Vico argued systematically that the understanding of a past society—even of an earlier period in the history of one's own society—was a demanding, if rewarding, intellectual task. The modern reader opening a work by Homer or Livy had to realize that it did not describe individuals like himself, men and women whose experiences, feelings, and ideas would be immediately recognizable. Only by mastering the general laws of social and cultural evolution that Vico himself had formulated could one avoid committing basic errors. Vico's contemporaries envisioned the ancient Greeks and Romans as robed sages moving decorously down perfect colonnades. In fact, they had been brutal, primitive warriors. Any modern who sincerely desired to enter into their minds and understand their actions must first undergo a long process of training and self-discipline, learning that language itself had evolved over the centuries, that feelings had been far more intense and ideas far more crude in primitive societies and cultures than they were in modern ones, that ancient poetry contained not moral lessons but historical clues to the life of the heroes who had created it. Vico's *New Science,* the massive decoding of ancient history, mythology, and law in which he argued these points, is commonly recognized as one of the founding works of the modern human sciences, a work in some ways as deep and original as the contemporary work that transformed the natural sciences, the *Principia* of Isaac Newton.

In life, however, Vico was no hero. Newton received many honors for his scientific work, becoming one of the greatest celebrities of his age. Vico, by contrast, lived the life of an obscure—a very obscure—academic. His modest professorship of rhetoric paid only one sixth as much as the professorship of law that he failed to win. He treasured every reference to his books in the foreign journals that could bring his name and ideas to a European public. But these were few, and some were negative. At home in Naples he walked the crowded streets in misery, avoiding the gaze of the acquaintances who failed to acknowledge the copies of his works that he sent them. He never managed to travel abroad—not even to Rome, to unraveling whose history he devoted much of his life. Even his funeral degenerated into a public quarrel, as the professors of the University of Naples and the members of the Confraternity of Santa Sofia, to which Vico had belonged, argued over which group should provide his pallbearers. In the end, his body had to be carried back into the house, where it awaited burial overnight.

Vico's great book fared just as badly, at first, as its author. A massive defense of the humanities, it appeared in an age when the philosophy of Descartes had triumphed in much of continental Europe and natural philosophy seemed the cutting edge of human thought. Vastly erudite—though also vastly inaccurate—it challenged the canons of taste in a period when the *philosophes* were beginning to denounce the study of historical details, which Voltaire memorably described as "a vermin that kills great works." Throughout the period in which the three editions of the *New Science* appeared, prices for erudite Latin books were falling. The whole style of the book seemed archaic and remote. With its allegorical title page, pullulating erudition, and strange language (even some central and north Italians prefer to read Vico in English), the *New Science* was generally declared dead on arrival: out of scale, out of date, and doomed to be thoroughly out of mind.

Yet Vico and his book have had an afterlife as exciting as their original life was depressing. Italian readers continued to admire him. In the second half of the eighteenth century, the creators of the new sensibility that became known as Romanticism began to appreciate the depth and value of his work. Vico's evolutionary approach to ancient culture was independently revived by the heroes of German historicism after 1770. Some of Vico's more specific theses—like his arguments that Homer was a man of the people, not a polished poet, and that the myths about Romulus and Remus, Tarquin and Lucrece concealed a true and instructive social history of Rome's growth—found academic exponents at the same time. Long before the classical scholars and historians of late-eighteenth-century England and Germany embarked on their discovery of the pastness of the past, Vico was already there—as more than one prophet of modern historicism discovered belatedly, to his chagrin. The *New Science* gradually began to be cited, summarized, and translated.

Early in the nineteenth century, the French historian Jules Michelet fell in love with Vico's evocation of the terrible creative power of ordinary people—a central motif of Michelet's own work on the history of France. He produced an abridged French text of Vico's prescient (because pre-Revolutionary) demonstration that man makes his own history. Social scientists from Auguste Comte to Karl Marx approved and embroidered on Vico's theory that each society passed through a recognizable series of stages of development. Later in the nineteenth century, pioneers of modern hermeneutics like Karl Lamprecht and Aby Warburg saw him as one of the creators of their method, with its emphasis on historical empathy, on the need to feel one's way into the strange textures of past cultures. Still later Vico provided Benedetto Croce with the core of his attack on the positivism that the comparatist parts of the *New Science* had helped to nourish and inspired James Joyce to devise the complex structures of *Finnegans Wake*. Since Croce's time the study of Vico has engaged the attention of some of the most influential intellectuals in western Europe and America, like Erich Auerbach, Isaiah Berlin, Arnaldo Momigliano, and Hayden White. They have given Vico a firm place in the intellectual pantheon of modernity.

The creator of the *New Science* had to struggle to find the social and mental freedom to do creative work. Born in 1668, Vico was one of the eight children of a poor man—Antonio de Vico, who owned the smallest of the many bookshops that crowded the street of San Biagio in central Naples. In the sharply hierarchical society of Naples, ruled by a Spanish viceroy and dominated by the landed aristocracy, Vico struggled from birth against the terrible handicaps of poverty and modest birth. These were made worse by his traumatic headfirst fall from a ladder at the age of seven, which left him with a fractured skull and interrupted his studies.

Though he made excellent progress while confined to his home, he found little appreciation at school, and an early effort to master Scholastic philosophy with the Jesuits ended in failure. Vico's encounters with injustice and misunderstanding, in other words, began early.

Nonetheless, he studied Roman law more successfully on his own, defended his father in a lawsuit, and attracted the attention of a rich and distinguished jurist named Rocca. Vico became the tutor to Rocca's nephews, with whom he spent several years, dividing his time between his teaching and study at the University of Naples. He also began to read the classics of Italian poetry and to write verse of his own, and to study the fashionable new natural philosophy of Pierre Gassendi and others. Their efforts to replace the traditional Aristotelian natural philosophy of the schools with atomism attracted much interest in Naples, both from younger intellectuals and, in a different way, the Inquisition.

At thirty, Vico entered a competition to become professor of rhetoric—a poorly paid post, and an elementary subject—at the University of Naples. Despite the vagaries of his education, his mastery of the Latin classics and his erudition evidently stood out. He won the post, married, and raised a family, supplementing his meager income by writing commissioned poems and eulogies, giving private lessons, and evaluating libraries that came up for auction. For all the problems that afflicted Vico, he found much to enjoy and profit from in his immediate environment. Naples had a diverse and lively local culture, as Harold Stone has recently shown in detail. A social and cultural pressure-cooker, the lid of which was periodically blown off by revolutions, the city harbored convents, museums, and libraries where innovative intellectuals had gathered for decades. Its natural philosophers and opera librettists were equally innovative. They read the most radical books of the seventeenth century, like the *Tractatus* of Spinoza; treasured manuscript copies gave them access to works too hot to be printed. Ideas were exchanged in Naples as much by public performance as by formal publication: effective formal speeches could make a career. Vico's skills as poet and orator established his name. He made alert and well-informed friends—like the brilliant Paolo Maria Doria, who shared his commitment to humanistic studies and with whom he discussed a wide range of philosophical questions. An elegant set-piece Latin oration won him membership in the liveliest intellectual organization in the city, the Accademia Medinaceli, which the Spanish viceroy had founded in 1698. To his fellow intellectuals who avidly studied the Epicureanism of Gassendi and the metaphysics of Descartes, Vico owed much stimulation and perhaps some questioning of his original religious convictions.[1]

Gradually Vico gained recognition as a leading figure in this competitive and articulate intellectual field. At the same time he developed a sense of his own distinct intellectual position. In opposition to Descartes and his followers, he began to insist on the vital independent value of humanistic and historical studies. By the 1710s, he was developing what he called both a "philosophical philology" and a "new science"—a radically new approach to the understanding and study of human history. The Latin works on jurisprudence in which he described this project won a favorable review from the Protestant scholar and journalist Jean Le Clerc. In the early 1720s Vico was invited to contribute to a collection of autobiographies of distinguished Italian scholars. In the 1730s he became the official historiographer of Naples. At times he could feel that he was well on his way to attaining celebrity, not only in Naples but in the Republic of Letters, the imaginary society of scholars across Europe who were bound together by networks of correspondence and depended for information about the works of the learned on review journals like those edited by Le Clerc.

Sadly, none of these individual successes radically improved Vico's lot. He failed either to climb the academic ladder at home or to win widespread admiration for his most ambitious efforts as a writer. In 1717 he tried and failed to win one of the much more lucrative chairs of law in the university. The first edition of the *New Science*—the publication of which Vico had to finance by selling a ring—fell almost dead from the press. Vico did not receive so much as a letter from Le Clerc or Newton, to whom he sent copies. The only reference to the book that appeared abroad was a deliberately inaccurate and malicious notice in the influential *Acta eruditorum*, published in Leipzig, which Vico tried to rebut. His sense of isolation and disaffection grew. Vico saw his career as a catastrophe, the normal lot of a prophet in his own country. Other Neapolitan intellectuals, he decided, regarded him as a madman. By the end of his life, as he wrote in one bitter letter, he expected nothing from his native city but the complete isolation which enabled him to work so hard.[2]

Despite his increasing despair, Vico continued to work with admirable determination, revising his great book in 1729–30 and again in 1744. The final edition of the *New Science,* which appeared in the year of Vico's death, became his unruly summa. It defies recapitulation. The sprawling mass and spiraling cross references of Vico's book effectively subvert its geometric form of presentation—a modern device that Vico borrowed from Descartes, as part of his claim to create a new science of humanity. But its general purport is clear enough.[3] Vico set out to show that his predecessors and contemporaries had misunderstood both the capacities of the human mind and the development of the human race. All too many intellectuals had dedicated themselves to the study of nature—the most fashionable of topics in the age of the New Philosophy of Descartes and Bacon, Copernicus and Gassendi. In doing so, however, they had failed to see that they were attempting something for which the human mind lacked the proper equipment. Understanding, Vico argued, in passages which have spawned much commentary, comes from making: one can truly understand only what one has created. Only God, accordingly, could truly understand the cosmos. Human beings, by contrast, could and should address themselves to the study of the human world—the laws and institutions, customs and practices created by earlier humans. The proper study of mankind was—must be—man.

Even those philosophers who studied society, moreover, had gone radically wrong as they tried to draw from a wide range of texts and experiences, themselves pulled out of context, a theoretical history of the origins of society and the state. Some, like the legal theorist Hugo Grotius, looked for clear, abstractly formulated laws that all men, pagan or Christian, early or late, acknowledged as valid. Others, like Thomas Hobbes, used the absence of an original code of laws as an explanation for the viciousness and fear that drove men to frame the state in the simple, brute hope of finding safety.

The philosophers, for all their disagreements, had converged in reading the wrong lessons into human history. They had created imaginary stories about society, culture, and the state instead of teasing out the lineaments of the true history from the clues that remained in myths and texts. Their failure was easy to explain, if hard to redress. From Bacon and Descartes onward, modern thinkers had despised the mere scholars who read ancient texts instead of dealing with the modern world. Bold speculation and experimentation in the world seemed far more productive than old-fashioned interpretation of books. Bacon condemned the philologists who had confined themselves to imitating Cicero instead of attacking the objects around them. Descartes dismissed the study of old texts as nothing more than a form of virtual travel. History, he explained, could teach only that customs varied from time to time, as they did from place to place. The serious thinker must look elsewhere for certain knowledge about God and the universe.

But the philosophers' willful ignorance ruined their systematic theories. They could not assess the quality and solidity of the slabs of evidence which they hauled into different positions in the theoretical structures they erected. Samuel Pufendorf, for example, studied societies ancient and modern, civilized and barbarous. But he concluded only that history could not yield the rules that should frame a society, since no single set of laws and institutions appeared everywhere. History seemed mere chaos to this learned natural lawyer. As always, those who did not know how to study history were condemned to distort it.

The philologists, for their part, knew a great many things about the human past. Since the fourteenth century, after all, the Renaissance humanists had worked frenetically to collect and emend the ancient texts and to reconstruct ancient customs and institutions. Professional specialists in texts and commentary, they had direct access to the rich textual data that the philosophers refused to exploit. Antiquaries amassed heaps of information about the rituals and customs, institutions and life-styles of the ancient world. But the philologists were as blind as the philosophers. They took their texts—and the stories these told—far too literally. They believed that the ancients had been men and women like themselves, with thoughts and feelings like their own. They broke their hearts and bankrupted their publishers bringing out folio after folio in which they tried to weld the divergent claims of Jews and Greeks, Egyptians and Babylonians about the early origins of their states into a single, coherent chronological framework—as if the ancients who had dated the origins of Egypt and Babylon had been rational moderns like themselves, working from precise quantitative evidence.

In fact, the ancients' stories about the early histories and primeval wisdom of Egypt and Mesopotamia derived not from their learning but from their ignorance. The original isolation of each nation led it to overestimate its originality and antiquity—a shared delusion which Vico called "the conceit of the nations." Modern scholars, for their part, had failed to see that they must not expect an ancient historian to use the methods and meet the standards of a modern archivist, a systematic error which Vico named "the conceit of the learned." The *folie à deux* of ancient writers and modern scholars had twisted the historical record into something as distorted as the image in a fun-house mirror. To that extent, the philosophers had been perfectly right to refuse to learn from books. At best the specialists in books knew only disconnected and insignificant facts—the same sort of facts that Cicero's serving maid had known by virtue of living in the ancient world. Scholarship of this tedious, compilatory kind could not shed light on the origins of humanity or the state.

Vico's *New Science* set out to reform both philosophy and philology by connecting the two enterprises—by making philology into philosophy. Philosophy would trace the basic path that the march of human history must have followed, in all cases except that of the Jews. Thanks to direct divine revelation, they had had an organized civilization from the start. But other societies and civilizations—whose history Vico separated radically from the sacred history of the Jews—had not taken shape until after the Flood. And the founders of these gentile nations could not have been the sage legislators long celebrated in classical and modern texts, like the Egyptian Hermes Trismegistus and the Spartan Lycurgus. Rather, they must have been *bestioni*—brutish primitives, without masters and without mates, of gigantic size and untrammeled appetites. These antediluvian Frankenstein's monsters of Vico's romantic imagining had wandered the drying marshes left by Noah's Flood. They took what property and women they wished—a vision of the state of nature that owed something both to the ancient Epicurean Lucretius and to the modern atheist Hobbes.

Gradually and inevitably, Vico argued, the *bestioni* turned into heroes, and the heroes into men. Exhalations from the drying earth caused terrifying thunder in the sky. Being primitives, the *bestioni* imagined that the threatening natural phenomenon was an anthropomorphic god, literally threatening them. Hence religion came into being, and with religion shame. The fact that sexual intercourse had been carried out whenever and wherever one of the giants wished, without solemnity and in the open, now seemed horrifying. Sexual relations began to take place only after a religious ceremony sanctified the union of the couple in question, and in private. Over time, stable families were formed. Then a complex, hierarchical society took shape, as those *bestioni* who could not defend themselves became the slaves of those who could, exchanging freedom for safety. Divisions rent the once-unified family when the slaves realized that they were as human as their heroic masters. Struggles for power and autonomy led to reforms and the creation of laws. Gradually each society developed laws, codes, and institutions. The state replaced the family. This dynamic history, in which strife played a basically creative role, was exemplified for Vico, as for Machiavelli, by the case of Rome.

In the end, Vico admitted, even Rome's triumphant story closed in disaster and sorrow. Prosperity and sophistication corrupted the original order, and Rome relapsed into a new barbarism as terrible—and happily as temporary—as the old. This course each nation except the chosen one must run—though not, of course, simultaneously. The barbarous peoples of the New World and China, for example, were clearly the contemporaries in development not of the Europeans of their day but of the primitives of ancient Germany or Scythia. Philosophy, rather than philology, provided this conjectural history of man—a history for lack of which the philologists inevitably went wrong. It also sounded the warning that the Europeans of Vico's time could themselves fall back into barbarism.

Philosophy, however, could lay out only the largest features on Vico's map of the human past. Philology filled in the contours and details, and in doing so it not only bore out Vico's theories about the origins of societies but shed a blinding new light on the most familiar texts. The oldest substantial document of Roman law consisted of the fragments of the Twelve Tables—the tables of statutes, traditionally thought to have been written down by the members of a commission appointed in 451 B.C.E., and traditionally ascribed to the influence of Athenian example on the less civilized Romans. Vico admitted the vital importance of the Twelve Tables. But he rejected the story of their origins, insisting that these laws were not an import from a superior civilization but a "code" autonomously created by the Romans over a century and more. Many earlier scholars had followed ancient precedent, drawing easy, rapid connections between one people and another and positing cultural borrowings even where the evidence was very slight. They imagined the entire ancient Mediterranean world as a small, well-lighted space, where Jewish patriarchs, Athenian statesmen, and Roman generals cosily exchanged ideas.[4] Vico, by contrast, insisted on the autonomous development of societies. Moreover, he not only argued for the native origins of the tables, but reinterpreted the document as a whole, trying to show that it began as the enactment of an agrarian law, itself passed in the course of the savage struggle for equality that raged between patrician heroes and plebeian *bestioni* in the early period of Roman history. A century before Barthold Georg Niebuhr recast the early history of Rome as one of radical social struggle gradually transformed into the mythical account of Roman origins, Vico rethought the whole Roman historical tradition, insisting that a true account of the early history of the city would bear little resemblance to the stories that had been retold for centuries in classrooms or to the interpretations offered by earlier jurists.[5]

Even in fields where Vico lacked the technical expertise he brought to the law, he proved capable of making extraordinary discoveries. In preparing the last edition of the *New Science,* for example, he devoted himself to a systematic study of Homer. The *Iliad* and *Odyssey,* Vico pointed out, had many curious characteristics, to some of which literary critics had objected since the Renaissance. Homer's heroes lived an absurdly simple life. Achilles cooked his own meals, the princess Nausicaa did her own laundry, and piles of manure reeked outside the palaces of kings. The heroes were often unheroic: Achilles railed like a fishwife at Agamemnon and wept like a child at the death of Patroclus. The gods were even worse: bad-tempered, jealous, sometimes vulnerable to mortal attack. Homer, moreover, often contradicted himself. How, for example, could Odysseus's men have stolen the cattle of the sun, whom Homer described as "all-seeing"? Long and inept comparisons between humans and animals filled page after tedious page, while absurd epithets ruined what could have been powerful emotional effects.

Vico's new science explained away these indelicacies. Homer's heroes lived simply because they had only recently climbed out of the mire. They showed their emotions because they were primitives, more like modern children than like modern adults. They created anthropomorphic gods because primitives and children always imagine deities in their own form. Homer's apparent self-contradictions arose because his poems were oral, not written. Over the centuries, the reciters had made many changes and additions to the original work.

Even Homer's repetitive, inappropriate similes made sense of a particular kind. In the history of culture, analogy precedes logic as poetry precedes prose. Comparison between the known and the unknown was the chief mental tool at a primitive's disposal. Homer's poetry revealed in its warp and woof the perplexities of a mind still frightened by natural forces, still unbroken to the dry analytical logic of civilization. Both the curious style and the indecorous content of his poetry stemmed from his historical position. Both provided vital evidence about the way the primitive mind worked and the imaginative power that the primitive could attain. Vico saw even Homer's errors, in short, as historical clues that revealed the differences of feeling and expression that had grown up between Homer's time and his own. This insight has received its full development only in the twentieth century, thanks to the very different work of such Homeric scholars as Milman Parry and Moses Finley.

Vico's own imaginative brilliance seems as impressive as that of the ancient bards he liked to evoke, singing their tales around the fire. He knew Homer only at second hand, through Latin translations. He knew the Greek world more distantly still, through scholarly compilations, themselves based on the epics, of the customs and manners of the Homeric heroes. Yet he saw what dozens of more learned scholars had not: that Homer described, and lived in, a world very distant from the present. Vico, in other words, had the sort of prescient structural insight into difficult problems which is more often found in scientists than in humanists. A Richard Feynman of the social universe, he could predict almost without effort, and certainly without research, results that later scholars would take lifetimes of work and masses of new data to confirm. Raising his six children in genteel poverty amid the pastel palaces, stuccoed churches, and noisy streets of Europe's most rebellious city, imagining the life of the ancient giants as he trudged to his home in the Vicolo dei Giganti, Vico saw that men could live by radically different codes of value and speak in radically different codes of meaning. His program for understanding the human past, with its insistence on using the evidence of custom and emotion to recreate the peculiar texture of each past society, adumbrates the achievements of modern anthropology and cultural history. His theory of interpretation often resembles the historical hermeneutics of the late eighteenth and nineteenth centuries. Throughout the twentieth century, the most up-to-date students of culture have repeatedly found inspiration and stimulation in the *New Science*.

The modern reader who seeks not only to follow Vico's arguments, but also to understand the intellectual context in which he framed them, should be aware that he was not the lonely explorer of strange continents of thought that some modern accounts portray. He learned from others who had gone in some of the same directions before him. Often, he took facts and factoids, theses and interpretations from ancient and modern sources with the undiscriminating zeal of an intellectual magpie. True, it is not easy to identify all the sources on which he drew for inspiration or information. The Inquisition did its best to stamp out atomism and biblical criticism in late-seventeenth-century Naples, making it risky even to refer to Spinoza or Hobbes—both of them authors who attacked issues of central importance to Vico. Vico, moreover, was a master of misquotation, whose deft misreadings of ancient and modern classics bewilder and bemuse the modern critic. He knew no English or German. When he listened in on the great debates of his time from his post in lively but distant Naples, he resembled a country telephone operator trying to eavesdrop on lovers whispering on a crackling party line. And even when he claimed to identify his intellectual icons and enemies, he cited authors whose work shows, on the surface, few precise connections with his. It seems genuinely impossible to know exactly what Vico knew, and when he knew it, about such iconoclastic, and even scandalous, figures as Thomas Hobbes, Pierre Bayle, Richard Simon—the "moderns" whom he both learned from and attacked. Nor is it easy to see the *New Science,* as Vico described it, as a work deriving from the teachings of Plato and Tacitus, Bacon and Grotius—though he learned something from each of these thinkers. Though Fausto Nicolini, author of a comprehensive commentary on the *New Science,* and later scholars like Paolo Rossi have done a spectacular job of clearing the scholarly ground, much remains to be rediscovered about what Vico read and how he used it.[6]

In general, however, it is clear that Vico responded not only to the discoveries he made on his own, but also to some of the most widespread and dramatic discussions of his own period. When Vico insisted on the value of humanistic and historical study, when he dwelt on the vital importance of classical studies, he took a side in a debate between Ancients and Moderns which had begun well before he was born. Previous participants had staked out positions which strongly resembled his. From the sixteenth century onward, European intellectuals debated in a lively, even ferocious, way about the value of ancient texts, and the knowledge they enclosed. Advocates of modernity emphasized the gaps in the ancients' knowledge of the world. They wrote panegyrics to the modern inventions which had enabled Europeans to discover the New World, circumnavigate the globe, and establish empires of unprecedented size: the compass and gunpowder. Printing, which preserved and disseminated the new knowledge brought back by explorers and conquistadors, also came in for praise. Francis Bacon—who placed a ship sailing past the Pillars of Hercules on the title page of his programmatic work *The Great Instauration*—found a new way of saying something which many others had felt when he described antiquity as "the youth of the world" and insisted on the need to surpass the ancients. In the later seventeenth century, advocates of the ancients fought back, admitting the superiority of modern inventions but insisting that the ancients retained preeminence in literature and philosophy. The Quarrel of the Ancients and Moderns in France and the Battle of the Books in England represented parallel episodes in a literary war that engulfed academies, universities, and coffee-houses.

By the later seventeenth century, as Joseph Levine has shown, historical thought began to play a vital role in this discussion. Advocates of the Modern position argued that the works cited as inimitable classics by the ancients were in fact the products of a society so alien from modern life, so primitive, that they could not possibly serve as moral or literary models. Charles Perrault, the French critic whose polemical *Parallel of the Ancients and Moderns* did much to frame the central issues of the debate, insisted as heatedly as Vico that Homer described a primitive, not a noble world. Richard Bentley, the most proficient Hellenist and editor of classical texts in early eighteenth-century Europe, dismissed the idea that Homer had meant to instruct and entertain readers for ages to come: "Take my word for it, poor *Homer* in those circumstances and early times had never such aspiring thoughts. He wrote a sequel of Songs and Rhapsodies, to be sung by himself for small earnings and good cheer, at Festivals and other days of Merriment; the *Ilias* he made for the Men, and the *Odysseis* for the other sex."[7] Vico's reading of Homer was far more sustained, and the consequences he drew from it more radical, than these men's remarks. But his approach to the subject bore a clear resemblance to those already sketched out in the last generation or two before his time.[8]

Even Vico's reading of the Homeric text rested on a more distant scholarly precedent. Julius Caesar Scaliger, the sixteenth-century scholar who wrote the first independent treatise on poetics of modern times, saw Homer's literary crimes as clearly as Vico. In his *Poetics,* he treated the *Iliad*

and *Odyssey* as models of literary incompetence and low taste. He identified every misplaced epithet and inappropriate action he could in order to
prove, to his own satisfaction at least, the superiority of Virgil to Homer.
Vico's lists of Homer's primitive forms of expression derived not only from
his reading of the text, but also from Scaliger's commentary on it—which
had also inspired Bentley.[9]

Some scholars in seventeenth-century Italy held the beliefs that Vico
denied. Athanasius Kircher, the German Jesuit whose museum in the Collegio Romano at Rome became one of the most popular gathering places
for native and foreign intellectuals in the 1660s and 1670s, firmly believed
that the Egyptians had had a primeval revelation, direct rather than scrip-
tural, of all the basic truths about the universe. Only elaborate allegorical
decoding of their hieroglyphs and the myths these recorded, he argued,
could unveil these lost truths to the forgetful moderns. Vico insisted that
the most ancient pagans had been primitive giants, rejected allegorical
explications of their myths, and treated hieroglyphs as a primitive form of
writing rather than a subtle philosophical code devised by learned priests
who did not want their learning sullied by the eyes of ordinary mortals. In
this way, he attacked Kircher's impressive books—as well as the magnificent Roman monuments, with obelisks at their core, that the Jesuit had
helped to design. In Naples as well, scholars like Antonio Costantino,
whose *Divine and Worldly Adamo-Noetic Philosophy,* written around 1730,
circulated in manuscript, juggled the data of chronology and biblical exegesis in order to show that all nations, gentile as well as Jewish, had inherited a primeval revelation of the basic truths of religion and philosophy.[10]

But Vico had allies as well as enemies when he took the field. Jean
Le Clerc, for example—the very journalist whose review he prized so
highly—also insisted on the need to read texts historically, and rejected the
allegorical tradition as anachronistic and unsubstantiated. He even wrote
an elaborate theoretical manual on textual interpretation and emendation,
the *Ars critica,* to which he appended detailed treatments of specimen texts
and problems. Vico did not cite the works in which Le Clerc advanced
theses like his own, but the many resemblances between Le Clerc's work
and his own make it highly likely, as Gianfranco Cantelli has argued, that
he knew them. Vico's *New Science* was a synthesis of novel work done by
others as well as a statement of his individual discoveries.[11]

Vico learned from his enemies as well as his friends. No Modern, he still used the characteristic tools of the Moderns against their creators. Though he rejected Cartesianism, he certainly took from Descartes the idea of presenting his way of understanding the past as a radically new philosophy—a new, independent, and structurally coherent method for attacking problems that intellectuals had dealt with piecemeal and ineffectually in the past. His effort to state his findings axiomatically, to make the normally vague disciplines of historical interpretation take on the visible clarity of geometry, reflected his effort to fight the Cartesians on their own ground.

Though Vico disagreed on many points with Bacon, in some ways he owed the man he called "the pioneer of a completely new universe" even more than Descartes. Bacon, like Vico, held that the ancients were not classic models for the moderns, but their primitive ancestors—an idea that lies at the core of the *New Science*. More important, Bacon argued that the reform of culture in his own time must be prepared for by a systematic effort to collect and explain the cultural achievements of the past. Each century, he argued, had had a different "spirit," which had promoted certain studies while discouraging others. The modern manager of knowledge needed to understand these in order to create the proper "spirit" in his own day. And the only way he could attain this knowledge was, quite simply, by surveying as many products of the human mind in each period as possible, in order to see which conditions had brought them into being. A comprehensive history of culture—which Bacon, like others before him, called a "historia litteraria," or "literary history"—would have to be compiled before natural and moral philosophy could be completely reformed. Throughout the seventeenth century, intellectuals struggled to produce such a history. Varied contributions to it—dozens of large-scale and monographic investigations of the history of philosophy, for example— poured from the presses.[12]

As early as 1708–09 Vico devoted a Latin oration, *On the Study Methods of Our Time,* to attacking Descartes and Bacon for their failure to appreciate the vital importance of the humanities. In the course of this work, he used Bacon's own method for historical analysis to explain why intellectual tastes changed, so that a given book might find many readers in one period only to drop from sight a decade later. "Every epoch," he wrote, "is dominated by a 'spirit,' a genius, of its own. Novelty, like beauty, recommends certain faults which, after fashion changes, become glaringly apparent. Writers, wishing to reap a profit from their studies, follow the trend of their time."[13] This argument already summed up, in a nutshell, the larger program of the *New Science*—the great work in which Vico used his understanding of the differences between historical periods to explain the different forms of feeling and expression that had flourished in them. Despite his dislike of the new natural philosophy, Vico learned a vast amount from its prophets.

The *New Science* presents itself not only as a study of providence, grounded in theological debate, but also—indeed, above all—as a study of myth and law, grounded in scholarly traditions. It offers explanations of a great many textual, mythological, and historical details. And its interpretations of particular details in human history often incorporate intellectual traditions which now seem highly recondite, but were in Vico's time simply in the scholarly air. Vico, for example, made clear that the Roman scholar Varro, who had divided past time into three periods, "chaotic," "mythical," and "historical," inspired his own effort to divide the past into coherent periods. In using and giving credit to Varro, Vico quoted a text and took positions in a discipline familiar to every scholar of his time. True, Varro's own historical works did not survive. But the later Roman scholar Censorinus, writing in C.E. 238, quoted the passage in question. In the sixteenth century, when Joseph Scaliger and others began to try to establish the framework of dates for ancient history, they seized upon, quoted, and interpreted this same passage in the massive, highly technical works they dedicated to what became, for a century and more, a highly fashionable subject. In making Varro's tripartite periodization a cornerstone of his own work, Vico was not rejecting, but adapting, the chronological scholarship of his own day.[14]

Similarly, in treating the development of law as one of the keys to human history, Vico built on precedents solidly established in the sixteenth century. Philologically trained lawyers like Andrea Alciato, Jacques Cujas, François Baudouin, and Jean Bodin had broken, long before Vico, with the largely unhistorical treatment of Roman law normally offered in the medieval universities. They had insisted that Roman law changed radically over time. They had done their best to dissect the *Corpus iuris* of Justinian and other surviving documents, reconstructing lost or partially preserved sources like the Twelve Tables, on which an enormous literature had grown up before Vico. And they had insisted, polemically, on the need to use legal systems as central evidence about past societies and states. Their works included elaborate treatises, like Baudouin's *Prolegomena* and Bodin's *Method,* on how to study law historically. No earlier jurist anticipated Vico's bold effort to turn the Twelve Tables into evidence for the existence, in early Rome, of social struggles as radical as those that had flared up in Naples a generation before Vico's birth. But the tradition of humanistic jurisprudence was much on his mind for decades. Vico owed at least a part of his historical sensibility to the jurists who, as he wrote in 1708–09, "gave back to Rome her own laws, instead of adjusting these laws to the needs of our epoch."[15]

The French jurists of the sixteenth century, like Vico himself, are often seen as preeminently modern figures. Accordingly, a number of scholars have been willing to accept that he learned from them. But Vico also drew on much older scholarly traditions. Some of these were classical—like the rhetorical tradition, with its emphasis on the kinds of knowledge that were directly relevant to life in society and its elaborate treatments of hermeneutics, on which he drew heavily.[16] Others he found at less respectable addresses. The case of Vico's giants, for example, tells a story very different from that of his legal scholarship. A number of scholars have suggested that Vico drew his vision of the first men from the *De rerum natura* of Lucretius. The Roman poet described the gigantic sizes early beings attained and evoked the fear that thunder inspired in early men. His account of the primitive world provided the basis for a modern anthropology, just as his discussion of atoms provided part of the basis of a modern physics. In fact, however, Vico's giants were composite figures, historical golems patched together from diverse sources. In his first treatment of the giants, which formed part of his works of the 1710s on law, Vico cited not only Lucretius's poem but also Chapter 6 of Genesis. This tells the story of the sons of God, who saw that the daughters of men were beautiful and went in to them, siring mighty men of valor. The text remarks that "there were giants in the earth in those days." This verse provided the foundation for Vico's belief that early humans reached enormous size. His later tale of the barbarian giants who lived after the Flood repeated, in updated terms, the history of the antediluvian giants of the Bible.

In fusing history with gigantology—as Walter Stephens has shown in a massive, fascinating book entitled *Giants in Those Days*—Vico followed exegetical traditions of long standing.[17] One of the most influential world historians of the Renaissance, the saintly Dominican forger Giovanni Nanni da Viterbo, portrayed all men before the Flood as giants. Many other writers took him up—not least François Rabelais, whose giants, Gargantua and Pantagruel, also have a biblical ancestry and inspiration as well as classical and modern characteristics. Vico's *bestioni,* then, were not by any means the first gigantic brutes to populate world histories. And though Vico gave the story his own twist, he drew on another source—a genuinely classical text—in doing so. Urine and feces, Vico noted, have a great fertilizing power, as anyone can see by planting a field where an army has made camp. The Jews were clean, as their divine law made them. But pagan babies, abandoned by their mothers, played with their own excretions—as Tacitus showed, in a passing remark in his account of the ancient Germans. Pagan babies, accordingly, never stopped growing. These points seem trivial to the modern reader, and are often overlooked by modern interpreters seeking points of contact with the *New Science.* Vico, however, endlessly repeated and developed them—clear evidence that he took them very seriously indeed. Biblical and apocryphal, classical and Renaissance, historical and scientific theories coalesced in the foundations of Vico's work.

The *New Science* in other words, is nowhere simple, never of a piece. Vico's heroic effort to modernize philology by making it philosophical was a project he shared with many seventeenth-century intellectuals of the most diverse theological views, as Carlo Borghero has shown in his detailed account of historians' and philologists' efforts to counter the Cartesian attack on book-based, historical forms of knowledge.[18] Vico's history of the human race, in short, is less a fresco painted spontaneously than a Watts Tower of found objects, combined in dazzling new ways but often old and battered in themselves. A baroque encyclopedist, he seized upon an incredibly wide range of materials, not only acting upon them but being acted upon by them. As one might expect, his system resembled the muddy vortices of Descartes' physics rather than the lucid structures of his mathematics. Vico's new science grew like a glacier, awkwardly and incoherently, absorbing new elements whle shedding older ones.

The peculiar origins, composite character, and complex, twisting argumentation of Vico's book made it hard to interpret even in his own time. For all its use of and references to well-known books and theories, it did not belong to any of the standard genres of Vico's period. Philosophical works, in Vico's day, regularly dealt with the origins of human society and law. But they rarely referred in detail to a vast range of literary and legal sources. Scholarly works, by contrast, often rested on massive erudite foundations. But the leading scholars of the late seventeenth century—men like the great Benedictine scholars Jean Mabillon and Bernard de Montfaucon—pioneered in the precise historical study of objects, from documents on parchment and paper to sculptures in stone. Connoisseurs of detail, they analyzed the materials they studied word by word or surface by surface, often providing illustrations to enable their readers to participate in the work of philology. Vico's imaginative decoding of literary texts differed radically in style—if not always in spirit—from their austere, step-by-step decipherment of clearly delimited bodies of evidence. That helps considerably to explain why this ambitious scholar's most ambitious book found so few sympathetic readers among those contemporaries who had read the same texts and confronted the same problems as Vico himself.[19]

The *New Science* fits modern ideas about method and genre even more loosely than it did those of Vico's contemporaries. Moreover, it has spawned a vast range of interpretations, some of them richly informed about Vico's own world, others motivated by more contemporary concerns. In these circumstances, debate is only natural. Scholars disagree sharply over many important points connected with the interpretation of the *New Science*—for example, the religious views that it expresses. Some have seen Vico's history of the human race as radically secular. Man, Vico argued, could understand only what man had made: not the physical, but the social universe. By turning from the cosmos to the human past, the modern scholar would come to see that the ancient stories about the gods had been not a twisted version of Christian sacred history, as many scholars thought, but the creation of primitive men desperately trying to master the universe they inhabited. On this account, Vico's history of humanity strikes a modern, secular note, insisting on its own independence from the sacred histories and emphasizing the creative independence of the human race.

Others see Vico's universe as absolutely determinist. By separating gentile from Jewish history, they argue, he made clear that the human race, unsupported by revelation, could evolve only in one direction—one programmed into it in advance, by the Creator, who destined all races to create religions, institutions, and laws as they wandered the earth after the Flood. Vico's new science of the past did not draw most of its details from the Old Testament account of early human history. Nonetheless it asserted—more powerfully, perhaps, than the traditional histories which did draw on the Bible—the absolute power of Providence. Like the little figures in the eerie drawings of *Prisons* by Vico's contemporary Giambattista Piranesi, all humans appear, on this account, as prisoners dwarfed and manipulated by a gigantic historical machinery that they could neither comprehend nor control.[20] Disputes on this and many other points will certainly continue: no amount of critical and editorial commentary will produce consensus on all controversial points. For Vico's book, infinitely remote and startlingly contemporary, is perhaps more cited and less understood than any of the other challenging books produced in the age of the New Philosophy that called all in doubt.

15

Jacob Bernays,
Joseph Scaliger,
and Others

ᘒᘡᘡᘓ

ISTORIANS of scholarship write, for their sins, about their own professional ancestors: other scholars. Historians of art, literature, and philosophy can happily justify their pursuits by citing the intrinsic interest of their famous subjects' accomplishments. Historians of scholarship, by contrast, must morosely identify the dead grammarians they study every time they give a public lecture or apply for a fellowship. Historians of sexuality spend their time reading through riotously funny ethnographies and court records. Historians of scholarship, by contrast, disinter long-unused boxes of notecards from their cobwebbed tombs in ancient file cabinets, and derive what pleasure they may from discovering long-forgotten errors in unread footnotes. Historians of science follow the processes by which humanity gained understanding of the orbits of the planets, the nature of DNA, and the idiosyncrasies of the fax machine—problems that remain current today. Historians of scholarship, by contrast, follow the complex, paradoxical, and drawn-out process by which humanity gradually learned that the past is a foreign country. But this achievement of intellectuals in Hellenistic Alexandria, fifteenth-century Florence, and eighteenth-century Göttingen has little evident relevance to the resolutely unhistorical culture of early-twenty-first-century America.

Even worse than these problems of audience and rhetoric, moreover, are the substantive ones. Historians of scholarship set out to identify and study their betters: to rediscover, by sifting and analyzing the work of great scholars, what it meant in terms of intellectual innovation, provocation, and controversy to study the past when classical philology and history were the central intellectual disciplines of the new Dutch universities in the late Renaissance or the new German ones in the late Enlightenment. Historians of science constantly confront the work of greater thinkers than they can ever hope to be: no sane scholar will claim to have the mind of an Einstein or a Newton. But historians of scholarship constantly explore the work of their own colleagues and superiors—the work of philologists and historians who, unlike them, did work of sufficient originality and interest that it demands the attention of readers centuries later. Samuel Johnson tried to defuse the envy of his readers by describing his own trade, that of the lexicographer, as work fit for a harmless drudge. It is not a *captatio benevolentiae* but a grim recognition of existential truth that makes me define the historian of scholarship as a malevolent drone—one who works obsessively, not to create something new but to find out what makes warriors and queen bees tick. Historians of scholarship are doomed, in short, to struggle with more Oedipal demons than any single hive can contain. This essay deals with the way that one of the most learned and original historians of scholarship, Jacob Bernays, met—and failed to meet—this challenge.

The son of a controversial and much-loved writer and teacher, Hakham Isaak Bernays of Hamburg, Jacob grew up steeped in traditional Hebrew learning. At the end of his life, after many years as a university librarian and a professor of the Greek and Latin classics, he still read the Talmud or other rabbinic texts for an hour every day.[1] While still a schoolboy, Bernays began to transcribe unpublished Hebrew manuscripts in the Hamburg library. At the same time, the Hakham insisted that his son grow up steeped in the secular classics as well. Jacob studied the whole range of Greek and Latin texts at gymnasium in Hamburg and at the innovative Prussian university in Bonn. At the university he rapidly became the favorite student of the great Bonn textual critic Friedrich Ritschl, as well as of Ritschl's Jewish wife, Sophie, who worried touchingly when Jacob refused to eat anything but bread and butter and fruit at her table.

Bernays began to publish at about the age of twenty. In a pioneering article he showed how one could reconstruct the textual history of Lucretius's poem *De rerum natura* by grouping the extant manuscripts into families—a relatively new idea at the time.[2] The stream of articles and monographs that followed—all of which combined technical brilliance, broad erudition, and a sharp sense for the historically important problem—made his name. Bernays ventured not the first, but the most systematic effort to show that the *katharsis* of pity and terror described by Aristotle as the effect of tragedy was not an aesthetic or moral term, but a medical one. In so doing, Bernays anticipated Friedrich Nietzsche (who, predictably, became furious when "der Jude Bernays" mentioned this inconvenient fact).[3] Bernays reconstructed, mostly from difficult passages in the late antique commentaries on Aristotle, the nature and purport of the philosopher's lost dialogues. He thus made it possible to attempt something like a critical biography of Aristotle. For good or ill, Werner Jaeger could not have written his *Aristotle* if he had not had Bernays's studies of the language and the transmission of Aristotle's lost texts to disagree with and build upon.[4] Particularly dazzling were the studies in which Bernays showed that late antique neo-Platonists like Jamblichus and Porphyry had quoted rich, forgotten fragments of much earlier philosophical works— like the lost treatise by Theophrastus which, he argued, contained the first account of Jews by a Greek.[5]

Bernays had a gift for friendship and showed almost infinite generosity toward those he respected—who were not many. He collaborated, for instance, with the Prussian ambassador to England, the Freiherr von Bunsen, on his elaborate, rather fantastic studies of ancient Near Eastern mythology and history. To more lasting effect, he helped Theodor Mommsen overcome the depression natural in grimy, industrial Breslau and the fatigue caused by a fourteen-hour-a-week teaching load to produce the greatest of all histories of Rome. Bernays read proofs, offered advice, and drank beer with the great jurist who was turning ancient history upside down.

One revealing case will give a sense of the sorts of scholarly magic Bernays could perform, alone or in company. In a commentary on Aristotle published by Christian August Brandis, one of his teachers in Bonn, Bernays found a reference to a grammatical theory ascribed, unintelligibly, to *ho Patraios dous areios*. This he connected, at once, with a remark of the grammarian Hesychius, who had said that the Nabataeans called Dionysus Dousares. The meaningless *dous areios*, Bernays immediately saw, must be a corruption of *Dousareios*—a personal name formed from that of the god, as Dionysius was derived from Dionysus. It was the work of a moment to turn *Patraios* into *Petraios*. Suddenly Bernays had conjured up a forgotten Greek writer, "Dousareios from Petra," the Nabataean city. Further evidence from the Byzantine lexicon of Suidas enabled him to show that Dousareios had belonged to a forgotten group of Greek-speaking rhetoricians and grammarians, men who had cultivated the refinements of Hellenism in the distant rock city.[6] This emendation of two words opened up a lost chapter in cultural history.

The measure of Bernays's achievement is easy to take. He lived in bitter times for German Jews with academic ambitions. Born in 1824, just after the anti-Semitic "hep hep hep" riots of 1819 and the prohibition of university careers for Jews, he became a popular Privatdozent at the university in Bonn.[7] However, he had no hope of abandoning this unpaid status—which the son of a poor Hakham obviously could not occupy for long—for a permanent chair. The Prussian government proved obdurate not only to his teachers in Bonn but to the influential Bunsen; Bernays, however, refused to convert. He could neither find an appropriate job nor stand to do what he saw as paid hackwork, like compiling the commentary on Lucretius which the Clarendon Press commissioned from him. Eventually, to avoid starvation, he had to move to barbarous Breslau, where he taught elementary Latin and Greek at Zacharias Frankel's Jewish Seminary (and one advanced course in classics for a time at the university, which gave him teaching status).[8] Only in middle age was Bernays finally called back to Bonn. Even then he became not an ordinarius, but university librarian and professor extraordinarius. Nonetheless, he did win European recognition. The unequaled master of the black arts of scholarship, the emender and interpreter of a thousand obscure texts, Bernays was the only teacher who impressed the Prussian aristocrat Ulrich von Wilamowitz-Moellendorff, less through his learning than through his pride in the nobility of his own Jewish blood. (Wilamowitz later recalled that, with Bernays, everything was genuine; everything had real style—"da war alles echt, hatte alles Stil.")[9]

Bernays died in 1881. Despite his firm position at Bonn, his life ended in despair. Bernays held that the new forces of democracy, radicalism, and positivism, joined with the old ones of reaction, antisemitism, and religious orthodoxy, would destroy European civilization. He felt sure that the sort of scholarship he and his generation had done would not survive. He was, of course, quite right. In the short run, however, his example would prove a powerful and attractive one. The historian of religion Hermann Usener, who edited Bernays's collected shorter writings, was only one of a number of masters who learned their philological trade by steeping themselves in his work and by trying to emulate his command of multiple forms of evidence and his meticulous attention to revealing detail.[10]

In 1855 Bernays published his first large book, the one with which this essay deals: a biography of Joseph Scaliger, an extraordinarily energetic and productive late Renaissance humanist.[11] Scaliger, who lived from 1540 to 1609, revolutionized fields of classical studies as varied as Latin textual criticism, Greek epigraphy, and chronology—as I have tried to argue in two substantial volumes of my own.[12] Studying his work has certainly taught me many lessons in humility. If Bernays could reconstruct the lost and repair the corrupt, Scaliger devised the whole instrumentarium of modern scholarship with which his successors, down to Bernays, worked. Arriving in Paris from Agen and Bordeaux, where he had grown up, Scaliger taught himself Greek; it took him all of three weeks, he later recalled, to read the entire text of Homer, compiling his own grammar as he went. Inspired by contact with Guillaume Postel, with whom he briefly shared a bed at a printer's shop, he moved on to study Hebrew. This he learned from the Bible, and well enough that he could dispute in Hebrew with Jews in southern France and northern Italy; they remarked, perhaps not without irony, that he spoke the Hebrew of the Bible, quite a different language from that of *"Rabbotenu zicronam"* (our Rabbis of [blessed] memory). Aramaic, Arabic, and Ethiopic followed.

Still in his early twenties, Scaliger wrote a brilliant commentary on one of the most puzzling and difficult of Latin texts, Varro's *De lingua latina*. His precocious ability to transform scribal gobbledygook into archaic Latin by conjecture startled even the erudite and literate scholars of the mid-sixteenth-century Collège Royal—men like Denys Lambin and Jean Dorat, who had taught the poets of the Pléiade how to emulate classical verse. So did the polyglot erudition with which Scaliger commented on the poems of the late antique schoolmaster Ausonius, drawing on texts as diverse as the *Greek Anthology* and the bilingual dialogues from which the schoolboys of late imperial Rome had learned their Greek. More impressive still was his restoration of the battered text of Sextus Pompeius Festus's

Latin lexicon, itself an epitome of an earlier work, which survived only in a single manuscript, much of which had been lost, and in a late epitome by the Christian scholar Paulus Diaconus.

In 1577 Scaliger tried, in a brilliant edition of Catullus, to reconstruct by conjecture the textual history of a classical author. He inferred from identical textual errors in later manuscripts and editions that the lost archetype of Catullus (the medieval manuscript from which all later ones must have descended) must have been written in what he called "Lombardic" script. The very similar forms of *a* and *u,* tall *i* and *l, c* and *g,* characteristic of this early medieval bookhand, he insisted, had confused later scribes. Only a bold conjectural history of the text could explain the errors shared by later textual witnesses and make it possible to reconstruct an earlier state of the text than they presented. This form of argument would not be revived with such precision and dramatic flair until the nineteenth-century heyday of German philology, when Karl Lachmann informed his stunned contemporaries how many pages the lost archetype of Lucretius had possessed, and how many lines of verse to the page. Yet even the brilliance of Scaliger's textual history of Catullus pales before the greatest of his editorial efforts: his critical edition of and commentary on the astrological poem of Manilius, which combined tours de force of textual emendation with equally brilliant explanations of the details of Hellenistic astrology.

Scaliger's work as a textual critic—which occupied him until his late thirties—in itself would have ensured him a prominent place in the scholarly pantheon. But he did much more. In the second half of his career, he devoted himself to technical chronology—the discipline, now little known but fashionable in the sixteenth century, which aimed at establishing the main eras of ancient and medieval history and reconstructing the calendars used in the ancient and medieval worlds. Scaliger's work in this field resulted in two massively unreadable books: the *De emendatione temporum* of 1583 and the *Thesaurus temporum* of 1606. In them he filled more than two thousand folio pages of Latin with computed dates for solar eclipses and planetary occultations, and lists of Egyptian dynasties and Argive priestesses of Hera.

Scaliger drew more heavily on his predecessors than he ever admitted. Many new details of his work, moreover, provoked sharp criticism, some of it justified, from such rival experts as the astronomers Tycho Brahe and Johannes Kepler and the very expert chronologer Joannes Temporarius.

Still, the structures Scaliger erected have remained, on the whole, astonishingly sound, for four centuries.

Scaliger reconstructed the lost Greek *Chronicle* of Eusebius and used it, deftly and plausibly, to date the main events of Near Eastern as well as Greek and Roman history. He discovered what remain the most important preserved fragments of ancient chronological literature, such as the Egyptian dynasty lists of Manetho. He showed that these were genuine even though they contained what looked, to a sixteenth-century Calvinist, like wildly improbable statements (for example, Manetho placed the beginning of Egyptian history not only before the Flood, but before the Creation itself). Scaliger steeped himself in the literature of Hellenistic Judaism, becoming the first Christian scholar to recognize—as did the Italian Jew Azariah de' Rossi—that large numbers of Jews in the ancient world had read the Bible and had worshiped not in Hebrew but in Greek, and had created a Greek literature of their own.[13] He made brilliant use of the Passover Haggadah to show that the Last Supper represented an adaptation of the Jewish seder. And he expunged from the historical record, with pungent sarcasm and tungsten-steel philological arguments, a wide range of forged texts—most prominently the letter of Aristeas, which purported to explain the origins of the Septuagint. No one described this massive historical enterprise more effectively than Scaliger himself. With characteristic immodesty he told his students that "I am writing the history of 8,000 years, according to the pagans."

His erudition—unique even in that age of polyhistors, whose common intellectual currency took the shape of back-breaking folios laden with quotations in many languages and scripts—won him all that erudition then could: fame throughout the Republic of Letters, hatred from Jesuits and Puritans alike, and the only research professorship known to have existed between the fall of the Alexandrian Museum and the rise of the MacArthur Foundation. Scaliger held this post for fifteen years at the University of Leiden, the most aggressively modern institution of higher learning in Europe. Though he did not lecture, he created something like an early research seminar, choosing gifted pupils and supervising their work with an iron hand in an iron glove. The ingenious Daniel Heinsius, his favorite, followed Scaliger's hints and devised the theory that the Hellenistic Jews had created their own form of Greek, one in which Greek words bore Semitic senses. Heinsius's thesis provoked sharp and productive debate for decades, even centuries. Still greater success awaited Hugo Grotius. With Scaliger's help, he produced, by the age of fourteen, critical editions of the Latin Aratea and of the obscure late antique encyclopedia of Martianus Capella, *The Marriage of Mercury and Philology*. Later he became, exactly as Scaliger predicted, an able and efficient public official as well as a prolific writer and scholar.

My twenty-year pursuit of Scaliger has been painful, and not only because I continually found myself confronted by his inimitable learning and ingenuity. For my contact with him was never simple or direct. From my first fumbling months of research in 1973 to the last days of proofreading the second volume of my biography of Scaliger twenty years later, Bernays served as my essential guide through the details of Scaliger's life and work, as well as their political, religious, and intellectual contexts. Bernays's book on Scaliger offers only a short (seventy-page) eloquent survey of his hero's life. But it was preceded by a brilliant introduction in which Bernays argued, in detail, that Scaliger was the first real world historian to fuse the Bible and the records of the Near Eastern, Greek, and Roman nations into a single, coherent account of world history. And it was followed, more important still, by dozens of excursuses, filling hundreds of pages, which Bernays called his "Giftschrank" (poison cupboard).[14] Here he settled problems of dating, attribution, and interpretation, provided texts and details to substantiate and flesh out the lapidary characterizations in his text, and illuminated many dark corners of late-sixteenth-century intellectual history. Bernays assembled, in mosaic form, what remains the best account of the multiple worlds of scholarship in the late Renaissance, a time in which philologists ruled the intellectual roost. Over and over I have redated a letter from or to Scaliger, seen the biographical relevance of a passing phrase in a technical argument, or discovered a hidden reference to an obscure classical or patristic source—only to find, a day, a week, or a decade later, that Bernays had already made the same find, and recorded it in one of his pullulating appendices.

The book has hardly a misprint to gratify the critical eye; moreover, it is not only rife with solid scholarship but written in a classical German prose. "His majesty J. J. Scaliger stands there alive and gives the epigoni a standard, against which they can measure themselves"—Max Muller's verdict, written just after the book came out, still holds.[15] Even the depressingly familiar fact that thirty years after the book first appeared, when Bernays set out to prepare a new edition, the publisher still had a quarter of the original stock of six hundred on hand, offers only modest consolation.[16] For Bernays quarried all the materials that went into this masterpiece himself, unsupported by grants or large public libraries, before the end of his thirtieth year.

Bernays seems slightly out of place as a historian of scholarship. In the first place, he was himself a master, not an epigone, of the art whose development he traced. In the second place, he was a rigorously independent man, in both spiritual and intellectual terms—not the sort of retiring, timorous soul whom one might think of as inhabiting the Oedipal world of scholarly genealogies. He kept up his observance of the Sabbath and the dietary laws even in difficult circumstances—as when, in his twenties, he lived for a while in the Prussian embassy in London, where he could drink only tea. Challenged by his dear friend Bunsen to convert to Christianity not for careerist reasons but simply, so Bunsen said, because to remain a Jew was to struggle in vain against the great current of world history— Bernays categorically refused. "Jesus of Nazareth himself," he replied, in a letter that became a classic of German-Jewish polemical writing, "born now as a Jew, would not be able to do it [become a Christian]"—at least not as a member of one of the churches of the mid-nineteenth century.[17] He even dared what now seems quite impossible: to tease Theodor Mommsen. Asked by his friend about a problem of interpretation in the satires of Juvenal, Bernays thanked him for the "striking and flattering proof" that Mommsen had not read his essay on the subject, which had appeared in Mommsen's own recently published festschrift.[18]

In retrospect, Bernays seems a figure far more likely to inspire than to feel the anxiety of influence, the weight of scholarly example. One case, an intimate one, will stand for many parallels. Bernays was one of three brothers; the third one, Berman, remained a faithful Jew, became a merchant, and had a daughter named Martha. She, of course, became Sigmund Freud's beloved fiancée and, later, his wife. But the second brother, Michael, had a more tormented life and a more complex fate. Like Jacob, he studied at Heidelberg, where he became obsessively interested in German literature. The two young men found some common ground in Edward Gibbon, whose *Decline and Fall* they read together. But Michael eventually succumbed to the mounting political and cultural pressures that Jacob always resisted. He returned to the ancestral city of Mainz, where he announced his conversion to Christianity. He devoted himself to the philological and historical study of German literature. In the end he became, after some hard times, a prominent professor at the University of Munich. The close friend of such prominent antisemites as Heinrich von Treitschke and Richard Wagner, Michael also taught Heinrich Wölfflin and created the discipline now known as Germanistik.[19]

Jacob felt Michael's conversion as a personal wound: he mourned his brother as dead and never spoke of him again, even to their mutual friends, like the poet and Romance scholar Paul Heyse. But he let his rich personal library pass, after his death, to the lapsed younger brother. And Michael clearly spent a lifetime paying tribute, in a variety of ways, to Jacob. He took a deep interest in the history of classical scholarship, as his detailed study of Goethe's relations with the Halle professor and Homeric critic Friedrich August Wolf clearly shows.[20] He was the only Munich professor to offer help and sociability to the brilliant young Jewish paleographer Ludwig Traube, whose seminar became a center of work on the classical tradition and the history of texts.[21] More strikingly still, Michael emulated, in the realm of German literature, what Jacob had done for Latin. Jacob had grouped the manuscripts of Lucretius into families, establishing a stemma, or family tree, and identifying those that a textual critic must use: Michael did the same for the editions of Goethe's works, establishing that the great poet had often used poor, error-ridden reprints as the basis of the revised editions of his own works. These swarmed, as a result, with missing words and unintelligible remarks that Goethe had not bothered to correct. Michael even arranged the editions into families and drew up stemmata—perhaps a first in the study of printed texts.[22]

Most revealing of all, to the end of his life Michael felt compelled to return to the interests he shared with his brother. His marvelous essay on the history of the footnote—still the fullest and most enlightening treatment of this absorbing subject ever written—includes a rich analysis of the funniest footnotes ever written, those in Gibbon's *Decline and Fall,* and clearly began from the discussions he and his older brother, who also loved Gibbon's more audacious mock-learned remarks, had held in Heidelberg almost half a century before.[23] True, Bernays did not weigh so heavily on the less gifted of his students as did his English friend Mark Pattison, the biographer of Isaac Casaubon who reviewed Bernays's book on Scaliger in the *Quarterly Review* and then set out to produce his own, never-finished biography. Pattison told a student who, he thought, might edit John Selden's *Table Talk* that he would have to spend at least twenty years memorizing the text and reading the entire literature of the period. The student duly recalled that "he put the thing before me in so unattractive a way that I never did it or anything else worth doing. I consider the ruin of my misspent life very largely due to that conversation."[24] But Bernays showed impatience enough toward those unwilling to follow his precepts and example: for example, he drove the young Hermann Cohen, who had no sympathy for his teacher's rigorous historicism, out of his seminar in Breslau.

What then did Jacob Bernays find in Joseph Scaliger? Why did this man of stiff-necked independence devote himself, in the biography and in a large number of his other writings, to finding heroes to emulate? And does his work on the history of scholarship perhaps reveal some of the tensions common to this tense, aggressive field?

Bernays's motives were both emotional and intellectual. On the first count, readers have realized ever since Bernays's biography appeared that it had something of the character of an allegory. In laying out the main lines of Scaliger's work and the forces that had shaped his character, Bernays described not only his protagonist but himself as well. He accepted as credible Scaliger's remarkable statements about the rapidity and independence with which he absorbed information—such as Scaliger's boast that he had read Homer in three weeks and made his own grammar of Homeric Greek while doing so.[25] While this may seem highly credulous, it is understandable in the light of Bernays's own rapid, self-motivating progress as a scholar. The young man who was already, at the outset of his twenties, reading Joseph Scaliger's Latin letters and studying his annotated books—borrowed, by the happy custom of the time, from the Leiden University Library—felt a kinship with the other prodigy.[26] More important are the other similarities that emerge on comparison: the two mens' refusal to marry; their exile to learned institutions in provincial cities far from their native lands; and above all, their sense of their own nobility.

No facet of Scaliger's fascinating character is more bizarre than his insistence that he belonged to the ancient della Scalla family of Verona—a belief he owed to his father, a brilliant academic con man named Giulio Cesare Bordon. Giulio Cesare, the son of a gifted illuminator of manuscripts, Benedetto Bordon, moved from north Italy to southern France and established himself at Agen. There he passed himself off as a della Scala to the credulous provincial gentry and literati, married the daughter of a local notable, and became famous as a natural philosopher and literary critic. His son, Joseph, accepted at his father's knee the belief that he belonged to a noble Italian house, one whose annals stretched back to the time of Theodoric and beyond. He clung to his noble identity as a young traveler in Italy, thrilling himself and his friends as he whispered that he must remain incognito lest Venetian assassins murder him. He repeated his father's dynastic fantasies as a middle-aged scholar in France, even when friends began to report from Italy that another story about his origins was in circulation. And he defended them just as fiercely as an old professor in Leiden, where he insisted on his right to wear, and have his portrait painted wearing, the purple robes of a prince. Scaliger refused to drop his claim to nobility even when his enemies in Italy published his father's doctoral diploma, which clearly bore the name Bordon (he tried, with a brilliantly perverse piece of historical criticism, to show that the document was forged).[27] Even many of Scaliger's friends and supporters found his attitude puzzling: why not, one of them asked, simply dismiss the problem? Scaliger and his father had ennobled their ancestral city by their achievements. Why worry about whether their ancestors had a claim to nobility by birth as well? Yet Scaliger went to his death quixotically embattled on this point. And Bernays supported him, arguing that Scaliger's conduct as a man and as a scholar flowed from his conviction of his own noble descent and the duties it required of him.

Wilamowitz remarked on what he saw as Bernays's "pride in his nobility": his sense of himself as one born to a high station.[28] It seems obvious that Bernays saw in Scaliger someone who shared his high, stern sense of self, and who followed a rigorous ethical code because he felt he had inherited the duty to do so. To that extent Scaliger offered him (as Arnaldo Momigliano pointed out in his brilliant article on Bernays) an absolute model of personal rectitude that no scholar of ordinary descent could have provided. When Bernays eloquently evoked Scaliger's crushing attacks on fanatical Calvinists who read the Bible literally and on corrupt Jesuits who refused to accept that the works of Dionysius the pseudo-Areopagite were forged, he saw himself, caught between the racism of Protestant Prussia and the ignorance and superstition of the German Catholic population.

But Scaliger mattered for more strictly intellectual reasons as well. In his biography of Scaliger Bernays stated unequivocally what he believed to be Scaliger's chief motive for studying the history of his field. Scaliger, he argued, had devised a method for classical scholarship that remained valid centuries after his death. His technical work could still supply precedents, stimuli, and themes for the young philologists of the mid-nineteenth century. Bernays evidently believed that Scaliger's combination of biblical and classical philology, his insistence on studying Herodotus and the Old Testament together, offered a model for the study of ancient history that suffered neither from the excessive classicism of some German philologists nor from the wild speculation of their enemies, the mythographers and pan-Babylonist world historians. But Bernays also meant something more specific: that Scaliger had devised and practiced exactly the sort of interdisciplinary classical scholarship that the Germans of his own day called "Altertumswissenschaft" and claimed as their special discovery.

The intellectual revolution that created the new Prussian universities was touched off by classical scholars such as Christian Gottlob Heyne and Friedrich August Wolf in the later eighteenth century. Both insisted that philologists must no longer confine themselves to studying texts; rather, they must recreate the historical contexts in which the ancients had lived and written, using everything from the material remains of ancient art to the scattered evidence of ancient material culture to give their vision of the past color and solidity.[29] Wolf issued his call for a new scholarship in a densely written, enthusiastic manifesto, his *Darstellung der Alterthums-Wissenschaft*. This manifesto, and his brilliant, critical *Prolegomena to Homer*, won him the fascinated attention of young scholars—like Leopold Zunz, who modeled his own approach to the study of Jewish texts and traditions on Wolf's approach to Greece and Rome.[30] It also won him the support of Wilhelm von Humboldt, who embodied Wolf's theories in his plans for the new University of Berlin. At Bonn, where Berlin standards were systematically applied, Bernays mastered the new scholarship and directly experienced both its rich rewards and its underlying problems and contradictions.

Bernays, however, did something more—and more unusual—than his predecessors. He insisted that the interdisciplinary study of the past was neither new nor fully developed in his own time. In his biography of

Scaliger, he called the reader's attention to the fact that his hero, a student of literary and historical texts, had also devoted himself to the study of ancient inscriptions. Scaliger collected these in notebooks, supervised and encouraged the efforts of the Heidelberg scholar Janus Gruter to edit a new corpus of Greek and Roman inscriptions, and even spent ten months, eighteen hours a day, drawing up the indices to Gruter's work when Gruter himself proved unwilling to do so. Bernays's characteristically hyperbolic remark "Auch das scheinbar Niedrigste veredelte sich unter seinen Händen" shows how deeply he respected Scaliger's effort to master all the crafts of scholarship at once.[31] He regretted only that after the middle of the seventeenth century, scholars had ceased to follow Scaliger's example and connect the study of ancient literature with that of the material remains of the ancient world.[32] Where Wolf and August Böckh, in other words, represented themselves as the creators of a new form of scholarship, Bernays portrayed himself as the rediscoverer of a lost one.

This argument was not merely rhetorical. One year after Bernays's *Scaliger* appeared, he published one of the most rigorous and original of all his technical papers: an analysis of the Greek poem long attributed to Phocylides. This set of moralizing verses, a favorite in Renaissance schools because it seemed so nearly Christian in spirit, had last been studied seriously by Scaliger. He had argued, at length, that the text must be by a Jew or a Christian rather than a Greek. Scaliger himself settled for the second hypothesis. Pseudo-Phocylides instructed the reader that "if a beast of your enemy falls on the way, help it to rise [140]."[33] This injunction to help one's enemies Scaliger took as a Christian reinterpretation or rewriting of Deuteronomy 22:4, which instructs the Jew to help raise his *brother's* ass or ox if it falls by the way. But Scaliger also urged erudite young men to continue the study of Pseudo-Phocylides, saying that they would find plenty of unexplored details there to confirm or challenge his own analysis.[34] In fact, however, no one accepted Scaliger's challenge: the demonstration that the text was forged seemed to deprive it of any interest or importance, and it dropped from scholarly sight in the seventeenth and eighteenth centuries.

Bernays, in taking up the gauntlet Scaliger had dropped, did not slavishly follow his mentor's line. Rather he started out by noting an omission in Scaliger's analysis of the text's religious character. If Deuteronomy 22:4 instructed the good Jew to help his brother's beast of burden, Exodus 23:5

told him to do the same if the beast of his enemy fell under his yoke. Bernays concluded: "Wenigstens in diesem Falle erscheint also die 'Feindesliebe' als echt mosaisch." Evidently, Scaliger had lacked a "living and certain" knowledge of the Pentateuch, even if he had noticed his error and omitted his argument in the second edition of his work.[35] The remainder of Bernays's analysis, however, moved along rails that Scaliger had laid out and spiked down.[36]

Scaliger, as we have seen, had proved to his contemporaries that the last centuries before and the first ones after the beginning of the Christian era saw the rise of a "Hellenistic" form of Judaism, whose practitioners read the Torah and performed their liturgy in Greek, not Hebrew. Scaliger argued that the most prominent Hellenistic writer, Philo, had been so steeped in Hellenic culture that he had lost contact with Judaism itself: Philo's supposed etymologies of Hebrew terms and explanations of Jewish customs were largely inventions. Even Christian *tyrunculi,* to say nothing of Jews, could find the errors in this poor Platonist's efforts to deal with Jewish topics. Scaliger also showed that these Hellenists often had given way to the temptation to invent the texts their tradition did not provide. For example, one of them had forged the letter of Aristeas, which purported to show that the Septuagint deserved more faith than the Hebrew text of the Old Testament.[37] Bernays renewed Scaliger's effort to reveal the peculiarities of the Hellenists' Greek, and continued his effort to identify and produce a literary history of their works; in so doing, Bernays showed once again that he saw Scaliger as a living model for his own work.

Bernays's use of Scaliger clearly shows his distance from the normal preoccupations of German scholars in his time. August Böckh, Karl Lachmann, and Theodor Mommsen, for all their differences of method and achievement, agreed in insisting on the novelty of their approaches. No earlier scholar, however erudite, had anticipated their efforts to reconstruct the ancient world as a whole. In the Protestant culture of north Germany, claims to innovation sounded virtuous. In the fiercely competitive German universities and academies, in particular, those who could slaughter their intellectual ancestors stood a better chance of prospering than those who worshipped them.[38] Bernays, by contrast, saw himself as one link in a chain of tradition; and he held that anyone who hoped to join that chain must do so by finding a connection, as Bernays did, to earlier links. It seems only reasonable to identify his attitude as a peculiarly Jewish one:

the attitude of one who held that the only way back to canonical texts lay through the whole history of their interpretation, that the best way to form a scholarly life was to ponder the personal examples of great scholars, and that the best way to form a style of inquiry was through the systematic study of one's predecessors. Bernays, the most brilliant of German classical scholars, differed from the rest because he preserved a rabbinic sensibility in the midst of a modern, scientific age. Like all great rabbis, also, Bernays found that he could choose a master without being silenced by doing so. The earlier masters, like Scaliger, spoke not only to instruct but to stimulate; they provided not only rich material to study but also suggestions for further research and incitement to further debate. Discipleship, in Bernays's rabbinic version of it, seemingly did not prejudice independence of thought and frankness of expression. Or did it?

Histories of scholarship, like all other texts, contain silences as well as statements; and these silences sometimes speak volumes. Bernays said nothing at all in the biography about one especially prominent area of Scaliger's scholarship: his theories about Hellenistic Judaism. He argued, in his own analysis of Pseudo-Phocylides, that the poem was clearly the work of a Jew. The author had desperately wanted to prove, either to his fellow Jews or to cultured Greeks, that the core of Judaism basically matched the teachings of pagan philosophy. Hence his use of a classical meter, but also his omission of vital Jewish tenets, such as the prohibition against worshipping idols. Bernays condemned Pseudo-Phocylides as sharply as Scaliger condemned Philo: Pseudo-Phocylides' poem, like the Hellenized Jewish culture from which it sprang, was doomed to failure because it rested on an effort to conceal its own true essence and tried to pass as something other than what it was. Pseudo-Phocylides fully deserved his eventual fate of scholarly neglect. In fact, Bernays argued, "the history of this little Jewish-Hellenistic product mirrors the fate that deservedly befell the entire Jewish-Hellenistic literature and every other one that resembles it: the fate of failing to influence the spiritual life of peoples, which transforms itself through sharp oppositions and pushes contemptuously to the side all efforts to flatten the concrete by compromise or abstraction."[39] Jewish Hellenism—like the Reform Judaism of the nineteenth century—falsified the tradition it claimed to preserve.

At this point, as Bernays must have known, his analysis diverged sharply from his master's. For Scaliger did not attribute the defects of Hellenistic

Judaism simply to the efforts of individual writers to play down the differences between the Mosaic commandments and the precepts of classical philosophy. He ascribed them, quite directly, to the nature of the Jews themselves. The author of the letter of Aristeas had pretended that twelve Jewish tribes still existed in the age of Ptolemy Philadelphus, centuries after the Exile. He claimed to quote original documents written both by Demetrius of Phalerum and by Ptolemy Philadelphus, even though the supposed letters in question were formally and stylistically identical. Scaliger found it quite easy to explain these obvious "mendacia": they stemmed from the natural Jewish urge to deceive. "Who," he asked rhetorically, "is unfamiliar with the fabrications of the Jews?"[40] The Hellenistic Jews were no less given to invention, to wild attempts to mislead their students and their readers, than the rabbis of the normative tradition, for whose biblical exegesis and chronological and calendrical hair-splitting Scaliger more than once showed open contempt. In so doing, he founded a tradition of a sort. Later Christian scholars who dealt with similar material found it easy, traveling in his deep wake, to explain the peculiarities of a given Hellenistic text by what Böckh described as "an impious, rather than pious, deceit, innate to the Hebrews."[41]

Curiously, Bernays never tried, either in his biography or elsewhere, to inquire into Scaliger's diagnosis of the errors of Jewish Hellenism or to follow up its after-effects. He left this unpleasant task to his one gifted pupil at Breslau, Jacob Freudenthal, a pioneering student of Hellenistic Jewish historiography, who confronted directly what his master had ignored. "It is incomprehensible," Freudenthal wrote, that men like Scaliger, Lodewijk Caspar Valckenaer, and Böckh should have ascribed the forgeries of the Hellenists simply to "the natural predisposition of the Jewish people."[42] These intolerant philologists had failed to understand the several related but not identical facts that had hemmed in the Greek-speaking Jews: above all, the expressive limits of their dialect of Greek, which made it impossible to reach real literary mastery, and the vicious criticisms to which non-Jews like Manetho subjected them, which forced them to resort to trickery in a desperate, doomed effort at cultural self-defense.[43] Freudenthal was in other ways as well more decisive than Bernays. He moved, over time, away from tradition. He left Frankel's seminar for the University of Breslau, traded up (or down?) from philology to philosophy, and became the author of a magniloquent, enthusiastic biography of Spinoza, whom he eloquently praised as the inventor of historical criticism of the Bible. From this standpoint—one in which he had to invent his own models for conduct as man and scholar—Freudenthal could do more than admire the general greatness and correct specific errors of the great figures of the past. He could bring himself, as Bernays could not, to see their limitations as well as their strengths: to see that they too now belonged to a past that had become irretrievably foreign.

Bernays, by contrast, found in Scaliger a model for both the analysis and the evaluation of Hellenistic Judaism. To undertake these, however, Bernays had to distort the record, which he knew better than anyone. He never acknowledged that Scaliger had seen Hellenistic Judaism only as an illustration of the general weaknesses of Judaism, as a religion and as a culture. And the omission was not accidental. The more closely one examines Bernays's book, the more gaps and silences one uncovers. Bernays called attention to the fact that Scaliger did not have an educated Jew's command of Hebrew and Aramaic. But he barely mentioned Scaliger's effort, late in life, to compensate for this weakness by working regularly with a Jewish convert in Leiden. (Scaliger typically remarked that his tutor did not know Hebrew grammar, but admitted that he could recognize, as Scaliger himself could not, Talmudic proverbs and allusions.)[44] Furthermore, Bernays called attention to the fact that Scaliger learned Arabic and Ethiopic. But he omitted Scaliger's own references to the fact that he received assistance with eastern calendars from a remarkable figure of Counter-Reformation Rome, the onetime Syrian Jacobite patriarch and later convert to Catholicism Ignatius Na'amatallah. Ignatius sent Scaliger elaborate treatments in Arabic of the Oriental twelve-year animal cycle and other matters, which Scaliger quoted with lavish endorsements.[45] Bernays lived among Christian friends who prized the rare information he could give them and wanted him to convert for his own sake. He could not endure the fact that Scaliger had resembled his own patrons, like Bunsen or Mommsen, in his limited tolerance for Judaism and in his willingness to work with converts, marginal figures, and informants who looked all too much like a fun-house reflection of Bernays himself.

Most important of all, Bernays could not deal honestly with some of Scaliger's most radical and challenging theories about history and exegesis. Bernays insisted that he himself had no faith in biblical criticism. Historical readings of the Old Testament he dismissed as pseudo-scholarly profanations of a sacred text, based only on wild hypotheses.[46] Scaliger, however, had other views. He not only found but published (and refused to abridge) the Egyptian dynasty lists that plunged the world of European historical learning into a century and more of crisis. Worse still, he speculated in radical ways about the gaps and defects of the Masoretic text of the Hebrew Bible. Scaliger noted that the Masoretic text was relatively late: he dated it to around the time of Gamaliel, whose remark that *masoret seyag la-torah* (tradition is a fence to the law) he took as a reference to the Masoretic apparatus. And he insisted that even this well-preserved official text represented only a version of a lost original. Its language, Hebrew, was not—so Scaliger claimed—a special, holy language, with which God had created the world and in which Adam had named the animals, but the ordinary tongue of ancient Assyria. Neither was its script original or sacred, since the Jews originally had used a different one, much like that of the Samaritans. Only after their return from the Babylonian exile did they transliterate the text into the square Aramaic characters used in the extant manuscripts and the printed Hebrew Bible. The Old Testament, like the new, suggested Scaliger, incorporated many errors and showed some worrying gaps. The Masoretes, narrowly Jewish in culture and tradition, had known little or nothing about non-Jewish history. Their vocalizations of non-Hebrew names, for example, were often faulty; much less accurate, Scaliger thought, than those of the more cosmopolitan Alexandrian Jews who had translated the Septuagint. Finally, all texts of the Old Testament referred to stories and texts now lost, such as the story of the young man killed by Lamech, referred to—but not recounted—in Genesis.[47]

Bernays knew that Scaliger took a serious amateur interest in the Bible. He recorded with glee some bold remarks about the New Testament that he found in Scaliger's table talk, the *Scaligerana*. No doubt Bernays relished Scaliger's worried statement that "there are more than 50 additions or changes to the New Testament and the Gospels. It's a strange thing, I don't dare to say it [in print]; if it were a pagan author, I would speak about it differently."[48] But he left Scaliger's efforts to historicize the Old Testament entirely out of account, even though they seem highly relevant to his belief that Scaliger's work retained its relevance in the mid-nineteenth century.

In the end, then, Bernays's *Scaliger* does not do full justice to its subject. Less by misrepresentation than by omission, Bernays fabricated for himself a master who mirrored his own strengths of character and who worked with more than his own sense of purpose, ignoring Scaliger's prejudices and insights when they did not serve his purposes.[49] Those using Bernays's book must do so with due caution, aware that the same passion for his subject that fires his prose sometimes interferes with his analysis. And those who consider his case (as I have, every day for more than twenty years) will probably come away with a deep feeling of uncertainty. If Jacob Bernays could not distinguish between historical fact and personal need, between what the record said and what he wanted to find, can anyone hope to do better? Does his case suggest a gloomy conclusion: that historians of scholarship who are not harmless drudges, stodging away in the records without presupposition, will more likely paint a heroic portrait of a past master, robed in purple, than analyze a past physiognomy, warts, period features, and all? These thoughts disturb me deeply, but I think that setting them down may be in keeping with Bernays's heroic side, his willingness to confront some, if not all, deeply uncomfortable truths.

NOTES

SOURCES

INDEX

Notes

ᏄᏍᎥᎧ

Introduction

1. A. Brasavola, dedicatory letter in C. Calcagnini, *Opera aliquot* (Basel, 1544), sig. alpha 2 recto: "Nihil dulcius quam omnia scire."

2. See in general *Contemporaries of Erasmus,* s.v. Celio Calcagnini, by D. Aguzzi-Barbagli. The old monograph by T. G. Calcagnini, *Della vita e degli scritti di Monsignor Celio Calcagnini* (Rome, 1818), retains considerable interest.

3. See J. Shearman, *Mannerism* (Harmondsworth, 1967; repr. 1969), 156.

4. *Pedacii Dioscoridae Anazarbei De materia medica libri sex,* ed. M. Virgilio Adriani (Florence, 1518); Calcagnini's copy is now in the Princeton University Library. On Adriani's work see in general J. Stannard, "Dioscorides and Renaissance Materia Medica," *Analecta Medico-Historica I: Materia Medica in the XVI Century,* I (Oxford 1966), 1–21, repr. in Stannard, *Herbs and Herbalism in the Middle Ages and Renaissance,* ed. K. E. Stannard and R. Kay (Aldershot, Brookfield, Singapore, and Sydney, 1999), IX, at 4, 9–10; P. Dilg, "Die botanische Kommentarliteratur in Italien um 1500 und ihr Einfluss auf Deutschland," *Der Kommentar in der Renaissance,* ed. A. Buck and O. Herding (Boppard 1975), 225–252 at 244–245; J. Riddle, "Dioscorides," *Catalogus translationum et commentariorum,* ed. F. E. Cranz, P. O. Kristeller, and V. Brown, IV (Washington, D.C., 1980), at 36–37; and above all P. Godman, *From Poliziano to Machiavelli* (Princeton, 1998), chap. 5.

5. Calcagnini to Tommaso Calcagnini, n.d., *Opera aliquot,* 26: "Pandulphus Collenutius nostro aevo vir multae eruditionis, in studendo annotandoque hac

usus est religione, ut praeclara gesta, quaeque ad virtutes pertinebant, sinopide allineret: quae ad vitia morbosque attinebant, atramento: quae ad herbas arbores fruticesque silaceo: quae ad medicamenta et metallica ferrugine designaret. Quae opera quam operosa sit, quantum morae addat ad plurima, praesertim festinanti quis sine admonitore non cognoscit? Sed vir ille inexhausti laboris maximus omnium lucubrator (parcissimus enim somni fuit) incomparabili omnia perficiebat diligentia. Novi quosdam ad praesidium memoriae in margine librorum, quos legunt, turriculas, manciolas, columellas, et id genus alia sigillaria quasi symbola tesserasque effingere, quae rerum quaesitarum imagines e memoriae promptuario facile evocent."

6. Ibid.: "Ego profecto quicquid lego, quicquid meditor, ita omne in arcanis animi recondo, quasi mox ad usum humanarum actionum expositurus. Et quoniam arduum nimis reor omnia seorsum excerpere, multa sane in commentarium refero, aut seorsum in pagella exscribo. Sed in margine compendiose omnia, quae digna sunt aliqua animadversione, sepono: quod siqua praestant, quasi coryphaea et optimatia in summa marginis coronide. Hinc ea mihi utilitas nascitur, ut vel sesquihora multa possim volumina recognoscere. Tentavi aliquando Plinii Naturalem historiam in epitomen revocare, quando eius autoris mira semper cupidine exarsi: sed rem sine controversia ridiculam feci, qui omnem ferme Plinium exscripserim."

7. Calcagnini remarks that he likes to place his summaries of the most important points "in summa marginis coronide" (ibid.). Few examples of this practice occur in his copy of Discorides. On the other hand, he also remarks that the reader should pay attention, first and foremost, to "elocutio" (points of style). His notes on Dioscorides' herbal, accordingly, reveal over and over again his serious interest in Adriani's Latin style—as when he singles out, in Adriani's prefatory letter, the phrase "sarctum tectum" (sig. AA iii verso)—a phrase which he himself used in letters to Tommaso and others (ibid., 42 and 122)—and in the first instance in an extended sense, which he then defended against unnamed critics (40).

8. Dioscorides, *De materia medica libri sex,* ed. Adriani, Princeton University Library, 83 recto: "theô dóxa Ferraria 21 Aprilis 1520"; 220 recto: "26 Ian. 1522"; 330 recto: "Ferr. 22 Iun. 1522"; 352 verso: "theô dóxa. Ego Coelius Calcagninus ferr. xxix Iulii MDXXII."

9. Ibid., 267 verso on Dioscorides 4.145 (147): "Vidimus aliquando ex Gallia in Italiam advectum hominis in natura monstrum: quod per urbes ad spectaculum questus causa a plerisque circumferebatur. Id puer nondum plenae pubertatis erat, cui ab anteriore parte inter imum pectus et umbilicum eiusdem sexus paulo minus quam integer alius pendebat homo: alterius illius et integri ex quo pendebat tertia

fere pars. Caput illi tantum et superiores humerorum partes deerant, quae veluti insitione quadam in integro illo latentes tam apte quo diximus loco coaluerant ut sine labore vitaeque tedio duo simul paulo minus quam tota corpora in uno homine viverent. Brachia incaepta illi tantum videbantur, reliquum undique integrum corpus erat, quod ad alterius sensus necessitatesque omnes etiam moveretur. Simile illi Alexandrinae Lauri folium est."

10. Ibid.: "Monstrum e Gallia: quod et nos vidimus." Calcagnini's comment falls between two dated notes, the former from 26 January and the latter from 22 June 1522; hence the conjecture offered about the date of this note in the text.

11. On monsters and their interpreters in Renaissance culture see the masterly works of J. Céard, *La nature et les prodiges* (Geneva, 1977); O. Niccoli, *Prophecy and People in Renaissance Italy,* tr. L. G. Cochrane (Princeton, 1990); and L. Daston and K. Park, *Wonders and the Order of Nature, 1150–1750* (New York, 1998). On the sort of show that Adriani and Calcagnini saw, see also O. Niccoli, "'Menstruum quasi monstruum': Monstrous Births and Menstrual Taboo in the Sixteenth Century," *Sex and Gender in Historical Perspective,* ed. E. Muir and G. Ruggiero, tr. M. A. Gallucci et al. (Baltimore and London, 1990), 1–25, esp. 5.

12. See Calcagnini's fascinating letter to Giovanni Francesco Pico della Mirandola, responding to the latter's "Strix": *Opera aliquot,* 111–112.

13. On Leoniceno see D. Mugnai Carrara, "Profilo di Nicolò Leoniceno," *Interpres* 2 (1979), 169–212, and *La biblioteca di Nicolò Leoniceno* (Florence, 1991).

14. A. Poliziano, *Epistolae* II.3; reprinted by Leoniceno at the start of his own work, *De Plinii in medicina erroribus,* ed. and tr. L. Premuda (Rome, 1958), esp. 148: "Etenim cum gravissima sit apud eruditissimum quemque Plinii auctoritas, aut non tentanda fuit, aut aliquanto fortius quam certe adhuc fecisse videris convellenda."

15. For accounts of the controversy see esp. L. Thorndike, *A History of Magic and Experimental Science* (New York, 1926–1958), IV, 593–610; A. Castiglioni, "The School of Ferrara and the Controversy on Pliny," *Science, Medicine and History,* ed. E. Ashworth Underwood (London, New York, and Toronto, 1953), I, 269–279; M. Santoro, "La polemica pliniana fra il Leoniceno e il Collenuccio," *Filologia romanza* 3 (1956), 162–205; C. Nauert, "Humanists, Scientists, and Pliny: Changing Approaches to a Classical Author," *American Historical Review* 84 (1979), 72–85; G. Ferrari, *L'esperienza del passato* (Florence, 1996), chap. 4; Godman, *From Poliziano to Machiavelli,* 99–106. Though all are useful, the accounts by Santoro and Ferrari are especially insightful and detailed. For more general accounts of the history of Plinian scholarship in the Middle Ages and the Renaissance, see C. Nauert, "Caius Plinius Secundus," *Catalogus translationum et commentariorum,* ed. F. E. Cranz, P. O. Kristeller, and V. Brown, IV (Washington,

D.C., 1980), 297–422, and A. Borst, *Das Buch der Naturgeschichte,* 2d ed. (Heidelberg, 1995). On the immediate context for the discussion between Poliziano and Leoniceno, see also the important articles by V. Fera, "Un laboratorio filologico di fine Quattrocento: la *Naturalis historia," Formative Stages of Classical Traditions: Latin Texts from Antiquity to the Renaissance,* ed. O. Pecere and M. D. Reeve (Spoleto, 1995), 435–466; "Poliziano, Ermolao Barbaro e Plinio," *Una famiglia Veneziana nella storia: I Barbaro,* ed. M. Marangoni and M. Pastore Stocchi (Venice, 1996), 193–234; and M. Davies, "Making Sense of Pliny in the Quattrocento," *Renaissance Studies* 9 (1995), 239–255; and the great edition of E. Barbaro, *Castigationes Plinianae et in Pomponium Melam,* ed. G. Pozzi (Padua, 1973–1979).

16. Leoniceno, *De Plinii in medicina erroribus,* ed. and tr. Premuda, 152, where he says that Pliny, "cum non ea scriberet, quae ipse novisset, sed quae potius a diversis auctoribus varie scripta collegisset, saepius diversa pro eisdem, atque eadem pro diversis retulisse videatur."

17. Ibid., 197: "Nam quum hic non de verborum momentis sed de rebus agatur, ex quibus hominum salus ac vita dependent, impium sane sit atque inhumanum, sicuti tibi alienos, ita mihi meos velle errores obnixe, atque obstinate contra veritatem tueri."

18. Ibid., 149–150.

19. Ibid., 150–151: "Scito non fuisse tunc animi mei propositum Plinii auctoritatem pessundare. Nam cum illa dictabam, praecipua erat mihi contentio cum barbaris, atque immo cum de haedera sermo haberetur, cuius naturam non satis Avicennae cognitam fuisse probare contendebam, obiter ac veluti quodam in transcursu Plinii quoque in aliorum mentione nominavi, quem tamen non dixi una cum Averroe ac reliquis errasse, sed videri in eodem cum aliis errore versari"; 166, 168–169, 175, and esp, 197, where he says of Avicenna: "in cuius auctoris erroribus explicandis exspatiari si velim, nullus huic operi terminus futurus erit." On the role of the Arabo-Latin tradition in Renaissance medical teaching and learning, see N. G. Siraisi, *Avicenna in Renaissance Italy* (Princeton, 1987).

20. Leoniceno, *De Plinii in medicina erroribus,* ed. and tr. Premuda, 151: "Illud vero mihi primum tecum conveniat, tam apud graecos quam apud latinos atque etiam barbaros, Dioscoridem esse summum auctorem atque praecipuum, cui in herbarum ac fruticum descriptionibus fides sit adhibenda. Nam et Plinius ipse non hunc minus quam Theophrastum in hac parte secutus videtur, ut qui utramque linguam et graecam et latinam noverit, sententias integras Dioscoridis quasi verbum ex verbo a Plinio translatas agnoscat"; 155: "nam omnia verbum fere ex verbo Plinius ex Dioscoride transtulit"; see also 156, 157, 160, 180ff.

21. Santoro, "La polemica," 174–175. On Venice's role in Renaissance efforts to improve pharmacological theory and practice, see R. Palmer, "Pharmacy in the

Republic of Venice in the Sixteenth Century," *The Medical Renaissance of the Sixteenth Century,* ed. A. Wear et al. (Cambridge, 1985).

22. See e.g. Leoniceno, *De Plinii in medicina erroribus,* ed. and tr. Premuda, 160: "Si itaque in re quam adeo curiose investigavit Galenus eidem magis quam Plinio credere oportet"; 189: "gravissimi testis Dioscoridis me facile movet auctoritas"; 193 (on lapis lazuli): "Sed dicat aliquis, quisnam usus aut ratio hoc in lapide lazuli depraehenditur, nisi forte in eadem re Arabibus autoribus fidem adhibere velimus."

23. See e.g. Calcagnini, "De mensibus dialogus," *Opera aliquot,* 608–609, recalling a conversation in which he and Leoniceno had debated Pliny's merits; and many passages in his letters—e.g. a 1518 letter to Mainardi in which he described another debate about Pliny, this one staged at Cracow (ibid., 51–52).

24. For Adriani's career see Godman, *From Poliziano to Machiavelli.*

25. See esp. Dioscorides, *De materia medica libri sex,* ed. Adriani, 352 verso, where Adriani explained certain faults and lacunae in his work by the desire not to fatigue either his printers or his readers, "festinantibus presertim amanuensibus nostris ad totius operis emendationem."

26. See P. Findlen, *Possessing Nature* (Berkeley, Los Angeles, and London, 1994); Findlen, "The Formation of a Scientific Community: Natural History in Sixteenth-Century Italy," *Natural Particulars,* ed. A. Grafton and N. Siraisi (Cambridge, Mass., and London, 1999), 369–400; and *Pietro Andrea Mattioli, Siena 1501–Trento 1578: la vita, le opere,* ed. S. Ferri (Perugia, 1997).

27. Dioscorides, *De materia medica,* ed. Adriani, 9 verso on the discussion of nard in Dioscorides I.6: "Sed nulla nobis utilior ob quottidianos stomachi cruciatus ea, qua hic ait stomachi erosionibus quas graeci cardiogmos dicunt mederi. In quibus ab antiqua graecae vocis aestimatione *kardía* scilicet incipiendum est: nisi enim intelligatur quid ea quondam significaverit gravi medicinae periculo multaque partium corporis nostri incertitudine tota miscebitur res, fietque ut credentes *kardían* cor omnium extorum praestantissimum ut communis et recepta iampridem eius vocis aestimatio est significare: quae stomacho remedia debentur cordi reddantur, et dum curatur quod vitio caret totum pereat quod remedio et ope indigebat. Sciendum itaque illud est: quam graeci ex multo tempore *kardían* id est cor dicunt, antiquissimis in ea gente Peloponesiaci belli tempore quo Hippocrates medicinam suam commentatus est, non cor sed ventriculum et hostium stomachi significasse: eaque voce intellexisse antiquissimos graecos stomachum et eius hostium tantum, non cor, aliud penitus ab eo. Testis significationis eius Hippocrates est gravis auctor: et qui pro oraculo in his merito habendus sit pluribus locis ea voce pro stomacho usus [*Prorrh.* 1.72]. Testis Thucidides maximus graecae historiae scriptor, qui secundo Peloponesiaci belli libro cum pestilentem morbum

quo tota Attica pene exhausta est describeret, inter alias eius morbi notas vomitiones fieri etiam dicebat, suntque eius haec verba: Nec multo post descendebat dolor in pectus excitabaturque tussis [2.49]. Et cum *es tên kardían* non in corde sed in stomacho haesisset: eam subvertebat sequebanturque bilis vomitiones quotquot a medicis suis nominibus dictae sunt: quod totum ad stomachum pertinet, nec nisi in stomacho fieri poterat. Qui enim ad vomitiones cor subverti potest?" Calcagnini's notes show that he found this analysis most instructive.

28. Ibid., 42 verso on Dioscorides 1.79: "hoc vero nostrum purgandi instaurandique quae in impresso Dioscoride vitiosa diversave sunt aut esse videntur, et in graecis latinisque vocibus aperiendi et explicandi quae minus nota et rariora sunt, humilius certe, nec antiquorum scriptorum, quos ille aliquando totos reddidit, maiestati comparandum: non penitus tamen ut speramus ingratum et inutile, presertim aetate hac nostra, in qua tam multi in graecis quottidie proficiunt: ut ea simulque latina discere et tractare cupientes laborem hunc nostrum neglecturi penitus non sunt. Conarique id nos maxime persuasit, qui ex Gallia non multo antehac prodiit latinus hic auctor, tam multis locis editioni huic nostrae contrarius, aut non idem saltem, ut diversitatis ab eo nostrae reddenda merito ratio et declaranda ubique causa fuerit."

29. See L. MacKinney, "Medieval Medical Dictionaries and Glossaries," *Medieval and Historiographical Essays in Honor of James Westphal Thompson*, ed. J. L. Cate and E. N. Anderson (Chicago, 1938); D. Goltz, *Mittelalterliche Pharmazie und Medizin, dargestellt an Geschichte und Inhalt des Antidotarium Nicolai* (Stuttgart, 1976); and Dioscorides, *Codex Neapolitanus Graecus I,* ed. M. Ciancaspro, G. Cavallo, and A. Touwaide (Athens, 2000).

30. Dioscorides, *De materia medica,* ed. Adriani, 3 recto: "Quod sane nobis primum hactenus consilium fuit, et continuum posthac studium erit praeterquam ubi doceri aut in melius restitui aliquid impossibile nobis erit. Quod in tam multis medicae materiae tamque diversis eius appellationibus quae cunctis fere capitibus a principio statim in Dios. leguntur praecipue accidet. In quibus non nisi post multum tempus constitutum mihi est an expungendae omnes exceaptis graecis latinisque, et his tantum quae recaeptae iampridem et in communi usu essent, an ex quo in cunctis fere exemplaribus legunt<ur> longaque temporum serie quasi per manus traditae ad nos pervenerunt servandae et ut erant ad latinos transferendae essent. Persuadebat enim expungi eas, et ex tanti scriptoris possessione eiici, quod ex eis plures barbarae sunt, aut tam corruptae, ut a barbaris non differant, nullam habentes hoc tempore, nec habiturae posthac, graecis latinisque incognitae utilitatem. Quodque verisimile est crevisse per tempora, et tam multas hodie numerari, pereuntibus quotidie renascentibusque aliis atque aliis rerum vocabulis, inserentibusque deinceps codicibus suis medicis et herbariis omnibus suorum temporum et suae gentis plantarum appellationes: fuisseque potius quondam in

tanta earum copia quam esse nunc utilitatem aliquam. Accedebat his etiam quod in diversis codicibus aliquando plures, aliquando pauciores, nec eaedem in cunctis, aut eodem loco adscriptae, et in aliquibus excaepta una aut altera nullae aliae legebantur: ideoque non accusandum in nobis esse quod ante nos aliis licuisset. Fuerat illud praeterea a nobis observatum, ex aliarum plantarum similitudine aliquando multis nomina accrevisse, miscerique simul difficili intellectu in una eademque appellatione diversa penitus aliquando genera, quod nunc etiam fieri deprehendimus ignota sibi plantarum nomina ex similitudine ad notum aliquod genus referentibus saepenumero herbariis nostris."

31. See most recently the studies collected in *Poliziano nel suo tempo,* ed. L. Secchi Tarugi (Florence, 1996), and *Agnolo Poliziano poeta scrittore filologo,* ed. V. Fera and M. Martelli (Florence, 1998), and the materials collected by P. Viti, *Pico, Poliziano e l'Umanesimo di fine Quattrocento* (Florence, 1994). Naturally, Poliziano's applications of these principles varied widely in nature and effectiveness, as the materials available to him, the context in which he worked, and the state of scholarly discussion varied. For recent case studies of great interest, see C. Auvray-Assayas, "L'ordre du deuxième livre du *De natura deorum* de Cicéron. Ange Politien et la philologie moderne," *Revue d'Histoire des Textes* 27 (1997), 87–108, and M. Campanelli, "Angelo Poliziano e gli antichi manoscritti di Marziale," *Interpres* 17 (1998), 281–308, as well as the studies of V. Fera cited in n. 15 above.

32. On Adriani's editorial method see in general Stannard, "Dioscorides and Renaissance Materia Medica"; more specifically on his use of clm 337, the Lombard MS of the Latin Dioscorides, see K. Hofmann and T. M. Auracher, "Der Longobardische Dioskorides des Marcellus Virgilius," *Romanische Forschungen* 1 (1883), 49–105 at 49–51. Citations appear throughout Adriani's commentary, e.g.: 70 verso (misnumbered 69) on 1.158: "Quod vetustissimus qui apud nos est longobardis litteris scriptus latinus Dios. indicat: in quo legitur: maxime quae ex foliis componuntur"; 208 verso–209 recto on 3.128 (138) (violet): "Florent hae passim triplici colore, candido, luteo, et purpureo. Qui quartus deinde ab hoc numeratur ceruleus in violarum genere hoc quod sciam in Italia nullibi videtur. Ex eo oborta nobis suspitio est posse in graecis abundare eam vocem, etsi in cunctis pariter legatur. Is etiam quem nos habemus egregiae antiquitatis et fidei latinum Dios. longobardis litteris scriptum tres tantum colores illos notos omnibus numerat: quartus hic ceruleus nullus in eo est. Nec nos tantum illi deferimus ut unum velimus pro cunctis aliis nobis esse, sed accedente rei naturaeque et suspitioni huic nostrae hoc veluti teste, qualiscunque ille est, non fore credidimus inutile hoc etiam legentes monere, presertim nullibi ut paulo ante diximus ostendente in hoc flore eum colorem natura"; 142 verso on 2.190: "Vidimus tamen in antiquissimo latino Dios. et qui longobardis litteris scriptus sexcentorum annorum vetustatem

refert hydropiperis appositam imaginem, diligenti ut erant ea tempora pictura effigiatam. In qua descriptioni huius scriptoris omnia conveniunt: caulis, geniculi, alarum concavitates, folia, foliorumque color. Vnum in fructu discrimen tantum est. Quod enim hic ait in ramulis secundum folia nasci et acinosum esse, in ea pictura in summis ramulis est vasculi potius quam folliculi aut siliquae figura, indicatque in eo claudi semen quod hic cum fructu miscet fructum vasculum, et in eo semen simul appellans. Quod deficientibus coniecturis aliis non penitus ab re audisse fuerit" (Hofmann and Auracher confirm this description, *Romanische Forschungen* 1, 50; 262 verso on 4.129 (131): "Esse leontopodio eandem Camon de qua Plinius xxvii. volumine capite viii [27.57]. negavit se quicquam scripturum, quum ad amatoria tantum usus eius esset, pro comperto nobis est. Vidimusque nos antiquissimos et optimos graecorum codices in quibus non Leontopodion sed camos capitis huius titulus est. Habemus et vetustissimum longobardis litteris scriptum latinum Dios. in quo pariter non Leontopodion sed Camos est, iisdemque omnibus hoc capite aliis. Sola in graecis et latinis tituli capitis et plantae appellationis diversitas est, magno argumento non differre leontopodion a Camo nisi sola appellatione." Humanists normally applied the phrase "Lombardic script" to pre-Caroline minuscules. See S. Rizzo, *Il lessico filologico degli umanisti* (Rome, 1973), 122–126.

33. Dioscorides, *De materia medica libri sex,* ed. Adriani, AA ii verso: "Et quum in eo maxime res vertebatur ut ex integro aliquo exemplari bona fide omnia traderentur, cum non liceret ex uno alterove quod satis ad eam rem esset reddere, in cunctis enim quae vidimus graecorum exemplaribus aliquid desiderabatur, quod Crotoniatibus in pingenda dea ingeniosus quondam pictor fecerat: collatis quinque Dios. graecis codicibus ubi aliquid variaret aut corruptum occurreret certiorem aptioremque elegisse lectionem: ubi vero aliquid simpliciter damnari deberet ratione aliqua signatum a nobis ubique id fuisse."

34. Ibid.: "Crotoniatum pictor Zeuxis."

35. Ibid., 2 recto: "Ego illud tantum expunxerim."

36. See Dioscorides, *De medica materia libri V,* ed. Adriani, (Cologne, 1529), blurb on title page: "Eiusdem Marcelli Vergilii in hosce Dioscoridis libros commentarii doctissimi, in quibus praeter omnigenam variamque eruditionem, collatis aliorum interpretum versionibus, suae tralationis ex utriusque linguae autoribus certissima adferuntur documenta. Morborum praeterea atque humani corporis vitiorum genus omne, quorum subinde meminit Dioscorides, diligentissime explicatur"; Preface, signed by Io. Soter Chalcographus Coloniensis, AA 2 recto-verso, 31 November 1529: "Eius [sc. Dioscoridis] ubi primum nobis evulgandi subiit studium, hoc conabamur sedulo, ut omnium eius interpretum placita poneremus ob oculos. At cum viderem nimiae molis opus futurum, animadverteremque Marcellum Vergilium magna sedulitate in eo scriptore versatum, ea

praestitisse, quae alii (absit invidia verbo) non praestiterint, eum potissimum delegi. Siquidem is utriusque linguae vetustissimorum codicum praesidio adiutus, tum admirabili quodam in expendendis veterum scriptis iudicio praeditus, *ton gnêsion* nobis, quantum licuit, Dioscoridem reddidit, resectis interim multis, quae quorundam vana curiositate inutiliter illi accreverant. Adiectis insuper doctissimis commentariis, rem ita illustravit, ut non magnopere quispiam reliquos desideraturus sit interpretes, ubi illius perlegerit commentarios. Collatis siquidem illorum tralationibus, sicubi urgente veritate atque re ipsa ab illis dissentire cogitur, suae tralationis firmissima adducit praesidia"; L. Fuchs, *De historia stirpium commentarii insignes* (Basel, 1542), [alpha 5 recto]: "Ad Marcellum igitur Virgilium Florentinum, qui post Ruellium hanc medicinae partem illustrare aggressus est, accedamus. Quamvis vero ille non magnam admodum herbarum notitiam habuisse videatur, ut qui professione medicus non fuerit, eoque tempore quo densissimis tenebris res herbaria obducta iacuit sua ediderit, tamen quia complura obscura et depravata Dioscoridis loca enucleavit et pristino nitori restituit, debet vel hoc saltem nomine illius studium et conatus nobis probari, cum nihil aeque ad recte intelligendum Dioscoridem aliosque autores conducat ac exemplariorum integritas et puritas. Quod vero nonnunquam a verbis Dioscoridis paulo longius recesserit, nec eorum legitimum et genuinum sensum assecutus fuerit, id illi vitium cum caeteris interpretibus commune est, utpote qui non raro Plinii magis quam Dioscoridis sensum exprimere ac sequi studuerint. Quod vero nonnulli Marcellum Dioscoridis interpretem plane grammaticum esse iudicant, non magnopere reprehendo. Sed quod adiiciunt eum in hac arte non satis tritum, hoc faciunt more suo, ne non palam omnibus insanire ac furere videantur, dum ita sinistre ac temere de hoc viro multisque aliis de literis et re medica optime meritis iudicare audent. Ego vero omni asseveratione affirmare nihil metuo, Marcellum in tanta etiam rerum omnium caligine, plures herbas cognitas habuisse, magisque grammaticum fuisse, quam illi hodie, qui tam impudenter de fama illius et aliorum eruditorum hominum detrahere non verentur." Cf. also I. Lonicerus, *In Dioscoridae Anazarbei de re medica libros, a Virgilio Marcello versos, scholia nova* (Marburg, 1543), ep. ded. (Lonicerus to the printer, Christianus Aegenolphus), alpha 2 recto, both praising Adriani's eloquence and criticizing his tendency "in plerisque locis in suis commentariis prolixius aequo rhetoricari"—a quality which Calcagnini, as we have seen, appreciated.

37. Dioscorides, *De materia medica*, ed. Adriani, 1518, 126 recto on 2.151: "Fecimus id veterum codicum fide et ope adiuti. Sed repetentes animo etiam credentesque quod Augustus in quotidiano sermone consueverat dicere, celerius quam asparagi coquantur [Suet. *Divus Augustus* 87.1], huc pertinere, nec celerioris et brevioris cocturae causam in natura oleris sed in usu hominum esse: qui subcrudo ad molliendam alvum simul et cibum quotidie uterentur: qualia multa alia sunt."

38. Ibid., 3 recto: "Instabat postremo illud quod rerum non vocum nominumve scientia haec est."

39. Ibid., AA iii recto: "Antiqua enim et graeca antiquorum et graecorum rationibus tradere et confirmare praecipuum nobis consilium est. Medicos herbarios in agro agentes aliquando consuluisse. Multarum plantarum oculatos esse testes. Ex longinquis regionibus quatenus id fieri potuit curasse nobis hoc aut illud apportari. Ab his qui cognovisse rem poterant litteris et coram pleraque didicisse. Et ne legentes ultra remoremur, qua licebit homini herbariam non profitenti diligentia sedulitateque, semper autem bona fide, tradenda a nobis omnia."

40. Ibid., 263 verso on 4.132 (134) (vetch): "Damnavit Naso in amoribus suis Philtra et amorum veneficia omnia, satisque uno versiculo qualia ea essent indicavit cum cecinit, Philtra nocent animis vimque furoris habent [*Ars amatoria* 2.106]. Damnaverunt et alii sapientiam inter gentes et bonos mores professi. Nullaque aetas non aliquem habuit qui contra malas amorum huiuscemodi causas pugnaret, omnium autem maxime a salutari exortu religionis nostrae Christiani principes et ecclesiae auctores, magicas vanitates quotidie et ubique exagitantes. In quibus perierunt quidem antiqua: sed aliunde nova irrepserunt. Tam vana mortalitas est, et in amoribus affectibusque aliis suis plus posse herbam quam formam, virtutem, laborem, industriamque et operam hominis credit, certioremque spem ab anu agyrteve aliquo in votis suis concipit, quam a natura, moribusque et industria sua."

41. Ibid., 135 verso on 2.176: "Peregrinam Graeciae Italiaeque et ex alieno orbe petitam fuisse medicam herbam nisi id Plinius manifeste testaretur, satis unum indicaret nomen: quod non ei tantum sed Assyriae malo commune eosdem utrique et ex eadem gente natales ostendit. Fuit haec quondam in maximo ruris et pecuariae rei honore: nec quicquam diligentius maioreque laboris compendio et utilitate ad universi rustici pecoris pabulum ferebatur: quo magis miretur aliquis periisse eam tantopere et a nobis evanuisse, ut nulla nunc eius in Italia ex antiquo nomine et usu vestigia deprehendantur: auditaque medica herba nihil auribus nostris certius obversetur quam si inaccessos Scythiae lucos aut Indiae odorata prata audiamus. Quaesivimus nos iampridem tota Italia: antiquum enim renovandae vetustatis studium in nobis est, diligentique multarum diversis locis gentium et incolarum percontatione sicubi incognita medica lateret in lucem proferre et ruris disciplinae restituere conati sumus: nec aliunde quam ex Hispania quod ad hanc rem faceret nunciatum nobis aliquid est." For the meaning of "ruris disciplinae" see Adriani, AA iii verso: "Quae [sc. medicina] non aliter quam ea, quae in ruris et hortorum disciplina calcata attritaque speciosius florere et flammis incensa copiosius nasci feruntur, multorum labore, ingenio, censuraque exagitata et exculta, qualis quondam fuit iterum nostra aetate videri et exerceri ut credimus poterit." And for a similar effort to compare Dioscorides' information with obser-

vation of modern customs, see Dioscorides, *De medicinali materia libri sex,* tr.
J. Ruellius, ed. W. Ryff (Frankfurt, 1543), 356, on the Laurus Alexandrinus: "Fuisse
tamen olim non parvum illum ex hypoglotti et hypoglossidii nomenclatura constat, quae hinc proculdubio facta illi est, quod sub lingua teneri solita sint folia, ut
vel hodie, non tantum apud Insubres, ut Vergilius Marcellus ait, aliasque alibi
gentes, sed etiam in Germania nostra fit, quoties abundantem puerorum salivam
et destillantem in fauces humiditatem, unde vel prolixa columella, id est, uvula,
vel fauces balbucie linguae impedimentum oritur, cohibere: et siccare opus est."

42. See J. Ackerman, "Early Renaissance 'Naturalism' and Scientific Illustration," *Distance Points* (Cambridge, Mass., and London, 1991), 185–207, for some
fascinating examples.

43. Fuchs, *De historia stirpium commentarii insignes,* alpha 4 recto: "Sic sane
Theophrastum, qui nobis novem de historia libros certe praestantissimos reliquit,
multas peragrasse provincias constat: neque enim alias tam exquisita ratione sin-
gulas stirpium differentias, quas diversarum regionum ratione habent, tradere
potuisset. Dioscorides quoque, ut metipse testatur, incredibili quodam cogno-
scendarum herbarum desiderio ductus, multa admodum in militari labore loca
perlustravit, tantam hinc consecutus peritiam stirpium, ut post se de iisdem,
Galeno etiam teste, absolutissimos reliquerit libros, quos multi hodie herbariae
medicinae studiosi, magno cum fructu, non tantum assidue domi legunt, sed et
secum nunquam non circunferunt." On the place of experience in ancient natural
history see G. E. R. Lloyd, *Science, Folklore and Ideology* (Cambridge, 1983; repr.
1986).

44. A. D. Momigliano, "Ancient History and the Antiquarian," *Journal of the
Warburg and Courtauld Institutes* 13 (1950), 285–315.

45. See e.g. F. Haskell, *History and Its Images* (New Haven and London, 1992);
P. Brown, *Venice and Antiquity* (New Haven and London, 1997).

46. Cf. A. Grafton, A. Shelford and N. Siraisi, *New Worlds, Ancient Texts*
(Cambridge, Mass., and London, 1992).

47. See L. A. Jardine and A. T. Grafton, "'Studied for Action': How Gabriel
Harvey Read his Livy," *Past & Present* 129 (1990), 30–78; cf. K. Sharpe, *Reading
Revolutions* (New Haven and London, 2000).

1. Panofsky, Alberti, and the Ancient World

1. See the splendid edition and commentary by R. Fubini and A. M. Gallorini, "L'autobiografia di Leon Battista Alberti," *Rinascimento,* ser. ii, 12
(1972):21–78, and the translation, also with very helpful discussion, by R. Watkins,
"L. B. Alberti in the Mirror: An Interpretation of the *Vita* with a New Translation." *Italian Quarterly* 30 (1989):5–30.

2. See W. Kaegi, *Jacob Burckhardt,* III (Basel and Stuttgart, 1956), 657–58, 720–22.

3. E. Panofsky, *Idea,* 6th ed. (Berlin, 1989).

4. The quality of Panofsky's plates was at its lowest in his works on general cultural problems; far higher, of course, when he investigated Dürer or early Netherlandish painting.

5. Research on Panofsky's life and thought is clearly entering a growth spurt, parallel in some respects to the recent spurt of interest in Warburg. Some orientation is provided by a helpful review of a recent congress: S. Grobé, "Platon in Hamburg," *Kunstchronik* 46 (1993):1–14. In the current essay I concentrate on Panofsky's American career, making no effort to trace the earliest versions of his thinking or to solve such complex questions as that of his relation to Warburg— which does not mean that I accept all or any of the answers that have been proposed up to now.

6. E. Panofsky and F. Saxl, "Classical Mythology in Mediaeval Art," *Metropolitan Museum Studies* 4 (1993):228–80; see also the brilliant short statement in *Kenyon Review* 6. My generation met this argument in *Renaissance and Renascences in Western Art* (Stockholm, 1960).

7. M. Baxandall, *Painting and Experience in Fifteenth-Century Italy,* 2d ed. (Oxford, 1988).

8. L. B. Alberti, *Opuscoli inediti,* ed. C. Grayson (Florence, 1954), 45ff.

9. L. B. Alberti, *Della famiglia,* "Proemio del libro terzo"; in *Prosatori volgari del Quattrocento,* ed. C. Varese (Milan and Naples, 1955), 413–17; for the context see R. Fubini, *Umanesimo e secolarizzazzione da Petrarca a Valla* (Rome, 1990), with references to the earlier literature.

10. L. B. Alberti, *L'architettura,* ed. and tr. G. Orlandi and P. Portoghesi (Milan, 1966), 6.3; cf. the classical analysis offered by R. Krautheimer in his inaugural lecture, now available in his *Ausgewählte Aufsätze* (Cologne, 1988).

11. E. Garin, "Fonti albertiane," *Rivista critica di storia della filosofia* 29 (1974):90–91, developed further in his *Rinascite e rivoluzioni* (Bari, 1975). Cf. Fubini and Gallorini, "L'autobiografia."

12. See esp. Alberti, *L'archittetura,* ed. and tr. Orlandi and Portoghesi, 6.1 and 9.10.

13. Alberti, *On Painting,* in *On Painting and On Sculpture,* ed. and tr. C. Grayson (London, 1972), 2.26.

14. D. and E. Panofsky, *Pandora's Box* (New York, 1956); cf. the German edition with a Nachwort by P. Krumme (Frankfurt and New York, 1992).

15. E. Panofsky, *Meaning in the Visual Arts* (Garden City, 1955), chap. 7.

16. I do not mean to suggest that there were only two Panofskys (or Albertis); in each case, surely there were many original heads under one capacious hat.

17. Alberti, *On Painting*, ed. and tr. Grayson, 3.56.

18. I use the annotated text in *Scritti d'arte del cinquecento*, ed. P. Barocchi, II (Milan and Naples, 1973), 1529–31.

19. N. Maraschio, "Aspetti del bilinguismo albertiano nel De pictura," *Rinascimento*, ser. ii, 12 (1972):193–228.

20. G. Boccaccio, *Tutte le opere*, ed. V. Branca (Verona, 1965), 6:305–6.

21. G. W. Pigman, "Barzizza's Treatise on Imitation," *Bibliothèque d'Humanisme et Renaissance* 44 (1982):351.

22. For two complementary recent discussions of Pienza, both of which take Alberti's involvement as to some degree likely, see A. Tönnesmann, *Pienza* (Munich, 1990), and C. Smith, *Architecture in the Culture of Early Humanism* (New York, 1992).

23. See *Meaning in the Visual Arts*, epilogue.

2. The Ancient City Restored

1. See *Montaigne's Travel Journal*, translated by Donald M. Frame (San Francisco: North Point, 1983), 78–80.

2. See *Codice topografico della città di Roma*, edited by Roberto Valentini and G. Zucchetti, vol. 3 (Rome: Tipografia del Senato, 1946), 17–65. Renaissance editions contain some amusing (and scathing) notes on this text.

3. Georg Fabricius, *Roma* (Helmstedt: Heitmuller, 1670), 3.

4. Ibid., 105.

5. Arnaldo Momigliano, "Ancient History and the Antiquarian," *Studies in Historiography* (London: Weidenfeld and Nicolson, 1966), 1–39.

6. See in general Roberto Weiss, *The Renaissance Discovery of Classical Antiquity* (Oxford: Blackwell, 1973).

7. Ibid., 38–42.

8. The text and an Italian translation of the relevant passages are in Cesare D'Onofrio, *Visitiamo Roma nel Quattrocento* (Rome: Romana Società Editrice, 1989), here p. 67.

9. Ibid., 69.

10. Ibid., 70–72.

11. Anne Reynolds, "The Classical Continuum in Roman Humanism: The Festival of Pasquino, the *Robigalia*, and Satire," *Bibliothèque d'Humanisme et Renaissance* 49 (1987): 289–307.

12. D'Onofrio, *Visitiamo Roma*, 271–90.

13. *A Documentary History of Art*, edited by Elizabeth G. Holt, vol. 1 (Garden City, N.Y.: Doubleday, 1957), 177–79.

14. For Poggio's account see D'Onofrio, *Visitiamo Roma*, 72.

15. Vat. lat. 8492, fol. 21 recto. See Erik Iversen, *Obelisks in Exile,* vol. 1, *The Obelisks of Rome* (Copenhagen: Gad, 1968), 147.

16. Vat. lat. 3906, fol. 92 recto. See Vittorio Fanelli, *Ricerche su Angelo Colocci e sulla Roma cinquecentesca* (Vatican City: Biblioteca Apostolica Vaticana, 1979), 117.

17. See the letter from Fabio Vigili to Benedetto Egio in Vat. lat. 8495, fol. 189 recto.

18. William McCuaig, "The *Fasti Capitolini* and the Study of Roman Chronology in the Sixteenth Century," *Athenaeum* 79 (1991): 141–59.

19. For a modern text see D'Onofrio, *Visitiamo Roma,* 163–64.

20. Leon Battista Alberti, *On the Art of Building in Ten Books,* translated by Joseph Rykwert et al. (Cambridge, Mass., and London: MIT. Press, 1988), 279.

21. Silvia Maddalo, *In figura Romae* (Rome: Viella, 1990).

22. See, in general, Anthony Grafton, *Forgers and Critics* (Princeton, N.J.: Princeton University Press, 1990).

23. See Philip Jacks, "The *Simulachrum* of Fabio Calvo: A View of Roman Architecture *all' antica* in 1527," *Art Bulletin* 72 (1990): 453–81.

24. Pirro Ligorio, *Delle antichità di Roma,* edited by Daniela Negri (Rome: E & A, 1989), 63.

25. See Erna Mandowsky and Charles Mitchell, *Pirro Ligorio's Roman Antiquities* (London: Warburg Institute, 1963), with the review by Carlo Dionisotti in *Rivista storica italiana* 75 (1963): 890–901.

26. For this and the next paragraph see the splendid study by Howard Burns, "Pirro Ligorio's Reconstruction of Ancient Rome: The *Anteiquae urbis imago* of 1561," *Pirro Ligorio, Artist and Antiquarian,* edited by Robert Gaston (Florence: Silvana, 1988), 19–92.

27. Vespasiano da Bisticci, *Renaissance Princes, Popes, and Prelates,* translated by W. George et al., edited by M. P. Gilmore (New York, Evanston, and London: Harper & Row, 1963), 50.

28. Silvia Grassi Fiorentino, "Note sull' antiquaria romana nella seconda metà del secolo XVI," *Baronio storico e la Controriforma,* edited by Romeo de Maio et al. (Sora: Centro di Studi Sorani "Vincenzo Patriarca," 1982), 205–6.

29. J. Wilpert, *Die Katakombengemälde und ihre alten Copien* (Freiburg i.B., 1891).

30. See G. B. De' Rossi, *La roma sotterranea cristiana,* vol. 1 (Rome, 1864); *Inscriptiones christianae urbis Romae septimo saeculo antiquiores* (Rome, 1857–61).

31. Anthony Blunt, "The Triclinium in Religious Art," *Journal of the Warburg and Courtauld Institutes* 2 (1938–39): 271–76.

32. See Anthony Grafton, *Defenders of the Text* (Cambridge, Mass., and London: Harvard University Press, 1991), chap. 5, and, more generally, Eric Cochrane,

Historians and Historiography in the Italian Renaissance (Chicago and London: University of Chicago Press, 1981), chap. 16.

33. See William McCuaig, *Carlo Sigonio* (Princeton, N.J.: Princeton University Press, 1989), chap. 4.

34. Erik Iversen, *The Myth of Egypt and Its Hieroglyphs in European Tradition* (Copenhagen: Gad, 1961).

35. Iversen, *Obelisks in Exile*, 1:67–69.

36. See Frances A. Yates, *Giordano Bruno and the Hermetic Tradition* (Chicago and London: University of Chicago Press, 1964).

37. Iversen, *Obelisks in Exile*, 1:76–92.

38. See also Robert Evans, *The Making of the Habsburg Monarchy, 1550–1700* (Oxford: Clarendon, 1979), part 3.

4. The Rest versus the West

1. José de Acosta, *Historia natural y moral de las Indias,* edited by J. Alcina Franch (Madrid: Historia 16, 1987), Book I, Chapter 9, pp. 82–86.

2. The letters of Acosta and Tovar appear in J. García Icazbalceta, *Don Fray Juan de Zumárraga, primer obispo y arzobispo de México,* edited by R. Aguayo Spencer and A. Castro Leal, Vol. 4 (Madrid: Porrúa, 1947), pp. 89–93.

3. J. H. Elliott, *The Old World and the New, 1492–1650* (Cambridge University Press, 1970); Anthony Pagden, *The Fall of Natural Man: The American Indian and the Origins of Comparative Ethnology* (Cambridge University Press, 1982).

4. Sergio Landucci, *I filosofi e i selvaggi, 1580–1780* (Bari: Laterza, 1972).

5. Giuliano Gliozzi, *Adamo e il nuovo mondo* (Florence: La Nuova Italia, 1977).

6. Sabine MacCormack, *Religion in the Andes: Vision and Imagination in Early Colonial Peru* (Princeton University Press, 1991); Fernando Cervantes, *The Devil in the New World: The Impact of Diabolism in New Spain* (Yale University Press, 1994).

7. See e.g. the remarkable exchange between Gananath Obeyesekere, *The Apotheosis of Captain Cook* (Princeton University Press, 1992), and Marshall Sahlins, *How "Natives" Think: About Captain Cook, For Example* (University of Chicago Press, 1995), and the discussion of both books by Clifford Geertz (*The New York Review of Books,* November 30, 1995). See also Geertz's essays on a number of related questions in *Local Knowledge: Further Essays in Interpretive Anthropology* (Basic Books, 1983).

8. Serge Gruzinski, *La colonisation de l'imaginaire* (Paris: Gallimard, 1988). This is now available in English, as *The Conquest of Mexico: The Incorporation of Indian Societies into the Western World,* translated by Eileen Corrigan (Cambridge: Polity, 1993).

9. N. Badaloni, *Un vichiano in Messico* (Lucca: Maria Pacini Fazzi, 1990), provides an Italian translation of and detailed historical commentary on Boturini's *Idea de una Nueva Historia General de la América Septentrional* (1746); there is an edition of the Spanish text by Miguel León-Portilla (Madrid: Porrúa, 1974). See also the fascinating account of a reader of Boturini, Francisco Javier Clavigero, in Cervantes, *The Devil in the New World,* pp. 149–154.

10. Walter D. Mignolo, "On the Colonization of Amerindian Languages and Memories: Renaissance Theories of Writing and the Discontinuity of the Classical Tradition," *Comparative Studies in Society and History,* 34 (1992), pp. 301–330.

11. Space prevents me from doing justice to the full richness of Cummins's series of case studies.

12. See in general Robert B. Tate, *Ensayos sobre la historiografía peninsular del siglo xv,* translated by J. Díaz (Madrid: Gredos, 1970), esp. pp. 25–27.

13. Bartolomé de las Casas, *Historia de las Indias,* edited by A. Millares Carlo (Madrid: Fondo de Cultura Económica, 1951; reprinted 1968), Vol. 1, pp. 5–7; Melchior Cano, *L'autorità della storia profana (De humanae historiae auctoritate, 1563),* edited by A. Biondi (Turin: Giappichelli, 1973), especially pp. 121–152.

14. See e.g. the very full collection of material on early Roman history and its sources in O. Panvinio, *Fastorum libri V* (Heidelberg: Officina Sanctandreana, 1588).

15. See in general H. J. Erasmus, *The Origins of Rome in Historiography from Petrarch to Perizonius* (Assen: Van Gorcum, 1962), and the review by A. D. Momigliano in *Rivista storica italiana,* 75 (1963), pp. 390–394.

16. García Icazbalceta, *Zumárraga,* Vol. 4, p. 91: "demás de que vi un libro que hizo un fraile dominico, deudo mío [Durán], que estaba el más conforme a la librería antigua que yo he visto." Cummins renders this as follows: "I saw a book made by a Dominican friar, a relative of mine, which was very similar to the ancient library that I had seen" (p. 166).

17. See e.g. Helen Whitehouse, "Towards a Kind of Egyptology: The Graphic Documentation of Ancient Egypt, 1587–1666," in *Documentary Culture: Florence and Rome, from Grand-duke Ferdinand I to Pope Alexander VII,* edited by E. Cropper et al. (Johns Hopkins University Press, 1992), pp. 63–79; Francis Haskell, *History and Its Images: Art and the Interpretation of the Past* (Yale University Press, 1993).

18. Acosta, *Historia,* p. 400: "porque sus figuras y caracteres no eran tan suficientes como nuestra escritura y letras."

19. García Icazbalceta, *Zumárraga,* Vol. 4, p. 92: "Pero es de advertir que aunque tenían diversas figuras y caracteres con que escrebían las cosas, no era tan suficientemente como nuestra escritura, que sin discrepar, por las mismas palabras, refiriese cada uno lo que estaba escrito; sólo concordaban en los conceptos."

20. See in general Erik Iversen, *The Myth of Egypt and Its Hieroglyphs in European Tradition* (1961; reprinted by Princeton University Press, 1993), and the important article by C. Dempsey, "Renaissance Hieroglyphic Studies and Gentile Bellini's *Saint Mark Preaching in Alexandria*," in *Hermeticism and the Renaissance: Intellectual History and the Occult in Early Modern Europe*, edited by Ingrid Merkel and Allen G. Debus (Folger Books, 1988), pp. 342–365.

21. See G. Cantelli, *Mente corpo linguaggio: Saggio sull'interpretazione vichiana del mito* (Florence: Sansoni, 1985), and his introduction to M. Mercati, *Gli obelischi di Roma* (1589; reprinted Bologna: Cappelli, 1981). Paleotti's views appear in his *Discorso intorno alle imagine sacre e profane*, in *Trattati d'Arte del Cinquecento*, edited by P. Barocchi (Bari: Laterza, 1960–1962), Vol. 2, pp. 142–149.

22. My thanks to Jorge Cañizares for comments and criticism.

5. The New Science and the Traditions of Humanism

1. For this paragraph and what follows, see his autobiography, ed. J. A. Worp, in *Bijdragen en mededeelingen van het historisch genootschap*, 18 (1897), 1–122; for a modern translation with excellent introduction and notes, see Constantijn Huygens, *Mijn jeugd*, ed. and trans. C. Heesakkers (Amsterdam, 1994).

2. See e.g. L. Forster, *The Icy Fire* (Cambridge, 1969).

3. Quoted by R. Jenkyns, *The Victorians and Ancient Greece* (Oxford, 1980), p. 67.

4. Michel de Montaigne, *Essais*, ed. P. Villey (Paris, 1965), pp. 1065–116; for an English translation, see Montaigne, *The Complete Essays*, trans. M. A. Screech (London, 1993), pp. 1207–69.

5. See R. F. Jones, *The Triumph of the English Language* (Stanford, 1953; reprinted 1966).

6. Johannes Kepler, *Gesammelte Werke*, ed. W. von Dyck and M. Caspar (Munich, 1937–), XVI, p. 329.

7. H. Aarsleff, *From Locke to Saussure* (Minneapolis, 1982).

8. Quoted by F. F. Blok, *Nicolaas Heinsius in dienst van Christina van Zweden* (Delft, 1949), pp. 111–112.

9. C. Borghero, *La certezza e la storia: cartesianismo, pirronismo e conoscenza storica* (Milan, 1983), pp. 170–195.

10. L. Gossman, *Medievalism and the Ideologies of the Enlightenment* (Baltimore, 1968); S. Timpanaro, *La genesi del metodo del Lachmann*, second edition, reprinted with corrections and additions (Padua, 1985), chap. 1; J. M. Levine, *Humanism and History* (Ithaca, 1987).

11. See G. Oestreich, *Neostoicism and the Early Modern State*, ed. B. Oestreich and H. G. Koenigsberger (Cambridge, 1982); M. Stolleis, *Staat und Staatsräson in*

der frühen Neuzeit (Frankfurt, 1990), pp. 197–231; P. S. Donaldson, *Machiavelli and Mystery of State* (Cambridge, 1988).

12. A. Clapmarius, "Nobilis adolescentis triennium," in Hugo Grotius et al., *Dissertationes de studiis instituendis* (Amsterdam, 1645), pp. 145–146.

13. G. J. Vossius, "Dissertatio bipartita," in Vossius et al., *Dissertationes de studiis bene instituendis* (Utrecht, 1658), especially pp. 15–18.

14. For the fullest study of the late humanist curriculum see the analysis of the influential academy designed by Jean Sturm for Strasbourg in A. Schindling, *Humanistische Hochschule und freie Reichsstadt* (Wiesbaden, 1977).

15. Grotius, *Dissertationes,* pp. 4–5.

16. Erasmus's *De ratione studii* is reprinted in Grotius, *Dissertationes,* pp. 319–339, as is another early-sixteenth-century treatise by Joachim Fortius Ringelberg, pp. 252–316 with an appendix on 317; Bruni's *De studiis et litteris* appears on pp. 414–431.

17. Grotius, *Dissertationes,* p. 4.

18. Caspar Barlaeus, "Methodus studiorum," in Grotius, *Dissertationes,* p. 353.

19. Grotius, *Dissertationes,* pp. 2–3.

20. Philip Sidney to Robert Sidney, 18 October 1580, in S. A. Pears, ed., *The Correspondence of Sir Philip Sidney and Hubert Languet* (London, 1845), pp. 199, 201.

21. See, in general, L. Jardine and A. T. Grafton, "'Studied for action': How Gabriel Harvey Read His Livy," *Past and Present,* 129 (1990), 30–78.

22. Barlaeus, "Methodus," in Grotius, *Dissertationes,* p. 353.

23. Vossius, "Dissertatio bipartita," p. 17.

24. Jean Bodin, *Methodus ad facilem historiarum cognitionem* (Paris, 1566), reissued several times up to 1650; see also A. Blair, *The Theater of Nature* (Princeton, 1997).

25. Pears, *Correspondence of Sidney and Languet,* p. 201.

26. John Jonston, *Thaumatographia universalis* (Amsterdam, 1665), epistola dedicatoria. See I. Maclean, "The Interpretation of Natural Signs: Cardano's *De subtilitate* versus Scaliger's *Exercitationes,*" in B. Vickers, ed., *Occult and Scientific Mentalities in the Renaissance* (Cambridge, 1984), pp. 231–252; and, more fully, W. Schmidt-Biggemann, *Topica universalis* (Hamburg, 1983).

27. F. Seck, "Keplers Hochzeitgedicht für Johannes Huldenreich (1590)," *Abhandlungen der Bayerischen Akademie der Wissenschaften,* mathematisch-naturwissenschaftliche Klasse, new series, 155 (1976).

28. See e.g. H. Arning, *Medulla variarum earumque in orationibus usitatissimarum connexionum* (Altenburg, 1652), chaps. 12–14.

29. *Secunda Scaligerana* (Cologne, 1667), pp. 140–143, at 141.

30. See M. Croll, *Style, Rhetoric, and Rhythm: Essays,* ed. J. M. Patrick and R. O. Evans (Princeton, 1966); W. Kühlmann, *Gelehrtenrepublik und Fürstenstaat* (Tübingen, 1982).

31. A. T. Grafton, "Teacher, Text, and Pupil in the Renaissance Class-room: A Case Study from a Parisian College," *History of Universities,* 1 (1980), 37–70.

32. See M. Fumaroli, *L'Age de l'éloquence* (Geneva, 1980).

33. See J. Tribby, "Body/Building: Living the Museum Life in Early Modern Europe," *Rhetorica,* 10 (1992), 139–163; T. DaC. Kaufmann, *The Mastery of Nature* (Princeton, 1993); P. Findlen, *Possessing Nature* (Berkeley, 1994).

34. Sebastian Münster, *Briefe,* ed. and trans. K. H. Burmeister (Ingelheim am Rhein, 1964), p. 67.

35. See G. F. Tomasini, *De vita, bibliotheca et museo Laurentii Pignorii canonici Tarvisini dissertatio,* in Lorenzo Pignoria, *Magnae Deum matris Idaeae et Attidis initia* (Amsterdam, 1669).

36. See A. Ellenius, *De arte pingendi* (Uppsala, 1960). The most accessible product of these efforts is the new edition of the 1638 edition of Franciscus Junius's *De pictura veterum: The Painting of the Ancients,* ed. K. Aldrich, P. Fehl, and R. Fehl, 2 vols. (Berkeley, 1991).

37. See e.g. G. Nadel, "Philosophy of History before Historicism," *History and Theory,* 3 (1964), 291–315; R. Koselleck, *Vergangene Zukunft* (Frankfurt, 1984).

38. Pears, *Correspondence of Sidney and Languet,* p. 200.

39. Jardine and Grafton, "Gabriel Harvey," p. 36.

40. J. G. Schellhorn, *De vita, fatis ac meritis Philippi Camerarii . . . commentarius* (Nuremberg, 1740), p. 120.

41. Francesco Guicciardini, *Maxims and Reflections of a Renaissance Statesman,* trans. M. Domandi (New York, 1965), C 110.

42. Marc-Antoine Muret, *Scripta selecta,* 2 vols. (Leipzig, 1887–8), I, p. 155.

43. See T. H. Lunsingh Scheurleer and G. H. M. Posthumus Meyjes, eds., *Leiden University in the Seventeenth Century: An Exchange of Learning* (Leiden, 1975); Stolleis, *Staat und Staatsräson,* pp. 37–72; Kühlmann, *Gelehrtenrepublik;* and H. Wansink, *Politieke wetenschappen aan de Leidse Universiteit, 1575–1650* (Utrecht, 1981).

44. A. Clapmarius, *De arcanis rerumpublicarum libri sex,* new edition (Amsterdam, 1644).

45. See B. Bauer, "Die Rolle des Hofastrologen und Hofmathematicus als fürstlicher Berater," in A. Buck, ed., *Höfischer Humanismus* (Weinheim, 1989), pp. 93–117.

46. The best introduction to this development is still A. D. Momigliano, "Ancient History and the Antiquarian," *Journal of the Warburg and Courtauld Institutes,* 13 (1950), 285–315.

47. Schellhorn, *De vita Camerarii,* pp. 36–37.

48. See E. Mandowsky and C. Mitchell, *Pirro Ligorio's Roman Antiquities* (London, 1963).

49. Justus Lipsius, "De ratione legendi historiam," in Grotius, *Dissertationes,* pp. 157–169. A nice example of this sort of note-taking is provided by Friedrich Lindenbruch's "De servis, deque eorum conditionibus, poenis, ac manumissionibus commentarius" (MS Hamburg, Universitätsbibliothek, philol. 291), which includes ample notes on legal and literary texts, and instructions on which historians to trust (and to examine for further information). See in general E. Horváth, "Friedrich Lindenbruch, Späthumanist und Handschriftensammler des 17. Jahrhunderts," dissertation, University of Hamburg, 1988, pp. 185–186: Lindenbruch seems to have taken these notes as a young student at the University of Leiden, which he attended in the mid-1590s, not long after Lipsius's departure.

50. D. C. Allen, *Mysteriously Meant* (Baltimore, 1970); A. T. Grafton, *Joseph Scaliger,* 2 vols. (Oxford, 1983–1993), II.

51. H. J. Erasmus, *The Origins of Rome in Historiography from Petrarch to Perizonius* (Assen, 1962).

52. E. Hassinger, *Empirisch-rationaler Historismus,* second edition (Freiburg im Breisgau, 1994).

53. J. W. Binns, *Intellectual Culture in Elizabethan and Jacobean England: The Latin Writings of the Age* (Leeds, 1990).

6. Civic Humanism and Scientific Scholarship at Leiden

My thanks to Henk Jan de Jonge and Glenn Most for their detailed comments on earlier drafts of this essay.

1. *Epistolae Ho-Elianae: The Familiar Letters of James Howell,* ed. J. Jacobs (London, 1890), p. 32.

2. *Shakespeare's Europe: Unpublished Chapters of Fynes Moryson's Itinerary,* ed. C. Hughes (London, 1903), pp. 372–377.

3. *The Diary of John Evelyn,* ed. A. Dobson (London, 1908), p. 17.

4. Chr. Köler, quoted by H. Schneppen, *Niederländische Universitäten und Deutsches Geistesleben* (Münster Westfalen, 1960), p. 36.

5. Ibid., p. 7.

6. *Diary of John Evelyn,* pp. 17–18.

7. B. Siegmund von Stosch, *Danck-und Denck-Seule des Andreae Gryphii* (1665), *Text und Kritik* 7/8 (n.d.): 6.

8. Th. H. Lunsingh Scheurleer, "Un amphithéâtre d'anatomie moralisée," in *Leiden University in the Seventeenth Century: An Exchange of Learning,* ed. Lunsingh Scheurleer et al. (Leiden, 1975), pp. 217–277.

9. See A. Grafton, "The World of the Polyhistors: Humanism and Encyclopedism," *Central European History* 18 (1985): 31–47.

10. For a full bibliography of earlier work, see R. E. O. Ekkart in *Bibliographie internationale de l'histoire des universités* (Geneva, 1976), II, 83–140.

11. A. Flitner, *Erasmus im Urteil seiner Nachwelt* (Tübingen, 1952), pp. 94–105; B. Mansfield, *Phoenix of His Age* (Toronto, 1979); and the exhibition catalogue *Erasmus en Leiden* (Leiden, 1986), esp. pp. 30–45.

12. P. Cunaeus, *Sardi venales* (1612), in *Two Neo-Latin Menippean Satires*, ed. C. Matheeussen and C. L. Heesakkers (Leiden, 1980); D. Heinsius, *Orationum editio nova* (Leiden, 1627), pp. 449–452.

13. See, for example, D. W. Davies, *The World of the Elseviers, 1580–1712* (The Hague, 1954), chap. 1; C. R. Boxer, *The Dutch Seaborne Empire, 1600–1800* (Harmondsworth, 1973), pp. 176–178.

14. W. Dilthey, *Weltanschauung und Analyse des Menschen seit Renaissance und Reformation*, 7th ed. in *Gesammelte Schriften*, vol. II (Stuttgart and Göttingen, 1964), pp. 443–444. The standard older compendium on the university also stresses the vital importance of its success in attracting world-famous scholars. G. D. J. Schotel, *De Academie te Leiden in de 16ᵉ, 17ᵉ en 18ᵉ eeuw* (Haarlem, 1875), chap. viii.

15. See, in general, G. Oestreich, *Neo-Stoicism and the Early Modern State* (Cambridge, 1982); and H. Wansink, *Politieke Wetenschappen aan de Leidse universiteit, 1575–1650* (Utrecht, 1981).

16. See F. Lucä, "Memoirs," in *Deutsche Selbstzeugnisse*, vol. VI, ed. M. Beyer-Frölich (Leipzig, 1930), p. 132.

17. H. J. de Jonge, *De bestudering van het Nieuwe Testament aan de Noordnederlandse universiteiten en het Remonstrants Seminarie van 1575 tot 1700* (Amsterdam, 1980), pp. 11–18; idem, "The Study of the New Testament in the Dutch Universities," *History of Universities* 1 (1981): 113–129. For Hebrew scholarship, see the illuminating dissertation of P. T. van Rooden, *Constantijn L'Empereur (1591–1648), professor hebreeuws en theologie te Leiden* (Leiden, 1985).

18. J. Platt, *Reformed Thought and Scholasticism* (Leiden, 1982).

19. E. G. Ruestow, *Physics at Seventeenth- and Eighteenth-Century Leiden* (The Hague, 1973); A. M. Luyendijk-Elshout, "Oeconomia animalis, pores and particles," *Leiden University in the Seventeenth Century*, ed. Lunsingh Scheurleer et al., pp. 295–307.

20. *Bronnen tot de geschiedenis der Leidsche Universiteit*, ed. P. C. Molhuysen, vol. I: *1574–7 Febr. 1610* (The Hague, 1913), doc. 258, pp. 289–291 (9 January 1594). See also R. Bartlett, *Trial by Fire and Water* (Oxford, 1986), pp. 146–152, for this incident and its larger context.

21. A. Klempt, *Die Säkularisierung der universalhistorischen Auffassung* (Göttingen, 1960), pp. 114–123; E. Hassinger, *Empirisch-rationaler Historismus* (Bern

and Munich, 1978), pp. 127–136; G. Hornius, *Arca Noae* (Leiden and Rotterdam, 1666).

22. See, in general, J. J. Woltjer's introduction in *Leiden University in the Seventeenth Century,* pp. 3–19. In addition to this magnificent book, the quatercentenary produced anniversary volumes of the journals *Quarendo* 5 (1975) and *Lias* 2 (1975), and the extremely rich and informative Rijksmuseurn Amsterdam exhibition catalogue, *Leidse Universiteit 400. Stichting en eerste bloei 1575–ca. 1650* (Amsterdam, 1975).

23. M. Jurriaanse, *The Founding of Leiden University* (Leiden, 1965).

24. See, for example, P. Zumthor, *Daily Life in Rembrandt's Holland* (London, 1961); Boxer, *The Dutch Seaborne Empire,* pp. 60–61, 70, 322. S. Schama, *The Embarrassment of Riches* (New York, 1987), which appeared after this essay was written, sheds a flood of light on many matters fitfully illuminated in what follows in this essay.

25. J. J. Scaliger, *Poemata anecdota,* ed. H. J. de Jonge (Leiden, 1980), p. 9. *Autobiography of Joseph Scaliger,* trans. G. W. Robinson (Cambridge, Mass., 1927), pp. 50–52.

26. *Shakespeare's Europe,* p. 382.

27. Lucä, "Memoirs," p. 132. Scaliger noted that the Walloons urinated against the inside as well as the outside walls of their churches.

28. W. Temple, *Observations upon the United Province of the Netherlands,* ed. G. Clark (Oxford, 1972), pp. 88–89; *Autobiography of Joseph Scaliger,* pp. 48–49; Lucä, "Memoirs," pp. 131–32.

29. E. Bronckhorst, *Diarium,* ed. J. C. van Slee (The Hague, 1898), pp. 122, 136; Schotel, *De Academie te Leiden,* pp. 230–232; D. J. H. ter Horst, *Daniel Heinsius (1580–1655)* (Utrecht, 1934), chap. ix. One of Heinsius's acquaintances described him in his later years as "no longer a man but an amphora."

30. Bronckhorst, *Diarium,* pp. 64, 68, 118.

31. *Autobiography of Joseph Scaliger,* p. 49.

32. P. Dibon, *La Philosophie néerlandaise au siècle d'or* (Amsterdam, 1954), I, 4. See also G. H. M. Posthumus Meyjes, *Geschiedenis van het Waalse College te Leiden, 1606–1699* (Leiden, 1975), for the Walloon College. For evidence that William of Orange himself saw the promotion of theology as the chief aim of the university, see *Leidse Universiteit 400,* p. 76, item A 131.

33. Dibon, *La Philosophie néerlandaise,* pp. 7–11, on G. Feugueray's 1575 *Hypotyposis,* in *Bronnen,* ed. Molhuysen, I, doc. 26, pp. *39–*43 (which envisages training for the church, the state, and medicine, p. *40).

34. *Bronnen tot de geschiedenis der Leidsche Universiteit,* ed. P. C. Molhuysen (The Hague, 1916), II, 127; L. Holstenius, *Epistolae ad diversos,* ed. J. F. Boissonade (Paris, 1817), pp. 4–5. In fact, the curators objected to Meursius's religious views.

35. Dibon, *La Philosophie néerlandaise,* I, 80–90.

36. See the exhibition catalogue from the Herzog August Bibliothek, Wolfenbüttel: *Hermann Conring, 1606–1681* (Wolfenbüttel, 1981), pp. 23–29.

37. The role of religious tolerance—and even Nicodemism—in the university's early history certainly deserves detailed study but may be slightly overemphasized in the important work of the late J. van Dorsten. See, for example, his "Temporis filia veritas: Wetenschap en religievrede," *Tijdschrift voor Geschiedenis* 89 (1976): 413–419. For a more nuanced view see A. Hamilton, *The Family of Love* (Cambridge, 1981), pp. 99–111.

38. J. Huizinga, *Dutch Civilization in the Seventeenth Century and Other Essays,* ed. P. Geyl, trans. A. Pomerans (New York, 1968), p. 151.

39. J. A. van Dorsten, *Poets, Patrons and Professors* (Leiden and London, 1961); P. Tuynman, "Petrus Scriverius, 12 January 1576–30 April 1660," *Quaerendo* 7 (1977): 5–45.

40. G. Schwartz, *Rembrandt* (New York, 1985), esp. chap. 4.

41. J. Meursius, *Athenae Batavae* (Leiden, 1625). This was adapted from the *Alma Academia Leidensis* of 1614, and much of its content is made up of autobiographies of the professors which retain great value. See, in general, S. Ridderbos, *De philologie aan de Leidsche Universiteit gedurende de eerste vijfentwintig jaren van haar bestaan* (Leiden, 1906); J. H. Waszink, "Classical Philology," *Leiden University in the Seventeenth Century,* ed. Scheurleer et al., pp. 160–175; "Lo sviluppo della filologia nei Paesi Bassi del nord dalla morte di Erasmo fino alla morte dello Scaligero," *Annali della Scuola Normale Superiore di Pisa,* cl. di lettere e filosofia, ser. 3, 8 (1978): 97–133.

42. See, in general, M. W. Croll, *Style, Rhetoric, and Rhythm* (Princeton, N.J., 1966); A. Momigliano, *Essays in Ancient and Modern Historiography* (Oxford, 1977), chap. 13.

43. A. D. Momigliano, *Polybius between the English and the Turks,* 7th J. L. Myres Memorial Lecture (Oxford, 1974), pp. 10–12.

44. Wansink, *Politieke wetenschappen.*

45. J. Ruysschaert, *Juste Lipse et les Annales de Tacite* (Louvain, 1949).

46. B. Rekers, *Benito Arias Montano (1527–1598)* (London, 1972), p. 102. See also N. Mout, *Bohemen en de Nederlanden in de zestiende eeuw* (Leiden, 1975); Hamilton, *The Family of Love.*

47. G. Güldner, *Das Toleranz-Problem in den Niederlanden im Ausgang des 16. Jahrhunderts* (Lübeck and Hamburg, 1968). Lipsius insisted that his phrase *ure et seca* had been meant only as a call to use serious remedies (its sense in classical Latin), not as a demand for execution. But both his contemporaries and modern historians have differed about the plausibility of this effort to make the literal metaphorical when challenged. In addition to Güldner's careful study, which

favors Lipsius, see H. Bonger, *Leven en werk van D. V. Coornhert* (Amsterdam, 1978), pp. 140–156, which favors Coornhert.

48. The standard biography remains J. Bernays, *Joseph Justus Scaliger* (Berlin, 1855); more recent literature is listed in A. Grafton and H. J. de Jonge, *Joseph Scaliger: A Bibliography, 1852–1982* (The Hague, 1982). For details of Scaliger's life in Leiden, see H. J. de Jonge, "Josephus Scaliger in Leiden," *Jaarboekje voor geschiedenis en oudheidkunde van Leiden en omstreken* 71 (1979): 71–94.

49. A. Grafton, "From *De die natali* to *De emendatione temporum:* The Origins and Setting of Scaliger's Chronology," *Journal of the Warburg and Courtauld Institutes* 48 (1985): 100–143.

50. See *Bronnen,* I, index s.n. Scaliger.

51. M. Billanovich, "Benedetto Bordon e Giulio Cesare Scaligero," *Italia Medioevale e Umanistica* 11 (1968): 187–256.

52. G. Crapulli, *Mathesis Universalis* (Rome, 1969), pp. 101–123; W. E. van Wijk, *Het eerste leerboek der technische tijdrekenkunde* (Leiden, 1954).

53. F. Raphelengius to Lipsius, November 1595, quoted by Bernays, *Joseph Justus Scaliger,* p. 174.

54. See, in general, Bernays, *Joseph Justus Scaliger;* for other cases in point, see A. L. Katchen, *Christian Hebraists and Dutch Rabbis* (Cambridge, Mass., 1984).

55. For the incident, see *Bronnen,* I, *443–*57. For Baudius's speech—the duration of which I infer from the length of the text—see his *Epistolarum centuriae tres,* new ed. (Amsterdam, 1647), pp. 555–608. For Scaliger's presence, see pp. 556–557, 608. Naturally, the timing is an approximation.

56. Lucilius, *Satyrarum quae supersunt reliquiae,* ed. F. Dousa (Padua, 1735), p. 236 (on a fragment now assigned to Ennius).

57. Scaliger to Wowerius, 12 December (Julian) 1602; Scaliger, *Epistolae,* ed. D. Heinsius (Leiden, 1627), p. 718.

58. Wowerius's interest in the comparison of Greek and Jewish (Masoretic) critical methods clearly comes from Scaliger. For specific points that reappear compare Scaliger, *Epistolae,* pp. 718–719, with J. Wowerius, *De polymathia tractatio,* 18.4 and 24.6; *Thesaurus Graecarum Antiquitatum,* ed. Jac. Gronovius (Leiden, 1701), X, cols. 1080, 1114.

59. *Scaligerana,* ed. P. Desmaizeaux (Amsterdam, 1740), pp. 395–396; see also de Jonge, "The Study of the New Testament," p. 84.

60. *Scaligerana,* p. 399; de Jonge, "The Study of the New Testament," p. 82.

61. A. Grafton, "Joseph Scaliger's Indices to J. Gruter's *Inscriptiones Antiquae,*" *Lias* 2 (1975): 109–113.

62. Syncellus *29* M = *FrGrHist* 680 F 1; 59 M ff. = *FrGrHist* 609 F 2. See A. Grafton, "Joseph Scaliger and Historical Chronology: The Rise and Fall of a Discipline," *History & Theory* 14 (1975): 156–185.

63. P. Rossi, *The Dark Abyss of Time,* trans. L. Cochrane (Chicago, 1984).

64. E. H. Waterbolk, "Zeventiende-eeuwers in de Republiek over de grondslagen van het geschiedverhaal. Mondelinge of schriftelijke overlevering," *Bijdrage voor de Geschiedenis der Nederlanden* 12 (1957): 26–44; "Reacties op het historisch pyrrhonisme," ibid., 15 (1960): 81–102; both rpt. in *Mythe & Werkelijkheid,* ed. J. A. L. Lancée (Utrecht, 1979), pp. 9–24, 68–85; H. J. Erasmus, *The Origins of Rome in Historiography from Petrarch to Perizonius* (Assen, 1962). For a summary of the Frisian Urgeschichte, see S. Petrus, *Apologia . . . pro antiquitate et origine Frisiorum* (Franeker, 1603), pp. 15–17. See also Schama, *The Embarrassment of Riches,* chap. 2.

65. U. Emmius, *De origine atque antiquitatibus Frisiorum,* in his *Rerum Frisicarum historia* (Leiden, 1616), separately paginated, 7 ff. See *Scaligerana,* p. 304 ("bon & rare").

66. Petrus, *Apologia,* pp. 40–41; previously quoted by Erasmus, *Origins of Rome,* p. 90.

7. Printer's Correctors and the Publication of Classical Texts

1. J. O'Brien, *Anacreon Redivivus* (Ann Arbor, 1995).

2. J. A. Gruys, *The Early Printed Editions (1518–1664) of Aeschylus* (Nieuwkoop, 1981); M. Mund-Dopchie, *La survie d'Eschyle à la Renaissance* (Louvain, 1984).

3. Aulus Gellius, *Noctes Atticae,* ed. H. Estienne (Paris, 1585), 2. See in general F. Schreiber, *The Estiennes* (New York, 1982), 127–183.

4. Aulus Gellius, ed. H. Estienne, 12–13.

5. Ibid., 12.

6. Ibid.

7. Ibid.

8. Ibid. For a modern discussion, see E. Armstrong, *Robert Estienne, Royal Printer* (Cambridge, 1954).

9. J. C. Zeltner, *C. D. Correctorum in typographiis eruditorum centuria speciminis loco collecta* (Nuremberg, 1716), 43; F. Waquet, *Le latin ou l'empire d'un signe* (Paris, 1999).

10. Schreiber, 87.

11. The statute of Aldo's academy—a unique printed broadside—is preserved in Biblioteca Apostolica Vaticana, Stamp. Barb. AAA IV 13, inside front cover.

12. M. Lowry, *The World of Aldus Manutius* (Oxford, 1979), chap. v; see more recently N. G. Wilson, *From Byzantium to Italy* (London, 1992).

13. See e.g. the illustration in J. Hornschuch, *Orthotypographia,* ed. and tr. P. Gaskell and P. Bradford (Cambridge, 1972), xvi, reproduced and analyzed in

P. Simpson, *Proof-Reading in the Sixteenth, Seventeenth and Eighteenth Centuries* (London, 1935), 126–134.

14. G. Hoffmann, "Writing without Leisure: Proofreading as Work in the Renaissance," *Journal of Medieval and Renaissance Studies* 25 (1995), 17–31.

15. M. Sicherl, in D. Harlfinger et al., *Griechische Handschriften und Aldinen* (Wolfenbüttel, 1978), 119–149.

16. Cf. S. Rizzo, *Il lessico filologico degli umanisti* (Rome, 1973), 327–338.

17. See e.g. L. A. Jardine, *Erasmus, Man of Letters* (Princeton, 1994); J. D'Amico, *Theory and Practice in Renaissance Textual Criticism* (Berkeley, 1988).

18. F. Geldner, "Das Rechnungsbuch des Speyrer Druckherrn, Verlegers und Grossbuchhändlers Peter Drach," *Archiv für Geschichte des Buchwesens* 5 (1963), 1–196; P. Trovato, *Con ogni diligenza corretto: La stampa e le revisioni editoriali dei testi letterari italiani (1470–1570)* (Bologna, 1991), 19–21. See also the important work of B. Richardson, *Print Culture in Renaissance Italy* (Cambridge, 1994), chaps. 1–2.

19. Trovato, chaps. 2–3.

20. Hornschuch, 15–17; Simpson, 132–136.

21. See J. Gerritsen, "Printing at Froben's: An Eye-Witness Account," *Studies in Bibliography* 44 (1991), 144–163; A. Grafton, "Correctores Corruptores? Notes on the Social History of Editing," *Editing Texts / Texte edieren,* ed. G. W. Most (Göttingen, 1998), 54–76; R. Chartier, *Au bord de la falaise* (Paris, 1998), chap. 12.

22. Hornschuch, 28–32.

23. Zeltner, *Centuria,* 585.

24. Zeltner, errata (after 598).

25. See esp. Trovato.

26. Hornschuch, v. Trovato, chap. iii, confirms this impressionistic account with rich detail.

27. Zeltner, 589.

28. H. Estienne, *Artis typographicae querimonia,* in his *Pseudo-Cicero,* ed. F. W. Roloff (Halle, 1737), ccclxxvi.

29. Trovato, chap. iii.

30. Ibid., 65.

31. E. J. Kenney, *The Classical Text* (Berkeley, 1974), 12–17.

32. Ibid., 17.

33. Ibid., 13, 18–19, 23–26.

34. C. Frova and M. Miglio, "Dal Ms. Subiacense XLII all'*editio princeps* del 'De civitate dei' di Sant'Agostino," *Scrittura, biblioteche e stampa a Roma nel Quattrocento: Aspetti e problemi,* ed. C. Bianca et al. (Vatican City, 1980), 245–273.

35. Trovato, 30–43.

36. See in general R. Sabbadini, "Le edizioni quattrocentesche della *Storia naturale* di Plinio," *Studi italiani di filologia classica* 8 (1900), 439–448; A. Maruc-

chi, "Note sul manoscritto di cui si è servito Giovanni Andrea Bussi per l'edizione di Plinio del 1470," *Institut de recherche et d'histoire des textes, Bulletin* 15 (1967–68), 155–182; P. Casciano, "Il ms. Angelicano 1097, fase preparatoria per l'edizione del Plinio di Sweynheym e Pannartz (Hain 13088)," *Scrittura biblioteche e stampa a Roma nel Quattrocento,* ed. C. Bianca et al. (Rome, 1985), 383–394. For the larger context see C. G. Nauert Jr., "Caius Plinius Secundus," *Catalogus translationum et commentariorum,* 4, ed. F. E. Cranz (Washington, D.C., 1980), 223–422; Nauert, "Humanists, Scientists, and Pliny: Changing Approaches to a Classical Author," *American Historical Review* 84 (1979), 72–85; A. Borst, *Das Buch der Naturgeschichte* (Heidelberg, 1994; repr. 1995).

37. Quoted by Nauert, "Plinius," 308 n. 38.

38. J. Monfasani, "The First Call for Press Censorship: Niccolò Perotti, Giovanni Andrea Bussi, Antonio Moreto, and the Editing of Pliny's *Natural History,*" *Renaissance Quarterly* 41 (1988), 1–31 = Monfasani, *Language and Learning in Renaissance Italy* (Aldershot, 1994), XI; M. C. Davies, "Humanism in Script and Print," *The Cambridge Companion to Renaissance Humanism,* ed. J. Kraye (Cambridge, 1996), 57; Davies, "Making Sense of Pliny in the Quattrocento," *Renaissance Studies* 9 (1995), 239–255.

39. Monfasani, 25.

40. Ibid., 27 (text), 11 (translation and interpretation).

41. Campano, *Opera* (Venice, 1502), LXIII verso–LXIIII recto.

42. Ibid.

43. P. O. Kristeller, "De traditione operum Marsilii Ficini," in *Supplementum Ficinianum* (Florence, 1937).

44. H. Harth, "Niccolò Niccoli als literarischer Zensor: Untersuchungen zur Textgeschichte von Poggios 'De avaritia,'" *Rinascimento* NS 7 (1967), 29–53.

45. Rizzo, esp. 249–268; cf. Jardine.

46. Grafton, 72–75.

47. M. Ferno, "Campani vita," in Campano, *Opera,* xiii verso.

48. Ibid., ii recto–iii verso.

49. Ibid., xiii verso.

50. Campano, *Opera,* [l iiii] ro-vo.

51. Text in Rizzo, 342–344 at 342.

52. Ibid., 343.

53. Vat. lat. 1801, 184 recto.

9. The World of the Polyhistors

1. J. B. Mencke, *The Charlatanry of the Learned,* tr. F. E. Litz, ed. H. L. Mencken (New York, 1937), 61–62.

2. Ibid., 68–69.

3. Ibid., 85–86.

4. For the history of the former belief see E. Iversen, *The Myth of Egypt and Its Hieroglyphs in European Tradition* (Copenhagen, 1961); for that of the latter D. P. Walker, *The Ancient Theology* (London, 1972).

5. *Hinkmar von Repkows Noten ohne Text* (1745). On this and similar literature see W. Martens, "Von Thomasius bis Lichtenberg: Zur Gelehrtensatire der Aufklärung," *Lessing Yearbook* 10 (1978): 7–34.

6. See R. Spaethling, "On Christian Thomasius and His Alleged Offspring: The German Enlightenment," *Lessing Yearbook* 3 (1971): 194–213.

7. *M. Manilii Astronomicon liber primus*, ed. A. E. Housman, 2d ed. (Cambridge, 1937), xv.

8. For the linking of Barth with Morhof see J. A. Fabricius's *praefatio* to D. G. Morhof, *Polyhistor literarius, philosophicus et practicus*, 4th ed. (Lübeck, 1747; reprint Aalen, 1970), 1: ix: "Multum semper debere me professus sum, ac profiteor libenter duumviris eruditis Germanis nostris CASPARI BARTHIO, & DANIELI GEORGIO MORHOFIO." In the absence of a modern appreciation of Barth's work, one may consult Fabricius's (ibid.); he makes clear that Barth's example of command of "illum orbem scientiarum" inspired him to become the greatest bibliographer of his (or any other) era.

9. E. Trunz, "Der deutsche Späthumanismus um 1600 als Standeskultur," in *Deutsche Barockforschung*, ed. R. Alewyn, 3d ed. (Cologne and Berlin, 1968), 147–181 (originally published in 1932); of more recent general essays the most stimulating are perhaps C. Wiedemann, "Polyhistors Glück und Ende: Von D. G. Morhof zum jungen Lessing," *Festschrift Gottfried Weber* (Bad Homburg v.d.H., Berlin, and Zurich, 1967), 215–235; R. J. W. Evans, "Rantzau and Welser: Aspects of Later German Humanism," *History of European Ideas* 5 (1984): 257–272.

10. Some particularly useful monographs include: T. Bleicher, *Homer in der deutschen Literatur (1450–1740)* (Stuttgart, 1972); N. Hammerstein, *Jus und Historie* (Göttingen, 1972); G. Hornig, *Die Anfänge der historisch-kritischen Theologie* (Göttingen, 1961); A. Klempt, *Die Säkularisierung der universalhistorischen Auffassung* (Göttingen, Berlin, and Frankfurt, 1960); G. Oestreich, *Neostoicism and the Early Modern State* (Cambridge, 1982).

11. W. Kühlmann, *Gelehrtenrepublik und Fürstenstaat* (Tübingen, 1982); the footnotes and bibliography of this massive book stimulate and inform even when it does not command assent; all future work in the field must begin from it. See also the complementary case study by Kühlmann and W. Schäfer, *Frühbarocke Stadtkultur am Oberrhein: Studien zum literarischen Werdegang J. M. Moscheroschs (1601–1669)* (Berlin, 1983); and, for the larger setting, H. Bots and F. Waquet, *La République des lettres* (Paris, 1997).

12. For the tradition of humanist rhetoric see H. H. Gray, "Renaissance Humanism: The Pursuit of Eloquence," *Journal of the History of Ideas* 24 (1963), reprinted in *Renaissance Essays*, ed. P. O. Kristeller and P. P. Wiener (New York and Evanston, 1968), 199–216; for its German form see above all Kühlmann, *Gelehrten-republik*, pt. I.

13. F. J. Stopp, *The Emblems of the Altdorf Academy* (London, 1974), provides interesting samples and analyses of schoolboy oratory.

14. G. J. Vossius, *De quatuor artibus popularibus* (Amsterdam, 1660), 67, 71–74. Cf. A. Ellenius, *De arte pingendi* (Uppsala, 1960).

15. See the useful study by M. Benner and E. Tengström, *On the Interpretation of Learned Neo-Latin* (Göteborg, 1977), and E. Tengström, *A Latin Funeral Oration from Early Eighteenth Century Sweden* (Göteborg, 1983), which illuminate the German as well as the Swedish scene.

16. Erasmus, *De utraque verborum ac rerum copia lib. II*, I.31 (Amsterdam, 1645), 62.

17. H. Arningk, *Medulla variarum earumque in orationibus usitatissimarum connexionum* (Altenburgi, 1652).

18. Ibid., 11.

19. Calvisius to J. J. Scaliger, n.d.; Göttingen, Niedersächsische Staats- und Universitätsbibliothek, MS philos. 103, vol. 3, p. 95 (draft); copy ibid., vol. 2, p. 31: "Elenchus etiam tuus ad me pervenit . . . Magna eum cum voluptate legi quod adeo evidentissimis [lined through: argumentis] demonstrationibus et oratione [lined through: nervosa] gravi et nervosa eum ita prosternis et obruis ut depositus fere videatur. Ideo quamvis in me scripsit, quiescendum tamen mihi jam puto, ne mortuo cani videar insultare et post Homerum Iliada scribere."

20. J. Sparrow, *Visible Words* (Cambridge, 1969). Kühlmann provides an exhaustive treatment of the modernization of Latin rhetoric in *Gelehrtenrepublik*, pt. I, chap. v.

21. See in general L. E. Loemker, *Struggle for Synthesis* (Cambridge, Mass., 1972), chap. 2.

22. W. Ong, "Commonplace Rhapsody: Ravisius Textor, Zwinger and Shakespeare," *Classical Influences on European Culture, A.D. 1500–1700*, ed. R. R. Bolgar (Cambridge, 1976), 111–118.

23. See e.g. P. R. Sellin, "The Last of the Renaissance Monsters . . . ," in *Anglo-Dutch Cross Currents in the Seventeenth and Eighteenth Centuries* (Los Angeles, 1976), [1]–[39].

24. G. J. Vossius et al., *Dissertationes de studiis bene instituendis* (Utrecht, 1658).

25. See H. I. Marrou, *A History of Education in Antiquity*, tr. G. Lamb (New York, 1956), pt. III, chap. 5; A. T. Grafton and L. Jardine, "Humanism and the School of Guarino: A Problem of Evaluation," *Past & Present* 96 (1982): 70–73.

26. H. Aarsleff, *From Locke to Saussure* (Minneapolis, 1982), 106.

27. *Schurzfleischiana* (Wittenberg, 1741), 15.

28. B. Siegmund von Stosch, "Danck- und Denck-Seule des Andreae Gryphii (1665)," *Texte & Kritik*, 7/8 (n.d.): 6.

29. See the sympathetic account by L. M. Newman, *Leibniz (1646–1716) and the German Library Scene*, Library Assoc. Pamphlet no. 28, 1966.

30. G. Naudé, "Bibliographia politica," in H. Grotius et al., *Dissertationes de studiis instituendis* (Amsterdam, 1645), 25–26.

31. Ibid., 23.

32. *Schurzfleischiana*, 102.

33. Ibid., 17–18.

34. For a late specimen of this literature see A. Böckh, *Encyklopädie und Methodologie der philologischen Wissenschaften*, ed. E. Bratuscheck (Leipzig, 1877).

35. Cf. A. Grafton, "Polyhistor into *Philolog* . . . ," *History of Universities* 3 (1983): 159–192.

36. Morhof, *Polyhistor*, 1:2.

37. Ibid., 10.

38. G. Hornius, *Arca Noae* (Leiden and Rotterdam, 1666); see Klempt, *Die Säkularisierung*, pt. II, chap. C; E. Hassinger, *Empirisch-rationaler Historismus* (Bern and Munich, 1978), 127–136, offers important qualifications, but is a trifle too ungenerous.

39. C. S. Schurzfleisch, *Orationes panegyricae et allocutiones varii argumenti* (Wittenberg, 1697), 1:126.

40. *Schurzfleischiana*, 213.

41. Ibid., 207.

42. Ibid., 151.

43. Ibid., 221.

44. Ibid., 157.

45. Ibid., 181–182.

46. Ibid., 180.

47. Ibid., 182.

48. See in general Hornig, *Die Anfänge der historisch-kritischen Theologie;* O. Merk, "Anfänge neutestamentlicher Wissenschaft im 18. Jahrhundert," *Historische Kritik in der Theologie: Beiträge zu ihrer Geschichte*, ed. G. Schwaiger (Göttingen, 1980), 37–59.

49. Cf. W. Jens's interesting remarks on the strange evolution of legal thought in Tübingen, *Eine deutsche Universität: 500 Jahre Tübinger Gelehrtenrepublik*, 2d ed. (Munich, 1981), chap. 6.

50. Mencke, *Charlatanry of the Learned*, 64. For a witty and vivid account of the behavior of the real polyhistors, see Jens, *Eine deutsche Universität*, chaps. 2–8.

10. Jean Hardouin

Earlier versions of this essay were presented as a Sawyer Seminars Lecture at the University of Chicago, 9 April 1996; as the William F. Church Memorial Lecture, Department of History, Brown University; and on 19 January 2000, to the Seminar on French Studies, University of Pennsylvania. Much of my research was made possible by the Dibner Institute, which enabled me to spend summer 1997 in Cambridge, Massachusetts, and the Ecole Normale Supérieure, which invited me to spend March 1999 in Paris as Condorcet Professor. My thanks to the audiences who heard the original paper and to the editors of the *Journal of the Warburg and Courtauld Institutes* for helpful criticism, to M. Mulsow for valuable information, and to P. Petitmengin for many kindnesses during my stay in Paris.

1. Leibniz to Huet, 18 October 1678, in Paris, Bibliothèque Nationale MS nouv. acq. fr. 6202, fol. 19v: "Haec vero omnia ita ut narrantur gesta fuisse, demonstrari non potest nisi tota historia universali sacra et profana accuratissime constituta, collectisque et manuscriptis et numismatis et inscriptionibus aliisque cimeliis eruditorum. His enim fit historiae fides, itaque saepe mecum cogitans optavi esse qui nobis inventarium ut ita dicam exhibeat pretiosi huius thesauri omnium quae hodieque supersunt reliquiarum antiquitatis: quoad eius fieri potest."

2. Ibid., fols 19v-20r: "Tale quiddam circa inscriptiones expectamus a summo in his studiis viro Marquardo Gudio nec numismatis deerunt Ezechiel Spanhemius aliique excellentes Viri, maxime autem Carcavius vester tantarum in hoc genere opum custos meritissimus."

3. Ibid., fol. 20r: "Sed historiam manuscriptorum hactenus desidero, qua enumerentur meliores qui nunc quoque extant in Europa codices, illi inprimis ex quibus autores expressi sunt, et qui sunt unici." For a slightly different version of this letter see Leibniz, *Die philosophischen Schriften*, ed. C. I. Gerhardt, Berlin 1875–1890, iii, p. 13.

4. On the work of Mabillon and his *confrères* see B. Barret-Kriegel, *Les historiens et la monarchie*, 4 vols., Paris 1988; J. Mabillon, *Brèves réflexions sur quelques règles de l'histoire*, ed. B. Barret-Kriegel, Paris 1990.

5. Leibniz to Huet (as in n. 1), fol. 20r: "Sed haec obiter: interim suffecerit omnem eruditionis apparatum ad historiam sacram comprobandam, velut scopum potissimum dirigi debere. Quod cum a te felicissime factum esse non dubitem." On Huet's *Demonstratio evangelica*, Paris 1679, see O. Gruppe, *Geschichte der klassischen Mythologie und Religionsgeschichte*, Leipzig 1921, p. 52; A. Dupront, *Pierre-Daniel Huet et l'exégèse comparatiste au xviie siècle*, Paris 1930; D. C. Allen, *Mysteriously Meant*, Baltimore and London 1970, pp. 80–82; D. P. Walker, *The Ancient Theology*, London 1972; A. Shelford, "Faith and Glory: Pierre-Daniel Huet and the Making of the *Demonstratio evangelica* (1679)," Ph.D. diss.,

Princeton University 1997; C. R. Ligota, "Der apologetische Rahmen der Mythendeutung im Frankreich des 17. Jahrhunderts (P.-D. Huet)," in *Mythographie der frühen Neuzeit. Ihre Anwendung in den Künsten*, Wiesbaden 1984, pp. 149–161; A. Juillard, "Pierre-Daniel Huet," in *Grundriss der Geschichte der Philosophie*, ii: *Die Philosophie des 17. Jahrhunderts*, i, ed. J.-P. Schobinger, Basel 1993, pp. 142–153; A. Niderst, "Comparatisme et syncrétisme religieux de Huet," in *Pierre-Daniel Huet (1630–1721)* (Actes du Colloque de Caen, Nov. 1993), ed. S. Guellouz, Paris, Seattle, and Tübingen 1994, pp. 75–82; E. Rapetti, *Pierre-Daniel Huet: erudizione, filosofia, apologetica*, Milan 1999.

6. A. D. Momigliano, "Ancient History and the Antiquarian," *Journal of the Warburg and Courtauld Institutes*, xiii, 1950, pp. 285–315, repr. in his *Contributo alla storia degli studi classici*, Rome 1955, pp. 67–106.

7. Momigliano (as in n. 6), p. 89.

8. For his own second thoughts, see his *Classical Foundations of Modern Historiography*, ed. R. Di Donato, Berkeley 1993, chap. 3. See further *Ancient History and the Antiquarian: Essays in Memory of Arnaldo Momigliano*, ed. M. H. Crawford and C. R. Ligota, London 1995; A. Grafton, *The Footnote*, Cambridge, Mass. 1997, repr. 1999, pp. 171–189.

9. E. Eisenstein, *The Printing Press as an Agent of Change*, Cambridge 1987, p. 137; F. Waquet, "Qu'est-ce que la République des Lettres? Essai de sémantique historique," *Bibliothèque de l'Ecole des Chartes*, cxlvii, 1989, pp. 473–502.

10. For a rich and up-to-date survey of the Republic's institutions and customs see H. Bots and F. Waquet, *La République des Lettres*, Paris 1997. Also helpful are A. Goldgar, *Impolite Learning: Conduct and Community in the Republic of Letters, 1680–1750*, New Haven and London 1995; L. Daston, "The Ideal and Reality of the Republic of Letters in the Enlightenment," *Science in Context*, iv, 1991, pp. 367–386; and P. Dibon and F. Waquet, *Johannes Fredericus Gronovius pèlerin de la république des lettres*, Geneva 1984.

11. Thus Huet recalled his relations with his Protestant teacher Samuel Bochart as idyllic, despite their religious differences: P. D. Huet, *Commentarius de rebus ad eum pertinentibus*, Amsterdam 1718, p. 43: "Quamquam liquido asseverare possum, in tam familiari plurimorum annorum consuetudine, nullam unquam habitam esse inter nos de rebus ad fidem Christianam pertinentibus et litigiosis, non dico disputationem, sed ne collocutionem quidem, atque id utrumque nostrum studiose vitasse. Semel tantum delibata a nobis quaestio est de cultu imaginum, cum in Germania depictas et suspensas cerneremus tabulas in Lutheranorum templis; et leviter quidem delibata, atque amice et citra omnem contentionem." Similarly, Protestant scholars like Gisbert Cuperus made clear how much pleasure they received when Catholic scholars like Ludovico Antonio Muratori and Benedetto Bacchini sought their friendship. See "Lettres inédites de Gis-

bert Cuper à P. Daniel Huet et à divers correspondants," ed. L.-G. Pélissier, *Mémoires de l'Académie Nationale des Sciences, Arts et Belles-Lettres de Caen*, 1905, pp. 174, 183–184.

12. See Goldgar (as in n. 10); S. Shapin, *A Social History of Truth: Civility and Science in Seventeenth-Century England*, Chicago and London 1994. For a classic contemporary description of the way the Republic was supposed to function see *The Dictionary Historical and Critical of Mr Peter Bayle*, 2nd edn., London 1735, ii, p. 389, s.v. "Catius," under "D—making use of the Liberty, which prevails in the Common-Wealth of Learning": "This Common-Wealth is a State extremely free. The Empire of Truth and Reason is only acknowledged in it; and under their Protection an innocent War is waged against any one whatever."

13. See e.g. R. Weiss, *The Renaissance Discovery of Classical Antiquity*, revised edn., Oxford 1988; E. Mandowsky and C. Mitchell, *Pirro Ligorio's Roman Antiquities*, London 1963; *Pirro Ligorio, Artist and Antiquarian*, ed. R. W. Gaston, Florence 1988; W. McCuaig, *Carlo Sigonio: The Changing World of the Late Renaissance*, Princeton 1989; idem, "The *Fasti capitolini* and the Study of Roman Chronology in the Sixteenth Century," *Athenaeum*, lxxix, 1991, pp. 141–159; *Documentary Culture*, ed. E. Cropper et al., Florence 1992; *Antonio Agustín between Renaissance and Counter-Reform*, ed. M. H. Crawford, London 1993; J.-L. Ferrary, *Onofrio Panvinio et les antiquités romaines*, Rome 1996.

14. K. Pomian, *Collectionneurs, amateurs et curieux. Paris, Venise: xvie–xviiie siècle*, Paris 1987; A. Schnapper, *Le Géant, la licorne, la tulipe*, Paris 1988.

15. P. Findlen, *Possessing Nature: Museums, Collecting, and Scientific Culture in Early Modern Italy*, Berkeley, Los Angeles, and London 1994; H. Bredekamp, *The Lure of Antiquity and the Cult of the Machine*, tr. A. Brown, Princeton 1995; cf. G. Olmi, *L'inventario del mondo*, Bologna 1992; T. DaC. Kaufmann, *The Mastery of Nature*, Princeton 1993, pp. 174–194; and M. Kemp, "'Wrought by No Artist's Hand': The Natural, the Artificial, the Exotic and the Scientific in Some Artifacts from the Renaissance," *Reframing the Renaissance*, ed. C. Farago, New Haven and London 1995, pp. 177–196.

16. F. Haskell, *History and Its Images*, New Haven and London 1993, chaps 1–6.

17. Cuperus to Noris, 1 September 1688, "Lettres de Cuper," ed. Pélissier (as in n. 11), p. 169: "Magnum revera est hoc saeculo decus in patribus, auctoribus Graecis et Latinis, marmoribus et nummis interpretandis, unum eundemque virum tam probe versatum esse."

18. See in general G. Martini, "Le stravaganze filologiche di padre Jean Hardouin," *Scritti di paleografia e diplomatica in onore di V. Federici*, Florence 1944, pp. 351–364. A full bibliography of works by Hardouin and early responses to them appears in A. and A. De Backer, *Bibliothèque de la Société de Jésus*, ed. C. Sommervogel, repr. Héverlé-Louvain 1960, s.v. "Hardouin, Jean." For his

theological position see A. Kors, *Atheism in France,* i, *The Orthodox Sources of Disbelief,* Princeton 1990, pp. 343–344 n. 69, 366–367.

19. Montfaucon to Gattola, 12 September 1699, quoted by H. Quentin, *Jean-Dominique Mansi et les grandes collections conciliaires,* Paris 1900, p. 39 n. 1.

20. *Acta conciliorum et epistolae decretales ac constitutiones summorum pontificum,* ed. J. Hardouin, Paris 1714–1715, 11 vols., i, cols. 1–2 (frontispiece), and xi, cols. 1631–42 (*Unigenitus*).

21. See L. Doutreleau, "L'Assemblée du clergé de France et l'édition patristique grecque au xviie siècle," *Les Pères de l'Eglise au xviie siècle,* ed. E. Bury and B. Meunier, Paris 1993, pp. 99–116.

22. *Acta conciliorum* (as in n. 20), i, p. ii: "Praefationes edere ab iis praemissas qui Concilia ante nos ediderunt, nullius visum est usus esse: cum nihil fere complectantur, praeter laudationem Conciliorum, quae quis esse sacrosancta nescit? vel commendationem sui laboris suaeque diligentiae; quam quis summa laude dignam esse non ultro fateatur?" In the end, Jesuit *pietas* triumphed over editorial economy, and Hardouin did include Jacques Sirmond's notes on the councils in vol. xi (cols. 1683–1772).

23. Ibid., i, p. xii: "Manuscriptis codicibus usi sumus in primis e Bibliotheca nostra Parisiensi, in qua sunt collecti dudum a P. Sirmondo plurimi: praeter varias lectiones quas in Concilia pleraque Gallicana collatione plurimorum exemplarium manu eiusdem descriptas servamus. Nam Concilia ipsa Gallicana omnia vetera, quae Labbeus postea edidit, descripserat ipse perquam accurate. Alios dum appellamus codices, quibus usi sunt Labbeus et Baluzius, hos eorumdem fide, quae sane est certa tutaque, laudamus. Regios saepenumero praeterea Colbertinosque consuluimus: sed cum eosdem concordare cum nostris plerumque animadvertimus, nostros appellare satis habuimus. Denique alios etiam non paucos, qui suis locis a nobis indicabuntur."

24. Ibid.: "Cetero Conciliorum pauciora, quam ceterorum librorum, in bibliothecis exemplaria manuscripta sunt, sed et plerumque emendatiora: quae causa est cur pauciores in his, quam in illis, expectandae lectiones variae sint."

25. Ibid., p. vii: "Nicaeni Concilii subscriptiones ceterorumque Conciliorum exhibemus ex manuscriptis codicibus, qui expressi ex primigenio exemplari possunt videri."

26. Ibid., p. xii: "A Graeca interim oratione subinde discrepare Latinam ex vetusto codice acceptam, in ipsis etiam episcoporum subscriptionibus nemo miretur: manuscriptos codices, qui in utroque sermone visi sunt optimi, nunc quidem summa religione sequimur, alias Deo dante, causam discriminis indagaturi."

27. Quentin (as in n. 19), pp. 38–54; see also C. J. Hefele, *Histoire des Conciles,* i, Paris 1907, pp. 97–110.

28. J. Hardouin, *Ad censuram scriptorum veterum prolegomena,* London 1766, pp. 15–16: "Nos mense Augusto anni 1690 coepimus in Augustino et aequalibus fraudem subodorari; in omnibus mense Novembri suspicati sumus: totam deteximus mense Maio anni 1692, prolixis ex singulis scriptoribus Graecis Latinisque descriptis excerptis: quo in labore paene ad fastidium, sed interiecta persaepe summa ex vero detecto oblectatione, desudavimus." I use the English translation by E. Johnson, *The Prolegomena of Jean Hardouin,* Sydney 1909, pp. 10–11, with some changes.

29. J. Hardouin, *Chronologiae ex nummis antiquis restitutae prolusio de nummis Herodiadum,* Paris 1693, p. 60: "Afferam hoc loco non inanis quidem semper conjectoris, sed nunc tamen plus justo fortassis suspiciosi ingenioque nimium indulgentis hominis conjecturam. Accipiet quisque, ut volet. Deprehendit ille, ut quidem mussitabat nuper nobiscum, coetum certorum hominum ante saecula nescio quot extitisse, qui historiae veteris concinnandae partes suscepissent, qualem nunc habemus, cum nulla tunc exstaret: sibi probe notam illorum aetatem atque officinam esse: inque eam rem istis subsidio fuisse Tullium, Plinium, Maronis Georgica, Flacci sermones et epistolas: nam haec ille sola censet, quod vereor ut cuiquam suadeat, ex omni Latina antiquitate sincera esse monumenta, praeter inscriptiones admodum paucas Fastosque nonnullos." Tr. Johnson (as in n. 28), pp. xix–xx.

30. Hardouin (as in n. 28), p. 172: "Ut historiam Romanam Graecamque conficerent, nomina virorum multa desumpsere ex nummis antiquis, quorum habuere magnam supellectilem."

31. Mathurin Veyssière de Lacroze, *Vindiciae veterum scriptorum contra J. Harduinium,* Rotterdam 1708, p. 22.

32. For Genevrat's "Permissio" see Hardouin, *Chronologia* (as in n. 29), p. [112]. On the effort to suppress the *Prolusio* see B. Neveu, *Erudition et religion aux xviie et xviiie siècles,* Paris 1994, p. 58, quoting the account of Father Léonard de Sainte-Catherine: "le 7 janvier 1693, le P. Ayrault [Hurault] jésuite, recteur du Collège de Louis le Grand, et autres allèrent chez Anisson [pour] emporter tous les exemplaires" of the *Prolusio.* Léonard remarked of Hardouin: "Il n'ose dire tout ce qu'il pense. Il avoit promis de faire réimprimer sa dissertation *De nummis Herodiadum*—ou s'il le fait, il sera contraint d'en retrancher tout ce qu'il y avoit de plus curieux." For the notion that the Jesuits hoped to drive up prices see Veyssière de Lacroze (as in n. 31), p. 8.

33. J. Hardouin, *Opera selecta,* Amsterdam 1709, pp. 357–370, 645–654.

34. See Hardouin, *Opera selecta* (as in n. 33), pp. 525–527; and Veyssière de Lacroze (as in n. 31), p. 80, quoting Hardouin, *Chronologia:* "Manethon fit ex MAN voce Germanica, quae hominem sonat; (ut *Mansur* hominem Syrum significat:)

deinde ex *et cum*, et *on virtus*. Homo igitur, vel *filius hominis cum virtute*, ut apud Matthaeum legitur, cap. xxiv.30, Christus est."

35. Veyssière de Lacroze (as in n. 31), p. 96: "deus redemtor." In this case Veyssière de Lacroze relied on the criticisms directed at Hardouin by George Hickes in the "Praefatio" to his *Linguarum veterum septentrionalium thesaurus*, i, Oxford 1703, pp. xxiii–xxiv.

36. J. Hardouin, "Pseudo Virgilius. Observationes in Aeneidem," in his *Opera varia*, Amsterdam and The Hague 1733, p. 280: "Virgilio numquam venit in mentem Aeneidem scribere."

37. Ibid., p. 284: "sed sunt mere ludicra et fabulosa, ut ligneolae atque automatae hominum effigies, *des marionnettes*."

38. Ibid., p. 294, on *Aeneid*, ii.753–754: "Quomodo potuit, in tenebris praesertim, notare vel observare vestigia?"

39. Ibid.

40. Ibid., p. 289, on *Aeneid*, i.462: "Dictum prorsus insolenter, pro eo quod est: Hic etiam commiserationi locus est, ob res adversas, quae calamitosis accidunt."

41. For Plato see Paris, Bibliothèque Nationale MSS lat. 6573, 6574, and 8799; for the tragedians and Pindar see MS 6574, ii ("De poetis Graecis").

42. Paris, Bibliothèque Nationale MS lat. 2746, p. 117, "Antitheta puerilia," on *Confessions*, viii.5 ("sed modo et modo, non habebat modum"); and p. 119 on viii.7: "Non satis digna certe adolescente ingenioso ad Deum oratio haec fuit."

43. Paris, Bibliothèque Nationale MS lat. 12015.

44. Paris, Bibliothèque Nationale MS lat. 2746, p. 118, on *Confessions*, viii.6: "Vitae Antonii ab Athanasio scriptae conciliare vult fidem et auctoritatem."

45. See in general A. Grafton, *Forgers and Critics*, Princeton 1990; R. Bizzocchi, *Genealogie incredibili*, Bologna 1995; the essays published in *Quaderni storici*, n.s. xciii.3, 1996, on the theme of "Erudizione e fonti"; and C. Ginzburg, *History, Rhetoric and Proof*, Hanover and London, 1999, pp. 54–70.

46. *Huetiana, ou pensées diverses*, Amsterdam 1723, chap. xix, pp. 51–52: "Le public n'a pas été moins injuste envers M. Chapelain. Je n'ai jamais consenti au jugement que le public a fait de sa Pucelle . . . Il n'appartient pas à tout le monde de juger du Poëme Epique. Ce droit est reservé à un très-petit nombre de personnes; et tout le monde l'a usurpé contre la Pucelle. On a jugé du Poëme Epique sur les régles des Sonnets et des Madrigaux . . . Quel jugement feroient aujourd'hui ces Critiques délicats de l'Iliade d'Homére, si elle n'avoit jamais paru, avec tant de vers négligez, tant de répétitions ennuyeuses, et tant de défauts qu'on y a remarquez?" In fact, many seventeenth-century critics—including a number of members of the Society of Jesus—condemned Homer on exactly these grounds. See N. Hepp, *Homère en France au XVIIe siècle*, Paris 1968, pp. 396–434, 521–563.

47. *Huetiana* (as in n. 46), chap. xxvii, pp. 70–71: "Les Jesuites communé-
ment écrivent et parlent bien en latin, mais leur latinité péche presque toûjours en
ce qu'elle est trop oratoire. Cela vient de ce que dès leur premiere jeunesse on les
fait regenter. Ces regences les engagent à parler incessamment en public; ils s'ac-
coûtument insensiblement à le faire d'un stile soûtenu et arrangé, et à s'élever
au-dessus du genre mediocre. Cela se remarque clairement dans les Lettres du
P. Petau: il va toûjours par courbettes, et jamais au pas; par periodes nombreuses,
par figures étudiées, et jamais par cette admirable simplicité des Epîtres de
Ciceron, qui tout grand Orateur qu'il étoit, savoit bien cesser de l'être, quand il le
falloit. Quand les Lettres du P. Petau parurent, on en fit comparaison avec celles de
Scaliger. Cette question donna lieu à une grande dispute chez Messieurs Dupuy,
où étoit le réduit ordinaire des Savans de Paris. Les gens de Collége se déclarerent
pour le P. Petau: Mais M. Guyet, homme d'un goût rafiné, mais avec des manieres
dures, leur dit pour toute réponse, qu'ils meritoient qu'on leur présentât du foin.
M. Guyet avoit raison."

48. Ibid., chap. lxiv, p. 173: "Les bon juges de le Poesie sont plus rares que les
bons Poetes."

49. Veyssière de Lacroze (as in n. 31), pp. 101–107.

50. See in general A. Borst, *Der Turmbau von Babel: Geschichte der Meinungen
über Ursprung und Vielfalt der Sprachen und Völker,* 4 vols., Stuttgart 1957–1963;
D. Droixhe, *La linguistique et l'appel de l'histoire (1600–1800),* Geneva 1978.

51. Paris, Bibliothèque Nationale MSS lat. 3422, 3452A.

52. Paris, Bibliothèque Nationale MS lat. 3647, pp. 275–276: "Chaldaicae
quae dicuntur voces apud Esdram et Danielem, tam mihi videntur esse Hebraeae,
quam sunt eae Gallicae, quibus nunc utimur, quamvis eis caruerit aetas Francisci I
aut alio nunc sint exitu verborum."

53. Paris, Bibliothèque Nationale MS lat. 1583, p. 1.

54. Hardouin, *Prolegomena* (as in n. 28), p. 2: "Atqui si vel una in aliquo
instrumento notatio temporis vitiosa sit, in foro confestim magno animorum con-
sensu, magnisque, sed iustis, clamoribus, reiicitur ac repudiatur instrumentum;
quanto vehementius ac iustius vociferandum est, cum sacrosancta Religio petitur
et labefactatur?" Tr. Johnson (as in n. 28), p. 2.

55. Ibid., pp. 203–205.

56. Hardouin, *Opera selecta* (as in n. 33), p. 282: "Proh! quot adminiculis fulta
Aeneis est, ut sincera ac genuina Virgilii lucubratio fuisse credatur! 1° Testimoniis
innumeris, Ovidii, Juvenalis, Statii, Silii Italici, Martialis, Propertii, Quintiliani,
Asconii Pediani, Taciti in dialogo de Oratoribus, aliorumque; ut eos qui Ecclesiastici dicuntur scriptores omittamus, qui plurimi certe sunt, sed aeque supposititi-
tii, proximi sequentis aevi et fabricae. 2° Comparatione cum Homero ficta a

Macrobio. 3° Fictis tum Aeneidomastigibus, qui Aeneida vituperarint, tum illius defensoribus, ut a Donato fingitur in vita Virgilii: tum denique Servio Scholiaste, qui ut aeque vetusta eiusdemque vatis partus credatur Aeneis ac cetera, in Bucolica Georgicaque, quemadmodum in Aeneidem, scholia conscripsit."

57. Hardouin, *Prolegomena* (as in n. 28), p. 188: "Habuit coetus impius Mathematicos computatores eclipseon, Iureconsultos conditores codicum ac legum, Medicos qui de medicina scriberent, Poetas, qui carmina ederent, linguarum peritos interpretes sibi addictos, qui scripta a se Latine, in Graecum potissimum sermonem, sed et in Hebraeum Arabicumque converterent." Tr. Johnson (as in n. 28), p. 133.

58. Paris, Bibliothèque Nationale MS lat. 1584, fol. 43v.

59. Descartes, *Discours de la méthode*, part 1; *Oeuvres philosophiques*, ed. F. Alquié, Paris 1988, i, pp. 573–574.

60. See Momigliano (as in n. 6); C. Borghero, *La certezza e la storia*, Milan 1983; M. Völkel, *Pyrrhonismus historicus*, Frankfurt am Main 1987. B. Dooley, *The Social History of Skepticism*, Baltimore and London 1999, sets these developments into a wider context.

61. Jacques Spon, *Recherches curieuses d'antiquité*, Lyons 1683, Préface, sig. a4r: "En effect, ce Siecle semble estre un Siecle de nouvelles inventions." Ibid., sig. a4v: "et enfin les Antiquaires ne se sont pas moins donné de peine à faire des découvertes dans le pays vaste et curieux de l'Antiquité. On a deterré des Medailles anciennes de tous les Regnes et de tous les Empires; on a déchifré mille curiositez des anciens Romains, qui ne paroissoient à nos Peres que des Lettres muettes destituées d'esprit et de mistere." Note how the modern notion of geographical discovery justifies the study of the historical past.

62. Jacques Spon, *Miscellanea eruditae antiquitatis*, Lyons 1685, Praefatio, sig. a3r: "Archaeographia est declaratio sive notitia antiquorum monumentorum, quibus veteres sui temporis religionem, historiam, politicam, aliasque tum artes tum scientias propagare posterisque tradere studuerunt." Cf. R. Rappaport, *When Geologists Were Historians, 1665–1750*, Ithaca and London 1997, esp. chaps 2–3.

63. Momigliano (as in n. 6), pp. 79–94.

64. Johann Burkhard Mencke, *Dissertationes litterariae*, Leipzig 1734, pp. 112–124, 80–92; Johann August Ernesti, *Opuscula philologica critica*, Leiden 1776, p. 82.

65. Hardouin, *Opera selecta* (as in n. 33), p. 358, where he quotes an extract from Jacques Basnage's *Histoire des Juifs*, which Ballonffeaux had sent him, according to which Hardouin's genealogy "renverse toutes les idées qu'on en avoit eües jusqu'à présent;" and p. 367, "Je fais profession de rejetter comme mensonge tout ce qui est opposé à la verité; c'est-à-dire, tout témoignage purement humain, qui est contraire à l'Ecriture sainte: et tout témoignage particulier touchant les faits

purement historiques, quand il est détruit par un témoignage public, tel qu'est celui des médailles, qui n'ont jamais été frappées que de l'aveu des Princes, ou des Magistrats legitimes."

66. For Hardouin's status see P. Kinns, "Two Eighteenth-Century Studies of Coin Hoards: Bayer and Pellerin," *Medals and Coins from Budé to Mommsen*, ed. M. H. Crawford et al., London 1990, pp. 101–114.

67. See M. Jones, "'Proof Stones of History': The Status of Medals as Historical Evidence in Seventeenth-Century France," in *Medals and Coins* (as in n. 66), pp. 53–72.

68. J. Cunnally, *Images of the Illustrious*, Princeton 1999, chap. 12.

69. P. Burke, *The Fabrication of Louis XIV*, New Haven and London 1992.

70. Jean Mabillon, *De re diplomatica libri vi*, Paris 1681, iii.6, p. 241: "IV Non ex sola scriptura, neque ex uno solo characterismo, sed ex omnibus simul de vetustis chartis pronuntiandum. Neque enim unum est in uno saeculo unave provincia scripturae genus, sed varia, ut de nostro experiri licet: nec possumus omnes unius saeculi scripturas ad amussim repraesentari. V Unum aut alterum defectum, modo essentialis non sit, legitimis autographis obesse non debere: cum in sinceris diplomatibus nonnullis, quae vidimus, quidam occurrant ejusmodi leviores defectus . . . VII Historicorum aut inscriptionum testimonia legitimis chartis non ita praejudicare debere, ut illorum praeferatur auctoritas."

71. Ibid., p. 242: "Sed ut ad nostra veniamus, quis in assignando die unctionis Ludovici Magni, modo feliciter regnantis, numismatum hac de re cusorum fidem et auctoritatem non praeferat quibusvis aliis monumentis? Et tamen mutato indicto die, quatuor aut quinque diebus posterior fuit regia coronatio, ut omnibus notum est. Non ergo semper in diplomatum praejudiciam citari debent historici et tituli, quantumvis authentici et aequales."

72. Paris, Bibliothèque Nationale MS lat 6216A, p. 28: "Neque enim anulus ibi repertus aut regius est, aut Childerici. Ponderosior est ille, quam ut digito ferri commode possit. Ex illo genere anulorum aureorum est, quos in pugnis ludicris equestribus donare victoribus solebant feminae nobiles, quae aderant spectatrices . . . Ejus generis, inquam, anulus ille aureus est, cujus pondus persaepe mirati sumus in Bibliotheca Regia, ubi asservatur. Quod si Regis ille anulus fuit, cur Rex ipse ibi diademato capite non est, aut cincto lapillis, ut in suis nummis Clodoveus, Clotarius, ceterique omnes?" There is a draft of this text in MS lat. 6226A. The publication in question was J.-J. Chifflet, *Anastasis Childerici I, Francorum regis, sive thesaurus sepulchralis Tornaci Nerviorum effossus, et commentario illustratus*, Antwerp 1655.

73. Paris, Bibliothèque Nationale MS lat 6216A, p. 131: "Similitudo maxima fabricae et characterum inter nummos Pipini et Caroli qui sequitur, omnino suadet Pipino Carolum proxime successisse."

74. Simon to the Marquis de Caumont, 6 November 1717, Paris, Bibliothèque Nationale, MS nouv. acq. fr. 11636, fol. 145r-v: "J'ay leu avec attention le Catalogue des Medailles qui ne se trouvent point dans le Livre de Mr Vaillant. Il n'est point estonnant que l'on decouvre tous les jours des Medailles dont il n'a point eu connoissance, bien qu'il eust veu des principaux Cabinets de l'Europe. Ce qu'on pouroit plus justement lui reprocher, c'est de s'estre trop fié a sa memoire dans la citation qu'il en fait. C'est aussi ce qui est arrivé au P. Hardouin, quelque habile antiquaire qu'il soit, qui attribue quantité de medailles au Cabinet du Roy qui n'y ont jamais esté." On the Cabinet in this period see T. Sarmant, *Le Cabinet des Médailles de la Bibliothèque Nationale*, Paris 1994.

75. See e.g. Paris, Bibliothèque Nationale, MS lat 8799, p. 6, where Hardouin argued that Montfaucon had inferred the age of the Vienna Dioscorides only from an illustration and its captions. Cf. also ibid., p. 1: "Sed spem tanti absolvendi operis aetas provectior adimit. Igitur de aetate dumtaxat eorum codicum, qui sunt celebriores, ferre iudicium aggredimur. Huius generis in primis sunt circiter ducenti, quos in Palaeographia sua Graeca domnus Bernardus de Montfaucon Benedictinus laudat, desumptis optima fide librariorum, sive, ut appellant, calligraphorum subscriptionibus: ex quibus codicum singulorum agnosci certo aetatem vulgo existimant. Nihil autem esse eo iudicio incertius fallaciusve, nunc nobis propositum est demonstrare: atque ex illis ipsis subscriptionibus sive notationibus temporis, praeter alia argumenta, quae ex ipsa librorum materia petuntur, evinci posse contendimus; nullum ex centenis codicibus quos vir eruditus profert, ante saeculum xiv. exaratos, ut arbitratur, saeculo ipso decimo quarto vetustiorem esse: nullum ex totidem, qui sequuntur, non multo recentiorem esse anno eo, quem subscriptio codicis praefert. Ex eo autem consequitur, vix ullum esse ex his codicibus, qui non haberi debeat pro primigenio codice, accuratius post adversaria exarato, ipsiusmet auctoris iussu. Excipiendi ex hoc numero sunt duo omnino, supra omnem dubitationem vel suspicionem vetusti scriptores, Homerus et Herodotus; quibus nihilominus similes subscriptiones subdiderunt, ut aequalis omnino conditio putetur esse." Cf. also Hardouin's attack on Mabillon in MS lat 6216A, p. 114: "Non nostri est instituti omnia quae iam prodiere a Mabillonio aliisve edita diplomata singulatim excutere: quaedam solummodo obiter indicamus, quae cum indubitato nummorum veterum testimonio pugnant, ac proinde cum ipsa rerum veritate. Omnia paene corruere ex positis hactenus observationibus intelligent viri sagaces."

76. A. Grafton, *Joseph Scaliger: A Study in the History of Classical Scholarship*, 2 vols., Oxford 1983 and 1993, ii, chap. 4.12.

77. Isaac Casaubon, *De rebus sacris et ecclesiasticis exercitationes xvi*, Geneva 1654, p. 207: "Nullam occasionem praetermittit Baronius, sive iustam, sive iniustam, detrahendi Iosepho, historico nobilissimo, quicquid ingrati Iosephomastiges

muginentur . . . cuius libros nisi providentia Dei singularis ad nostra servasset tempora, in quantis rerum Iudaicarum tenebris hodie versaremur? quot fabulas, quot mendacia iubar historiae Iosephi discutit?" See A. Grafton, *Defenders of the Text*, Cambridge, Mass., and London 1991, chap. 7.

78. Hardouin, *Opera selecta* (as in n. 33), p. 358: "Quand on trouve que Josephe, et Dion qui l'a suivi, sont opposés aux témoignages du S. Esprit dans les livres sacrés, et à celui des Magistrats publics, qui ont fait frapper les Médailles, on est quitte pour dire dans ces occasions-là de Josephe, ce que le Cardinal Baronius et bien d'autres en ont déjà dit: *Scriptor mendacissimus.*"

79. See R. R. Palmer, *Catholics and Unbelievers in Eighteenth-Century France*, Princeton 1939, pp. 65–69; B. Schwarzbach, "Antidocumentalist Apologetics: Hardouin and Yeshayahu Leibowitz," *Revue de théologie et de philosophie*, cxv, 1983, pp. 373–390.

80. I. Uri, *François Guyet (1575–1655) d'après des documents inédits*, Paris 1886.

81. Pierre Bayle, *Historical and Critical Dictionary*, London 1734–1738, s.v. "Guyet."

82. See Grafton (as in n. 76), i, chap. 6; and ii, pp. 706–707.

83. O. F. Gruppe, *Minos. Über die Interpolationen in den römischen Dichtern*, Leipzig 1859, pp. 135–140. Huet identified Guyet as one of those nonpedantic readers, like himself, who could appreciate the need for stylistic variation. *Huetiana* (as in n. 46), p. 71.

84. Hardouin, *Opera varia* (as in n. 36), p. 288.

85. J. Masson, *Jani templum Christo nascente reseratum*, Rotterdam 1700, sig. ***v.

86. Cf. R. Colie, *Light and Enlightenment*, Cambridge 1957.

87. . See P. Rossi, *Le sterminate antichità*, Pisa 1969; and idem, *I segni del tempo*, Milan 1979 = *The Dark Abyss of Time*, tr. L. G. Cochrane, Chicago and London 1984.

88. Hardouin, *Opera selecta* (as in n. 33); for Hickes's *Thesaurus* see above, n. 35.

89. See C. L. Hulbert-Powell, *John James Wettstein, 1693–1754*, London [1938], chap. ii; A. Fox, *John Mill and Richard Bentley*, Oxford 1954, pp. 119–121; and *The Correspondence of Richard Bentley, D. D.*, London 1842, ii, pp. 518–519, 521–522.

90. Neveu (as in n. 32), p. 59.

91. Hardouin, *Acta conciliorum* (as in n. 22), i, ep. ded., sigs. aiiv–aiiir, aivr–v.

92. Veyssière de Lacroze (as in n. 31), pp. 3–18.

93. B. Pascal, *Les provinciales*, ed. L. Cognet, Paris 1965, Lettre 17, pp. 332–333. For a full discussion of the way in which Hardouin, the author of a conspiracy theory on the grand scale, became the object of one in his turn, see M. Mulsow, *Die Drei Ringe* (forthcoming). Mulsow also offers a full account of Lacroze.

94. On the effects of confessional loyalties see *Commercium litterarium, 1600–1750: la communication dans la République des Lettres,* ed. H. Bots and F. Waquet, Amsterdam 1994.

95. H. Lacombe de Prezel, *Dictionnaire des portraits historiques, anecdotes et traits remarquables des hommes illustres,* 3 vols., Paris 1768, ii, p. 179: "Hardouin lui répondit brusquement: 'Hé, croyez-vous donc que je me serai levé toute ma vie à quatre heures du matin pour ne dire que ce que d'autres avoient déjà dit avant moi?'"

96. Hardouin, *Opera selecta* (as in n. 33), Praefatio, sigs. A3r–*4v. For Grotius's letter to J. Bignon see H. Grotius, *De veritate religionis christianae,* ed. J. Le Clerc, Glasgow 1745, ep. ded., 17 August 1639, sig. b3r.

97. On efforts at conflict resolution in the Republic of Letters see Daston (as in n. 10).

98. See A. Lombard, *L'Abbé Du Bos: un initiateur de la pensée moderne (1670–1742),* Paris 1913, repr. Geneva 1969, pp. 5–38, on Du Bos's *Histoire des Quatre Gordiens, prouvée et illustrée par les Médailles,* Paris 1695. For Cuperus's critique of Du Bos see Lombard, pp. 37–8.

99. See Cuperus to Bacchini, 11 July 1699, in "Lettres de Cuper," ed. Pélissier (as in n. 11), pp. 189–190: "Est certe Harduinus in explicandis nummis veteribus versatissimus, sed nemo eruditorum ignorat eum multa paradoxa et a prompto ingenio non satis examinata in medium proferre . . . Plurimi equidem facio viri eruditionem; sed tamen nescio qua fronte rejicere possit tot veterum auctorum testimonia . . ."

100. See e.g. L. Gossman, *Medievalism and the Ideologies of the Enlightenment,* Baltimore 1968, pp. 223–228; S. Timpanaro, *La genesi del metodo del Lachmann,* repr. of 2nd edn., Padua 1985, pp. 13–15.

101. A. Pope, *The Dunciad Variorum with the Prolegomena of Scriblerus,* London 1723, repr. Princeton 1929, pp. 99–103.

102. T. J. Meijer, *Kritiek als herwaardering. Het levenswerk van Jacobus Perizonius (1651–1715),* Leiden 1971, esp. pp. 151–152.

103. Hardouin's propensity to scholarly radicalism did not make him sympathetic to any and all revisionist theses. In 1729 he wrote "the most venomous French assault" on Newton's effort to revise the chronology of the ancient world. See F. E. Manuel, *Isaac Newton, Historian,* Cambridge, Mass., 1963, p. 177.

104. J. B. Mencke, *De charlataneria eruditorum declamationes duae,* Leipzig 1715, pp. 33–35.

105. *Journal des Sçavans,* Supplément, janv. 1707, p. 194.

106. See J.-A. de Thou, *Historiarum sui temporis libri cxxv,* Paris 1609, i, p. 22: "Cum Iulio II non eandem amicitiam coluit Ludovicus, quippe eum infestissi-

mum hostem semper expertus, quem gratissimum amicum habere debuit. Quae odia eo evaserunt, ut temere et iniuriose rex a pontifice proscriptus primo Lugduni Synodo praesulum regni convocata ipsum in ius vocaverit, dein auctoritate quorumdam Cardinalium Mediolani congregatorum concilium Pisis indixerit, in quo de emendando ecclesiae statu ageretur, et iuxta regulam ultimi concilii Constantiae sub Sigismundo celebrati, in caput et membra anquireretur. Quin et eo usque provectus est, ut spretis multis multorum, quibus alioqui plurimum tribuebat, suasionibus, moribundi senis inaneis diras contraria obnuntatione generose revicerit, cuso etiam Neapoli aureo numo, qui effigiem suam ex una parte, et insignia Neapolis ac Siciliae ex altera referebat, cum hoc elogio, PERDAM BABYLONIS NOMEN; quales adhuc hodie multi reperiuntur."

107. C. S. Liebe, *Prodromi reformationis pia memoria recolendae sive nummi Ludovici XII regis Gallorum epigraphe: Perdam Babylonis nomen,* Leipzig 1717, in which Hardouin's discussions of the question are both reprinted and opposed at length. See esp. pp. 72–73: "Harduinus igitur, qui religionis, quam profitetur, studio ductus, concoquere non potuit, Romam Babylonis nomine ab optimo principum traduci ac reddi detestabilem." Liebe also reprints the scholarly correspondence discussed in the text, ibid., pp. 125–164.

108. B. Anderson, *Imagined Communities,* London 1983; rev. edn., London and New York 1991; *The Invention of Tradition,* ed. E. Hobsbawm and T. Ranger, Cambridge and New York 1983.

11. Petronius and Neo-Latin Satire

1. Schöbinger to Goldast, 1603, in *Titi Petronii Arbitri Satyricon quae supersunt,* ed. P. Burman, Utrecht 1709, p. 276; on Goldast and Schöbinger see B. Hertenstein, *Joachim von Watt (Vadianus), Bartholomäus Schöbinger, Melchior Goldast,* Berlin and New York 1975.

2. Burman (as in n. 1), ii, pp. 265–266.

3. J.-K. Huysmans, *À rebours,* Paris 1918, chap. iii, pp. 41–42.

4. See the three editions by K. Müller, 1961, 1965, 1978, and *Texts and Transmission,* ed. L. D. Reynolds, Oxford 1983, pp. 295–300 (by M. D. Reeve).

5. *The Satyrical Works of Titus Petronius Arbiter,* London 1708, preface; *Satyricon,* ed. C. G. Antonius, Leipzig 1781, p. xii.

6. K. F. C. Rose, "The Petronian Inquisition: An Auto-da-Fé," *Arion,* v, 1966, pp. 275–301. Rose's own name has now been added to the Petronian *chronique scandaleuse* by W. Hübner, "Ein Skandalon der Petronphilologie," *Gymnasium,* xcvi, 1989, pp. 129–132.

7. A. Rini, *Petronius in Italy,* New York 1937.

8. Gronovius to Heinsius, 9 July 1664, in *Sylloge epistolarum a viris illustribus scriptarum,* ed. P. Burman, Leiden 1727, iii, p. 504; Heinsius to Falconerius, 17 August 1664, v, p. 499.

9. Schefferus to Heinsius, 16 August 1664, Burman (as in n. 8), v, p. 69; Heinsius to Falconerius, 17 August 1664, v, p. 499; Heinsius to Schefferus, 6 February 1672, v, p. 139. For a fine account of these debates and the world they raged in see F. F. Blok, *Nicolaas Heinsius in dienst van Christina van Zweden,* Delft 1949.

10. E.g. K. F. C. Rose, *The Date and Author of the Satyricon,* Leiden 1971, p. 7.

11. Heinsius to Falconerius, 17 August 1664; Burman (as in n. 8), v, p. 499: "Soloeca quippe et semibarbara illic non pauca occurrunt, quae Petronio ipsi excidisse absit, ut credamus;" Heinsius to Gronovius, 16 August 1664, iii, p. 508.

12. Burman (as in n. 1), i, p. 174.

13. See the Appendix at the end of this essay.

14. J. F. Gronovius, *Observationum libri tres,* Leiden 1662, I.xxiii, p. 184; Burman (as in n. 1), i, *praefatio.*

15. *Petronii Arbitri Satyricon,* Paris 1577, "De Petronio" = Burman (as in n. 1), ii, pp. 254–255; P. Daniel, *praefatio,* ibid., p. 256 (Daniel was skeptical); J. Durant de Chazelle, *Variae lectiones* I.v, ibid., p. 260; J. Dousa, *Praecidanea* III.ii, ibid., p. 50, drawing on Jerome's attribution to Petronius of a line of Martial (*Ep.* 130.19); Goldast, *Prolegomena,* ibid., p. 265; Gonzales de Salas, *Commenta,* ibid., e.g. p. 100. Cf. Rose (as in n. 10) for a crisp account. Modern scholars name the author T. Petronius Niger and date the work to 63–66 C.E., but disagree about its original scope and size. Cf. J. P. Sullivan, *The Satyricon of Petronius,* Bloomington 1968, and P. G. Walsh, *The Roman Novel,* Cambridge 1970, chaps. 4–5 and appendix 1.

16. I. Casaubon, *De Satyrica Graecorum poesi et Romanorum Satira libri duo,* Halle 1774, II.ii, pp. 199–202; II.iv, p. 259.

17. For a fine survey see J. IJsewijn, "Neo-Latin Literature: *sermo* and *satyra menippea," Classical Influences on European Literature, A.D. 1500–1700,* ed. R. R. Bolgar, Cambridge 1976, pp. 41–55.

18. See D. Fleming's edition of Barclay, Nieuwkoop 1973, and Casaubon's letter in *Satirae duae,* Leiden 1617, sig. [*8]ʳ⁻ᵛ: "quam docti et salsi sales: quam alta denique et profunda atque effluens eruditio tua in singulis prope verbis apparet"; "Placuit etiam filium meum natu maximum ad epularum tuarum delicias admittere ac propterea Satiram tuam cum eo relegi, ut quae minus assequeretur, ea ipse interpretarer."

19. For England cf. Barclay, *Satyricon* II.xxx–xxxii and *Icon animorum* iv; for Italy I.xxx and vi; I use the edn. of Leiden 1674. For Leibniz, *Allgemeiner politischer and historischer Briefwechsel,* v *(1687–1690),* Berlin 1954, pp. 439–440.

20. "A huge vessel full of unmixed Falernian was carried in . . . Hilarion im-

mediately ordered it to be brought to him and, when he had washed his sweating face and hands in it, belched violently two or three times and, thrusting down his throat a vomiting thong, he threw up the contents of his stomach—an appalling spectacle . . . His companions did not hold back, one contributing slimy snot from his nostrils, another stinking spittle, another the liquid product of tallow candles . . . others disgusting dog-shit, others whatever nastiness the sluttish brooms of servants had missed—and some even emptied into it the contents of their bladders." [F. Guyet], *Gaeomemphionis Cantaliensis Satyricon 1628,* ed. J. Desjardins, Leiden 1972, xcv; cf. her translation, Geneva 1972, pp. 99–100.

21. For Scioppius see the anonymous *De satyra* in Barclay, *Satyricon* (as in n. 19), sig. [* 6]ʳ. On this one point Joseph Scaliger agreed with his most vicious assailant: *Secunda Scaligerana,* s.v. Barclaeus, ed. P. Desmaizeaux, Amsterdam 1740, ii, p. 216: "Il y a bien des fautes que tout le monde ne connoistra pas, comme aux vers de Monsieur de Bèze il y a beaucoup de Gallicismes."

22. A. Collignon, *Pétrone en France,* Paris 1905, p. 42; cf. IJsewijn (as in n. 17).

23. G. Pellissier [C. I. Brugère de Barante], *Observations sur le Petrone trouvé à Belgrade en 1688,* Paris 1694, pp. 50–59, and Nodot's reply, *La contre-critique de Petrone,* Paris 1700, pp. 65ff. The whole story is elegantly told by W. Stolz, *Petrons Satyricon und François Nodot (ca. 1650–ca. 1710),* Stuttgart 1987.

24. G. B. Pio, *Annotationes posteriores* xl, as entered by an early reader in the copy of the 1604 Raphelengius edition in Columbia University Library (Gonzalez Lodge 1604 P 448), on a blank leaf at the front.

25. Lipsius, *Epistolicae quaestiones* III.ii, *Opera omnia quae ad criticam proprie spectant,* Leiden 1596, pp. 299–300; Burman (as in n. 1), ii, pp. 271–272 (on the identity of Tacitus's Petronius and the author of the *Satyricon*).

26. Erasmus, *Paraphrasis in elegantias L. Vallae,* ed. C. L. Heesakkers and J. H. Waszink in his *Opera omnia,* i, 4, Amsterdam 1973, p. 306.

27. L. Valla, *Opera,* Basel 1540, pp. 19–20, 412.

28. R. A. Kaster, "The Grammarian's Authority," *Classical Philology,* lxxv, 1980, pp. 216–241; W. J. Slater, "Problems in Interpreting Scholia on Greek Texts," *Editing Greek & Latin Texts,* ed. J. N. Grant, New York 1989, p. 61.

29. De Valois, *Dissertatio,* in Burman (as in n. 1), ii, p. 318.

30. Wagenseil, *Dissertatio,* ibid., ii, pp. 314–316.

31. De Valois, *Dissertatio,* ibid., ii, pp. 317–319.

32. See e.g. Leibniz's critique of Nodot, *Allgemeiner politischer und historischer Briefwechsel,* ix (1693), Berlin 1975, pp. 295–300, and Burman's *praefatio* (as in n. 1).

33. Wagenseil, *Dissertatio,* ibid., ii, p. 314; De Valois, *Dissertatio,* ibid., ii, p. 318.

34. J. H. M. Salmon, "French Satire in the late Sixteenth Century," *Renaissance and Revolt,* Cambridge 1987, pp. 73–97; G. Hess, *Deutsch-lateinische Narrenzunft,* Munich 1971, gives the wider background.

35. *Satyre Ménipée* ed. Ch. Marcilly, Paris n.d., pp. 76, 87.

36. [P. Petit], *Marini Statilei . . . responsio,* in Burman (as in n. 1), ii, p. 340.

37. Ibid., ii, p. 334. For a much fuller treatment of many of the questions touched on here, see now I. A. R. de Smet, *Menippean Satire and the Republic of Letters, 1581–1655,* Geneva 1996.

14. An Introduction to the *New Science* of Giambattista Vico

1. For the larger context of Vico's thought see H. Stone, *Vico's Cultural History: The Production and Transmission of Ideas in Naples, 1685–1750* (Leiden, New York, and Cologne, 1997).

2. On Vico's life see especially his *Autobiography,* tr. M. H. Fisch and T. G. Bergin (Ithaca, N.Y., 1944; repr. 1963), and the perceptive commentary on it by D. P. Verene, *The New Art of Autobiography: An Essay on The Life of Giambattista Vico Written by Himself* (Oxford, 1991).

3. For more extended introductions to Vico's thought, see P. Rossi, "La vita e le opere di Giambattista Vico," *Le sterminate antichità: studi vichiani* (Pisa, 1969), 15–80; P. Burke, *Vico* (Oxford and New York, 1985).

4. See D. C. Allen, *The Legend of Noah: Renaissance Rationalism in Art, Science, and Letters,* Illinois Studies in Language and Literature, 33, 3–4 (1949; repr. Urbana, 1963); A. L. Owen, *The Famous Druids: A Survey of Three Centuries of English Literature on the Druids* (Oxford, 1962).

5. See A. D. Momigliano, "Roman 'Bestioni' and Roman 'Eroi' in Vico's *Scienza nuova,*" *History and Theory* 5 (1966), 3–23, repr. in Momigliano, *Terzo contributo alla storia degli studi classici e del mondo antico* (Rome, 1966), I, 153–177.

6. See F. Nicolini's *Commento storico alla seconda Scienza Nuova,* 2 vols. (Rome, 1949–1950), and his edition of *La Scienza Nuova giusta l'edizione del 1744,* 3 vols. (Naples, 1911–1916); Rossi, *Le sterminate antichità.*

7. [Richard Bentley], *Remarks Upon a Late Discourse of Free-Thinking, in a Letter to F.H.D.D. by Phileleutherus Lipsiensis,* 8th ed. (Cambridge, 1745), 25–26.

8. See K. Simonsuuri, *Homer's Original Genius* (Cambridge, 1979) and J. Levine, *The Battle of the Books: History and Literature in the Augustan Age* (Ithaca, N.Y., 1991).

9. See A. Grafton, "Renaissance Readers of Homer's Ancient Readers," in *Homer's Ancient Readers,* ed. R. Lamberton and J. J. Keaney (Princeton, 1992), 149–172.

10. See the splendid survey by D. C. Allen, *Mysteriously Meant: The Rediscovery of Pagan Symbolism and Allegorical Interpretation in the Renaissance* (Baltimore and London, 1970).

11. G. Cantelli, *Vico e Bayle: Premesse per un confronto* (Naples, 1971).

12. For Bacon's views and their context see E. Hassinger, *Empirisch-rationaler Historismus: Seine Ausbildung in der Literatur Westeuropas von Guicciardini bis Saint-Evremond* (Bern and Munich, 1978), and W. Schmidt-Biggemann, *Topica universalis: Eine Modellgeschichte humanistischer und barocker Wissenschaft* (Hamburg, 1983).

13. G. B. Vico, *Le orazioni inaugurali, il De italorum sapientia e le polemiche,* ed. G. Gentile and F. Nicolini (Bari, 1914), 116; *On the Study Methods of Our Time,* tr. E. Gianturco (Ithaca and London, 1990), ch. 13, 73.

14. See in general P. Rossi, *I segni del tempo: Storia della terra e storia delle nazioni da Hooke a Vico* (Milan, 1979), translated as *The Dark Abyss of Time: The History of the Earth and the History of Nations from Hooke to Vico,* tr. L. G. Cochrane (Chicago and London, 1984); A. Grafton, *Joseph Scaliger: A Study in the History of Classical Scholarship,* 2 vols. (Oxford, 1983–1993), II: *Historical Chronology.*

15. Vico, *Le orazioni inaugurali,* ed. Gentile and Nicolini, 110; *On the Study Methods of our Time,* tr. Gianturco, 65. On the French jurists see e.g. J. H. Franklin, *Jean Bodin and the Sixteenth-Century Revolution in the Methodology of Law and History* (New York and London, 1963); G. Huppert, *The Idea of Perfect History: Historical Erudition and Historical Philosophy in Renaissance France* (Urbana, Chicago, and London, 1970); and D. R. Kelley, *Foundations of Modern Historical Scholarship: Language, Law, and History in the French Renaissance* (New York and London, 1970). On Vico's debt to this tradition see e.g. I. Berlin, *Vico and Herder: Two Studies in the History of Ideas* (London, 1976; repr. London, 1992), 125–142.

16. See the lucid and informative work by M. A. Mooney, *Vico in the Tradition of Rhetoric* (Princeton, 1985).

17. W. Stephens, Jr., *Giants in Those Days: Folklore, Ancient History and Nationalism* (Lincoln and London, 1989).

18. C. Borghero, *La certezza e la storia* (Milan, 1983).

19. On this point, see Stone, *Vico's Cultural History.*

20. See M. Lilla, *G. B. Vico: The Making of an Anti-Modern* (Cambridge, Mass., 1993).

15. Jacob Bernays, Joseph Scaliger, and Others

1. On Bernays in general see M. Fraenkel, *Jacob Bernays* (Breslau, 1932); A. D. Momigliano, "Jacob Bernays" in *Quinto Contributo alla storia degli studi classici e del mondo antico* (Rome, 1980), 157–180; H. Bach, *Jacob Bernays* (Tübingen, 1974). E. E. Urbach, "The Breslau Years of Jacob Bernays and His Impact upon Jewish Studies," *Jacob Bernays: un philologue juif,* ed. J. Glucker and A. Laks (Lille, 1996), 17–28; J. Bollack, "Un homme d'un autre monde," ibid., 135–226.

2. J. Bernays, "De emendatione Lucretii," *Rheinisches Museum* 5 (1847), 533–587; on the importance of this work see S. Timpanaro, *La genesi del metodo del Lachmann* (Padua, 1985). M. Bollack, "Jacob Bernays ou l'abandon du commentaire," in *Jacob Bernays,* ed. Glucker and Laks, 31–44; J. Glucker, "'Lachmann's Method'—Bernays, Madvig, Lachmann and others," ibid., 45–56.

3. J. Bernays, *Grundzüge der verlorenen Abhandlung des Aristoteles über Wirkung der Tragödie* (Breslau, 1858), repr. with an introduction by K. Gründer, Hildesheim, 1970.

4. J. Bernays, *Die Dialoge des Aristoteles in ihrem Verhäıtniss zu seinen übrigen Werken* (Berlin, 1863). B. Effe, "Die Dialoge des Aristoteles: Jacob Bernays und die neuere Forschung"' in *Jacob Bernays,* ed. Glucker and Laks, 77–86.

5. J. Bernays, *Theophrastos' Schrift über Frömmigkeit. Ein Beitrag zur Religionsgeschichte* (Berlin, 1866).

6. J. Bernays, "Ein nabatäischer Schriftsteller," *Rheinisches Museum* 17 (1862), repr. in Bernays, *Gesammelte Abhandlungen,* ed. H. Usener (Berlin, 1885) 2:291–293. Cf. Momigliano's discussion of this article.

7. For the general context see M. A. Meyer, *The Origins of the Modern Jew* (Detroit, 1967).

8. M. Brann, *Geschichte des jüdisch-theologischen Seminars (Fraenckel'sche Stiftung) in Breslau* (Breslau, n.d.); Urbach.

9. U. von Wilamowitz-Moellendorff, *Erinnerungen, 1848–1914* (Leipzig, n.d.), 87–88.

10. See H. Usener, "Vorwort," in Bernays, *Gesammelte Abhandlungen,* iii–x, and the painstaking bibliographies that follow.

11. J. Bernays, *Joseph Justus Scaliger* (Berlin, 1855).

12. A. Grafton, *Joseph Scaliger* (Oxford, 1983–93).

13. On Azariah de' Rossi and Hellenistic Judaism see J. Weinberg, "The Quest for Philo in Sixteenth-Century Jewish Historiography," in *Jewish History: Essays in Honor of Chimen Abramsky,* ed. A. Rapoport-Albert et al. (London, 1988), 163–187.

14. Bach, *Bernays,* 128.

15. M. Fraenkel, *Jacob Bernays* (Breslau, 1932), 91.

16. Bach, *Bernays,* 211–212.

17. Fraenkel, *Bernays,* 58–60.

18. Ibid., 163 (Mommsen's funny reply to this comment appears on 163–164); the essay in question appears in *Gesammelte Abhandlungen* 2:71–80. On the relation between Bernays and Mommsen see L. Wickert, "Theodor Mommsen und Jacob Bernays: Ein Beitrag zur Geschichte des deutschen Judentums," *Historische Zeitschrift* 205 (1967), 265–294, reworked in Wickert, *Theodor Mommsen. Eine Biographie,* vol. 3: *Die Wanderjahre* (Frankfurt, 1969), 322–342.

19. See *Briefe von und an Michael Bernays* (Berlin, 1907); W. Rehm, *Späte Studien* (Bern and Munich, 1964), 359–458.

20. *Goethes Briefe an Friedrich August Wolf,* ed. (with an exhaustive commentary) by M. Bernays (Berlin, 1868).

21. See F. Boll, "Biographische Einleitung" in L. Traube, *Vorlesungen und Abhandlungen,* ed. P. Lehmann (Munich, 1909), 1:xix.

22. M. Bernays, *Über Kritik und Geschichte des Goetheschen Textes* (Berlin, 1866).

23. M. Bernays, "Zur Lehre von den Citaten und Noten," *Schriften zur Kritik und Literaturgeschichte* (Berlin, 1899), 4:255–347.

24. Quoted in L. A. Tollemache, *Recollections of Pattison* (London, 1885), 5.

25. For a more skeptical view see E. V. Blomfield, "Biographical Memoir of Josephus Justus Scaliger," *Museum Criticum* 1 (1826), 345.

26. Bach, *Bernays,* 51, 80, 95.

27. M. Billanovich, "Giulio Cesare Scaligero e Benedetto Bordon," *Italia Medioevale e Umanistica* 11 (1968).

28. Wilamowitz-Moellendorff, *Erinnerungen,* 88: "Es war eine sonderbare Sorte von Adelsstolz."

29. See A. Grafton, *Defenders of the Text* (Cambridge, Mass., and London, 1991), chap. 9.

30. Meyer, *Origins of the Modern Jew,* 158–162.

31. Bernays, *Scaliger,* 68.

32. See Bernays, *Gesammelte Abhandlungen,* 71.

33. I cite the translation in *The Sentences of Pseudo-Phocylides,* ed. P. W. van der Horst (Leiden, 1978).

34. Scaliger, *Animadversiones in Chronologica Eusebii,* 95–96, in *Thesaurus Temporum,* 2d ed. (Amsterdam, 1658).

35. J. Bernays, "Ueber das Phokylideische Gedicht," *Gesammelte Abhandlungen,* 192–261 at 198.

36. For the importance of Bernays's work see the review of scholarship in van der Horst's edition, 3–54.

37. Grafton, *Scaliger,* 2:413–420, 510, 707.

38. See W. Lepenies, *Autoren und Wissenschaftler im 18. Jahrhundert* (Munich and Vienna, 1988), 106; G. Walther, *Niebuhrs Forschung* (Stuttgart, 1993), 315–320.

39. Bernays, "Ueber das Phokylideische Gedicht," 254.

40. Scaliger, *Animadversiones,* 133–134.

41. Quoted in J. Freudenthal, *Alexander Polyhistor* (Breslau, 1875), 194.

42. Ibid.

43. See A. D. Momigliano, *Alien Wisdom* (Cambridge, 1975), 116–117.

44. Scaliger, *Epistolae omnes quae reperiri potuerunt,* ed. D. Heinsius (Leiden, 1627), 594.

45. G. Levi della Vida, *Documenti intorno alle relazioni delle chiese orientali con la S. Sede durante il pontificato di Gregorio XIII* (Rome, 1948), 22–25.

46. See e.g. Fraenkel, *Bernays,* 28–29.

47. Grafton, *Scaliger,* 2:728–737.

48. Bernays, *Scaliger,* 203–205. See also H. J. de Jonge, "The Study of the New Testament," in *Leiden University in the Seventeenth Century: An Exchange of Learning,* ed. Th. H. Lunsingh Scheurleer et al. (Leiden, 1975), 64–109, esp. 76–87.

49. For another case in point—one unconnected with Judaism—see M. Haupt, "Ueber Joseph Scaliger und die von Haase vorgeschlagene Umstellung tibullischer Versreihen," *Opuscula* 3 (Leipzig, 1876), 30–41.

Sources

ᎶᏃᏃᏬ

Most of the essays assembled here first appeared in the following journals and books. They are reprinted with permission, for which I am most grateful. Only the Introduction and Essay 7 are published for the first time here. The illustrations in Essay 2 come from MS 158 of the Robert Garrett Collection of Medieval and Renaissance Manuscripts, Manuscript Division, Princeton University Library.

1. From *Meaning in the Visual Arts: Views from the Outside. A Centennial Commemoration of Erwin Panofsky (1892—1968),* ed. Irving Lavin (Princeton: Princeton University Press, 1995), pp. 123–130.

2. From *Rome Reborn: The Vatican Library and Renaissance Culture,* ed. Anthony Grafton (Vatican City: Biblioteca Apostolica Vaticana; Washington, D.C.: The Library of Congress; New Haven and London: Yale University Press, 1993), pp. 87–123.

3. From *The New Republic,* 19/26 September 1994, pp. 44–51.

4. Reprinted with permission from the *New York Review of Books,* 10 April 1997, pp. 57–64; copyright © 1997–8 NYREV, Inc.

5. Reprinted with the permission of Cambridge University Press from *The Cambridge Companion to Renaissance Humanism,* ed. Jill Kraye (Cambridge: Cambridge University Press, 1996), pp. 203–223.

6. From *The University and the City: From Medieval Origins to the Present,* ed. Thomas Bender (Oxford: Oxford University Press, 1988), pp. 59–78; copyright © 1988 by Oxford University Press; used by permission of Oxford University Press.

8. From the *London Review of Books,* 5 October 1995, pp. 17, 19–20.

9. From *Central European History* 18 (1985), 31–47.

10. From the *Journal of the Warburg and Courtauld Institutes* 62 (1999 [2000]), 241–267.

11. From the *Journal of the Warburg and Courtauld Institutes* 53 (1990), 237–249.

12. From *American Scholar* 56 (1987), 382–390.

13. From the *Wilson Quarterly* 21 (Fall 1996), 36–46.

14. "Introduction" to Giambattista Vico, *The New Science,* tr. David Harsh (London: Penguin, 1999), pp. xi–xxxiii.

15. From *The Jewish Past Revisted: Reflections on Modern Jewish Historians,* ed. David Myers and David Ruderman (New Haven: Yale University Press, 1998), pp. 11–30; copyright © 1988 by Yale University Press.

Index